W9-BXW-718

Also by Pierre Birnbaum

Jewish Destinies: Citizenship, State, and Community
in Modern France

The Jews of the Republic: A Political History of State
Jews of France from Gambetta to Vichy

Anti-Semitism in France: A History from 1789 to
the Present

States and Collective Action: The European
Experience

The Heights of Power: An Essay on the Power Elite
in France

The Idea of France

The
Idea
of
France

PIERRE BIRNBAUM

Translated by M. B. DeBevoise

HILL AND WANG
A division of Farrar, Straus and Giroux
New York

Hill and Wang
A division of Farrar, Straus and Giroux
19 Union Square West, New York, NY 10003

Copyright © 1998 by Librairie Arthème Fayard
Translation copyright © 2001 by M. B. DeBevoise
All rights reserved
Distributed in Canada by Douglas & McIntyre Ltd.
Printed in the United States
First published in 1998 by Librairie Arthème Fayard, France, as
La France imaginée
First published in the United States by Hill and Wang
First American edition, 2001

Library of Congress Cataloging-in-Publication Data

Birnbaum, Pierre.
    [France imaginée. English]
    The idea of France / Pierre Birnbaum ; translated by M. B. DeBevoise.
        p.   cm.
    Includes bibliographical references and index.
    ISBN 0-8090-4650-4 (alk. paper)
        1. France—Politics and government—Historiography.   2. Church and
    state—France—History—20th century.   3. Decentralization in
    government—France.   4. France—Social conditions.   I. Title.
DC36.9 .B5713 2001
944—dc21   00-063430

Designed by Patrice Sheridan

This edition has been published with the financial assistance
of the French Ministry of Culture.

For Judith, who knows life

Table of Contents

Contents

Preface to the American Edition

Every nation seeks its origins in a remote history, in traditions, customs, and legends that are peculiar to it. Every nation provides itself with a flag, an anthem, and various other emblems that testify to its special character. Menacing eagles, triumphant lions, warrior goddesses, indomitable Hercules, and liberating female figures are among the symbols that—alongside the cross, the crescent, and stars of all sorts—embody the souls of nations, their cultures and their destinies.

Historians and social scientists nonetheless long believed, in an almost Hegelian way, that national peculiarities were doomed to fade away before the rising power of Reason and the expanding rule of Progress, Industrialization, and Modernization; that the signs of collective identity emblazoned on flags, engraved on statues, and imprinted on stamps would soon stand only for societies that had finally come to resemble one another. In this view, the conquest of the modern world by the Enlightenment signified the end of the exceptionalism of individual nations, fashioned over so many centuries; the convergence of a great many distinct, and distinctive, historical paths of development; the triumph of the public sphere and democratic consensus; and the end of poli-

Preface

tics—even of belligerent confrontation between nations, now pacified internally and henceforth destined to be peaceful in their foreign relations. As for the countries of the third world, they were regarded only as so many relics of an outmoded past that would disappear in their turn once the reign of progress had been inaugurated within their borders.

Today, however, notwithstanding the virtually universal achievement of democracy, each country seeks to reclaim and defend its own particular course of historical development. This return to the idea of the nation is taking place at a moment when market forces and the expansion of international trade (in both goods and ideas) are making themselves increasingly felt; and when supernational political arrangements are being established, in Europe for example, that limit national prerogatives and impose laws that are indifferent to local conditions. In attempting to rediscover its own history, each country thus finds itself confronted with new challenges to its identity. These challenges have suddenly emerged as much from outside its borders, under the influence of economic globalization, as from within, under the pressure of growing demands for recognition of regional differences, which everywhere encourage a multicultural understanding of the nation.

France—the nation-state par excellence, the very model of the early construction of national identity under the firm control of a powerful state—has been confronted by both kinds of challenge more directly than most nations. Highly centralized, owing as much to its experience of absolute monarchies as to that of Jacobin republics, and ruled for centuries by a strong state opposed to the expression of particular identities—whether religious, cultural, or territorial—France now finds itself faced with a difficult choice. If it hesitates, this is in large measure because the ideal of pluralism is not one that all of its citizens embrace. The conception of France that has endured until the present day is anchored in a distant and famously tumultuous past whose memory remains largely intact, as much among Bretons and Basques as among Catholics, Protestants, Jews, and Muslims; among workers and owners; among people of the Left and people of the Right; and among those who occupy either extreme of the political spectrum. Transmitted from generation to generation, these memories of remote civil wars that once tore apart French society still shape ideas of the nation in ways that are not always mutually compatible.

Imagining France—the France of yesterday, today, and tomorrow—therefore requires a special effort to reconstruct the past. It is a living past, one that is constantly revisited and incessantly reinterpreted—a past that remains forever present. Few nations in the world are more preoccupied by historical memory, by the permanent rereading of their past. Today, however, France is undergoing profound change. It is transforming itself with astonishing speed into an open society, abolishing boundaries that long separated members of different classes, thoroughly reexamining the role of its elites, rediscovering the charms of liberalism and, in the process, learning to live with the challenges of multiculturalism. Just so, the idea of France is being rapidly transformed as well. A recent poll conducted by *Le Monde* reveals that the great majority of the French people enthusiastically accept European integration. There is a new openness to persons of different races and beliefs—in short, a desire to break free from the limiting confines of the Hexagon.

Will the French nonetheless manage to exchange one image for another without being crippled by internal dissension? Can they give up their old passion for murderous contradiction in favor of a well-tempered Anglo-Saxon pluralism? Can they find a way to remain faithful to the special character of France's historical experience while creating a genuinely democratic and just society? Will the new idea of France bring forth a society that welcomes foreigners and respects differences, rejects once and for all the idea of revolution, refuses civil war, and renounces religious and social intolerance?

By contrast not only with the United States and Great Britain, but also with Spain and Italy—nations accustomed from their earliest times (despite a history sometimes no less violent than

Preface

that of France) to the idea of pluralism—France finds itself at a
crossroads. As its history shows only too vividly, change arouses
strong resistance, and creates new cultural tensions that are no
less rooted in a distant past than the ones they displace.

P.B.
Paris, June 2000

The Idea of France

Introduction: Solzhenitsyn

in the Vendée

On 25 September 1993, in the village of Lucs-sur-Boulogne, Alexander Solzhenitsyn paid vibrant homage to the uprising in the Vendée of 1793,[1] unveiling a memorial to the victims of the Terror and boldly proclaiming that all "revolutions destroy the organic character of society."[2] The Russian prophet's verdict was unmistakable: France, following Russia's example, must turn its back on the suffocating temptations of Reason and rediscover its true identity—abandoning, after a long period of indecision, the reveries of revolution and showing itself at last faithful to its own history. Solzhenitsyn's call for a return to national culture rang out as an urgent plea for revolt against Reason. At the very moment when France was commemorating the bicentennial of its own Revolution, Solzhenitsyn claimed that it was altogether futile to hope that revolution could regenerate human nature. "But that is what your revolution and especially ours, the Russian Revolution, had so very much hoped. . . . Many cruel procedures of the French Revolution were obediently reapplied to the body of Russia by the Leninist communists. . . . Together with you, we have crossed through a century of terror, the horrifying crowning of the progress that the eighteenth century had so longed for."[3] In

the person of the author of *The Gulag Archipelago*, old Catholic France and old Orthodox Russia suddenly met in this small town under the benevolent gaze of Philippe de Villiers, champion of a tasteful right-wing populism and architect of the revival of Vendean identity celebrated by shows mounted in nearby Puy-du-Fou.[4] Villiers, a viscount who, though he was a graduate of the École Nationale d'Administration (ENA), was captivated more by tradition than by the idea of serving a rationalist state, was preparing to lead his forces to a brilliant series of victories in the European elections of 1994. His successes turned out to be ephemeral, however, and his star soon faded—first in the presidential election the following year, and then in the legislative elections of 1997, when he was forced to yield the hotly contested position of national populist leader to Jean-Marie Le Pen. Le Pen generously welcomed Villiers's disappointed supporters into his ranks.

Shortly before Solzhenitsyn's visit, Villiers had received another distinguished guest, Monsignor Jozef Glemp, the Polish cardinal and ardent defender of a wholly Catholic Poland. Between these two visitors and various native advocates of a return to the deep sources of national identity there was a lively sympathy. The Vendean counterrevolution, a veritable crusade against evil, was said to have resembled the peasant revolts against Bolshevik authority. Both movements rejected the Enlightenment, which they saw as destructive of a vital attachment to the land, and both were loyal to Christianity, which they saw as the sole guarantee of an unbroken link with the distant past. They believed, as the Israeli historian J. L. Talmon has suggested, that the Enlightenment was responsible for the totalitarianisms that destroyed national identities. In Villiers's words, the "genocide" in the Vendée, with its "dozens and dozens of Oradours,"[5] appeared as a "final solution" comparable to the extermination of the kulaks—wealthy peasant farmers—in Soviet Russia in the 1930s. The Jacobins, like the Soviets, had created for themselves a purely "abstract" idea of liberty: "France invented in 1793 the infernal machine of ideological terror, which served as a womb for the terrors of the twentieth century. . . . The Vendée incarnated a moment of history when ideology, with all its abstract vocabulary, ran up against the resistance of human reality."[6] Adopting Solzhenitsyn's metaphor, Villiers asserted that the Russian prophet "ought to be able to speak to us of one of the cogs of that red wheel of totalitarianism, this offshoot of the French Revolution that prepared the totalitarian womb of the twentieth century."[7] Not long before, in May 1993, almost 50,000 royalists had gathered at the Mont des Alouettes and, after celebrating a mass in Latin, commemorated the Vendean uprising with cries of *"Vive le Roi!"*[8] Villiers resembled an unrepentent feudal landowner more than a royalist: implacably opposed to all centralizing powers, he presented himself as a "white knight who came forward to raise the standard of a faith that suffered neither adversaries nor contradiction."[9]

Similarly, after his brief trip to the Vendée, Solzhenitsyn declared that "humanity does not develop in a single mold but through often closed cultures, each of which has its own laws."[10] He dismissed the universalism of the Enlightenment and argued that the fate of each people depends on its fidelity to its own culture, which, in order to remain coherent and continue to bear historical meaning, must avoid all foreign influence. In France as in Russia, the end of revolutionary eschatology justified a return to an original culture that was constantly threatened by the abstractions of Reason. Solzhenitsyn symbolized the weakening of the revolutionary tradition and, by his own attachment to a remote Russian culture, delivered a new blow to the historical logic that for two hundred years had characterized French society. His hymn to a bygone Russia was easily transposed to France, a land haunted by so many *"lieux de mémoire"*[11] inscribed in the depths of national historical memory. He emphasized that "every people, even the very smallest, represents a unique facet of God's design,"[12] and that the political organization peculiar to each society must be fashioned by its "spiritual principles." Since in his view the structure of the state "must necessarily take national traditions into account,"[13] Russia could not with impunity import a centralized administrative system, as so many emperors who looked toward the West had sought to do, notably Catherine II (the Great) and Alexander I. Thus Solzhenitsyn proposed that Russia create a decentralized state and abolish politics as a profession. This state would do away with universal suffrage, which "assume[s] that the nation lacks all structure: that it is not a living organism but a mere mechanical conglomeration of disparate individuals,"[14] and instead make voting a public act done through a show of hands, after the example of the former canton of Appenzell in Switzerland. With the disappearance of the Western-style state, politics would lose its abstract character and become adapted to the culture in which the Russian people are rooted.

Respect for traditions and orthodoxy, a longing to return to the land, a privileging of "below" against a disfiguring and artificial "above," foreign to local culture—all these things explain Solzhenitsyn's trip to the Vendée and his attempt to relegitimate the populist and Slavophile currents that inundate Russia today. To the Slavophiles, the West is an entirely Protestantized world; even countries that are officially Catholic have lost their faith. Russia's Westernized elite, no less than the West itself, is marked by a spirit of individualism that is devoid of any spiritual dimension and destructive of the unity of the self and of all communal feeling.[15] To Solzhenitsyn's mind, the Marxist communism that sprang from Western rationalism had no less thoroughly wrecked the organic development of the life of the people in Russia, creating an impasse with regard to the national question.[16]

Such views have led some observers to suppose that the end of the Soviet Union once again caused great numbers of Russians to embrace their native culture. Similarly, some detect a renewed concern with identity in France, accompanied by a retreat from the republican state that came out of the revolutionary tradition. In each case, the tradition of the Enlightenment, including its most pathological consequences, finds itself abruptly called into question. This tradition involves a conception of history as the vehicle of progress that appears so naïvely scientistic that it at once runs up against an almost unanimous skepticism. Public confidence in the strong state is further undermined by its seeming indifference to the values of individuals. In this view, it was the delegitimation of the state machine that did away with the Soviet-style party-state. The fall of the rational state is therefore the indispensable condition for reappropriating the authentic culture that must serve as the basis for a new type of state.[17]

Of course, the attempt to achieve a perfect fit between nation and culture can have the tragic and unintended result of giving birth to a dwarf state—the servile and passive instrument of a unified and closed culture that becomes the mistress of the nation. This risk exists in a number of countries in Eastern Europe, where there have been countless calls for the formation of a "wholly Catholic"[18] Poland or a "wholly Orthodox" Russia. Such states would be stripped of all attributes of public power and independence in the conduct of policy, and their workings would be determined solely by a unique and uniform national identity. In these countries the Soviet Revolution of 1917 appears in retrospect—like the French Revolution of 1789—to have been the result of an internationalist conspiracy that relentlessly sought to deny authentic national values: thus the Jews, a "little people," threatened the "great" Russian people.[19] The "genocide" perpetrated against the Russian people is therefore comparable to the one that was perpetrated against the Vendée and all of France during the Terror. In both cases, the perpetrator was a gigantic Judeo-Masonic conspiracy, operating under cover of the grand principles of rationalist universalism.

The Russian question after 1990, like that of Poland, helped revive the nationalist relativism of the German philosopher and critic Johann Gottfried von Herder (1744–1803), whose writings were rediscovered both in the former Soviet bloc and in France.[20] In many respects, Herder addressed the same problem: Is it possible to preserve a universal morality that is not rooted in a particular cultural space? Pertinent in this connection as well is the work of the late Isaiah Berlin, which was devoted both to the Enlightenment and the emergence of nationalisms, with particular attention to the fate of the Russian and French revolutions. At first sight, Solzhenitsyn would seem to have nothing in common with a political theorist such as Berlin—a Jew, a fervent partisan of liberalism, and a knight of the British Empire. To be sure, Solzhenitsyn, the ardent champion of the spiritual renewal of Slavic orthodoxy, cuts a figure in every respect unlike that of the amiable Oxford philosopher. Yet the two are united in their fear of the Americanization of the world; in their desire to help bring about the renaissance of a variety of coherent national cultures; and in their hostility to the adoption of foreign cultural models. Consciously or unconsciously, the Russian prophet and the English scholar carry on the polemic inaugurated by Herder against the Enlightenment, whose universalism stands accused of destroying the souls of peoples. For just as Herder combated the importation of Enlightenment ideas to Germany from France in the eighteenth century, Solzhenitsyn challenges their more distant introduction to Russia today.

Berlin, while he did not object to the importation of French ideals into either Germany or Russia, felt that nationalists in both countries were justified in refusing the lessons in universalism given by French philosophers. In this sense, nationalism was an appropriate reaction on the part of nations whose own traditions had been wounded—a simple desire to reconstruct an injured indigenous culture. Like the Russian emperors who had sought to follow the French path, Frederick the Great became passionately attached to the rationalizing ideas conceived in the homeland of the *Encyclopédie*; like them, he exhibited a profound contempt for his own cultural heritage. In slavishly copying the French absolutist model, he inadvertently helped to bring into existence, in Prussia no less than in Russia, nationalist movements that were resolutely committed to a return to the people. In Berlin's view, Herder—along with the Russian journalist and politician Alexander Herzen (1812–70)—symbolizes the determined defense of cultural diversity in the face of universalism *à la française*, the product of a land that denied its own cultural identity.

Berlin naturally assigned a crucial role as well to the French diplomat and philosopher Joseph de Maistre (1753–1821), the first thinker to give an absolute and radical character to the rejection of a universalizing Enlightenment:

> Maistre amuses himself at the expense of the Encyclopedists [and] their clever superficialities . . . very much in the manner adopted by Tolstoy towards their descendants a century later—the scientific sociologists and historians. . . . Both Maistre and Tolstoy regard the western world as in some sense "rotting," as being in rapid decay. This was the doctrine which the Roman Catholic counter-revolutionaries at the turn of the century virtually invented. . . . From France this denunciation of secularism was carried . . . to Germany and to Russia. . . . No doubt Tolstoy derived this element in his outlook at least as much from Slavophils and other Russian chauvinists as directly from Maistre, but it is worth noting that this belief is exceptionally powerful in both these dry and aristocratic observers, and governs their oddly similar outlooks. . . . Nevertheless, of all writers on social questions, Maistre's tone most nearly resembles that of Tolstoy. Both preserve the same sardonic, almost cynical, disbelief in the improvement of society by rational means . . . ; there is the same distaste for anyone who deals in ideas, who believes in abstract principles.[21]

Maistre, the staunch adversary of revolutionary utopia, the inventor of modern nationalism, thus takes his place after Herder and before Herzen and Solzhenitsyn. The nationalist defense of authentic cultures in both the nineteenth and twentieth centuries has assumed the form of a negation of Enlightenment absolutism. From one epoch to the next, nationalism and culture have been inseparable, dismissing as too abstract—too disembodied—a conception of citizenship that lacks the spiritual rootedness inherent in an organic community and condemning the state as the chief threat to the defense of social values. As Berlin remarks, Dostoyevsky, faced with the Bolshevik Revolution, would have reacted in the same way as Solzhenitsyn does to-day. Solzhenitsyn thinks he is like Tolstoy, but he is much more like Dostoyevski. . . . [H]e is the voice of Dostoyevski. . . . He seems to me to be neither an intellectual, nor a Slavophil. Solzhenitsyn does not take the slightest interest in non-Russian Slavs. He is a Russian patriot and much more like one of the Old Believers in the seventeenth century who rose against Peter the Great and all the modernization which he introduced.[22]

However, Maistre and Solzhenitsyn—and (pace Berlin) Herder, Herzen, Dostoyevsky, and Tolstoy—all denounced as illusory the rationalism that the French and Bolshevik revolutions explicitly claimed to represent. All of them argued in favor of a homogeneous national culture; all of them, despite their differences, rejected internationalism as well as internal cultural pluralism; all of them, to differing degrees, claimed to speak on behalf of spiritual uniqueness and sought to revivify the ahistorical realities of the "depths" of human existence.

The return to Orthodoxy peculiar to Dostoyevsky and Solzhenitsyn, like Maistre's militant Catholicism, is consistent with Herder's doctrine of relativist (or simply pluralist) nationalism: to each nation its own unique spiritual principle. This formula supplies the guiding thread of the present book. The special character of modern French history—what is often called "French exceptionalism"—consists in a particularly efficient implementation of just such a principle of internal cultural unification. No matter that the vision of French society justified by the Enlightenment and realized by the French Revolution and the Third Republic represents the opposite—every bit as absolute—of the homogenizing pretension repeatedly championed by the counter-revolution in the name of an uncompromising Catholicism, the fact remains that France has always wished to identify itself with a unique spiritual principle. On the one hand, it has seen its soul as residing in a privileged relationship with Reason, and its deep personality expressed in an unquestioning adherence to the ideals of the Enlightenment—a source of lasting inspiration to foreign nationalist movements eager to defend themselves by rediscovering their own culture. On the other hand, it has conceived itself as the eldest daughter of the Church, the Catholic nation par excellence.[23] Of all nations, is not France the only one thus to doubly define itself,[24] finding its collective identity as much in Reason as in Catholicism? Is not the spiritual exceptionalism of France, with its two contradictory faces, the result of its early and highly original formation as a nation-state seeking to unify both minds and territories?

The emergence of the French state in the aftermath of feudalism inaugurated a logic so powerful that it imposed one, and only one, way of imagining the nation. In the minds of some, France was wholly Catholic; in the minds of others, resolutely nationalist and secular. Of all nations, and against all expectations, it was France that promised most completely to embody the true Herderian ideal—except that the clash between the two principles that underlie its identity took place on its own soil, within itself, and that the internal conflicts and unavoidable confrontations to which this dual and contradictory identity gave rise tore it apart ever further. Rather than examine the socioeconomic conflicts that also cut through French society, I attempt here to retrace the main forms of symbolic significance that presided over the nation's conception. *La France imaginée* is a France that possesses exceptional and antagonistic traits, a France wished for and loved by fraternal enemies—French citizens inspired by dreams emanating from almost unimaginably different mental worlds. This imagined France has its basis in conflicts of values: as the historian Maurice Agulhon has emphasized, "Having concentrated too much on the struggle between classes, we have managed to forget that the life of our country a century ago was—or, at least, was also—characterized by a 'war of religions.'"[25]

France was, after all, the first country to commit itself, violently and passionately, to contradictory forms of spiritual unification. Aided by a strong state, it invented a whole host of ways of standardizing thought and behavior and showing hostility to outsiders. The major events of French history have relentlessly challenged the very idea of plurality and tolerance. The name of Louis IX (1214–70) is associated with the crusades against unbelievers, which is to say Muslims guilty of occupying the Holy Places—and also the Jews. Saint Louis, it is well known, "did not like the Jews." Acting out of a desire for ultimate "purification aimed at purging Christianity of its impurities," and with "extreme aggressiveness," he obliged them for the first time to wear the felt badge (*rouelle de feutre*), that "infamous mark [that was the] . . . ancestor of the yellow star." The king (to quote his own words) devised this sign in order to better control this "filth" that defiled "his" land.[26] France was also the first country to banish its Jews, in 1182, out of a desire to become wholly Catholic. This decision "was to serve as a precedent, over the centuries, for the great expulsions"[27] of their coreligionists—from England (1290), again from France (1306 and 1394), and from Spain and Portugal (1492 and 1496, respectively)—with the result that, for a very long period, a large part of Europe was virtually empty of all Jewish inhabitants.

If France escaped a dreadful Inquisition on the Spanish or Portuguese model, this was due in part to the fact that its many expulsions had already effectively resolved the question of conversion. (The architects of the Inquisition, for their part, regarded the expulsion of the Jews of Spain and Portugal at the end of the fifteenth century as an imperfect outcome, for they sought to convert souls and not to lose them.)[28] In France, a still more efficient solution to the problem was found in the Saint Bartholomew's Day Massacre (1572), whose brutal eradication of religious pluralism constituted an "expiation offered to divine wrath"[29]—indeed, a veritable "rite of purification," a battle to the death against the "risk of stain," raising to its height "the hunting of Huguenots," which was then on the verge of becoming a national sport.[30] Neither the persecutions of Catholics in Protestant England nor the religious conflicts in Germany bear comparison with Saint Bartholomew's Day, in the course of which more than 10,000 Protestants were savagely killed. In the aftermath of the revocation of the Edict of Nantes in 1685,[31] which led to the permanent exile of more than 200,000 Protestants, radical measures were decreed by Louis XIV. Certain historians, pressing a highly doubtful analogy, consider these measures actually to have anticipated the Nazi terror that later descended upon the Jews.[32]

The passions of the Crusades, concentrated in the determination to root out heresy, survived in France throughout the seventeenth century. The "Catholic offensive" mounted by the Counter-Reformation was increasingly vigorous. Mysticism, strengthened by monarchical authority, gave birth to a Spanish-influenced "French spirituality" that sparked a profound transformation of the Church, marked by a proliferation of orders and brotherhoods and an unprecedented revival of religious practices and pilgrimages. These in turn led to a "strict monitoring of consciences, . . . to a totalitarian religion in which obedience to God and king was inseparable from the dogmas and practices of the Roman Church."[33] In such a culture, the Edict of Nantes represented the foundation of an unacceptable particularism, for it legalized, in a way that was altogether exceptional in Europe during this period, a degree of religious pluralism. The edict recognized a limited freedom of conscience on the part of Protestants, who had managed to establish a regional autonomy that was protected by a relatively democratic form of collective solidarity—so successfully that, in the eyes of their enemies, they constituted a state within the state, anchored in its own culture.[34]

The subsequent repression of all forms of Protestant identity was particularly severe. Rallying to the cry "one faith, one law, one king,"[35] the Catholic state destroyed Protestant strongholds and hanged their inhabitants; committed murders and rapes and carried out forcible conversions; kidnapped children, who were subsequently raised as Catholics; prohibited marriages between Catholics and Huguenots; purged the royal administration and required the Catholic oath from all future servants of the state; and excluded Protestants (among them bailiffs, notaries, and medical doctors) from many professions. This policy, worthy of the spirit of the Crusades, aimed at "excluding the Huguenots from the national community" despite their fierce loyalty to a monarchy that only increased its efforts at centralization. In retrospect, the "systematic aggression of the state against a non-conforming minority" appeared at a crucial moment in the transition from feudalism to the absolute monarchy.[36]

The revocation of the Edict of Nantes met with an enthusiastic welcome: poets and moralists such as Jean de La Fontaine, Jean de La Bruyère, and Madeleine de Scudéry made no attempt to hide their approval, congratulating Louis XIV for having put an end once and for all to heresy. The Académie Française offered prizes for the best works celebrating the decision of the Sun King. As one of his loyal subjects put it:

And reunited at last in a single faith,
Let us have only one God, one heart, one church, one king.[37]

Similarly, as Joseph de Maistre joyfully noted more than a century later, Madame de Sévigné commented to her cousin Bussy-Rabutin: "You have no doubt read the edict by which the king revokes that of Nantes: nothing is so fine as what it contains and never has, and never will, any king do anything more memorable."[38] Of all the Catholic countries, it was only in France that this "mystical union and this specific pact" (to quote the historian Robert Mandrou) was realized between the monarchy and the Catholic Church. This union, formalized by the Concordat of Bologna (1516), made it easier for the king to nominate bishops and gave the Crown a degree of autonomy with regard to the pope, which gave rise in turn to a political Gallicanism that reached its high point during the age of Louis XIV. Though the Very Christian King never broke with Rome, this Gallicanism nonetheless remained profoundly important.

If France invented the strong state,[39] on which attempts to unify the most opposed ways of thinking were based for centuries, it did so in response to a very fragile internal situation: the extreme heterogeneity of its population, combined with the abiding legacy of feudalism, had long made the birth of France as a nation an unlikely thing. While the countries of northern Europe were embracing Protestantism, and those of the south were embarking upon the Counter-Reformation, France hesitated. In the meantime, its growing diversity with respect to language and territory multiplied the dangers of fragmentation associated with an early and extreme feudalism. The ruthless struggle against the Protestants was proof of the Crown's desire to bring to completion a still uncertain process of national unification.

If the absolute monarchy reached its height during the age of Louis XIV—upon whom so many foreign monarchs were later to model themselves—this was in large part the result of a deliberate attempt to eliminate the risk of internal division by imposing an urgently necessary unification from above. The union of church and state aligned ways of thinking even more closely, excluding all differences. France's originality consisted in just this: it was a nation that (as Bishop Bossuet, the theorist of the divine right of kings, remarked) "can boast of having the best possible constitution of State and the one most in conformity with what God Himself has established. Which shows at once the wisdom of our ancestors and God's protection of this kingdom."[40]

With the turn toward revolution and the advent of Reason as the new unifying foundation of a nation of citizens, this protection disappeared. From 1789 to the present day, contrary dreams of a united France have clashed, neither one of them having the least interest in tolerating the other or in promoting a pluralism of values. Indeed, French history seems at times to amount to a gigantic confrontation between a nation of citizens governed by the goddess Reason and a Christian people anxious to recover the divine protection it had lost. In the late nineteenth century, under a Third Republic determined to bring about the rapid secularization of society in line with revolutionary ideals, Monsignor Charles-Émile Freppel, the irascible leader of the dominant hard-line Catholicism of the period, could still exclaim:

It was not in 1793, but in 1789, that France sustained the profound injury from which it has suffered since, and which may bring about its death if a strong and vigorous reaction does not succeed in putting it back on the path to complete recovery. It was in 1789 that, in renouncing the notion of a Christian people in order to apply deist or atheist rationalism to the social order, its representatives gave the world the lamentable spectacle of a national apostasy until then unprecedented in Catholic countries.[41]

This, finally, is the source of France's originality: no other country in the modern Christian West has experienced such a clash of radically opposed fundamental principles—a clash that plunged France into a succession of ruptures that were scarcely favorable either to tolerance, acceptance of internal cultural diversity, or liberalism.

Today, a century later, beyond the tumult of the interwar period and the quasi-civil wars that followed (from Vichy to Algeria, from the nationalist leagues of the late nineteenth century to Poujadism in the mid–twentieth century, from the Popular Front of the 1930s to the revolutionary strikes of the 1950s that culminated in the events of May 1968), France seems to have lost its bearings. The passions of a distant past have been extinguished, and the language of enmity issuing from France now seems old-fashioned. The present age is one of derision and irony, marked more by disillusionment than engagement. History seems suddenly empty of meaning, having given way to consensus, compromise, and pacification. Were it not for the presence of a radical and populist movement on the extreme Right, eager to gain adherents and thereby to achieve a fine revenge on behalf of its nationalist predecessors, France today might almost believe itself to be immune to strong feelings. Elites politely succeed each other in power; citizens tend to their own affairs; the great clamorings of yesteryear have subsided into silence. France is no longer capable even of boredom: it appears to have settled into a gentle tranquillity, troubled from time to time only by a mild excess of ordinary racism, unbridled speculation, and galloping poverty.

The age is no longer suitable for history—or so one might suppose, looking at France from within. Yet a large part of contemporary French historiography is still devoted to reviving the dramas of the "past that does not go away"[42]—from the Saint Bartholomew's Day Massacre to the French Revolution, the Dreyfus Affair, Vichy, and the Algerian war—reaching even as far back as Clovis himself. Official commemorations typically call upon the services of historians, who are paid by the government to make sure that national identity, though faltering and in danger of being "forgotten," fits with present reality.[43] As François Furet once observed, "The French are probably the all-around champions of the politics of memory."[44] Even in this respect, they remain exceptional.

The question arises, however, whether historians encourage the French people to remember these internal ruptures of the past as part of a long tradition of exceptionalism so that they may be more easily forgotten; or whether they bring to light the sediments of history so that their fellow citizens may better appreciate the scale of the change that is now taking place, marked by the end of France's exceptionalism and the advent of an age of reconciliation and mutual acceptance. In the latter case, the Franco-French wars of the past could be celebrated as so many distant, almost foreign, confrontations. The ambient relativism of the present day, often misinterpreted, insists on taking into account even the most divergent points of view, each of which thereby acquires an aura of legitimacy. Images of a remote past invade television, mixing fiction and fact and relegating to a distant time events whose logic is no longer understood. On the screen, or even in textbooks, historical figures seem to play roles, obeying the instructions of a hidden director or an invisible cameraman.

History has now become account, text, and spectacle all at once: its most dramatic events now furnish material for comic books—albums of holy images leafed through in a more or less distracted, distant, amused way—as if today we know how to free ourselves from the fixed and caricatural imaginings that ruled the actors of the past. Today's mood inclines to modesty: the great gurus who once dispensed truth have disappeared. Gone, too, is the oratorical jousting of an age when heralds of the two rival

Frances clashed with great pomp. In the eyes of many observers, the evidence is plain and admits of no argument: we are experiencing the end of the *exception française*.

The pivotal moment when the irrevocable transition to normality took place was May 1968. The lyrical flights of fancy to which the events of that tumultuous month gave rise (echoed in the Socialist victory of May 1981) represented the return of a revolutionary romanticism, bearing, as it had in earlier times, a regenerated vision of society—only this time, strangely enough, it signaled the definitive disappearance of the French model. Régis Debray, observing from a vantage point somewhere between the wartime underground and the *grand corps d'État* of the Fifth Republic, brilliantly put matters in perspective. Ten years after May 1968, rejecting the conventional wisdom of the age, he saw those events as marking the moment when French society was "normalized," its "political dramaturgy" ended. The sudden emergence of utopia, the general euphoria of those heady days, concealed an ongoing adaptation to the realities of the market, to liberalism—to California: "The intensification of the liturgies [of the Left]," Debray wrote, "covered up and permitted the liquidation of [its] dogmas."[45] The nation, the state, and the people were relegated to oblivion; civil society and the return to private life triumphed. Even earlier, the sociologist Michel Crozier had seen in May 1968 "the last great scene" to which an industrial society that had finally acquired an ethic of "responsibility" treated itself.[46] In this sense, paradoxically, May 1968 constituted the specifically French version of the end of ideologies announced almost a generation before by certain American authors who claimed to detect the "disenchantment" of the world[47]—a particularly crucial moment in French society, whose exceptionalism had been founded on a harsh and constant clash of unitary visions that blocked all attempts to retreat into the private sphere.

Paradoxically, too, the apparent triumph of socialism in 1981 masked for many observers the triumph of consensus—the victory of the "Republic of the Center," which imposed its rule both on upholders of the secular Republic and on those of the Catholic counterrevolution. Farewell, then, to Saint Bartholomew's Day and the Terror, to Joan of Arc and Nicolas Chauvin (the soldier who gave his name to chauvinism), to the barricades of 1848 and the Commune, to Boulanger and Dreyfus, to Vichy and sundry populisms, to peasant revolts and great workers' strikes—all symbols of the penchant for going to extremes that typified French exceptionalism. François Furet's assessment was meant to be both cruel and radical: "What we are experiencing is quite simply the end of French exceptionality . . . , the banalization of French politics. . . . France has closed its political theater of the exceptional and become an ordinary democracy like any other. . . . Along with its revolutionary gamble, French politics has lost its theatrical dimension." What we are witnessing, then, is the "twilight of a France that will have lasted two hundred years," the "liquidation of a bellicose political culture peculiar to France, which at once annoyed and fascinated foreigners." Again: "Twenty years ago, even ten, one wondered whether French society would one day cease to practice a politics in which the specter of civil war formed the background. This has now happened." As a result, "the decline of political passions" assures "the normalization of France in relation to the Anglo-Saxon democracies, in which [the passions of] politics cooled long ago."[48] Driving the point home, in an article written shortly before his death, Furet haughtily and mockingly added,

> I suspect that the "republican" [siren] song, which caresses France more or less everywhere, accompanies the twilight of the historic and exceptional election about which France has been able to boast since the days of the ancien régime and the Revolution. The country of Catholic and revolutionary universalism cannot ignore the fact that there now exists, at the end of the present century, a common model of democracy, to which [France's] history, grand though it may be, supplies no ready-made answers.[49]

André Malraux, bard of so many of the century's epic events, also saw the large-scale strikes that swept through French society in the spring of 1968—which in his view were devoid of "hatred"—as an instance of this same difficult "adaptation" to modernity.[50] In a similar vein, with the wisdom of hindsight, the historian Pierre Nora noted the decline of "the history that divides us and [the rise of] a culture that brings us together," all the more readily as France is faced with a "fading of nationalism" on both the Left and the Right.[51] Maurice Agulhon, somewhat nostalgically, conceded that "[t]here is indeed some truth in the idea that a certain philosophical civil war is in the [process] of being pacified."[52] As André Burguière and Jacques Revel put it, "for a very long time—too long—we have been convinced of a sort of French exemplarity. France has now entered into the ranks of [ordinary] nations."[53]

It has been France's peculiar fate, then, to end up witnessing the unexpected triumph of a passionless consensus, against which the two rival partners in French exceptionalism—the virtuous republicans and, even more, the uncompromising Catholic counterrevolutionaries—had fought since the French Revolution. As if by magic, Robespierre and Joseph de Maistre, Léon Gambetta and Charles Maurras, Léon Blum and Charles de Gaulle disappeared from collective memory, the market abruptly cousigning both the Republic and the Church to oblivion—the two of them carried off by the dreaded Hydra of individualism, with the menace of multiculturalism taking up the rear.

François Furet and his coauthors openly expressed their delight with this outcome in *The Republic of the Center* (1986). Régis Debray, on the other hand, their sworn adversary, faithfully raised once more the alarm of his *Modest Contribution* (1979) in the hope of rousing republican souls dulled and degraded by the formidable liberalism of the Anglo-Saxons: "Without calling attention to themselves," he announced a decade later, on the occasion of the bicentennial of the French Revolution, "the enemies of the Republic have taken power in society. In the forefront, Money and Image. Their alliance has replaced that of Throne and Altar."[54]

Since only the old alliance was capable of stirring up the righteous wrath of the republicans and rallying their forces, the demise of the old partnership of fraternal enemies implied a generalized withdrawal into private life.

In Debray's view, the French had turned into counterrevolutionaries without knowing it. Even at Koblenz—a metaphor for reactionaries in exile ever since the French émigrés gathered there to form Condé's army two centuries ago, in 1792—no one any longer cried "The Revolution is the enemy!" But it was not the French counterrevolution that had triumphed, since this would inevitably have provoked a massive uprising of the republicans, fortified by their rekindled faith; it was the insidious American counterrevolution that had carried the day, achieving its purpose under the cover of liberalism and individualism. Deprived of their favorite adversary, the heirs of the Enlightenment gave way. "Passion in general is dead," Debray lamented. The French version of history was coming to an end: "An old couple is splitting up before our eyes. In the arms of the state, 'society' supplants 'nation.' Each of us finds himself alone, then, lost in a crowd of individuals all alike in their desire not to resemble one another. . . . Return to the individual as the supreme end. Narcissism."[55]

Had America therefore infiltrated French minds to such an extent that Marianne was the victim of a "veritable ethnocide,"[56] a merciless "brainwashing . . . , a knowingly implemented enterprise of national depersonalization"[57]—a victim of American "perversions"[58] to such an extent that Debray, herald of a damned republic, was forced to adopt the passé vocabulary of David Riesman, the sociologist of the "lonely crowd," or the similarly outdated language of Christopher Lasch, the once-celebrated author of a rather unpersuasive essay about cultural narcissism? Not a trace of doubt seemed to cross his mind:

Individualism, of which democracy makes a religion, thus becomes the soul of a world without individuals, the spiritual aroma of sheep. . . . In the French Republic of 1989, the Republic has become a minority. . . . Democracy has conquered. . . . The Republic seems an old-fashioned idea. . . . Michelet has given birth to de Tocqueville. . . . This leveling has torn down the old barriers, letting in the wind from America that sweeps away everything in its way. . . . Our media establishment stages "the end of History" by Mr. Fukuyama, an official of the American State Department. . . . A French Republic that will only be a democracy like the others is insignificant.[59]

Since the consensual politics of the American "Left" no longer distinguished it in any way from a neoconservative Right whose ideas come from the University of Chicago, France had no choice but to say farewell to its history, to its passions: "Adieu '89"— womb of totalitarian ideology—"the Revolution is over."[60]

A worse nightmare could not be imagined: the Homeric clash between the two Frances, the one republican, the other counter-revolutionary, both determined to standardize thought and behavior, both hostile to pluralism and liberalism, gives birth, after so much blood and fury, to—a vulgar democracy that is more respectful of the rights of man than of those of the citizen! Hence the little game that was all the rage one winter in Paris, with everyone feverishly filling out questionnaires to find out at last whether they were a republican or a democrat, which is to say, a good person or a bad person. This typically French game assumed the disappearance once and for all of republican France's former adversary, the counterrevolutionary France that was deeply rooted in the political landscape for so long—a form of blindness that was all the more perplexing as it manifested itself at the very moment when the National Front had succeeded in becoming a durable presence at the heart of French society. Indeed, the inventor of the republican-vs.-democrat game acknowledged the resurgence of reactionary sentiment in France and beyond: "We are celebrating today perhaps not the Restoration, as the pessimists say, but the posthumous victory, on a European scale, of the Girondins over the nasty Jacobins.[61] This looks very much like the revenge of Maurras on Michelet, the land's revenge on the nation—and, by extension, the triumph of Joseph de Maistre over Condorcet, of Christianity over the Republic."[62]

All of which is very far removed from America and Tocqueville, from "Free Time and McDonald's, which have replaced Le Mahieu and Le Capoulade . . . on either side of the rue Soufflot, at the corner of the Boulevard Saint-Michel."[63] History remains decidedly dangerous when one speaks of the posthumous triumph of Maistre and Maurras, of the victory of intransigent Catholicism over its mortal enemy, liberalism; when Charles Pasqua, the former minister of the interior, observes, as though it were obvious, that "[i]t is [now] 1788. French society is on the eve of revolt";[64] when Jean-Marie Le Pen, the fiery leader of the National Front, hopes and prays for an indispensable regenerative "revolution."[65] Plainly the present situation cannot be described as one of soft consensus.

In short, things are far from being settled. We need to take a closer look, then—all the more since recent scholarship gives us a glimpse of an entirely different reality. Some scholars, it is true, hold that "what is coming to an end is an image of France [that was] inaugurated with the French Revolution. It is the end of a view of society conceived in negation of, but also in counter-dependence on, the religious model."[66] But others, a majority, emphasize "the persistence, for the most part, of the broad features of French political culture." Noting, for example, that religious convictions continue to have the greatest influence on voting,[67] they deny that any permanent "break" has fundamentally altered the traditional Left-Right cleavage.[68] For these scholars, the authoritarian temptation emerges—today as in the past—from the depths of a France that is supposed to be wholly pacified, centrist, and committed to liberalism. Today, however, an enterprising *lepénisme* takes aim at the Republic,[69] looking to attract left-wing working-class voters with its populist and anticapitalist program, just as similar movements attracted left-wing anti-Dreyfusards at the end of the last century.

Moreover, the present-day political and administrative system, which reflects the unresolved conflict between cultural allegiances and political utopia, is seen by most scholars as preserving many of its essential features, despite the many inroads made by "Americanization"[70] and despite its various internal rifts.[71] Thus the French state, ignoring proposals for reform and looking to the long term, continues to take responsibility for governing an often rebellious society, imposing its universalist norms and vigorously arguing against strong ethnic or religious attachments; at the same time, it strenuously resists the temptation to embrace liberal ideas and, out of a concern for maintaining French cultural exceptionalism,[72] seeks to dampen the hopes of those who turn their gaze across the Atlantic.

On this view, the state-republic alliance still remains the basis of the nation, even if it is attacked both by convinced liberals and by the supporters of the old counterrevolutionary current, now back in fashion again. But there are some historians of the Republic, such as Maurice Agulhon, who reject such an interpretation. "The Republic," Agulhon argues, "is the French form of liberal democracy. . . . It is no longer possible today, honestly, to deny the fact that a consensus exists about the principles of liberal democracy, and therefore of an admittedly minimal, but nonetheless authentic and sincere, definition of the Republic. . . . Conflicts remain between the value systems of the Right and the Left, but the conflict over the theme of the Republic, and over the word itself, is an obsolete conflict." In France, a reversion to fanaticism is no longer a concern.[73]

How far has the Republic actually renounced its ideal of militant citizenship, and the counterrevolution its Herderian view of the nation? How far have the two Frances actually abandoned their mutually exclusive unitary visions? How far have they become reconciled within the framework of an improbable liberalism that holds out the promise of guaranteeing a peaceful resolution of their conflicts? The pages that follow are an attempt to answer these questions.

Chapter One

The Innermost Thoughts
of Alexis de Tocqueville

In a letter to Francisque de Corcelle in 1843, Alexis de Tocqueville (1805–59) spoke from the bottom of his heart, telling Corcelle of an intimate and pessimistic conviction that he hardly dared acknowledge. Tocqueville, the aristocratic prophet of a new democratic age, confessed to his friend that he was deeply troubled by France's exceptional and implacable hostility to the emergence of an open society: "Catholicism, which produces such admirable effects in certain cases, which one must uphold with all one's power because in France the religious spirit can exist only with it, will never, I fear, adopt the new society," he wrote. "It will never forget the position that it had in the old one, and every time it is given powers, it will hasten to abuse them. I would say this only to you. But I say it to you because I want you to be privy to my innermost thoughts."[1]

Though he hoped to see the emergence in France of a liberal, consensual, and pluralist society on the American model, in which citizens would peacefully settle their differences through community institutions and political organizations, Tocqueville nonetheless felt compelled to predict instead intolerance, conflict, and hatred. And though he remained faithful to his religious heritage (despite the fact that he was no longer a practicing Catholic), he feared that the Church would "abuse" any power that it might be granted. From its earliest times the Church had been organized as a centralized bureaucracy and claimed the right to regulate the thinking of Catholics by imposing doctrinal order. It was inflexibly determined to monitor morals, to limit dissent, and, worse still, to suppress all forms of political liberalism and pluralism that might threaten the country's spiritual unity. The thought of all this made Tocqueville inconsolably "sad."[2]

In the United States, by contrast, it was possible to combine the spirit of religion with the spirit of liberty:

> Far from harming each other, these two apparently opposed tendencies work in harmony and seem to lend mutual support.
>
> Religion regards civil liberty as a noble exercise of men's faculties, the world of politics being a sphere intended by the Creator for the free play of intelligence. Religion, being free and powerful within its own sphere and content with the position reserved for it, realizes that its sway is all the better established because it relies only on its own powers and rules men's hearts without external support.
>
> Freedom sees religion as the companion of its struggles and triumphs, the cradle of its infancy, and the divine source of its rights.[3]

In America, where a great many churches and Protestant sects were constitutionally set apart from the state by a famous "wall" of separation that still allowed a place for religious values, pluralism reigned. How far was this relationship, which was one of symbiosis but also of radical separation, transposable to a society in which an insistent antagonism divided church and state, where two monolithic organizations engaged in a relentless competition to which the spirit of compromise was utterly foreign? Tocqueville's judgment that Protestantism played a crucial role in the birth of political consensus in America, from which he inferred an affinity between liberalism, democracy, and Protestantism, has been endorsed by many commentators, most notably the sociologist Robert Bellah and the political scientist Seymour Lipset.[4] The question remains, however, whether Tocqueville could have seriously imagined importing mechanisms that assumed a limited state and strong democracy, compatible with cultural pluralism, into a society as eminently Catholic as France. His entire work demonstrates the near futility of any such attempt.

In fact, Tocqueville long hesitated before reaching this somber conclusion. In 1834 he wrote:

> French society used to be split into two opposing camps. . . . Today, the two opposing standards are still upheld. But the ranks of the two armies have become mixed and it is difficult to tell to which of the two each [partisan] used to belong. . . . Men who started out from a purely political point of view were led by experience, little by little, to think that society could not do without religious beliefs. . . . To the extent that the political hatreds engendered by the temporal influence of the clergy lacked an object, this idea acquired authority and won over all minds. . . . There is agreement about wanting to bring the spirit of Christianity into politics. . . . We think that in France Christianity cannot help but take a Catholic form.[5]

The young Tocqueville had still been an optimist: rival armies would melt at the glance of an eye, and—contrary to his later "innermost thoughts"—the hatreds integral to French political culture in its relation with the Church would prove in the end not to be irremediable. In 1836, when he published the first part of *Democracy in America*, he remained yet full of hope, since the American example proved the compatibility of religion and democracy: although it presupposed the establishment of a "civil religion" that excluded the churches from the public sphere, this sphere was wholly suffused with the idea of the divine. He was therefore led to imagine that religion might be protected in

France if church were to be kept separate from state, for "it was much less as a religious doctrine than as a political institution that Christianity aroused these furious hatreds . . . not because the Church could not take its place in the new society that was being created, but because it occupied the strongest and most privileged place in the old society which was being ground into dust."[6] These "furious hatreds" had led straight to 1789. It was thus plausible to suppose that Catholics might agree to turn away from political power, as the American Protestants had; that they might admirably fit into the democratic movement and adopt its customs:

> [These Catholics] form the most republican and democratic of all classes in the United States. At first glance this is astonishing, but reflection easily indicates the hidden causes therefor. I think one is wrong in regarding the Catholic religion as a natural enemy of democracy. . . . [O]nce priests are excluded or exclude themselves from the government, as happens in the United States, no men are more led by their beliefs than are Catholics to carry the idea of equality of conditions over into the political sphere.[7]

There was good warrant, then, for optimism: it sufficed to detach the Church from political temptation, which is to say from the state, in order that the Catholic world, including France, would finally "adopt" the new society, and France would enter peacefully into the democratic age. Everything would turn out for the best—though Tocqueville nonetheless acknowledged that, in the United States, "[m]ost of the Catholics are poor, and unless all citizens govern, they will never attain to the government themselves. The Catholics are in a minority, and it is important for them that all rights should be respected so that they can be sure to enjoy their own in freedom. For these two reasons they are led, perhaps in spite of themselves, toward political doctrines which, maybe, they would adopt with less zeal were they rich and predominant."[8] And so Tocqueville's hopes foundered once more, the Catholics seeming decidedly unfit for democracy.

In a lucid commentary on this paragraph, Hervé de Tocqueville stressed the contradictions among his son's several observations and added: "At bottom, one cannot close one's eyes to the fact that the ecclesiastical hierarchy of the Catholics is much more a reflection of monarchical government than of republican institutions."[9] All the more lastingly, then, in a country like France, did the antagonism between Catholicism and democracy persist. Still hopeful, the young Alexis de Tocqueville refused to endorse either side. As for believers, he emphasized:

> Imagining unbelief to be something new, they compromise all that is new in one indiscriminate animosity. They are at war with their age. . . .
>
> I am profoundly convinced that this accidental and particular cause is the close union of politics and religion.
>
> Unbelievers in Europe attack Christians more as political than as religious enemies; they hate the faith as the opinion of a party much more than as a mistaken belief; and they reject the clergy less because they are representatives of God than because they are the friends of authority.
>
> European Christianity has allowed itself to be intimately united with the powers of this world.[10]

His father and brother did not share this fine optimism. In his father's view, Alexis "has not addressed the true cause of the estrangement between the clergy and persons who revere free institutions. It is to be sought in the memory of the persecutions religion suffered the moment the word 'liberty' rang out in France." And his brother, Édouard de Tocqueville, added: "I am of father's opinion. It is absolutely necessary to mention the memories of '93 as [a] powerful cause of the clergy's antipathy for liberal ideas."[11]

In 1840, when Tocqueville published the second part of

Democracy in America—whose tone, by contrast with that of the first, was strongly pessimistic—he was nevertheless still capable of writing: "If Catholicism could ultimately escape from the political animosities to which it has given rise, I am almost certain that that same spirit of the age which now seems so contrary to it would turn into a powerful ally and that it would suddenly make great conquests."[12] The second part of *Democracy in America* is concerned less with America than with the development of democracy in general and, implicitly, with the course of French society in particular. Tocqueville gives the impression of being less confident in this new work, forgetful of ad hoc arguments inspired by the American context; nonetheless, he continued to express the belief that Catholicism could profitably replace the Protestantism that, in the United States, was so favorable to the flourishing of a democracy that combined individualism and collective participation. This encounter between Catholicism and democracy seemed to him all the more imaginable since, across the Atlantic, Catholicism progressed so rapidly that it could be expected to end up one day "being the only religion of all those who have a religion."[13]

Considering the importance that Tocqueville accorded to religion in maintaining democratic customs, this proposition comes as a surprise; and it seems to beg the question since, in his heart of hearts, he remained persuaded of the contrary, as his private correspondence of the same period reveals. Tocqueville was not fooled: he had not brought back from the United States a miraculous solution capable of silencing his "innermost thoughts." Indeed, in the second part of *Democracy in America*, he doubted that Christian beliefs could be maintained in France, even assuming a genuine separation of church and state. The traditional alliance of throne and altar would contest any such separation too strongly.[14] And although he felt that Catholicism would finally be better adapted to democracy than Protestantism, he did not ask how the mechanisms for maintaining the wall of separation, peculiar to American society, might be imported to France.[15] Consequently, he took another tack: if religious beliefs endured across the Atlantic, it was because they depended more on the enlightened self-interest of Americans than on simple measures of separation; thus he hoped to convince his fellow countrymen to remain faithful to their religion without necessarily trying to separate church and state, an undertaking fraught with the possibility of violence.

But these hopes were not sufficient to overcome the dark forebodings Tocqueville felt. His innermost thoughts were above all a response to the French "accident," to the history peculiar to a society that fed to an unusual degree on hatred. The reader will have certainly remarked, from the passages just quoted, how frequently the idea of hatred recurs in the writings of this committed liberal—and this despite the fact, or perhaps because of it, that hatred was profoundly foreign to Tocqueville personally. In a superb letter to his friend Henry Reeve, he wrote:

> They are utterly determined to portray me as a partisan when I am not one at all; passions are attributed to me when I have only opinions. . . . Being myself part of the old aristocracy of my country, and this aristocracy having been destroyed, I had neither hatred nor natural jealousy against the aristocracy. . . . I would say the same of the democratic element. . . . I had no particular motive either to love or to hate independently of those that reason supplied me with. . . . I did not need to make any great effort to look calmly upon both sides.[16]

He stressed this abiding aspect of his character, which distinguished him from many of his fellow citizens. Although he was no stranger to the rough-and-tumble of provincial political life, where struggles to win local office were fierce to the point of recklessness, he nonetheless remained on his guard against all "hatred of individual persons" and refused to counsel his friends to resort to means that might generate "hatreds." In particular, he objected to the "violence of language" that he saw on all sides, rebuking one of his allies with these words: "[Y]ou express your hatred and scorn for the government as a whole too openly."[17]

Attacked by both the administration and the conservative parties, Tocqueville also met with hostility from the Left: in 1861, two years after his death, his close friend Gustave de Beaumont confided to the liberal English political economist Nassau William Senior that the leaders of the Left "hated [Tocqueville] as much as he hated them. Much more, actually, for his mind was not trained for hatred. They excluded him from practically all committees."[18] More generally, Tocqueville regretted that, in his own arrondissement of Valognes as in nearby Cherbourg, many "violent animosities" were expressed without restraint, to such a degree that he felt tempted to "withdraw from the fray," to escape the "war" that set local political life ablaze. Provincial France, he thought, was experiencing a "permanent" war. Faithful to his liberal principles, even if the government seemed also to want to make "war" against him, Tocqueville restrained his friends from declaring "war" against the state's representatives. On several occasions, and in the same terms, he lamented the local "civil war" that was tearing apart Normandy.[19] He confided his profound anguish to his friend and neighbor Jean-Jacques Ampère: in national political life, as at the local level, everything proceeded as though "hatred of one's neighbor was stronger than [hatred] of one's master."[20] In an admirable letter addressed to Ampère, he wrote: "My mind is at ease. . . . I am a liberal to the marrow of my bones. I will continue to be one or I will be nothing. . . . I am to be taken as I am or not at all." Scorning his critics, he added: "A valet's hatred is no excuse."[21]

This hatred, which Tocqueville himself did not feel, served him as a fundamental principle for distinguishing democratic societies from those, such as France, that remained subject to the forces of despotism and revolutionary passions. In a little-cited passage, he wrote, "In the United States there is no religious hatred because religion is universally respected and no sect is predominant; there is no class hatred because the people is everything, and nobody dares to struggle against it." In France, by contrast, hatred of all sorts spread without limit, to the point that it may truly be said to have fashioned French exceptionalism. This fury literally exploded during the French Revolution. In 1836, in the first part of *Democracy in America*, Tocqueville emphasized that the "Revolution pronounced at the same time against royalty and against provincial institutions. Revolutionary hatred was directed indiscriminately against all that had gone before, both the absolute power and those elements which could temper its rigors." Knowing that the "passions that stir the Americans most deeply are commercial and not political ones, or rather they carry a trader's habits over into the business of politics," how could he have imagined that importing their peaceful institutions into a society ruled by inexpiable hatreds—the buttresses of so many irreversible historical ruptures—would have the effect only of promoting healthy competition?[22]

The truth of the matter is that Tocqueville's impossible wager was lost in advance. One could not reasonably propose to put an end to hatred by introducing homeopathic doses of decentralization or by resolving to reinforce the communal fabric of society. Even Tocqueville was not convinced on this point. He suggested, optimistically, that "useful lessons" could be drawn from the American experience; that "borrowing" from America its "general and creative idea" was permissible.[23] He even hoped that an attempt could be made to "gradually introduc[e] democratic institutions among us" in order to avoid the "unlimited authority of a single man." Yet he declared in the same breath that simply "to imitate" American democracy would be a "great mistake."[24] A peerless comparativist, he knew that his successful tour of the United States would have little immediate consequence; that if one day he were to be understood, time and patience would be required.

The notion that "habits of the heart" can be transposed from one nation to another seemed to him doubtful. Tocqueville noted with sadness that in times of relative calm "beliefs are forsaken with indifference rather than from hate; without being rejected, they fall away."[25] In a country such as America, far from the religious turmoil of the old continent, the "unbeliever" (implicitly, Tocqueville himself) stands apart from his fellows, seemingly with regret. In France, by contrast, hatred appeared to have a tremendous hold on life, greatly tormenting believers and unbelievers alike and implacably undermining democratic hopes. In France "unbelievers . . . hate," while unbelief likewise aroused "hatred" and "terror" on the part of believers. But in the United States, such vehemence appeared only in connection with the slave question; as Tocqueville noted, "in proportion as slavery disappears, the Whites fear becoming mixed [and] become contemptuous. . . . The less harsh the law, the greater the hatreds."[26] Here for the first time, in connection with racism, "hatred" surfaces in his commentary on American society. These prejudices contradicted the smooth course of American democracy, giving free rein to a principle otherwise unknown in the New World but identical with the one that ruled French society. Indeed, Tocqueville himself felt "hatred" in the face of such injustice. In a moment that is unique in his work, he opens his moderate liberal heart to hatred. "[A]ll my hatred," he writes, "is concentrated against those who, after a thousand years of equality, introduced slavery into the world again."[27] Later, in his *Recollections*, he would say: "For my part I hate all those absolute systems that make all the events of history depend on great first causes,"[28] suppressing the freedom of individuals. "I hate demagogy," he emphasized in another little-known passage, once more personally adopting a verb that elsewhere he employed only to describe the history of French exceptionalism.[29]

Hatred—a paradoxical phenomenon in the United States—was an enduring feature of French society, torn apart not by racism but by the clash between believers and unbelievers. The true originality of France, in Tocqueville's view, resided in this very clash. In a rough draft of the second volume of *Democracy in America*, he wrote: "The first use that French philosophers made of their liberty was to attack all religions with a sort of fury, the Christian religion in particular. I believe that this must be considered a pure accident, a fact peculiar to France."[30] The American model thus became separated once and for all from the fate of France. Among the French, politics shattered all possible unity of belief, whereas Americans preferred to devote themselves to the "gentle commerce" of economic trade on a basis of shared morality and beliefs. In a surprising letter addressed to his brother Édouard on 28 May 1831, from New York, Tocqueville remarked:

> We really are in a different world here [in the United States]; political passions here are only on the surface. The profound passion, the only one that deeply stirs the human heart, the daily passion, is the acquisition of wealth, and there are a thousand ways to acquire it without disturbing the State. One would have to be quite blind, in my opinion, to compare this country with Europe and to wish to adapt to one what suits the other; I believed this before leaving France; I believe it more and more on examining the society in which I now live; this is a country of merchants who take care of public affairs when their work leaves them the leisure to do so.[31]

In Tocqueville's mind then, the two models irrevocably diverged: unlike America, France was a country of extreme "political passions" that brought the state into play and swayed rival camps. This view (which one also finds in arguments about France's famous economic backwardness) overrode Tocqueville's desire to imitate the American example, which yet occasionally crops up in his later writings when he seems to wish to reassure himself. In this passage, however, no such urge is to be found: to each society its own "habits of the heart." Political passions and hatreds are France's lot, emanating from a "special fact" and forming a durable basis for its exceptionalism.

In France, political passions were fueled by the presence of a strong state that had to conquer in order to impose its unitary interpretation of society; in America, the weakness of the state diluted political struggles and deprived them of ideological force, while the preeminence of economic passions pushed political passions into the background. The "new political science"[32] that Tocqueville hoped to bring forth aimed at explaining the differences between the Old and New Worlds, embodied respectively by France and the United States. In his essay *The Social and Political Condition of France*, the state lay at the heart of the strategies pursued by all of the contending parties: the clergy, the nobility, and the poor. The nobles "conducted the affairs of State"; they meant "to direct the whole State," to seize "the fortune of the State"; France "had a *religion d'État*"; and so on. In the United States and England, the state remained "weak," and these countries displayed democratic regimes "in which society acts by itself [and] power exists only within it."[33] But the world had not seen a concentration of power comparable to that of France "since the fall of the Roman Empire."[34] As a result, the weakness of democracy in France was proportional to the strength of the state: "[T]he state reaches the extreme limits of its power all at once, while private persons allow themselves to sink in one moment down to the lowest degree of weakness,"[35] recovering in order once more to do battle with a state that strips them of all power.

Americans, these "solemn men concerned with the serious pursuits of life," tried only to assure their own "material enjoyment" by applying "the doctrine of enlightened self-interest."[36] As Tocqueville further noted, "In the United States, when a citizen has some education and some resources he tries to enrich himself either by trade or industry. . . . All he asks from the state is not to get in his way while he is working and to see that he can enjoy the fruit of his labor. But in most of the countries of Europe, as soon as a man begins to feel his strength and extend his ambitions, the first idea that occurs to him is to get a public appointment."[37] In a shorter note, he remarked again, "In America, every man seeks to improve his situation through industry and commerce. In France, when [a man] desires to rise above his station, he asks for a public post."[38]

The weaker the state, the fewer officials there are. By contrast, where the state is strong, the market loses its preeminence, with the result that only an elite of political and administrative officials is recognized as legitimate. Within the agencies of the state, an inflexible system of fixed roles separates civil servants from other elites. As Tocqueville emphasized, "The bureaucracy, almost all bourgeois, already formed a class with its own character, its own traditions, virtues, honor, its own pride."[39] It constituted, especially in societies having a strong state, "a nation within each nation"[40] and was isolated from the larger society to the extent that it was supposed to act rationally in the name of the general interest. Thus one notices in the United States "the absence of what we would call government or administration," for "there is no central point on which the radii of administrative power converge." The civil servants there "blend with the mass of citizens; they have neither palaces nor guards nor ceremonial clothes"; but the stability of their employment is more uncertain owing to the operation of a spoils system that ensures they will have only "one brief moment of power."[41]

By contrast, Tocqueville remarked, "Under the old regime as now, there was in France no city, town, or village, no tiny hamlet, no hospital, factory, convent, or college, which could have an independent will in its own affairs, or freely administer its own goods. Then, as today, the government kept the French under its tutelage."[42] At another point he exclaimed, "Among the most absolute sovereigns of Europe, I defy anyone to show me *a single one* who has control over a comparable number of civil servants [as the French state] and who can act in as constant and direct a manner, not only regarding affairs of state but also the least interests of citizens."[43] The strong state goes far beyond simple administrative centralization, he recognized, since it implies not only public possession of the educational system, permitting control over political socialization (which thus escapes control by the upper class), but also control over an important part of economic production, through the nationalization of industry, further marginalizing the role of the market. This remark also clarifies Tocqueville's use of the term "despotism"[44] to describe the functioning of the strong French state: Americans, by contrast, "being from the beginning accustomed to governing themselves, . . . never had to call upon the state to act temporarily as guardian,"[45] and consequently did not direct hatreds and passions against it.

In *The Old Regime and the Revolution*, a mature work that openly expresses its author's innermost thoughts, as did the various notes and unpublished texts that appeared shortly after his death, Tocqueville still granted a conspicuous role to hatred in accounting for the Revolution—the perfect moment of French exceptionalism: "Throughout this Revolution, so repressive and so cruel, I see the hatred of the ancien régime continually surpass all other hatreds in the heart of the French and to root itself there to such a degree that it survives its very object and, [once] a temporary passion, [now] becomes a permanent and characteristic trait."[46] This now visceral hatred, in perfect contrast to the American case, grew out of both antagonistic beliefs and economic rivalries. The former were fundamental, because more lasting: "It was not the hatred of social inequalities, but the hatred of despotism, that first revealed itself,"[47] causing as a result, by association, "the furious hatred of priests and religion" that is "the most enduring and the last extinguished of revolutionary passions." Such animosity fed on "virulent hatred and contempt for the nonjuring clergy" (who refused to swear an oath of allegiance to the revolutionary government). The government and the dominant party, meanwhile, "professed hatred and contempt for each other, with this difference only, that hatred was strongest toward the latter and contempt most pronounced toward the former."[48] The atmosphere hardly favored reconciliation, so great was the hatred of priests "connected with the political hierarchy,"[49] and so hard did the aristocracy "try to revive Christianity as a political instrument."[50] Scholars played a leading role in the struggle against the Church, though the Terror inspired in them a profound "hatred" as well.[51]

Intolerance also fed on socioeconomic differences, especially since the French felt a "violent and inextinguishable hatred of inequality."[52] Again: "The hatreds that divided the classes were too inflamed for them to want to march together."[53] Certain aristocrats exhibited a "violent hatred" of the clergy, and to make matters worse, famine and cold took their toll: "Poverty worked to sharpen all jealousies and all hatreds on all sides";[54] and the prosperity that succeeded it increased discontent further and caused "hatred against the old institutions [to grow]. The nation [took] visible steps towards a revolution."[55] Violence was the result not of poverty as such but of the frustration associated with it. When the provincial assemblies sent circulars questioning the inhabitants of the local parishes about their grievances against the old regime, they did not anticipate the consequences; in a commentary that by itself would justify the thesis of French exceptionalism, Tocqueville remarked:

> [These circulars were] to inflame each and every individual by the recitation of his miseries, to point a finger at their authors for him, to embolden him by the sight of their small number, and to penetrate his very heart to inflame his greed, envy, and hatred. It seems as if [local episodes of violence such as] the Jacquerie, the Mallotins, and the Sixteen had been completely forgotten, and that it was unknown that the French, who are the gentlest and even the most benevolent people in the world as long as they remain peacefully undisturbed, become the most barbarous nation on earth as soon as violent passions arouse them.[56]

In only a few sentences, Tocqueville captured the import of the "barbarism" that had suddenly been raised to its highest point in French history—an intolerance that he then went on to characterize as a sort of constancy peculiar to the "national character" that generated "the most frightening confusion."[57]

During the time when peasants and minor notables were composing books of grievances (*cahiers de doléances*) for presentation to the Estates General, convened by Louis XVI on 5 July 1788, French society experienced a brief respite: "Souls calmed for a moment and were uplifted. It was then that hatreds and jealousies seemed forgotten in order to think only of the magnitude of what was about to be done." Nonetheless, certain individuals worked to fan the flames, to give new life to the passions. Abbé Sieyès, for one, was prepared to do anything to revive "violent class hatreds." He "cannot hide the bad humor in which the relinquishment [of tax privileges] has put him," Tocqueville noted. "Trying to prevent it from extinguishing hatreds."[58] Nor did Jean-Joseph Mounier make any attempt to hide his "hatred of the privileges of the provinces, of the provincial aristocracy,"[59] while Antoine Barnave's writings bore a "hatred of despotism"[60] and the Protestant pastor Jean-Paul Rabaut Saint-Étienne likewise preferred "hatred of the nobility to the love of freedom."[61] All of them exacerbated class struggles and strengthened "their defiance and their hatred." The course of the Revolution was then still uncertain: the aristocracy had already abandoned the reality of power but retained its appearances, and so "[it] seemed still great enough to be hated and yet no longer great enough to defend itself from attacks of hatred."[62] As a result, the Constituent Assembly (parliament), "caught up . . . in the general hatred . . . , [a] giant that seemed to have a hundred arms, . . . suddenly subsided and expired without being able even to emit a sigh."[63]

Tocqueville's overall assessment does not come as a surprise:

Hatred of the ancien régime: passion that dominates all others. It is so much the fundamental, essential, primordial character of the Revolution that it never left those who made [the Revolution] on any occasion. The feeling . . . persisted among those who suffered the most from the Revolution. More importantly, it won over the original enemies of the Revolution. It came to be shared by the princes themselves, who ended up supporting [the Revolution] and even finding good in the destruction of the old system.[64]

Once the new revolutionary society was stabilized, this feeling scarcely faded, for "hatred turned bitter in [the form of] obedience."[65] Hatred upset the whole social structure and lastingly marked the memories of adversaries: "When, sixty years ago, the different classes which made up the society of old France reentered into contact with one another, . . . [they] made contact only in order to tear each other apart. Even today their jealousies and their hatreds survive them."[66] As Tocqueville observed still more bitterly toward the end of the uncompleted second volume of *The Old Regime and the Revolution*, "[I]t is much easier for men to remain constant in their hatreds than in their affections." Accordingly, for Tocqueville the liberal, the ultimate conclusion was terrifying: hatred was "a permanent feature" of French society. He tirelessly repeated it: "I dare say that there is no other people on earth that could present such a spectacle. I know my nation. . . . There are undertakings that only the French nation is capable of conceiving, magnanimous resolutions that only she dares to make." The Terror was "impossible anywhere other than in France, with the characteristics it had among us."[67]

Shortly before the revolution of 1848, Tocqueville noted: "France, it is said, is sleeping; no, it is not sleeping, it is bored and [its head] droops"—then went on to add: "You believe that the nation is calm, I say that it is dozing."[68] Less than a year before the new outbreak of revolutionary violence, he wrote with an air of premonition: "The revolution is finished, revolutionary activity has ceased, passions have died out. One must not rejoice at this. . . . There is not room enough for life [i.e., the clash of ideas]. . . . I do not ask that citizens run to take up arms in the public square but that they have firm and settled opinions. . . . Soon, if one is not careful, indifference will give way to envy and hatred. Future danger: class warfare."[69] In this revolutionary context, he came back repeatedly to the same idea: "As for the moderate monarchy, it is dead. Only the Republic is possible any longer. . . . But there are other perils"[70]—the perils produced by social antagonism. In addition to hatreds due to social inequality, there was "the universal hatred combined with terror felt towards Paris for the first time," as well as the ancestral violence provoked by the specific status of the Church within society, with the result that a quite unexpected "community of hatreds" suddenly took shape: "[T]he tepid passions of our day were expressed in the burning language of '93."[71] Even among opponents of the Republic, as he observed later, "the hatred they felt was a gentle hatred, like all the passions then felt in the country."[72]

In a surprising draft of a speech to the Chamber of Deputies, Tocqueville, a Catholic and a supporter of the American system with its pacifying civil religion, again sounded the alarm: "We are witnessing, sirs, a singular and painful spectacle. Religious controversies are starting up again, the old war between the clergy and the academy has flared up again, and the ancient and eternal war between philosophy and religion is now reborn. . . . It is indisputable that, for several years now, religious zeal has been reawakened among us . . . hatred of Catholics toward Protestants."[73]

In a speech delivered to the Chamber shortly afterward, he drove the point home:

> The government has attempted to draw Catholicism toward itself, to exercise its authority over the clergy. . . . What has been the result of these actions? . . . All the old opponents of Catholicism were resuscitated, reawakened at the sight of the government's partiality. Not only were Protestants disturbed by the sight of this new . . . union between church and state; so were freethinkers and sincere men of all faiths and opinions. All these men were worried; a muffled agitation then developed not only against the clergy but against Catholicism as well. . . . The great and unfortunate war that had previously taken place between the new society and religion, . . . and which had seemed to be over or at least suspended—this war started up again with violence everywhere. . . . It was principally [the government's partiality toward Catholicism], so dangerous in its [consequences], that reawakened on all sides so many old hatreds that in the interest of the country should have been buried forever.[74]

Elsewhere, in connection with the Jesuits, Tocqueville added, "All of a sudden . . . the distance of the Church from the present age seems to become greater, the antagonisms more pronounced, the hatreds more fierce."[75] Throughout his writings, always these hatreds. . . .

Events were soon to prove Tocqueville right: passions became exacerbated once more, confirming his initial diagnosis and plunging France into events "stirred up by savagery and hatred."[76] As he confided to his friend Nassau William Senior, this "singular corner" of the world was once again experiencing "the most extraordinary situation into which a great nation [has] ever abruptly been thrown." Conscious of the exceptional character of France's fate, and continually finding himself confronted with the same tragic internal conflicts, he came close to admitting defeat "in the face of this situation unexampled in history. . . . Revolutions have been teachers to us all." Nonetheless, he could not hide his astonishment: "We have all made it this far; and when I consider the attitude of the nation as a whole, I cannot help but admire it. Right down to its faults and its weaknesses, this is a great people."[77] In the admirable conclusion to the first volume of *The Old Regime and the Revolution*, he still proclaimed his love of

> a people so unalterable in its basic instincts that we can still recognize it in portraits drawn of it two or three thousand years ago. . . . [T]he most brilliant and most dangerous nation of Europe . . . France alone could give birth to a revolution so sudden, so radical, so impetuous in its course. . . . Without the reasons which I have given, the French would never have made the Revolution; but it must be recognized that all these reasons together would not succeed in explaining such a revolution anywhere else but in France.[78]

France as a nation remained utterly unchanged: passionate, quarrelsome, violent, permanently vulnerable to the passionate hatreds that rise up from its depths and tear its people apart. In broad strokes, then, Tocqueville drew the portrait of French exceptionalism: "Has there ever been any nation on earth which was so full of contrasts, and so extreme in all of its acts?"[79] His mind was made up: France was fated never to know peace.

Chapter Two

The Body of the Nation

Tocqueville's pessimism had its source in the revolutionary moment. Social change he saw as the irreversible result of confrontation and denial of the past. Rival conceptions of France reduced the chances that democracy would take root, giving impetus instead to radical plots. Prior to the French Revolution, a profound sense of decadence had taken hold of people's minds and encouraged revolt. This sense, which arose from the degeneracy of the king and his hopelessly corrupt aristocracy, continued to be a part of the French political landscape even after the Revolution: at the end of the nineteenth century and later, during the interwar period, the radical and fascistic Right argued that democratic degeneracy justified recourse to the vigorous leadership of a new elite of strong men whose power, virility, and ability to bring forth a healthy and virtuous society were illustrated in pamphlets and political drawings.[1] The theme of regeneration, originally emphasized by the French revolutionaries, emerged yet again in the early twentieth century, in Russia, where it announced still more good news: the birth of Soviet man, once again powerful, virtuous, upright, and incorruptible.

The journalist and politician Camille Desmoulins (1760–94)

best described the utopia of the new man brought about by the French Revolution when he declared:

> Saint Paul, who once or twice in his life was eloquent, somewhere admirably wrote: "All of you who have been regenerated by baptism, you are no longer Jews, you are no longer Samaritans, you are no longer Romans, you are no longer Greeks, you are all Christians." Thus it is that, having just been regenerated by the National Assembly, we are no longer from Chartres or from Monthléri, we are no longer from Picardy or Brittany, we are no longer from Aix or from Arras, we are all French, all brothers.[2]

The project of regeneration—millenarian myth par excellence—was aimed at creating a new human race, free from evil. Whether it was provocatively articulated as a wholesale program of revolution or whether it took into account current realities as part of a program of gradual reform, it furnished the basis for an energetic world that would be the antithesis of the existing corrupt society. The corporeal metaphor of a nation of citizens innocent of all vices was often formulated in biological terms. Thus one reads in a revolutionary pamphlet of the period, for example, that patriotic devotion is "for the body politic what the circulation of the blood is for the veins of the human body; without this necessary circulation, every faculty [of movement] is unresilient, everything is sluggish, everything dies."[3] This idea of the new man, developed by several key Revolution figures in a great many speeches, treatises, and pamphlets, praised a refound energy—the rebirth, in Rabaut Saint-Étienne's phrase, of a race of strong and vigorous men.

Such extravagant imagery bespoke the unity of the nation, but it testified also to the extreme antagonism that the Third Estate felt toward the aristocracy, the radical break between the *peuple-nation* and all the other rejected social forces of the past that were doomed to exclusion. The counterrevolution thus felt justified in rejecting a form of regeneration that it considered synonymous with excess, madness, and baseless pretension. The metaphor of regeneration haunted the discourse of the revolutionaries: it was used to justify most measures, whether they involved the country's educational system or its new territorial divisions. Thus in November 1789, Jacques-Guillaume Thouret delivered his famous speech "On the New Division of the Kingdom," affirming at the outset that what was at issue was "regenerating the State." The transformations to come, he argued, must be large in scale: "Just as there would have been no regeneration if nothing had changed, [regeneration] would have been only superficial and fleeting if the changes were limited to mere palliatives, allowing the causes of the old vices to survive. Let us not undertake to draw up the Constitution if we do not wish to regenerate totally."[4]

Curiously, the task of theorizing this enterprise of radical regeneration fell to two priests who had been won over to the revolutionary cause: Abbé Henri-Baptiste Grégoire (1750–1831) and Abbé Emmanuel-Joseph Sieyès (1748–1836). Although as members of the clergy they were outsiders, they ardently threw themselves into the construction of the new revolutionary state in the hope that, by unifying the nation, they could control the national church within the Gallican tradition instituted by the monarchy. But they were both soon appalled by the consequences of their speeches and abruptly distanced themselves from the Revolution, emerging finally as liberal proponents of a constitutional separation of powers or, at least, a system that would protect religion against the ambitions of politics.

Along with Rabaud Saint-Étienne, Bertrand Barère, and many other orators, the two clergymen began by emphasizing the importance of the Third Estate as an entity unified around Reason and by encouraging it to break all links with the past. By a strange coincidence, the appearance of Abbé Sieyès's essay *What Is the Third Estate?* (1788) coincided with Abbé Grégoire's triumph in a competition, sponsored by the Royal Society of Arts and Sciences of Metz, aimed at devising ways to "make the Jews more useful and happier in France." Grégoire's *Essay on the Physical, Moral, and Political Regeneration of the Jews* (1788) recommended the systematic use of "regeneration," just as Sieyès hoped that the future national assembly would not be permitted to "degenerate into an aristocracy" and urged that "the body of representatives must be renewed by one third every year" in order to remain healthy.[5]

If Sieyès wished for a quasi-metamorphosis of the Third Estate into a new nation, Grégoire made the process of regeneration the engine of this transformation, giving the Revolution both its political form and its justification. It was not wholly by chance, or insignificant, that he formulated the dominant ideology of the Revolution in a work concerning the question of the emancipation of the Jews. He went on to defend before the Convention his many plans for reorganizing the territorial structure of the country, for suppressing the various patois of its people, and for overhauling the educational system—all crucial steps in the regeneration of the new man. The Jews had to be regenerated for the sake of their own happiness—often, like the peasants after them, against their will. The French people as a whole were likewise to exchange the old man for the new. The symbolic place occupied by the Jews in this forced rebirth of the French nation was linked with the place they had occupied several centuries earlier, when their expulsion prefigured the imminent unification of Catholic France. This France, eldest daughter of the Church, had been unified and given its raison d'être by rejecting first its Jews, then its heretics and Protestants.[6] The furious campaign of assimilation advocated by Abbé Grégoire reproduced the intolerance of an earlier age. In each case, regeneration, whether religious or rational, was symbolized by the eclipse of the Jews, who were made either to leave the country or to disappear behind their new dignity as citizens. Under the ancien régime, according to Grégoire, the Jews lived in a state of "profound moral deprivation," of complete "degradation"; they were, in fact, "parasitic plants." It was urgent to "melt them, so to speak, into the national mass, to the point of making them citizens in the fullest sense of the term"; to regenerate them through the wisdom imposed by state schools. Like all patois, their language, Yiddish—"a Teutonic-rabbinical jargon"—had to pass under the guillotine of rational unification. "Governments are unaware," Grégoire wrote in his essay on the Jews, "or do not sense enough, how important the abolition of dialects is for the spread of the Enlightenment."[7]

After the Jews came the peasants and their culture. To "electrify" the citizenry, to bring about the "resurrection" of the country, and to prevent it from being "reinfected" by new aristocrats, France must cease to be a "tower of Babel" of a thousand dialects that "prevent political amalgamation." This, then, was Grégoire's plan for complete openness, liberty, and French exceptionalism: "The language of a great nation needs to be be standardized so that all the citizens who compose it can communicate their thoughts without hindrance. This enterprise, which has not been fully achieved by any people, is worthy of the French people, who centralize all branches of social organization and who must jealously consecrate as soon as possible, in a single and indivisible republic, the unique and invariable usage of the language of liberty."[8] All the elements are here: centralization, standardization, transparency—France as the living embodiment of the Enlightenment.

Biological metaphors inspired the description of the redemptive transition from degeneracy to health, from prejudice to reason, from diversity to unity. The questionnaire that Grégoire addressed to his provincial correspondents revealed a willingness actually to carry out a "policy of extermination" (of local languages and identities) that alone would be capable of giving life to the national body. As the cultural historian Michel de Certeau has pointed out, "the national treatment of rural illnesses took on the aspect of a crusade." In this sense, the "linguistic *civisme*" that "recalls the 'constructivist' conception of Soviet architects between 1920 and 1930" led straight to "the crusade of 1794." This symbolic recourse to the vocabulary of crusade testifies once again to the inflexible will to unify the nation around a single symbol. The merciless denunciation of "untamed France"— *France sauvage*—led to one attack against ethnic enclaves and portended others.[9] Barère wholeheartedly associated himself with this project, exclaiming: "Let us therefore wipe out ignorance, let us set up instructors of the French language in the provinces, . . . let us break these instruments of injury and error"—Breton and Basque—and reject the use of the Italian language with its "soft and corrupting poetry." "Citizens!" he cried, "the language of a free people must be one and the same for all." This was true all the more, Barère argued, since "the laws of a Republic suppose that all citizens are particularly attentive toward each other and [exercise] constant vigilance with regard to the observance of the laws and the conduct of public officials."[10] Once again regeneration led to transparency, but also to surveillance and conformity.

The work of Abbé Sieyès provided the conceptual basis for the transition between the "body of the king" and the great "body of citizens," desacralizing the symbolic body of the king even before his physical execution. While Sieyès's thought drew upon the mechanical metaphors that were common during the eighteenth century, it also announced the sudden appearance of the biological (or "organicist") metaphors that were to dominate the nineteenth (without the relation between these metaphors always being very clear). The mechanical metaphor was introduced in *What Is the Third Estate?* Summarizing a vivid analogy, Sieyès wrote: "I imagine the law as being in the centre of a huge globe; all citizens, without exception, stand equidistant from it on the surface and occupy equal positions there."[11] This glacial vision of rigid juridical organization, admitting neither variation nor diversity, instituted equality within the community of citizens in a cold, almost repressive way.

In his *Essay on Privileges*, Sieyès had already described the conditions for the proper functioning of the "political machine" of the "great body of citizens" that formed the "social body" and inquired under what conditions "the political machine can move itself."[12] Later, on 20 July 1789, he declared before the National Assembly: "The public establishment is a sort of political body that, having, like the body of man, needs and means, must be organized in roughly the same manner. It must be endowed with the faculty of wishing and acting."[13] "Never will one understand the social mechanism," he stressed once more in *What Is the Third Estate?*, "if one does not decide to analyze a society as an ordinary machine, considering each part separately and then putting them back together, in the mind, one after the other, in order to grasp their agreement and to understand the general harmony that must result from it."[14]

As was so often done in the eighteenth century, Sieyès used the metaphor of a clock to describe the indispensable internal coherence that regulated the behavior of human beings in an essentially ahistorical way that once again tolerated neither deviation nor diversity in values. He then went on to propose a related mechanical metaphor. "What do you expect?" he asked of the privileged, who represented dysfunctional elements within the system. "Your house is held together only through artifice, with the help of a forest of crude supports arranged without taste or design, unless it be that of propping up the parts to the extent that they threaten collapse; [your house] has to be rebuilt, or you must resign yourselves to living day to day, in poverty and in the worry of one day being crushed under the debris. Everything holds together in the social order. If you neglect a part of it, this will not be without consequences for the other."[15]

This metaphor, which seems to belong to the tradition of social reformism, slightly anticipated the parable made famous by Claude-Henri de Rouvroy, comte de Saint-Simon (1760–1825),[16] the theorist of pre-Marxist socialism. Saint-Simon wished to see the privileged, who wrongfully occupied useless political and administrative positions, mercilessly eliminated. Saint-Simon and Sieyès were united in unreservedly supporting social equilibrium within the world of producers, whether or not they were property owners, in order to facilitate the regular functioning of the social system as a whole. The chief concern of these two authors, both trained in political economy, was to assure the functioning of a free-market economy in such a way that the real abilities of each citizen would be respected. Sieyès became one of the leading theoreticians of the French Revolution. Saint-Simon founded a positivist school that, in spite of its emphasis on order and industrialization, later influenced Marx's revolutionary thought.

If Sieyès's early writings therefore provided a glimpse of the coming revolutionary rupture, it is because he adopted metaphors framed in terms of sickness and health, life and death, degeneracy and regeneration—even though such metaphors lent themselves to a reformist perspective, implying adaptation, more readily than to revolution. Indeed, in the nineteenth century, programs for reform typically concealed a biological outlook that was a source of profound social conservatism. Many late-nineteenth-century philosophers and sociologists adopted the biological point of view, most notably the English philosopher Herbert Spencer, whose own organicist metaphors, like those of Saint-Simon before him, legitimized an industrialized order devoid of violent internal conflicts. Paradoxically, many of his most reactionary followers, such as Ia. A. Novikov, later relied on such metaphors in order to justify the continued direction of society by the aristocracy. For Novikov, the revolutionaries of 1789 had wrongfully cut off the head of the social body, which instead had to be treated in the way that a physician cares for a patient.

Given that Sieyès's metaphors did not necessarily favor revolution rather than adaptation, it is instructive to examine his mysterious transformation into the man who, "more than any other . . . articulate[d] the political theory of the French Revolution."[17] In Abbé Sieyès, more than any other revolutionary figure, one detects the ambiguities of the republican dream. His theoretical writings, together with the lampoons (*libelles*)[18] and political cartoons of the period, lastingly influenced the course of events, for the image of the nation that they conveyed led almost irresistibly from degeneracy to regeneration. For some scholars, such as the historians Antoine de Baecque and Lynn Hunt, such images of the body politic served almost to justify the readiness of a virtuous citizenry to eliminate the *faux frères*—fellow citizens who had turned traitor to their "band of brothers"—resorting even to terror if necessary. In the view of Baecque and Hunt, the pamphlets of the period had a logic and a metaphorical power that generated a history suited to the revolutionary imagination.

The historian William H. Sewell, Jr., argues to the contrary that Abbé Sieyès's metaphorical images had mainly unanticipated effects: "Sieyès, no less than his readers, was the dupe of the rhetoric he employed so brilliantly in *What Is the Third Estate?*" If the abandonment by the nobles of a great many of their privileges on the night of 4 August 1789 was consistent with the logic of this pamphlet, Sieyès (absent from the Assembly that night) "never imagined the terrifying revolution that would be necessary for the achievement of his ideal."[19] Indeed, among its victims was a clergy that he would have liked to protect. In view of the fact that Sieyès's organicist metaphors produced what might be called (borrowing the language of rational choice theory) perverse effects, provoking revolution rather than reform, and that these images conferred on historical reality a logic almost contrary to that of the actual events, one begins to see how such metaphors unexpectedly turned their author into the hero of the sans-culottes.

It is true that Sieyès's real purpose was difficult to fathom; indeed, his writings prior to the Revolution, if taken literally, unquestionably cast him in a radical light. The champion of regeneration used deadly phrases destructive of the old order, calling for the elimination of all privileges whatsoever, not only those possessed by the aristocracy he abhorred. Sewell advances a simple economic cause for what he calls Sieyès's "resentment,"[20] a notion that the political scientist Leah Greenfeld uses as an organizing principle in her study of the origin of modern revolutions. In Greenfeld's view, the revolutions in the United States and France at the end of the eighteenth century and, in the twentieth, in Russia and Germany, all had their origin in resentment: a feeling of jealousy, even hatred, that was anchored in "anomie," with the result that the various scorned elites experienced a true crisis of identity that supplied the motive force for a style of social criticism suited more to excess than to rational behavior. In support of this essentially sociopsychological thesis, Greenfeld quite naturally cites Abbé Sieyès and *What Is the Third Estate?*.[21] The resentment that Sieyès seems to have felt led him to devise metaphors for the body of society that went beyond his own private opinions as a young bourgeois: thus his personal "frustrations" furnished him with "emotional weapons" that could be used to mobilize others. His "hatred" of the aristocracy "blinded him," like all his readers, to the real consequences of the challenge to privilege, which was to end up having a grave effect on social groups other than the aristocracy itself.[22]

It is very unlikely that Sieyès deliberately wished to fool his fellow countrymen: far from conspiring, as Sewell rightly observes, he seems simply to have forgotten, through a sort of "rhetoric of amnesia,"[23] that he supported many of the socioeconomic privileges that were swept away during the night of 4 August. The images that flowed from the pen of this bard of liberalism[24] somehow "escaped" him—so painful was his humiliation, so strong his passion for taking revenge on those who had excluded him. His political language thus outran his analysis of the logic of economic events, which in many respects prefigured and rivaled that of Adam Smith insofar as it, too, concerned the productivity of work, free competition, and the division of labor. Sewell observes that Sieyès's *Lettre aux économistes* (1774) came two years before *The Wealth of Nations*, although Sieyès's basic metaphor of political economy was the contract, whereas Smith gave primacy to the market. As a result, Sieyès deduced only a political theory of representation, one that heralded a revolution whose course was to surprise him, for his theory, and the metaphors on which it relied, were to have radical and unintended consequences for cultural history.[25]

The metaphor of "adunation" revived by Sieyès—that is, of union or combination into one—is a good example. In the sixteenth century, the word was used to designate the circle of apostles around Christ as well as the union of duchies and principalities under the crown of France. Baecque observes that since, in Sieyès's view, the two privileged orders could not "make up a body, in the sense of absorbing the sovereignty of the nation . . . , [he] enjoined the Third Estate and its twenty-five million people to embody such a sovereignty, including and, above all, disregarding the separation and distribution into orders. . . . Adunation wove together metaphors of a corporeal unity recovered by binding together the old hierarchies."[26] Sieyès sharply distinguished the notion of "monastic integration" from the totalitarian integration of monastic societies. Monastic integration grew out of liberal theory and was conceived as a joining together of separate groups. It was meant to lead—for example, by means of the new territorial divisions in which Sieyès placed such great hope—to a unified system, regulated by a representative assembly that expressed the will of the nation.[27]

But adunation, linked in this way to the regeneration of the body of citizens, opened up a wide field for competing metaphors. The involuntary slide into revolutionary violence was seen as reinforcing the unity of the people-as-colossus, with Hercules symbolizing the union of the "band of brothers" through a sturdy and repressive administrative armature and a radical exclusion of all members of the privileged bodies. Privileged citizens were ultimately strangers to the fraternity of bourgeois, artisans, workers, and peasants that made up the Third Estate. It was in this symbolic context, to Sieyès's great dismay, that an apparently liberal image gave rise to extreme interpretations. These interpretations not only led to the night of 4 August but went on to exercise great influence on the Jacobin state, anxious to impose its order everywhere. The rhetoric deployed by Sieyès, and the force of conviction that his metaphors expressed, turned out to favor every kind of excess. The nineteenth-century political and social commentator Charles-Augustin Sainte-Beuve, in his *Causeries du lundi* (1851–62), wrote that Sieyès "saw the Revolution carried away like a chariot, escaping all calculations, all the art of its drivers."[28] Once opened by Sieyès, the "Pandora's box of the anti-nobiliary civil war"[29] was to have unpredictable consequences. The Terror,[30] which Sieyès condemned "in silence," did not result, in Sainte-Beuve's view, from exceptional circumstances. It was the result neither of war nor of the disruptions caused by the lower classes entering for the first time into politics; nor was it mechanically produced by the Enlightenment, by a deliberate will to construct the new man. Henceforth it was one of the unexpected, unpredictable, perverse consequences of revolutionary caricatures and images.

The unexpected consequences of *What Is the Third Estate?* and other writings of Abbé Sieyès irresistibly recall the works of Abbé Grégoire, who began by approving the idea of regeneration and went so far as to make it the emblem of the Revolution, without imagining the potential consequences of such an extreme position. Grégoire, who invented the word *vandalism*, later accused the sans-culottes and the Jacobins of reckless disregard for tradition: "[I]n the space of a year, [they] have almost destroyed the product of several centuries of civilization." He helped launch the dark legend of the Jacobins, transforming them into barbarians even though they, like him, pursued a policy aimed at preserving the national heritage. They were his old friends, who embraced the same policy of regeneration that he had advocated without any serious reservations: in this sense, "the Abbé found himself, above all, ceaselessly confronted by the trap of his speeches and past commitments. . . . Would it not be necessary, to judge from the content of his speeches, to rank Grégoire among the Vandals?" Owing to a genuine "political amnesia,"[31] Grégoire seemed to forget the logic inherent in his own speeches. Later, in 1808, he returned in his *Mémoires* to this period of dizzying upheavals and noted that Jacobin society had unquestionably "degenerated"— perverting the concept of regeneration, which had become symbolic of the Revolution itself and to which he had given an immense publicity. Indignant over the "oppression" he observed, Grégoire asked contemptuously "whether from now on the opinion that one will be obliged to hold would be posted on the door," and he concluded by condemning a revolutionary effort that turned out to be rather more tumultuous than he, the architect of the new man, would have liked: "In the nineteen centuries that have passed in nineteen years, the most complete and the most distressing course of experiment has been done on the human heart. What an infamous race are these great patriots . . . who today are dragged through the mire of adulation!"[32]

While the Revolution was still young, the images of Abbé Sieyès and Abbé Grégoire readily lent themselves to the most unpredictable excesses. The metaphors that issued from Sieyès's pen in particular were irresistibly persuasive. "Who is bold enough to maintain," he asked, "that the Third Estate does not contain within itself everything needful to constitute a complete nation? It is like a strong and robust man with one arm still in chains. If the privileged order were removed, the nation would not be something less but something more. What then is the Third Estate? All; but an 'all' that is fettered and oppressed." The aristocracy was a parasitical caste: "It is truly a people apart, but a bogus one which, lacking organs to keep it alive, clings to a real nation like those vegetable parasites which can live only on the sap of the plants that they impoverish and blight."[33] Moreover, Sieyès was ready to work out the implications of his own rhetoric.

Earlier, in November 1788, in his *Essay on Privileges*, he had multiplied organicist metaphors: honorific privileges "tended to demean the great body of citizens. . . . Well then! compensate the member that has earned the recognition of the body; but do not commit the absurd folly of belittling the body in relation to the member."[34] Such metaphors suggested an expeditious solution: why, he asked in *What Is the Third Estate?*, do the real people— the Third Estate—not expel this aristocracy? Why do they not "repatriate to the Franconian forests all the families who wildly claim to descend from the race of conquerers," who amount to a "monstrous" Hydra that is "foreign to the nation"? "We shall have to arrange for it to descend through the other line" in order for the nation to be "purged" once and for all, freed also from the almighty power of the Court, which is but "the head of this vast aristocracy which overruns every part of France, which seizes on everything through its members." The privileged person, who "stands outside citizenship," is "the enemy of common rights."[35] Sieyès ends his formidable essay with the following apostrophe, the ultimate organicist metaphor, urgently inviting regenerative action:

> Do not ask what is the appropriate place for a privileged class in the social order. It is like deciding on the appropriate place in the body of a sick man for a malignant tumour that torments him and drains his strength. It must be *neutralized*. The health of the body and the free play of its organs must be restored so as to prevent the formation of one of these malignancies which infect and poison the very essence of life itself.[36]

In September 1789, addressing the National Assembly, he dramatically declared: "Doubtless no class of citizens hopes to preserve in its favor a partial, separate, and unequal representation. That would be a monster in politics; it has been destroyed forever." In violent terms, he described this new France where "the central administration, departing from a common center, is going to uniformly strike the most remote parts of the empire," and where the Assembly would impose on each "the full weight of an irresistible force." The conclusion that he urged in ever harsher terms was plain, and full of radical implications: "France is, and must be, a single whole."[37]

Sieyès, the defender of constituent power, landed himself in contradiction by advocating a Constitution that limited the claim of the people to absolute authority. For as a theologian who was also a master of the rhetoric magnifying the Third Estate, he "transferred to the concept of constituent power, to the people . . . some of the attributes of God as these were laid down in Christian theology.[38] By secularizing attributes of divine power, he conferred on the Third Estate an unlimited sovereignty. The theory of constituent power had first been invented by the American colonists, but only in France did it acquire a "magical" dimension, reinforcing the image of a people naturally endowed with the capacity for self-government. Biological metaphors further strengthened this image:

The nation is in no way different from an individual in a state of nature, who cannot help but act out of self-interest. The individual, like the nation, has need of a government in order to conduct himself. Nature has taken care to provide the individual with a will in order to deliberate and to decide, arms in order to act, and muscles to support the executive power. In a nation, by contrast, since it is a body that has been deliberately established, it is up to the members that compose it to provide a will, a power of action, and a common force.[39]

As the political philosopher Marcel Gauchet points out, the nation, "through its artificial brain, arms, and muscles, [is] a whole in exactly the same way. And so it possesses 'all powers, all rights in their fullest extent.' The metaphor thrives."[40] The call to action was subject to no limits: "No," exclaimed Sieyès, "it is too late to work for the conciliation of all parties. What sort of agreement could one hope for between the energy of the oppressed and the rage of oppressors?"[41] For a political theorist who claimed to be a liberal, Sieyès had a strange way of predicting the coming of a plural society: his rhetoric heralded instead the coming of the famous Franco-French wars, with all their inflammatory symbolism—even if in the end he was surprised and pained by them.

The theorists of the French Revolution, Baecque observes, handled abstraction by means of "metaphors that 'created images' on the basis of political principles and events, metaphors that were expressly devised to catch the eye and capture the imagination of readers."[42] The dramatization of its events in order to bring forth a new world[43] relied on a series of stock caricatures, disseminated by revolutionary political cartoons that incited the new citizens to action and exacerbated the conflict to such a point that recourse to violence followed almost naturally.[44] In these caricatures, "staged" actors confronted each other and cultivated an "image." Events seemed to unfold according to a script that had been written in advance.[45] One example is particularly telling: the ritual governing Louis XVI's appearance before the National Assembly.

Whereas at the opening ceremony of the Estates General the king had sat on a throne, he now sat on a simple chair before the solemn-faced representatives of the people. The representatives were now seated on equal terms with the king, on their own chairs, with their heads covered—a sign of their rejection of royal authority. The protocol of the ancien régime had been shattered: having lost control of his own image, the king lost his hold on power as well.[46]

The power of revolutionary caricatures was to prove decisive in the abrupt change of regime, in the imagined transition from the metaphor of the king's body to that of the body of citizens. Caricatures were to be just as responsible for producing history as events themselves; in this sense, cultural history quite simply merged with history itself. Well before 21 January 1793, the date of Louis XVI's public execution, caricatures accustomed citizens to the idea of the impotence of the monarch and his worn-out body. The desacralization of the king was propagated by a great many licentious writings and indecent drawings of a flagging body and, in particular, a limp royal member. In verse, narratives, and pictures, virility was transferred from the royal member to the patriotic member.

The revolutionary caricaturists availed themselves of biological metaphors as a means of exaggerating the contrast between the old and the new, in order to sway public opinion and to narrow the gap between the literate and the illiterate, who were otherwise apt to decipher the same images in a different way. With the support of artists in all fields, a real cultural revolution occurred that was to leave an enduring mark on French society.[47] This largely spontaneous pictorial eloquence, manipulated by the Committee of Public Safety, was characterized by the animalization of the adversary. Monsters, as well as distortions of the most reviled animals (pigs, spiders, snakes, monkeys, turkeys), were used to portray the bodies of the king or queen, the aristocrat or the ecclesiastic, the émigré or the counterrevolutionary. In denying the humanity of the Revolution's opponents, "the image thus sought to destroy or pervert figures of authority."[48] The flight of the royal family to Varennes during the night of 20–21 June 1791 triggered an unprecedented explosion of caricatures of the king, often depicted as a hog. In prints his porcine features were accentuated so that, little by little, he became transformed into a savage and fierce beast nearer to a wild boar. Varennes appeared to everyone as a pivotal moment: the good king had betrayed the nation, fleeing from the world of human beings to take refuge in absolute animality. His allies likewise found themselves expelled from the community of citizens, assuming still more fully the traits of dangerous, venomous animals—unsuitable for a program of regeneration aimed at making them fit for inclusion in the nation. These caricatures prepared the French people for the execution of the king by zoologizing his body, even as his supporters were still desperately trying to magnify its dignity. Indeed, the French Revolution, and the explosion of caricature to which it gave rise, signaled "the advent of political imagery . . . as a cultural practice."[49]

The image of the fat reactionary, favored throughout the nineteenth and twentieth centuries by the extreme Right and Left alike, came to occupy a lasting place in the national imagination. Images of the king as a greedy pig stuffing himself in "grotesque holes" were damaging to sacred representations of the king as warrior,[50] as healer, as saint, as the embodiment of the state. Caricatures of the fat priest and the potbellied prelate proliferated as well. Symbols of the "degeneration" of the kingdom heralded the dream of the coming regeneration, in which the "new Frenchman" (as distinct from the "Frenchman of old")[51] assumed the characteristics of a giant: colossal, upright, healthy, happy. The plump prelates and corpulent aristocrats were dragged off by the National Guard to "patriotic *dégraisseurs*," pressing sheds converted for the purpose of large-scale purging, enabling the overweight to regain the egalitarian norm. Monopolists and all those who had been "fattened by the blood of the people" had to be unmasked and "purged." Their physical deformity, the monstrosity of their bodies, like those of great beasts, forever set them apart from humankind.

The obese Viscount André-Boniface Mirabeau—the younger brother of the famous orator and a mighty trencherman with a cast-iron stomach mockingly referred to as "Mirabeau-Tonneau" ("Mirabeau the Barrel")—became one of the favorite targets of the caricaturists, who had a field day depicting his unbalanced, bloated, and arrogant body. Sketched with the features of Sancho Panza (the "fat major of the black army" boasting a protruding belly), he single-handedly came to represent the paunchy army of counterrevolutionary émigrés who threatened national unity from the outside. Portly aristocrats and ecclesiastics were depicted as pursuing their dark plots to reappropriate the greater part of the national wealth that was produced by an army of ordinary, virtuous, hardworking, and resolutely naïve Frenchmen. In this utterly Manichaean stylization of foes, the bodies of the good patriot and the perverse aristocrat were supposed to reflect the quality of their respective souls. The stomach and buttocks, excessively accentuated, symbolized the scatology, the piggishness, the animality of the aristocratic adversary. Caricatures helped to embody and "give life" to the combatants on both sides.[52] As Baecque has noted:

> Here one encounters, through the image of the body, one of the essential themes that stimulated the imagination of so many revolutionaries: the ideal transparency of the new society. Absolute transparency required that politicians and political purpose everywhere be legible: with the erasure of the boundary between public and private, vigilant citizens had to be able to read in the outward behavior of men, in the very appearance of their bodies, the political message [they conveyed].[53]

The theme of the fat, wealthy, and powerful—*les gros*—has always been associated with conspiracy. During the Revolution, as in our own time, the strangeness of the bodies of the wealthy and powerful symbolized their betrayal of the national interest: a rich few, indifferent to the public good, manipulated the people.[54] This metaphor, propagated by the revolutionaries in their struggle against the aristocrats, henceforth became deeply embedded in the national imagination. All later French populist movements exploited it for the purpose of denouncing a small number of plotters who unhesitatingly sold out the interests of the ordinary people in order to more firmly establish their own power. Over time it was to pass indifferently from one extreme to the other, taking on a strongly anti-Semitic aspect during the period of triumphant Anglo-Saxon capitalism. In the revolutionary period, however, Robespierre hurled anathemas against the English people, despised as a nation of merchants: "As a Frenchman, as a representative of the people, I declare that I hate the English people. . . . I trust only in our soldiers and the profound hatred that the French have for this people. . . . I nurse an implacable hatred of them."[55]

The regeneration of France also presupposed the end of the corruption that threatened a nation of innocent worker-soldiers. If plots loomed at every turn, the people could only take up arms and do battle against these tyrants of darkness, authors of the most horrible misfortunes that plagued those below them. By their ubiquity, and by their distortion of the adversary's body, innumerable caricatures succeeded in giving a physical reality to vast imagined plots. Images of combat multiplied, showing the body of the patriotic people victoriously confronting the decadent bodies of the émigrés, who tirelessly devoted themselves at the country's borders to cowardly undertakings. Denunciations of traitors unified the revolutionaries and stimulated the imagination of the "Rousseaus of the gutter"—les Rousseau des ruisseaux. The radical dualism that so marked French exceptionalism, of le peuple and les gros, became systematically incorporated in biological representations of adversaries. For the revolutionaries, as for the spokesmen of various modern populisms, a single solution rapidly imposed itself: ruthless expulsion of the enemy, violent elimination in the name of a homogenizing virtue.

The unity of citizens assumed the absolute rejection of the enemy: the good king had to be eliminated from the body of the nation along with his allies, whether official or covert, willing or unwitting. The Terror resulted from this radical way of imagining French society, a Manichaeanism that long haunted the history of France and caused the specter of violence to reappear from time to time. This is what the historian Jean Starobinski had in mind when he wrote:

> The light of the Revolution that had been born of the rolling back of darkness now had to confront the return of darkness, which threatened its inmost being. . . . Theoretical reason and the enthusiasm that disseminated it had to face the play of "real forces." Thus they would witness the rebirth of the dark enemy whom they would have liked to be rid of once and for all. Any delay in the march toward enlightenment, any holdup in the practical organization of the revolutionary State, was attributed (often with good reason) to counter-revolutionaries, conspirators, or agents of the enemy coalition. By trying to establish the reign of virtue, revolutionary reason made the reign of suspicion inevitable, and, soon after, the reign of terror.[56]

Another historian, Bronislaw Baczko, echoes this opinion, noting:

> The People became transformed into myth and unifying symbol only by actively promoting the Manichaeanism implied by the image of the rupture of time. The new City, founded by the People, was attacked by the Enemy of multiple faces, always hidden, plotting. The Revolution did not lack real enemies, but the "force of circumstances," to recall Saint-Just's phrase, impelled it to fabricate fantastical representations of them . . . —so many *idées-images*, poorly inventoried and poorly studied, of the Enemy of the People and of the Revolution.[57]

63

According to this view, in addition to real plots, there were imaginary ones, attributed to an almighty adversary, capable of secretly corrupting even the most intimate friends of the Revolution.

Did Jacobinism amount to this, then—a permanent purge justified by fantastical representations of the enemy, issuing from a desire to establish Unity? "The essence of Jacobinism," the historian Mona Ozouf remarks, "lies in the impossibility of conceiving a divided popular will, a boundary between minority and majority, between the public and private sphere. The world of Jacobinism is one . . . where one's innermost thoughts are themselves criminal. This ideal of perfect social and psychological visibility is the basis of Jacobinism."[58] Accordingly, the "target of fraternal coercion is, at least as much as external traitors, the internal traitor potentially concealed within each individual." French society, of course, has long lent itself to hunts for traitors; indeed, had historical circumstances been different, they might have taken just as tragic a turn in the twentieth century. The image of a nation of regenerated citizens assumed "the complete absorption of individuals into the citizenry,"[59] an exaggerated militant form of citizenship that required reciprocal devotion. For this reason "complete unity, ethical strictness, and exclusion appear diametrically opposed not only to pluralism but also to moral relativism."[60] The Jacobin discourse assumed a unanimity that radically distinguished the people from its enemies, the threat of purifying scrutiny deflecting all deviance and foreseeing all schism. Its organicist metaphors were all the more effective as they closely bound citizens to one another. Thus the Jacobin deputy Didier Thirion declared:

> You wish, you say, to organize the social body, the political society of the French, in a word, the Republic. . . . Does it not also have its elements, its organic parts, like the physical body? Is it not endowed with movement and intelligence like each of us? Does it not, and must it not, also have a center of movement, of action and reaction; a head that contemplates, arms that execute, a heart that gives and receives life by turns, and distributes it equally in all its parts?[61]

The organicist metaphor rigidly distributes mutually dependent functions: autonomy and diversity are rejected; all manifestations of divergence are excluded as dysfunctional.

The logic of the unifying exceptionalism that punctuates so many episodes in French history is fully revealed in this declaration by the Committee of Public Safety, vehemently calling for a literal imposition of homogeneity: "After having repelled all these heterogeneous elements, you will be yourselves; you will form a core as pure as [it is] brilliant, as solid as [it is] dense, and similar to a diamond stripped of the crust formed on its surface by an accumulation of silt." According to Robespierre, it was necessary to "purge the whole society" in order to "re-create the people" with the help of a "strong action, a passionate impulse" (as Jean-Nicolas Billaud-Varenne put it). Almost everyone agreed, including certain Girondins such as the pamphleteer Jacques Brissot, who felt that "war alone can level minds and regenerate souls."[62] Evidence of good citizenship helped obtain jobs, led to the fusion of political and administrative elites, strengthened a partisan absolutism that was analogous to royal absolutism, and encouraged a conception of society anchored in the long term. "The revolutionary consciousness took form," François Furet remarked, "as an attempt to re-create undivided power in a society free of contradictions. The new collectively shared image of politics was the exact reverse of the ancien régime."[63]

The language of the revolutionary leaders, as Lucien Jaume observes, in "affirming the fusion between the community and the governors, on behalf of a new Catholicity, . . . revived an indubitable inspiration that had long marked French political culture. To be sure, it involved a metaphorical description in relation to the reality of the revolutionary state, but in just the same way as the incorporation of the people in the sovereign under the long reign of Louis XIV was metaphorical."[64] The Jacobin Garnier de Saintes, echoing Robespierre's extreme position, declared: "If we purge ourselves, it is in order to have the right of purging France. We will leave no heterogeneous body in the Republic."[65] And Gracchus Babeuf, the champion of absolute egalitarianism, pushed such logic to an extreme when he exclaimed, "A regenerator must take a broad view. He must mow down everything that stands in his way."[66] From one epoch to another, from one political culture to another, the same unitary temptation repeats itself: the revolutionaries, as Mona Ozouf has pointed out, "adopted from Christian tradition the promise of unity conveyed by the sentiment of fraternity in order to create a secular and voluntarist version of it, tested in the joint construction of the nation."[67] To "mold citizens," the Convention conceived of school textbooks as another way of reinforcing republican standardization by preparing future citizens to fulfill their duties toward the country.[68]

The masculinization of the combatants produced what Lynn Hunt calls the "family romance of the French Revolution"—the union of brothers against father—as well as a masculine union hostile to any feminine presence in the public sphere. The murder of the father deepened the sense of fraternity among brothers who were united against the adversary before they finally tore themselves apart. Hunt argues that the murder of the father represented a ritual sacrifice that gave the band of brothers a free hand; and once the political father had disappeared, the brothers' refusal to recognize the legitimacy of any other new father (not even the state itself), the absence of any badge of paternity in the iconography of the most extreme phase of the Revolution, gave the union a still more extreme dimension.[69] This hypothesis suggests a new way of understanding the incessant and brutal rifts of the period. Unlike the American revolutionaries, who rapidly conferred on George Washington the role of father-president, stabilizing the new union around a revered figure, Hunt argues that the regenerators of France were sucked into an endless spiral, protecting their unity by amplifying the plots of their adversaries. The band of brothers thus saw itself as fraternally united in solidarity against a common enemy.

Certainly the masculine representation of the people in the particular form of Hercules, the virile brother, the powerfully muscled giant, the sans-culotte symbolizing the regenerate man, constituted a key episode.[70] In a famous text of 7 November 1793, the painter Jacques-Louis David proposed to the Convention that a gigantic monument, having as its pedestal the remains of the statues destroyed in Notre-Dame Cathedral, be constructed in the heart of Paris, in front of the Pont-Neuf. This monument would be

> the image of a race of giants, the French people. May this image, imposing by its strength and simplicity, bear [the word], written in large letters on its forehead: Light; on its chest: Work; on its arms: Strength; on its hands: Work. May the figures of Liberty and Equality, on one of its hands, embracing each other, ready to travel around the world, show everyone that they rest only on the genius and the virtue of the people. May this standing image of the people hold in its other hand that terrible and real club of which ancient Hercules was only the symbol.[71]

In his draft decree, David went on to write, in article 2, "this monument will be colossal"; in article 3, "the people will be represented standing, by a statue"; in article 6, "the statue will be 15 meters, or 48 feet, high."[72] If colossal forms had captivated the imagination of artists, and particularly of architects, before the Revolution broke out, this event established them in the public sphere as a romantic form celebrating the regenerate people. In this sense, "David gave voice to the impulses of popular communion."[73] The antithesis of the feminine figure of Marianne, who symbolized Liberty, Hercules was chosen (by a vote of the Convention later the same month) to appear on the state seal. The Convention evidently attached a quite special importance to this symbol, repeatedly confirming its approval of David's project. Additionally, Hercules was pictured on many of the *Bulletins des lois de la République* between 1794 and 1797 and was associated in many engravings with the taking of the Bastille; his face appeared on certificates of membership in the National Guard; and his likeness figured on the flags of the National Guard, on calendars, and in children's books.

David assigned crucial importance to the image of Hercules in a festival he organized in August 1793 to commemorate not only the fall of the monarchy but also, and especially, the defeat of federalism, which was seen as embodying all the plots hatched against national unity. This, then, was depicted as one of the labors of Hercules, shown triumphantly striking down the counterrevolution. In the end, this immense statue was never built, but a similar monument, dedicated "to the 'glory of the French people,'" was erected a year later as part of a program of de-Christianization aimed at implementating the "cultural revolution" against the dominant culture of the ancien régime.[74] This colossus was to incarnate the image of the sovereign people:

> It was an image-representation of the people provided by the people's representatives, and as such it inherently included the representatives' interpretation of the people. . . . Thus, even as the image proclaimed the supremacy of the people, it reintroduced the superiority of the people's representatives. . . . The Terror was the people on the march, the exterminating Hercules. Hercules, the people, was in the eyes of the radicals who had called it into being a potential Frankenstein. . . . The masculinity of Hercules reflected indirectly on the deputies themselves; through him they reaffirmed the image of themselves as the band of brothers that had replaced the father-king. . . . Hercules put the women back in perspective, in their place and relationship of dependency. . . . [H]e was a transposed and magnified sign of monarchy itself. Hercules reflected Jacobin and radical aspirations. . . . The people, the new, formidable giant, had become king.[75]

This powerful and virile giant representing the revolutionary band of brothers reflected the image that the members of the

Convention cultivated of themselves as sans-culottes: strong, courageous, and hardworking—but also, and above all, violent. Was there a danger, then, that the people as incarnated by Hercules would appear to be *merely* violent, even stupid? Was it precisely because the interpretation of this image remained equivocal that it seemed necessary to add so many words, in order to make its meaning clear? For the philosopher Judith Schlanger, "It was as though the expressivity had to be reinforced and confirmed at the verbal level. . . . The inscriptions manifested a belief in the superiority of the clarifying power of words over the significance of what is shown."[76] Thus, as others have pointed out in challenging Lynn Hunt's interpretation,[77] Hercules bears on his forehead the word "Light," David having explicitly declared to the Convention that Hercules represented the victory of reason over prejudice. In this view, Hercules represented revolutionary force in the service of reason, not an unconscious revolt against a rejected father.

Because allegories, like caricatures, often lend themselves to contradictory interpretations,[78] it is difficult to know how different viewers would have regarded David's proposed statue or what influence it would actually have had. In the event, as we have noted, this gigantic monument was never constructed. Another statue of Hercules, similar to the one conceived by David, was erected on the occasion of the Festival of the Supreme Being, in June 1794. In early 1795, after the fall of the Jacobins, the colossus was destroyed: the hour of Marianne had come—only now as the image of Liberty, not as the image of the regenerate people, the homogeneous "band of brothers" formerly imagined as the sole possessors of power. Ultimately, the Republic, as pictured on diverse official documents of every sort, would assume the form of a woman, Liberty,[79] symbolizing the disappearance in revolutionary rhetoric of a masculine people, unified, regenerate, self-determined—this as a sort of symbolic compensation, given that women were then, and would long remain, excluded from the public sphere.[80]

The biological metaphors inspiring the "band of brothers" were not without consequence, however, from the point of view of political theory. As Hunt points out, in a work extending her earlier study of revolutionary culture:

> Under the Old Regime in France, the "mystic fiction" had it that the sacred was located quite precisely in the king's body, and as a consequence, the ceremonial and political life of the country revolved around that body. The French Revolution attacked this notion and replaced it with another, in which charisma was displaced and dispersed, to be located in language, symbols, and the new ceremonies of power; that is, in the collective representations of revolutionary fraternity. . . . In the fraternal model, all the brothers shared in the father's charisma just as they all shared in the guilt of his sacrifice. They had killed him and metaphorically eaten his body together. . . . The sacralization of any document, such as a constitution, was made nearly impossible by the unwillingness to fix charisma in any particular location, where it might become the reserve of a privileged few. . . . In this sense, the French family romance of fraternity worked against the establishment of a liberal, representative government.[81]

The utopian dream of transparency illustrated by this image of revolutionary brotherhood—of a regenerate masculine people, beset by enemy plots, opposed to internal diversity in the name of a shared solidarity—henceforth was to play a decisive role in shaping republican ideals.

Chapter Three

The Counterutopia of
Joseph de Maistre

With colossal Hercules bending his unlimited strength to the service of the sovereign people, nothing seemed capable of resisting the republican ideal. Yet all of a sudden there rose up before him another Hercules—a "Christian Hercules, strong in his own strength." "Frenchmen!" exclaimed Joseph de Maistre, "make way for the very Christian king, carry him yourselves to his ancient throne, raise again his oriflamme, and let his coinage, ranging again from one pole to the other, carry everywhere the triumphant device: CHRIST COMMANDS, HE REIGNS, HE IS THE VICTOR!"[1] In this titanic struggle, which began in the aftermath of the Revolution, two ways of imagining the nation confronted each other in the name of Reason and Faith, respectively.

Maistre's counterutopia represented the antithesis of the vision contained in the pamphlet published by Abbé Sieyès. The theorist of counterrevolution was not unaware of the celebrated revolutionary cleric, whom he described in unkind terms: "His pride is vile and his cowardice is fierce. It would be hard to find anything more repulsive among the filthy animals thrown up by the Revolution."[2] Maistre's violence was commensurate with revolutionary violence; his extremism was symmetrical with that of the men of

1789. Two visions of the world clashed, each opposed to making the least concession, each obsessed with "regeneration" and manly spirit. Each was willing to resort to blood and violence in order to build the new man, who was to be, for Sieyès, the disciple of reason and universalism; for Maistre, the devout partisan of the religion that France, more than any other nation, embodied. The reasons for Tocqueville's pessimism now became clearer: France was indeed different from other nations, for it engendered absolute contradictions and inexpiable hatreds. Each camp lined up behind its own Hercules, furiously feeding a spiral of confrontation that ruled out compromise and prevented the establishment of liberal democracy. There were, in fact, a great many points of agreement between the two, and within each camp some attempt was made to preach tolerance; yet leaders on both sides were pushed to radicalize their purifying discourse ever further.

The reactionary utopia conceived by Joseph de Maistre was inalterably opposed to revolutionary claims on behalf of regeneration. As Isaiah Berlin quite rightly observed,

> Temperamentally [Maistre] resembled his enemies, the Jacobins; like them he was a total believer, a violent hater, a *jusqu'au boutiste* in all things. . . . [But politically] Maistre was the polar opposite of [the extremists of 1792 who completely rejected the old order]. He attacked eighteenth-century rationalism with the intolerance and the passion, the power and the gusto, of the great revolutionaries themselves. He understood them better than the moderates, and he had some fellow-feeling for some of their qualities; but what was to them a beatific vision was to him a nightmare.[3]

Maistre wished "to raze 'the heavenly city of the eighteenth-century philosophers' to the ground, not leaving stone on stone."[4] Berlin saw in Maistre's "violent hatred" something "which at once echoes the fanatical voices of the Inquisition, and sounds what is perhaps the earliest note of the militant anti-rational Fascism of modern times." This hatred runs through all Maistre's writings, demanding ever bloodier refreshment—to the point of displaying "an affinity with the paranoiac world of modern Fascism, which it is startling to find so early in the nineteenth century." Maistre was "the first theorist in the great and powerful tradition which culminated in Charles Maurras, a precursor of the Fascists, and of those anti-Dreyfusards and supporters of the Vichy regime who were sometimes described as being Catholics before they were Christians."[5] Though he was attracted to the thought of Louis de Bonald, the early-nineteenth-century theoretician of the reactionary and monarchic Right with whom he is often associated, Maistre's conservatism was nonetheless distinguished from Bonald's by his rejection of a simple return to the old order and his impetuous demand for a new order that prefigured modern extremisms. Whereas Bonald desired reaction, Maistre prophesied a new society that would preserve Jacobin radicality. In Berlin's view, Maistre's conception signified the emergence of a bloody totalitarianism that went beyond authoritarianism. Some scholars, such as the political scientist Zeev Sternhell, claim to find in Boulangism[6] and the leagues of the late nineteenth century a specifically French origin for fascism; others, such as the historians Ernst Nolte and Eugen Weber, associate fascism with Action Française, the antirepublican movement founded at the time of the Dreyfus Affair. But Berlin reaches back further in time, to the late eighteenth and early nineteenth centuries, to connect fascism with a more remote current of thought rooted in French history.

These periods do indeed exhibit certain common features. There are nonetheless essential differences between, for example, Nazism, with its fierce hostility to Catholicism, and Maistre's counterutopia, which was devoted to reestablishing the absolute power of the pope. Dismissing such analogies, which are founded on nothing more than the violent rejection of rationalism in each case, one is left with a reactionary passion that was opposed to—and yet commensurate with—the revolutionary dream: systematic and mutually antagonistic visions of the world anchored in the French experience. One is left, too, with an intrinsic pessimism that was to intrigue staunch nineteenth-century Catholic thinkers, such as the writer and journalist Louis Veuillot, who were implacably opposed to the achievements of the French Revolution. Tocqueville, for his part, condemned the Revolution's excesses while recognizing the utter impossibility of turning back. He regretted the scope and permanence of the hatreds that tore apart French society and urged acceptance of democracy, so long as it showed itself to be pluralistic and respectful of Catholic beliefs. Maistre, on the other hand, who "seemed 'Jacobin' to the émigrés,"[7] embraced the cleansing violence of the Terror, savored the hatred to which it testified, and resolved to keep intolerance alive in order to reconstruct a truly Catholic France.

And one is left, finally, with the question of nationalism. Isaiah Berlin suggested that nationalism, in the systematic form first given it by Johann Gottfried von Herder, expressed a German reaction to the injury administered by the expansionist universalism of the French Enlightenment. Herder attached great importance to the renaissance of specific cultural communities sharing a particular language. Together with their distinctive traditions and customs, these communities permitted a collective spirit to flourish that he saw as a source of strength and refreshment for their members. Ironically, though he mistrusted nationalistic prejudice, his attacks on the cosmopolitanism and rationalist abstractions of the French *philosophes* were so many seeds favoring the emergence of a passionate and aggressive nationalism. Indeed, Herder's concern with authenticity made him the first theoretician of "nationalist resentment"—whence his "implacable crusade against French universalism, and his concept and glorification of individual cultures . . . and his hatred of the great levellers."[8]

Nationalism in this sense is more a cultural than a political reaction—a reaction against the abstract state, a recentering based on the values peculiar to each nation. Rejecting the utopia of a perfect society, Herder preached a return to the *Volk*—to the people—shaped not by race but by soil and religion. In his eyes, societies are incommensurable, plural, and unique; their logic is derived from their own cultural history. Advocates of the counter-

Enlightenment such as Herder therefore suggested that "Germans can only be truly creative among Germans; Jews only if they are restored to the ancient soil of Palestine. . . . [L]ife lies in remaining steeped in one's own language, tradition, local feeling; uniformity is death."[9] To each nation its own principle of coherence: rationalism, no less than internal pluralism, disfigures the soul of a people.

Maistre shared this animus toward internal pluralism and attempted to give back to France its spirit, endangered by the Revolution, which he denounced every bit as forcefully as the Enlightenment. Unlike Herder, however, he displayed an extreme intolerance toward pluralism abroad, since it seemed to him legitimate that France, once again Catholic, should become once again the leading light of Europe; by the same token, he utterly rejected the relativism popular among German Romantic irrationalists, Russian Slavophiles, and other messianic thinkers. There was only one truth—that of the Catholic Church, whose heroine was France. In this respect, he endorsed not only the cultural nationalism advocated by Herder but also the enthusiasm and certainties of his Jacobin adversaries: he believed, as did the Jacobins, in the universalist mission of France; and, though he fought in the name of the Church, he adopted their violence. In this respect, too, his affinity with Solzhenitsyn becomes clear.[10] In opposing rationalist Marxism, itself the heir of the Enlightenment, the Russian prophet shares Maistre's hatred of the Enlightenment, forcefully rejecting the regenerative spirit of 1789 that reemerged, transformed, in 1917. What is more, he shares Maistre's faith in the Church—for him, the Russian Orthodox Church.

Isaiah Berlin illuminatingly linked some of the protagonists of this long epoch in drawing a superb comparison, as we saw earlier, between Maistre and Tolstoy. He recalls this note in Tolstoy's journal, dated 1 November 1865—"I am reading Maistre"—and adds that the man who was then writing *War and Peace* had asked his publisher to send him Maistre's collected papers.[11] It should be kept in mind that Maistre spent fourteen years in St. Petersburg as Sardinian minister plenipotentiary to the Russian court. During this crucial period he intervened on behalf of Jesuits who were threatened with expulsion from the empire and sought to alert the tsar to the devastating consequences of importing rational modernity *à la française* into Russia—with such vigor that the interior minister, acting on the orders of Alexander I himself, demanded Maistre's recall, noting that the "unshakeable obstinacy of his ideas and the intolerance of his principles are solely the result of the hatred that he bears indiscriminately toward everything that seems to him associated with the opinions of the present age."[12]

Maistre, "the Voltaire of reaction,"[13] shared with Tolstoy a hearty contempt for intellectuals. Berlin observes that both

> Maistre and Tolstoy regard the western world as in some sense "rotting," as being in rapid decay. This was the doctrine which the Roman Catholic counter-revolutionaries at the turn of the century virtually invented, and it formed part of their view of the French Revolution as a divine punishment visited upon those who strayed from the Christian faith and in particular that of the Roman Church. . . . Both preserve the same sardonic, almost cynical, disbelief in the improvement of society by rational means.[14]

In Berlin's memorable phrase, both were "hedgehogs"—thinkers of stature who profess "a single central vision, one system less or more coherent or articulate, in terms of which they understand, think and feel"—rather than "foxes," who pursue several (sometimes contradictory) ends at once, ends that are not organized in accordance with a single moral principle.[15] This contrast between hedgehogs and foxes is marvelously well suited to describe the world that, to a far greater degree than Tolstoy, Maistre and his heirs created for themselves as ferociously hateful enemies of a rationalist utopia. Maistre was exceptional in the scope of his rejection, which, it bears repeating, was comparable to the ambition of the Jacobins. A perfect hedgehog, he did not hide his cold determination: in the history of ideas he stands out as a resolute adversary of the notion of fraternity among men and champion of a mode of government founded not on reason but solely on absolute power—in short, as the founder of antiliberalism.[16] One sees his reflection nearer to our own time in Carl Schmitt, a fierce critic of the fragile republican order instituted a century later in Germany (and, from May 1933, a member of the Nazi Party).[17] Maistre was ready to take any and all measures necessary to counteract the democratic menace. "It is perhaps the nature of reaction," he reflected, "to go to the opposite extreme."[18] Yet Maistre belonged, as the literary critic Émile Faguet pointed out, to "the age that he so detested. . . . It was the spirit of the eighteenth century against the ideas of the eighteenth century: the revolutionary dialecticians drafted [the declaration of] the rights of man and de Maistre the declaration of the rights of God; and what is more, he too led to a sort of terror."[19]

In this sense, the counterrevolution inaugurated by Maistre's thought cannot entirely be reduced to the usual paradigm of reactionary rhetoric. In the formulation recently given it by Albert Hirschman, reactionary rhetoric is structured by a series of propositions affirming, respectively, the perverse effects of reform, the futility of reform, and the fragility of reform. The first assumes that every action in favor of social or political change leads to its opposite, aggravating the existing situation; the second implies the impossibility of any lasting transformation, to the extent that nothing can really change; the third asserts that the high costs of reform inevitably undermine any gains that may be made. Hirschman notes that these arguments are generally endorsed by "conservative thinkers," foremost among them Edmund Burke in his *Reflections on the French Revolution*, and begins by stressing the profound break represented by 1789—this "great turning point," which by itself gave birth to reactionary thought. Burke had conceived the thesis of perverse effects by applying to the French Revolution the hypothesis (associated with the Scottish Enlightenment) of the unintended consequences of human action. For Hirschman, this essential ideological moment encouraged an irresistible pessimism: Maistre, he says, "pushes this thought to the limit," not hesitating to "come forward with an extravagant formulation of the perversity thesis. . . . One could not wish for a more extreme statement. . . . Maistre's construction of Divine Providence is no doubt exceptional in its elaborate vengefulness and in its seamless invocation of the perverse effect."[20]

Maistre's counterutopia impressed on the thesis of perverse effects a systematic dimension. Providence was seen as encouraging radical and thoroughgoing revolution, for if attempts at resisting it were immediately successful, the refreshing benefits of regeneration—vengeance and violence—could not be fully enjoyed. It was therefore necessary that the enemies of the monarchy and Catholicism be given free rein in order to assure the complete triumph later of the counterrevolution. Thus, Maistre taught, it happens that men obtain the opposite of what they believe themselves to be seeking. In spite of its extreme character, Hirschman groups Maistre's mechanical scheme together with other examples of perverse effects, such as the introduction of universal suffrage, which, Flaubert thought, made people permanently "stupid" (Burkhardt, for his part, believed that promoting liberty amounted to conferring a despotic power on "the mass of blowhards known as the people"); the creation of the welfare state, which increases poverty; and the unintended consequences of technological advances in controlling the environment (which, in the United States, for example, has worsened conditions of life for the underprivileged).[21]

While it is surely fruitful to point out the similarities between so many different cases, there is a risk that in doing so the history of ideas may lose sight of history itself, and with it particular paths of development. The thesis of perverse effects has the effect in turn of flattering Maistre's apocalyptic vision, which differs as much from the moderate worldview of a conservative thinker such as Burke as from the technical writings of William Forrester, a pioneer of feedback and inventor of the science of communication systems. Though it represents a form of reactionary rhetoric that is widespread on the Right (and even on the Left), Maistre's counterutopia has meaning only insofar as it corresponds to the messianic character of the French Revolution and the specific context of French hatreds; it is scarcely conceivable in Switzerland or the United States. It is true that Tocqueville suggested, with scathing irony, that the changes wrought by the French Revolution were already largely to be found in embryonic form under the ancien régime, the thesis of futility that inspired this remark (namely, that no matter what reform is undertaken, nothing changes)[22] is nonetheless not to be confused with the argument underlying Maistre's view, for it does not imply the redemptive presence of evil in the operation of ineluctable change. Maistre, fascinated by Jacobinism, differed in every respect from Tocqueville. Hirschman nonetheless feels that Tocqueville's position was "more stinging and insulting to a prorevolutionary opinion than the direct assaults of a Burke, a Maistre, or a Bonald."[23] But if the thesis of futility is scarcely sustainable, neither did it have any real resonance in the political debate of nineteenth-century France, unlike Maistre's eschatology. And whereas Burke's conservatism rested on the firm authority of the British nobility, Maistre's model remained that of the absolute monarchy peculiar to France. Maistre was a passionate partisan of the sovereign's omnipotence, reproducing the Jacobin discourse in his own terms—to the point that his Catholic faith came almost to be cast in the nationalist and statist terms that characterize French exceptionalism: "[T]he language is that of Robespierre. . . . [H]atred is often nurtured by the realization of similarities."[24] This hatred gives another dimension to the thesis of futility.

Maistre, the archangel of Almighty God, therefore deserves a special place. Utterly convinced of the urgency of France's religious mission, he combated Reason with all his might; his entire work is a hymn to France's exceptionality, to its unique destiny at the head of Catholicism, since its "spirit of proselytism . . . is the salient trait of the national character." "Every nation," Maistre wrote, "like every individual, has received a mission that it must fulfil. France exercises over Europe a veritable magistracy that it would be useless to contest and that she has most culpably abused. In particular, she was at the head of the religious system, and not without reason was her king called *most Christian.*" Though it proudly assumed this unique destiny, France was fated to endure an assault of unprecedented power and scope against its national spirit: "[I]t follows that the greatest efforts of the *Goddess of Reason* against Christianity should take place in France; the enemy attacked the citadel."[25] If France, as Berlin rightly says, is the place where the expansionist nationalism symbolized by Maistre was invented, it is because Maistre's counterutopia (unlike Herder's vision, born in a country that had not yet been unified politically) reproduced the absolutism of the revolutionaries, which itself was modeled on the absolutism of the Very Christian King. In common with Herder, however, Maistre proclaimed that every nation is endowed with a language—a culture—that it cannot abandon in favor of a reductive universalism; but beyond culture, Maistre saw in religion the true foundation of the French nation, which was already so harmoniously organized in its political body. For him, "[T]here are privileged nations that have a mission in this world. . . . The Frenchman is in need of religion more than any other man; if he lacks it, he is not only weakened, he is disfigured. . . . Christianity impregnated the French at once and with a facility that could only have been the result of a particular affinity. . . . The French people have had the singular honor . . . of (humanly) constituting the Catholic Church in the world."[26]

If Maistre had no tolerance for relativism, whether after the fashion of Herder or in its weak version, pluralism, it is because France alone showed itself to be worthy: "Look anywhere in the world for a state all of whose parts are linked together more closely and form a more imposing whole. France has at once both mass and volume; there exists nowhere in Europe a political body that is more numerous, more compact, more difficult to undermine and whose onslaught is more to be dreaded. To exercise the kind of supremacy that belongs to it, France has been given a dominating language."[27] This claim anticipated Tocqueville's historical account; but if Tocqueville considered that the course of

French history displayed a characteristic consistency, it was in order to deplore this consistency, out of a fear that French society would remain forever hostile to democracy. Maistre, on the other hand, loudly rejoiced in this exceptionalism. France's duty, he believed, was to serve as a beacon for Europe, even the world.

Like the revolutionaries, Maistre applied himself to the task of "regenerating" France. The "disease" with which the nation had been seized threatened its very soul: "Where, in France, are the elements of its supposed regeneration? Democracy has no bearing [on this question]." Maistre's vocabulary is identical to that of the revolutionaries Abbé Sieyès and Abbé Grégoire, whom he jubilantly mocked: these "luckless country curés," these nobles nursing "miserable resentments," these "obscure men" with "minds spoiled by fashionable books," these "villains," these "profoundly immoral men," these "apostates"—"These are the representatives, the legislators, the regenerators of France!"[28] In Maistre's view, these men who believed that France could be regenerated by exposure to the Enlightenment were in fact acting, without knowing it, in the name of Providence, involuntarily hastening the truly regenerative return to Catholicism: "We cannot remark too often that men do not lead the Revolution; it is the Revolution that uses men. They are right when they say *it goes all alone*. This phrase means that never has Divinity shown itself so clearly in any human event. If the vilest of instruments are employed, punishment is for the sake of regeneration."[29] The argument from perverse effects assumes a unique significance when applied to the French example: it means that men are conscious neither of the type of regeneration in which they are engaged, nor of the kind of upheaval they seek to bring about, nor of the nature of the history in which they are involved. "For my part," wrote Maistre, "I am unshakable. I want still to believe that the revolutionary monster worked only for the king. . . . Everything works against Louis XVIII; but everything works on behalf of the king of France."[30]

Faux frère of the Jacobins, Maistre shared their hatred, their execration of the adversary; his hatred matched that of the men of the Terror. Proud of his "forthright" character,[31] he assigned hatred a special place among human sentiments: as a call for the murder of the enemy-brother, it echoed down the ages. He assured the king that he "detested his enemies with a philosophical hatred that has in common with passion only heat and energy. I abominate the Revolution."[32] It had, in his view, produced only discord, "frenzy," "hatreds."[33] The writings of Voltaire likewise aroused in him an absolute "hate": "I would like to raise a statue to him—by the hand of the executioner,"[34] he wrote, noting that "the philosopher of the [present] age . . . can only hate social institutions that cannot be separated from religious principle."[35] Maistre approved the "hatred" with which François Fénelon, the sixteenth-century French prelate, pursued the Jansenists and warned that "so long as the royal billhook will not have attacked the root of this poisonous plant, it will not cease to run out through a ground it likes in order then to extend further its dangerous offshoots."[36]

Like all the leading figures of hard-line Catholicism, Maistre reserved for Protestants a thoroughgoing "hatred" that was all the more legitimate in his mind as there burned in "these intractable hearts [a] thirst for Catholic blood and hatred of the monarchy." The "hatred" that Louis XIV felt toward them in turn was therefore readily understandable, and "whether the hatred was reasonable or blind, it was certainly French and politically good."[37] Since "heresy feeds on hatred,"[38] there was no alternative but to rage with equal violence against this "deadly ulcer," to "choke" at once this "reptile" in order to reduce its "venom": "Humanity as a whole has the right to reproach Protestantism for [the] Saint Bartholomew [massacre], for to avoid it [Protestants] had only not to revolt. . . . A Protestant who reproaches the French crown for [the] Saint Bartholomew [massacre] perfectly resembles a Jacobin in our own time who declaims against the Chouans."[39] Convinced that Protestantism was literally the sans-culottism of religion; persuaded—just as Abbé Augustin Barruel and Bonald had been, and Veuillot, Maurras, and Action Française were later to be—that Protestantism was responsible for the outbreak of the

Revolution; and conscious of the "truly striking affinity" between Protestantism and Jacobinism, of the "filial tenderness" that the revolutionaries felt toward Protestantism ("the gospel [as] taught by the Protestant Church never frightened Robespierre"), Maistre called for the most extreme punishments against a heresy that had damaged the Catholic "cement" of the nation. This metaphor was to be adopted by the staunch Catholic Right and used throughout the nineteenth century. A willingness to take up arms was frankly admitted, all the more so since Maistre proudly acknowledged his fanaticism and intolerance—both of them "ingredients necessary to French greatness."[40]

Maistre thundered against all the enemies of Catholicism, regretting that the time of the Crusades had passed, a time when, "sword in hand . . . , the French were still at the head of this immortal enterprise. . . . The French name made so great an impression in the East that it has remained synonymous there with 'European.' " He prayed ardently that Protestantism might be made "to disappear" and impatiently awaited the day when it would be "remove[d] from the European dictionary."[41] If the violence of the Crusades or that of the Saint Bartholomew's Day Massacre did not suffice to suppress heretical dissidence, there remained another, utterly implacable instrument—the Inquisition. Maistre offered a lengthy plea in favor of the efficient techniques of the Inquisition, "in its very nature, good, mild, and preservative." Since Judaism, he argued, "threatened to kill the national plant," and "Mahometanism prodigiously increased the danger,"[42] it was urgent now, as it was then, to react using "similarly violent methods."[43] "If you confine your reflection to the severity of Cardinal Torquemada," he continued, "and fail to consider the awful desolation which it prevented, reasoning is useless."[44] Referring ironically to "the philosophical pathos of French writers" who were bothered by the use of torture and trial by fire, he calmly concluded: "If other nations do not wish the Inquisition, I have nothing to say. It might yet be said to the French, in particular, that they could not, without feeling shame, boast of having rejected this institution, and to all nations equally that any tribunal, established specially to monitor crimes directed chiefly against morals and antinational religion, will always and in all places be an infinitely useful institution."[45] Consequently, "communion through blood . . . , sacrifice through blood" are the condition of "redemption"—"blood is the bond of reconciliation."[46]

If the remedies of the Saint Bartholomew's Day Massacre or the Inquisition frightened the French, there remained the pure, measured, curiously more legitimate violence of the executioner. Maistre's apology for the executioner stands as a landmark in the history of calls for redemption through blood:

> So who is this inexplicable being who, when there are so many pleasant, lucrative, honest, and even honourable professions in which he could exercise his strength [and] dexterity to choose among, has chosen that of torturing and putting to death his own kind? Are this head and this heart made like our own? Do they contain anything that is peculiar and alien to our nature? For myself, I have no doubt about this. In outward appearance he is made like us; he is born like us. But he is an extraordinary being, and for him to be brought into existence as a member of the human family a particular decree was required, a FIAT of creative power. . . . He sets out. He arrives at a public square packed with a pressing and panting crowd. He is thrown a prisoner, a parricide, a blasphemer. He seizes him, stretches him out, ties him to a horizontal cross, and raises his arms. Then there is a horrible silence; there is no sound but the crack of bones breaking under the crossbar and the howls of the victim. He unties him and carries him to the wheel. The broken limbs are bound to the spokes, the head hangs down, the hair stands on end, and the mouth, gaping like a furnace, occasionally emits a few bloody words begging for death. He has finished; his heart is pounding, but it is with joy. He congratulates himself. He says in his heart, *No one can break men on the wheel better than I.* . . . Is this a man? Yes. God receives him in his shrines and allows him to pray. . . . And yet all

greatness, all power, all subordination rests on the executioner; he is both the horror and the bond of human association. Remove this incomprehensible agent from the world, and in a moment order gives way to chaos, thrones fall, and society disappears. God, who is the author of sovereignty, is therefore also the author of punishment. . . . Evil exists on the earth . . . , it must constantly be repressed by punishment.[47]

Maistre's hymn to the executioner is uttered in the hushed setting of the *St. Petersburg Dialogues*, which bring together the Count, the Senator, and the Chevalier on an evening in July 1809, as their boat glides silently along the Neva, taking them to a remote country house promising peace and quiet. It is a "beautiful summer evening," than which "nothing is more enchanting." "Brilliant American birds sail the Neva," flanked by orange groves, and the protagonists, struck by "the beauty of the spectacle and the calm of the night," converse peaceably around the tea table, lending an ear only to soft melodies, to the song of the departed oarsmen.[48]

The Count begins their conversation by announcing this self-evident truth: "*Evil is on the earth.* . . . The whole race of men is kept in order by punishment." Maistre's pessimism, with its apocalyptic overtones that foreshadow the operas of Richard Wagner, heralds the age of redemption by blood that will come after the present heretical revolutionary messianism: the envoy of God must ravage the land in order to give back to France its mission as the leader of Christian Europe. Under the pernicious influence of the "seeds" planted by Voltaire "in the hothouses of Paris," these "Frenchmen, thus degraded by the vile instructors who teach them to believe no longer in France . . . , produced the revolutionary monster that has devoured Europe." Consequently, "THE REMEDY FOR DISORDER WILL BE PAIN,"[49] and France, "the noblest, the strongest, the most powerful of monarchies," must confide its destiny to the executioner all the more quickly since, in keeping with its eternally exceptional destiny, "the French Republic alone was born of the putrid fermentation of all the accumulated crimes [of the Revolution]."[50] The urgency is great, for "Liberty, in being born, assumed a sacrilegious attitude. In place of the ancient hat, the Furies' snakes stood coiled upon her horrifying head; she rattled daggers, climbed up on cadavers to make herself heard farther away." At the head of this "population of madmen," this "hideous assemblage," "phalanxes of executioners" did their ominous job.[51] The Republic—Temple of Reason—concealed a "den of a thousand hideous insects"—"an edifice constructed out of sand and molded in blood."[52] Confronted by such a monster, by an event "the like of which has not been seen before," by this "satanic" plot,[53] this "diabolical work" carried out "to the noise of hellish songs, the blasphemy of atheism, the cries of death, and the prolonged moans of slaughtered innocence,"[54] there was no alternative: the executioners responsible for the Terror had to be succeeded by the executioners of the indispensable royalist regeneration, since the Revolution "will only be wholly extinguished by the contrary principle."[55]

Maistre announced the apocalypse, the time of vengeance when the executioner, the envoy of God, would mete out justice: "Every drop of Louis XVI's blood will cost torrents of French blood; four million Frenchmen perhaps will pay with their heads for this great national crime of an antireligious and antisocial insurrection crowned by a regicide."[56] In resisting the Revolution, the fanaticism of some would answer the intolerance of others. The counterrevolutionary martyrology, especially in the wars in the Vendée evoked by Maistre, rested on a faith that had been scorned by the revolutionaries as well as a firm rejection of the cultural and administrative unification accomplished with such violence by the Revolution. The apocalyptic prophesies of the counterrevolutionaries seemed justified by the horrors of the repression. The rebels of the earliest days, perceived as wholly fanatical and resolutely counterrevolutionary, joined the cruel combat of the Vendeans; the anti-Revolution, in the country and in the cities, embraced the logic of counterrevolution as one of many "sides of a single historical reality."[57] "Veritable dragonnades" conducted by the revolutionaries accumulated "a formidable capital of hatred"; the "imaginary Vendée" of the revolutionaries led to the mythological confrontation of "the Republic against the Vendée," in which neither side recoiled from excess. The Jacobin Barère sought "annihilation." In the words of a commissioner appointed by the Committee of Public Safety to report in the region, the Vendée needed to be "entirely regenerated by French colonists selected from the best departments of the Republic; [and] the children, wives of the rebels and the rest of the inhabitants of the Vendée be dispersed throughout France, if not deported to Madagascar." Henceforth, the Vendée—reductively identified with militant Catholicism and royalism—was to "submit to its punishment." Killings, massacres, "patriotic baptisms" by drowning, and deportations were freely indulged, while "hatred of priests" justified the bloodiest repression—a toll of 600,000, including all war-related deaths, is not improbable—thus transforming the Vendée into a *"région-mémoire."*[58]

Blood begat blood: for France to be truly regenerated, as Albert Hirschman has rightly noted in connection with the reactionary mentality, it was necessary that the counterrevolution not triumph too soon. Blood had to be spilled. This alone would open the way to reaction, as Maistre envisioned it:

> What then would French magistrates have done with three or four hundred Damiens and with all the monsters who covered France? Would the sacred sword of justice have fallen relentlessly, like Robespierre's guillotine? Would all the executioners of the kingdom have been summoned to Paris and all the horses of the artillery to draw and quarter men? Would lead and pitch have been melted in vast cauldrons and flung over limbs torn apart by red-hot pincers?[59]

Though Maistre impatiently awaited such a redemption by the sword, he strongly doubted its likelihood; only a few major culprits would be punished, he supposed, since in the last analysis only "great crimes, unfortunately, require great executions." Unlike conservatives, but also unlike émigré nobles serving in the coalition of armies marshalled against revolutionary France, Maistre argued that "if, at the beginning of our troubles, we had marched on Paris straight away, the Revolution would have been crushed like a worm; but France was finished, and its continental superiority [as well]: a nation penetrated is a nation lost."[60] By the same token, he glorified his enemies, the Jacobins, whose revolutionary passion helped them push the enemy back to the borders, to defend the kingdom, to go beyond death: "[O]nly Jacobinism could have saved France and the monarchy. How, then, was the coalition to be resisted?" Maistre asked. "Only the infernal genius of Robespierre could accomplish this prodigy. The revolutionary government hardened the soul of France by tempering it in blood. . . . The horror of the scaffolds, driving citizens to the frontiers, nourished external force in the measure that the least internal resistance was annihilated."[61]

Maistre also admired Jacobin excess, with its cold recourse to unbridled violence and its deliberate use of terror, which he saw as justifying resort to the royalist executioner:

> The great purification must be accomplished and eyes must be opened; the metal of France, freed from its sour and impure dross, must emerge cleaner and more malleable into the hands of a future king. . . . Only Jacobinism could have saved France and the monarchy. . . . This monstrous power, drunk with blood and success, the most frightful phenomenon that has ever been seen and the like of which will never be seen again, was both a horrible chastisement for the French and sole means of saving France. . . . All the monsters born of the Revolution have, apparently, laboured only for the monarchy.[62]

Maistre's counterutopia, though it was conceived in utter and complete contradiction to the republican ideal, nonetheless shared a number of features with it. The reactionaries sought to counter the revolutionary images that were being disseminated throughout the country with derogatory caricatures of their own. The royalist caricatures themselves were "comparable in every respect with the patriotic caricatures," as Claude Langlois has pointed out.[63] The revolutionaries were represented in their turn as degenerate or threatening animals: furious bulls, blind harpies with clawed hands, griffins, centaurs, monkeys, snakes, the man-eating beasts of Gévaudan—animals whose deformity betrayed their biological spirit. Once again, the adversary was devalued by reducing him to bestiality.

Maistre's resort to such symbolism, mirroring the use made of it on behalf of the revolutionary cause by Sieyès and Robespierre, his alter ego, endlessly intensified the struggle. To be sure, not all royalist caricatures were done in this vein; but many of them vividly embodied the spirit of Maistre's hatred. Their favorite targets were often the very ones at which he was later to aim his sharpest arrows—especially the Protestants, singled out for special abuse. Thus Rabaut Saint-Étienne, who was vehemently attacked by Maistre, figures in many royalist caricatures in the form of a menacing snake, a figure that, ever since the sixteenth-century massacres at Nîmes and Montauban, had long heralded the moment of Protestant revenge. Whereas Maistre loudly applauded such massacres when their victims were Protestants, Catholics now dreaded this "Saint Bartholomew's Day of the royalists." One drawing represented "a hideous scene completed by a group of cannibals who devour twitching limbs"; above their heads appears the legend: "Protestants of Nîmes enjoying a tasty meal."[64] Like Maistre, counterrevolutionary propagandists accused not only Protestants but also Jansenists and Calvinist "philosophists" of joining forces to overturn the Catholic order. In one cartoon, described by Langlois,

the prelate or philosophist, dragging religion behind him, presents it to a man with a billfold and repeats the words that Judas had said to the Jews when he wished to betray Jesus Christ: "How much will you pay me to deliver him to you?" The man with the banknotes, a satisfied Jansenist, replies by showing his money: "This efficacious grace ought to work on you!" . . . But the Calvinist minister impatiently snatches the censer from the hands of trembling Religion and prepares to plunge his dagger into its breast once the deal is concluded.[65]

A number of features are common to both revolutionary and counterrevolutionary caricatures. The latter likewise resorted to political pornography, rambling on, for example, about the disarray, or limpness, of the constitutional army—an image that recalls the famous royal limpness mentioned earlier. Scatological drawings were frequent as well, while blood—which was later to be made famous by Maistre—flooded representations of the adversary, with knives carrying out their redemptive work. Mythical figures were also frequently used, this time lending their irresistible force to the cause of counterrevolutionaries: thus, just as the revolutionary propagandists had portrayed Hercules quelling the counterrevolution, "the nobility accompanied by Hercules"—the same Hercules memorably evoked by Maistre himself—were shown victoriously attacking the Jacobins and the Constitution, whose defenders were transformed (again according to good Maistrean logic) into evil Satans; in other drawings, these diabolical figures are crushed by lightning bolts hurled by Jupiter.[66]

These antagonistic views of the world, both dedicated to the project of regeneration, were similar also in their profound desire to homogenize society, which is to say in their inveterate rejection of all signs of pluralism, whether division within the social body or diversity with respect to values. Corresponding to the sovereignty of the nation upheld by the Jacobins (whose ruthless single-mindedness Maistre could only admire) was the sovereignty of the king upheld by the royalists. Maistre, the "intolerant" and fierce enemy of liberalism,[67] agreed with the Jacobins in vigorously supporting the principle of sovereignty as "one, inviolable, and absolute." "All sovereignty," he added, "is necessarily *one* and necessarily *absolute*."[68] Like the Jacobins, he objected to the division of powers, for it threatened the majesty of sovereignty. The metaphors he used to describe this vitally important unity were likewise formulated in terms of a harmonious "machine"[69] whose parts effortlessly meshed with each other, devoid as they necessarily were of all internal conflict or heterogeneity. "In politics as in mechanics," Maistre observed, "theories fail if they do not take into consideration the different qualities of the materials that make up the *machines*." In the case of the political machine, "All parts have a natural tendency toward the place assigned them, and this tendency will favour all the king's efforts."[70] Influenced by the scientific theories that were then in vogue, Maistre drew a parallel between the unity of physical bodies and that of social bodies. Like other social thinkers of his time, he used the example of a watch to account for the "plans of the Creator"; like Saint-Simon and Auguste Comte, the founders of sociology, he saw in the revolutionary moment an unacceptable rupture of the unity of the social body—a sort of fit of ideological anger that triumphed over the biological logic that regulated human societies.

Maistre's denunciation of the French Republic as a lifeless structure, an artificial institution that turned its back on nature, linked him with conservative theorists such as Burke and Bonald and prefigured the classic distinction asserted by one of his principal heirs, Charles Maurras, between the legal country and the real country. In an entirely different spirit, strangely enough, it also prefigured the most sociological passages in Tocqueville and Marx, each of whom described the French bureaucratic apparatus as an entity devoid of life, pathologically cut off from the realities of society. "What an enormous machine!" exclaimed Maistre. "What a multiplicity of springs and clockwork! What a fracas of pieces clanging away! . . . Everything tells us there is nothing natural in these movements."[71] In a passage crossed out in the manuscript, he had written: "What an enormous machine! See how many people are required to make this mannequin move! The hinges with which all its joints have been furnished render it weak instead of supple. It is held upright by rods placed beneath its arms." The Republic thus stood as a "mannequin," and the

Constitution that ruled it appeared as "an automaton" emerging from the extravagant dreams of an "absurd . . . and exclusively mechanical" philosophy.[72] This striking description irresistibly calls to mind the parable of Saint-Simon, but this time the attack on the artificial, dysfunctional character of the state was mounted against the Republic, a lifeless monster, a purely automatic embodiment of Reason that was foreign to the soul and to the eternal mission of France.

This message was later taken up by the radical Right and ever since has been repeated ad nauseam. The famous charge made by Maistre and endlessly reiterated by Veuillot, Maurras, and Drumont—"*[I]t is a republic without republicans*"—raised a barrier between the French people and the Republic. "Do you not see," Maistre warned, "that your republican institutions have no roots, that they are simply *sitting* on your soil, in contrast to their predecessors, which were *planted* there? It took an ax to fell the latter; a breath will sweep away these ones and leave not a trace."[73] Maistre, prophet of reaction who prayed for a return to the "health" that would erase once and for all the disorder of "disease," deplored the "decadence" in which France was mired. As a convinced positivist (though the term would be coined only later by Comte), he cited the authority of the exact sciences in detecting the presence of divine Providence, and affirming the necessity of preserving the Catholic continuity of French society. His conviction was unalterable: "Frenchmen!" he exclaimed, "you will never become yourselves again unless once more you become *very Christian*."[74]

While this profession of faith was applauded by the leading figures of the radical Right, it aroused the astonishment and enduring incredulity of republicans. Thus in October 1886, under a Third Republic that was at last firmly planted in the national soil rather than simply inserted into it, at a solemn hearing of the appeals court in Nancy, the assistant public prosecutor, Villard, took as the subject of his opening speech "The Right to Punish and Joseph de Maistre." Well versed in Maistre's writings, in particular his commentaries on the function of the executioner, Villard declared before the assembled magistrates:

> Maistre linked the right to punish with a principle of vindictive expiation that the modern mind absolutely condemns. . . . He abhorred the Revolution and all the ideas that had worked to bring it about, together with all their consequences. The terrorism of 1793 he contrasted with what might be called religious terrorism. The desire for retaliation inspired him to write an apologia for the Inquisition, to propose a fierce and mystical theory about the necessity of human sacrifices. . . . Human justice he conceived as ruthless and unpitying. He made the scaffold the basis of the state. . . . The social and religious Inquisition became a necessity, for it alone can reach into the domain of private life as far as the sanctuary of the conscience.[75]

Horrified by such extreme virulence—which, as Isaiah Berlin later pointed out, heralded the totalitarian violence of the twentieth century—the counsel for the Republic deplored the fact that "the inflexible logic of a preconceived idea [extinguished] in Maistre all feeling of pity."[76] Nothing was more foreign to the republican spirit, which toward the end of the century seemed destined gradually to prevail. Even the pope came forward to rally Catholics to the Republic: far from wishing that France would experience a Catholic redemption after the fashion of Maistre, Leo XIII counseled Catholics to pursue their struggle within the framework of the newly legitimized Republic.

During the same period, however, Charles Maurras, the founder of Action Française and the most formidable adversary of the Third Republic, yet managed to give new life to Maistre's vindictive spirit. Maurras openly advocated recourse to the greatest possible violence, with the aim of overwhelming the artificial institutions of the Republic and restoring to the king his former majesty. Moreover, Maurras freely admitted his intellectual debt to Joseph de Maistre—"the master" from whom he acknowledged many "borrowings."[77] For Maurras, Maistre was a "penetrating and farsighted [thinker]. . . . All his opinions are founded . . . on observation." He was an "observer of profound power and lucidity. . . . His ideas are present and living, current. . . . Above all, let us try to understand and to spread his method."[78] Accordingly, he made a habit of citing Maistre's writings. In an essay published in 1905, after evoking in very Maistrean fashion "the price of blood," he hoped and prayed for the time when "each nation, each civilization would jealously lock itself up in the principle that constitutes it and in the character that distinguishes it from others. One will be a Swiss or French traditionalist, an English, German, or Russian nationalist; and one will be a man less and less." In the same vein, delivering a vibrant eulogy for Catholicism in *Enquête sur la monarchie* (1900–1909), Maurras began by explicitly referring to Maistre's *Du pape*.[79] His prejudices were Maistre's as well: "It must not be forgotten that before the recent Jewish scandal [the Dreyfus Affair], a policy of patience, no less Jewish, had had a deep effect by erosion. The two events explain one another, complete one another: evolution skillfully prepared the Revolution, and this explains Joseph de Maistre's most extreme, most unimaginable idea: Satan."[80]

Maistre and Maurras were "animated by the same spirit"; they both fought the same fight on behalf of royalist and Catholic restoration, of which "Action Française was the fullest expression"; and they both recognized the Catholic Church as the "only enduring international."[81] It was, moreover, in explicitly invoking Maistre's patronage that the Catholic philosopher Jacques Maritain, in *L'Antimoderne* (1922), observed with a sense of dread that modern history was "nothing other than the history of the final agony and death of Christianity," vanquished by the attacks of Luther, Descartes, and Kant: man, having become "deaf to revealed Teaching . . . hides from God." Maritain condemned "the anti-Christian revolution that puts man in the place of God" and, appealing to the authority of Maurras, added, "One ought to hate the modern world taken in what it regards as its proper and distinctive glory: independence with regard to God. We therefore hate the revolutionary-bourgeois iniquity that envelops and pollutes civilization today as we hate the revolutionary-proletarian iniquity that wishes to annihilate it. It is for God, not for modern society, that we wish to work."[82]

Indeed, Maritain came to Maurras's rescue following his condemnation by the pope in 1926. While regretting Maurras's philosophical and religious errors, and approving their rejection, he nonetheless asked, "Must what distresses us about Maurras prevent us from recognizing the truth that Maurras speaks, what links his thought with that of Joseph de Maistre and Bossuet?" After reviewing Maurras's critique of democracy, Maritain went on to say: "It must be admitted here that, in fact, *in concreto*, the historical movement triggered by the French Revolution is animated by a spiritual principle, by a profound *intentio* that is the enemy of humanity because it aims at creating a humanity that does without God. This is why Joseph de Maistre called that Revolution *satanic*. . . . Maurras's greatest merit . . . is having cleansed the mind, having delivered it from false liberal dogmas."[83] This hatred of the French Revolution, found in the writings of both Maurras and the early Maritain, continued to animate a counterrevolutionary spirit that remained astonishingly faithful to the radical visions of the founder of counterutopia.

As late as November 1943, Maurras "openly described himself as a disciple of de Maistre and accepted the totality of his ideas."[84] Just as Édouard Drumont, whose fiery talent the theoretician of Action Française so admired, asked how many people had read Maistre, Maurras acknowledged the magnitude of his debt, even during the darkest days of Vichy. In his 1941 work *La Seule France* (a veritable ode to Marshal Pétain marked by a pronounced anti-Semitism), he cited Maistre before even Bonald, Le Play, Taine, and Barrès, all of whom had denounced "the decadence of the French society produced by 1789" and who were now a source of inspiration for "the new French state" that finally was moving forward "at a brisk pace."[85] Maistre's influence upon movements of the radical Right was immense.[86] In 1940, introducing a selection of his writings, Bernard de Vaulx stressed that Maistre was "the first critic of stature of the philosophy and ideas of 1789," which Vichy was now ready to demolish. "What an arsenal against 1789!" cried Maistre's enthusiastic introducer, marveling at the depth of his hatred of the Revolution and offering valuable advice to those who wished to come back to the real country, to traditions, experience, and faith.[87]

Vaulx was far from alone. The importance of Maistre's thought was recognized in the academic world, where his vision was said to be "infinitely more social" than that of the socialist leader Jean Jaurès (1859–1914).[88] An entire course was devoted to Maistre at the Institut d'Études Politiques et Sociales (founded by Paul Marion, the very *pétainist* undersecretary of state for information). The teacher of the course, André Delay, stressed in his opening lecture that since the new institute proposed "to take as its point of departure the fact of the inequality of individuals, societies, and races," in order to demonstrate that "organic social relations" must remain subject to the authority of the "leader," a close study of Maistre's thought was obligatory. After reviewing his main ideas in subsequent lectures, Delay concluded:

What Frenchman of 1943 would not find instruction in the career of Joseph de Maistre? . . . The Frenchman of 1943 finds himself, through de Maistre's career, warned against the seductions and pretensions of the immense Russian power, committed to hoping for the development of our nation, invited not to judge politics on [the basis of] labels alone. . . . We, the servants of the *Maréchal*, consider his power to be legitimate because he has been led by a providential unfolding of circumstances. We continue to believe this and remain persuaded that the miracle [that has] begun will be completed. Thus, a book [i.e., Maistre's *Les Soirées de Saint-Pétersbourg*] that bears the subtitle *Entretiens sur le gouvernement temporel de la Providence* [*Conversations on the Temporal Government of Providence*] can pass for a current work. What chief of state today does not invoke God? . . .

Our institute of political and social studies has placed at the
heart of its work the fact of the inequality of men: as did
Maistre, since the core of every nation is its aristocracy. . . .
Maistre observed the reign of evil, and since the whole universe proceeds from God, from Unity, in which there can be
no evil, he concludes that only an error, a "breach of trust"
by humanity can explain why evil reigns over it; the original
sin of Hebrew legend is not, for our author, the cause of evil,
it is the sole plausible explanation of it. . . . Human nature is
good, but men are preyed upon by evil; evil is necessary;
men as individuals exist only for God; a nation regenerates
itself not by innovating but by remaining faithful to its past.
. . . Such is the lesson of Joseph de Maistre. A terrible event
of these days gives us the occasion to observe that this lesson is alive in contemporary consciousness. On Sunday 4
April 1943 a group of men came from the New Continent,
through the sky, to bombard an area of our city. In one
minute more than three hundred people were hurled [to
their deaths], crushed, mangled. . . . Cardinal Suhard,
archbishop of Paris, recalled that war has its laws, . . . that
measures must be taken in advance with regard to noncom-
batants: Maistre [would have] agreed with this . . . but above
all he [would have] approved the speech of M. Cathala, the
representative of the French state, who said, "In the presence of death, the duty of peoples is first and foremost to
unite." . . . This is the essence of Maistre's philosophy: horror must not frighten man. . . . Toward union beyond the
bloody horrors—that is the direction given us by the
Catholic whose work we complete.[89]

The eulogists of Vichy explicitly appealed to Maistre in order
both to justify the legitimacy of an authoritarian regime that
claimed Catholicism as the basis of its own authority and to vanquish the evil propagated by satanic sects, of which the Jews were
considered the most diabolical representatives, aided by the
Anglo-Saxon Protestants, who sought to undermine the French

spirit defended by the old *maréchal*. This apologia published in April 1943 under the auspices of the Institut d'Études Politiques et Sociales, a privileged organ of the Vichy regime, speaks volumes about the profound and abiding influence of the author of *Considérations sur la France*, a work whose message had suddenly assumed a new topicality.

Still, Maistre's extremism frightened certain elements of Vichy. On 19 August 1941, Joseph Barthélemy, the minister of justice, gave an important speech before the general assembly of the Council of State in the presence of Marshal Pétain. Criticizing the system of summary justice placed at the service of the occupier in response to mounting anti-German attacks—the source of the sinister special sections—Barthélemy declared: "We do not believe that swiftness is a method or the best method. . . . A decisive regime is strong, fit, and healthy only in the rule of law." Many years later, explicitly challenging "the curse of the pessimistic philosopher Joseph de Maistre," Barthélemy wrote in his memoirs:

> There is no doubt that there are men who love repression. Their prophet is Joseph de Maistre, with his essay, much too famous, on the essential, indispensable role of the executioner. This is why M. Charles Maurras salutes the Savoyard philosopher as the "exterminating archangel." . . . There are people who believe they have a passion for justice but in reality are animated by vengeance or by some other sadism. . . . But in face of the lovers of "irons, executioners, and tortures," there are people of whom one can ask nothing beyond a sad resignation to repression, as a painful and ineluctable necessity of social defense. I consider myself one of those.[90]

Maistre's appeals on behalf of rule by unlearned men who act more by instinct and impulse than by reasoning—who have no other instrument at their disposal besides a certain moral force that "bends wills the way the wind bows the crops"—nonetheless met with widespread approval. His inspiration was decisive in helping to create the image of new dictators—strong men who seize power. In this same terrible year of 1943, in the *Revue des deux mondes*, Baron Michaud saw Maistre as responding to contemporary anxieties and argued that "It is necessary to take as the basis of our regenerative action what Maistre called venerable laws, that is, the ancient laws and customs of the nation. . . . The French attempt to create a great republic seemed to him the supreme folly of the rationalists. . . . Maistre forcefully discerned the link between the dead and the living."[91]

Maistre's apologists were united in their conviction that Vichy's project of regenerating society—the "*Révolution nationale*"— could proceed only in accordance with his expiatory doctrines. The time had finally come to vanquish republican schemes by carrying out a Catholic program of regeneration oriented toward the values of the past. Insisting on the absolute rejection of the heritage of the French Revolution, Vichy imposed its new order without qualms for the most part. Of the many writings that celebrated Maistre and his work during the period, a few expressed certain reservations, but nothing more.[92]

Since then Maistre's influence has continued to make itself felt. Indeed, the various movements of the radical Right today still derive many of their arguments from him, almost two centuries after his death.[93]

Chapter Four

The Difficult Career
of Liberalism

And so it was, then, that France turned away from liberalism. The clash between two antithetical visions of the world aggravated extremist tendencies, inciting confrontation and closing off other possible paths of political development. Intransigence on both the Right and the Left, combined with a pervasive culture of authoritarianism, prevented the partisans of pluralism from making themselves heard and ruled out any reasoned consideration of the Anglo-American model. In the event, Tocqueville's dark pessimism turned out to be justified. Despite a brief moment of stunning glory, the solitary prophet was fated to be almost completely forgotten, his faith in the virtues of individualism recollected only with scorn and sarcasm.

To be sure, Tocqueville's defense of local democracy was consistent with the decentralizing spirit of his time, but this spirit came into enduring conflict with the logic of the indivisible state, endorsed by most of the heroes of the opposing camps. The supporters of the empire, like those of the republic (as well as their counterrevolutionary—and even revolutionary—adversaries), had no patience with his pleas for American-style self-government, community life, and civil religion. As a result, "the eccentricity of Tocqueville's thought in French culture" inevitably and lastingly transformed him into a "doctor without patients," a "forlorn partisan" who turned his back on the most popular absolutisms of his day. Not until the 1860s did Tocqueville—"deathly saddened" by the misfortunes of freedom (as the nineteenth-century liberal journalist Lucien-Anatole Prévost-Paradol put it)—achieve posthumous leadership of the liberal party.[1] The political theorists Édouard de Laboulaye, Émile Boutmy, and Charles de Rémusat, all of whom tried for a time to adapt liberalism to a society naturally oriented toward rival authoritarianisms, fully recognized their affinity with him. Certain supporters of liberal Catholicism, such as Henri Lacordaire, were also charmed by Tocqueville's eloquence—as was, surprisingly enough, Tocqueville's longtime enemy François Guizot. (Guizot, prime minister from 1847 to 1848, was a doctrinaire Catholic and unrepentent conservative who remained hostile to the ideals of democracy and equality to the end.)

But even the sense of intellectual kinship was ephemeral. The French political scene continued to be uncongenial to liberal democracy, and with the Paris Commune of 1871, hatred was once more given free rein, alienating the nation's progressive elements. Catholics subsequently rejoined the reactionary camp en masse while republicans remained faithful for the most part to the Jacobin spirit; the few liberals who were left tended to align themselves with the more individualist heritage of Benjamin Constant (1767–1830). Only the École Libre des Sciences Politiques continued to carry on with the project of reconciling democracy and the old elites. Its leading thinkers—Émile Boutmy, Eugène d'Eichtal, and Albert Sorel—still heard Tocqueville's message, but the school itself now produced senior civil servants who mocked him and perpetuated the tradition of the monarchist state, foreign to American democracy.[2] Tocqueville's hopes of importing the pluralist American model were doomed to failure.

The fate of his rival in liberalism, Benjamin Constant, whom he took such care to ignore, was scarcely happier. Constant shared Tocqueville's anti-Rousseauism, his condemnation of the "years of madness" and their use as a pretext for oppression, his rejection of administrative centralization, and his call for the separation of powers and for a rigorous distinction between the public and private spheres—all animating features of the antagonistic reveries that dominated the French political imagination. Unlike Tocqueville, however, Constant challenged the democratic principles of equality and majority rule, rejected community-based forms of association, and showed indifference to a pluralism that rested on the presumptive virtues of local customs. Politically, his program proved to be still more incongruous.[3] Attacked by the ultraroyalists and made a privileged target by Joseph de Maistre and many other Catholic thinkers throughout the nineteenth century,[4] he denounced the Jacobins' power—perhaps even more harshly than Tocqueville, who legitimized it to some degree by placing it in historical context—thanks to which "a thousand voices, disastrously docile, carry everywhere suspicions, hatreds, mistrust."[5]

Constant criticized the exclusively public and collective character of the liberties enjoyed by the Ancients, according to whom "men were only machines whose law ruled the springs and governed the wheels," and insisted on the necessity of combining these with the liberties of the Moderns, which ensured that "the peaceful enjoyment of private independence" flourished. Disdaining "uniformity," he feared revolutionary liberty (which "must have awakened hatred and dread"[6]) and called for the absolute defense of individual freedoms. He assigned a crucial function to the laws of the market ("gentle commerce"), but also, and more important, to the will of individuals in directing the course of history. A pacific future would blossom, he was certain, devoid of violent passions and resting on a quasi-Kantian moral code.[7]

All these opinions—because they went against not only the rival worldviews of the day but also the cautious conservatism of doctrinaire liberalism—seemed out of place. The patent "failure of liberalism"[8] left a lasting mark on French political tradition, which reserved its fascination for strong centralized government. Hard-line counterrevolutionary Catholics, joined by others in the Church concerned with social issues, ignored the Anglo-American sirens more resolutely than ever, remaining opposed to political and economic individualism and seeking to slow the ripening of liberal ideas in their midst.[9] The workers' movement, influenced by the authoritarian spirit of the socialist thinker Pierre-Joseph Proudhon (1809–65), condemned individualism in its turn, upholding unanimist conceptions that posited the People as a homogeneous entity rooted in real communities.[10] As a result, the brief spring of 1848 led once more to intolerance and prefigured the Commune and the "bloody week" of May 1871,[11] which exhausted the liberal imagination at a moment when the workers' leaders turned away from the infant Republic.

In his famous 1882 lecture "What Is a Nation?" Ernest Renan urged that France be reconstructed on other and more secure foundations, recognizing that its historical quarrels had to be permanently ended. In view of the challenge from a rising Germany, the French nation had to be refounded on the will of its people, the possibility of which in turn rested on the assumption that long-standing ideological conflicts could be resolved. Ideally, "the plebiscite of daily life" would heal the collective rifts of earlier times. Though he gradually came around to the idea of democracy, Renan was no convert to liberalism: the nation remained for him a community of citizens who had overcome their antagonisms, not a collection of individuals with diverse aims and purposes. Renan's conception of the nation haughtily ignored internal pluralism, community associations, and the many institutions that permit local participation as well as a balance of power at the national level—in a word, all those features of political life to which liberal thinkers were unalterably attached.

Renan's view of a united, closely knit nation assumed a miraculous end to the conflict between the republican dream and Maistre's counterutopia. In "What Is a Nation?" he argued:

Forgetting and, I would say, even historical error are essential factors in the creation of a nation, which is why progress in historical study is often a danger for a nationality. Historical investigation throws light once more on the violent events that took place during the origin of all political formations, even of those whose consequences are the most beneficial. . . . The essence of a nation is that all individuals have many things in common and also that all [of them] have forgotten many things. . . . Every French citizen must have forgotten the Saint Bartholomew's Day Massacre [and] the massacres in the Midi during the thirteenth century.[12]

But French citizens did still remember such things, as the political scientist Benedict Anderson has recently pointed out. Who else could have recalled the historical significance of these tragic events, which had taken place centuries earlier, if not the French themselves? Renan's readers were supposed to have already forgotten what, by his own argument, they were assumed naturally to remember. He peremptorily decreed it to be "a prime contemporary civic duty" incumbent upon all French citizens to "blur [the memory of] unnamed victims and assassins," to forget tragedies that they *themselves* might remember in only a confused way, and to calmly think of these "fratricidal wars" as unfolding among *"fellow Frenchmen."* "Having to 'have already forgotten' tragedies of which one needs unceasingly to be 'reminded,' " Anderson observes, "turns out to be a characteristic device in the later construction of national genealogies"[13]—genealogies that were inculcated by the state through its public schools.

Renan did not suppose that every citizen must have already forgotten an event as recent as the Commune, for example, which had so violently divided the French only a few years earlier. The obligation of forgetting recent history was something that in his view had to be taught. Underlying this deliberate amnesia is the idea that, prior to the eruption of internecine violence, solidarity reigned among the citizens it later divided. The sociologist Ernest Gellner congratulates Renan for having shown that the Jacobin state promoted not memory but amnesia, in order that the French forget their origins: "Renan therefore was right. There is indeed a perpetual plebiscite, a choice rather than an inevitability. . . . No doubt it does not take place every day, but with the start of each new school year. And anonymity and amnesia are essential."[14] Membership in the nation therefore meant forgetting the Franco-French wars. Frankly condemning "ethnographic considerations" as well as the notion of race, which play no role in the birth of a nation, and likewise denying any role to language, culture, or religion, which have now "become a personal matter,"[15] Renan saw in the nation only "a spiritual principle."[16]

But the rationalist Renan—sympathetic to the notion of the state as educator advocated by Jules Ferry and celebrated by the triumphant Third Republic, which nonetheless organized the remembrance of the Revolution with great pomp on the occasion of its centennial anniversary—represents only one side of his complex personality. Certain aspects of the 1882 lecture, particularly the insistence on the "cult of ancestors," are scarcely compatible with a will to forget. His linguistic doctrines, as well as his many anti-democratic statements on behalf of the monarchy in *L'Avenir de la science* (written in 1848 but not published until 1890) and *Histoire générale et système comparé des langues sémitiques* (1855), pose similar difficulties. Renan considered the inequality of races obvious, for the "Semitic race, compared to the Indo-European race, represents an inferior combination of human nature."[17] Even if he avoided linking race to blood or the shape of the skull, he established a clear connection between race, language, and religion—a perspective that hardly facilitates forgetting or the "plebiscite of daily life."[18] In this narrower sense, therefore, Renan was a supporter of racial theories before he became a celebrity of the Republic.[19] Whereas republican tradition preferred to forget this aspect of his work, the nationalist Right, discreetly closing its eyes to the rationalist Renan, appealed to the racist Renan alone; it remembered him still more explicitly both during Barrès's time and later during Vichy, and pays glowing homage to him still today.[20] Throughout an interminably long

Third Republic that was indifferent—when it was not violently opposed—to liberalism, the two Renans acted as spokesmen for antagonistic visions of French history.

With the advent of the "republican moment"[21] and the triumph of an " 'absolute' Republic [that was] more the heir to the ancien régime than a practitioner of liberalism," France entered into a long period of stability that worked against acceptance of liberal ideas: "Just like Jacob, condemned to wrestle alone with the archangel, the Third Republic was henceforth [fated] to live its whole life as a battle for the triumph of orthodoxy, as a struggle between good and evil."[22] Émile Faguet, in his famous work *Le Libéralisme* (1903), maintained that "France is a republican country that has no freedom."[23] More recently, the historian Tony Judt has suggested that during this period the "manner of [the republicans'] success placed the final nail in the coffin of liberal thought in French public life."[24] In a similar vein, the historian Pierre Rosanvallon has argued that "there was scarcely any place [in the Third Republic] for a pluralist democracy of interests. . . . A single antiliberal thread—[antiliberal] in the precise philosophical sense of a rejection of pluralism—ran through the different domains of French culture."[25] Whatever may be the justice of these views, the fact remains that the Third Republic did not intend to follow Renan's insistent advice: it was unaffected by amnesia and had no wish whatsoever to forget the "Saint Bartholomews" of yesteryear.[26]

The past was present to such a degree that it actively shaped political views. For Léon Gambetta (along with Jules Ferry one of the founders of the Third Republic), "the Revolution is purely and simply the new faith among men. . . . The French Revolution was the emancipation of all living creatures. . . . In such a way, gentlemen, that for those who seek to promote justice, there is nothing above or beyond the French Revolution."[27] Gambetta's "Jacobinism" was devoid of any neo-Robespierrist dimension, however, and implied no desire whatever to resort to authoritarianism. Conscious of France's exceptionalism, he exclaimed simply, "A government without precedent shall be established in the world, a government the like of which will never have been seen, the French Republic!"—a republic that expresses itself by its "unity, that particular and special physiognomy which stands out in full light."[28]

Jules Ferry, on the other hand, felt that "today all is quite changed . . . in an overflowing democracy, which, instead of enemies, has only sycophants"; and that it was therefore necessary to repudiate Jacobinism and "the memory of the scaffolds."[29] Georges Clemenceau, a bit later, attacked the prevailing consensus among moderate republicans, and in so doing revealed his concern with preserving the glory of Robespierre, which gave rise to the famous lines:

The Revolution is all of a piece . . . , a whole from which nothing can be taken away. Ah! You do not want the revolutionary Tribunal? Yet you know under what circumstances it was created. Do you not know where the ancestors of these gentleman of the Right were? . . . The point is that this admirable Revolution, with which we are not yet finished, still endures; that we too are the authors of it; that it is always the same men who are doing battle with the same enemies. Yes, we still want what our forebears wanted. We will meet with the same sorts of resistance. You have remained the same; we have not changed. The struggle will therefore have to last until victory is achieved once and for all.[30]

For Clemenceau, then, the time of "overflowing democracy" had not yet come; and the idea of an "open Republic" (another fine phrase due to Ferry)—a republic "open to all the French" and "devoid of the spirit of hatred" that would be worthy of a liberal society—did not always make sense in a society menaced by grave dangers, a society in which Gambetta could imagine his role as "a sort of mediator between people of differing interests" who worked to "dispel . . . prejudices."[31] French political life was to be shaped by the utopias and counterutopias of the past for many years to come, with the result that determined resistance of those who remained opposed to a resolutely "open" republic pushed the republicans into radicalism.

Commemorative celebrations relentlessly succeeded one another, reviving their memory of the conflicts of the past century. Ever since the entry of universalism into political modernity in the form of the French Revolution, the concern for remembrance was explicitly affirmed. The Constitution of 3 September 1791 clearly decreed, at the end of the preamble: "National festivals will be established to preserve the memory of the French Revolution, to maintain fraternity among citizens and to attach them to the Constitution, to the Country, to the laws."[32] Faithful to this injunction, which favored memory rather than forgetfulness, the Republic vigorously organized commemorations that from the moment of the "revolutionary festival" in 1789 until the "republican festival a hundred years later"[33] hardly ceased. Alongside this memory a counterrevolutionary memory has been constructed—likewise a memory similarly concerned to summon up tragedies reinforcing a contrary identification.[34]

The republicans declined to accommodate Renan's wishes. To his dismay, they lavishly celebrated the centenary of the Revolution, prompting him to issue a solemn admonishment: "Nothing is more unhealthy than to regulate the life of the present on the basis of the past, when the past is exceptional."[35] Considering that the Republic was still fragile and threatened, things turned out rather well. In order to remember the Revolution's great men and to pay homage to their values, an immense effort was undertaken in the way of public statuary: Rousseau, Condorcet, and above all Danton were honored. The centenary witnessed also the unveiling in the capital of a preliminary plaster version of Jules Dalou's *Triomphe de la République*, definitively installed in November 1899—the very moment when the Dreyfusard cause triumphed. The provinces were also covered with monuments and statues. In the Dauphiné, at Vizille, the events of 1788 in that region were celebrated—in the presence of the president of the Republic, Sadi Carnot—with military parades and the inauguration of a monument that provoked jubilation. The monarchists, for their part, organized a countercommemoration led by Albert de Mun, Monsignor de Canrières and the Marquis de La Tour du Pin-Chambly. Statues were also unveiled in Lille, Marseilles, and Toulouse in honor of the Revolution, with troops marching before the assembled authorities. In each case, in accordance with the instructions of the prefects,[36] emphasis was laid on the Revolution's dual character as a rupture with the past and a foundation for the future, while in other parts of Marseilles and Toulouse campaigns were conducted against the "crimes" of the Revolution, with "monarchist youth" rallying crowds of several thousand people in the streets. Rival memories similarly came into conflict in Lyons, rebel city of the Revolution, where freethinkers confronted staunch Catholics ("Marie defying Marianne"), and in the Vendée, where the landscape bristled with commemorative crosses at a time when "trials opened for the beatification of Vendean clerics killed out of hatred for the faith"—a style of remembrance that, by contrast with republican commemoration, exalted the thousand-year past of the Christian kingdom as well as the glories of the Vendée.[37]

In Paris, the Eiffel Tower was erected as a temple in honor of modernity, an homage "to the learned men who have honored France since 1789." Three hundred meters high, it triumphantly confronted an imposing monument of Christian France, the Basilica of the Sacré-Cœur, still under construction in this centenary year. In the 12 February 1887 issue of *Le Temps*, the poets Charles Leconte de Lisle, François Coppée, and Sully Prudhomme, who were later to become leading lights of the nationalist Right, thundered against a tower "that commercial America itself would not want" and that abolished "sublime Gothic Paris."[38] Opened for worship in June 1891, the Sacré-Cœur represented a crucial moment in the cultural war to which the French now devoted themselves;[39] for the new weekly *Le Sacré-Cœur*, the matter was straightforward: "We are a journal of combat and of the avant-garde. Whom do we combat? We combat the Opportunist and Radical Republic; we fight it tooth and nail." Consequently, through the whole troubled period of the Dreyfus Affair, the Sacré-Cœur was to be the symbol of the Catholic rejection of the Jewish and Masonic Republic, a site of nationalist mobilization that provoked republican demonstrations in the streets of Montmartre. For *La Croix*, "the Masonic lodges do not lack money. They prove it today, with their Tower." *Le Pèlerin*, in the same vein, adorned its cover with an image of Satan perched atop the Eiffel Tower, looking to seduce Catholic France. Thumbing its nose at the republicans, *Le Sacré-Cœur* announced in its 14 July 1892 issue that "the committee of the Basilica has installed atop the scaffolding a cross that dominates Paris at a height that reaches almost that of the Eiffel Tower. It sparkles, gleams; [its radiance] might be mistaken for stars sent by God to create a glorious and divine symbol. . . . Nothing prevails against it: it stretches out its gleaming arms over radiant Paris." The republicans were stunned. *L'Intransigeant* wrote: "On the hill [of Montmartre], the luminous cross of the men in black has stretched out its arms." Devout Catholics, speaking in the voice of *L'Autorité*, initially condemned the plan of celebrating a revolutionary festival—"the festival of a sans-culotte regime, of Jews and Freemasons, sworn enemies of the Catholic religion, the festival of a regime that has banned the cross from the school, from the hospital." In the end, however, they rejoiced in a "contrast the organizers [unwittingly] sought, the allegory of the sign of Redemption striking down by its radiance the City of Light, trapped in the clutches of orgy and debauchery, reminding it of [the] respect [that is due] divine law."[40]

The Universal Exposition of 1889, with its gigantic statue of the Republic, enthroned and wearing a Phrygian cap, drew millions of visitors eager to pay tribute to science. Paris was illuminated for the event. Musicians marched in parade[41] while the mayors of French cities and towns assembled for an immense republican banquet. Some of them (such as the mayor of Barville, in Oise, who wrote: "The festival to which you invite me could not be for someone who, like me, finds it impossible to separate the memory of the year 1789 from that of the tumultuous and bloody years that followed in such close succession") refused the invitation, but a great many agreed to attend the "fraternal banquet" of the Republic in homage to the Revolution, scheduled for 14 July, "the great day that made us citizens," that "emancipated all of us," that "made men of us by pulling us out of servitude and slavery." This festival provided them with an opportunity "to fraternize with the grandsons of the gallant men and martyrs who spilled their blood for the emancipation of the people"—an occasion rendered all the more urgent by the recognition that "in this year of the centenary of the French Revolution, and above all in the presence of supreme efforts on the part of the united forces of reaction to overturn the Republic and restore personal government in some form or other, . . . the Republic must survive." This gigantic "staging of the nation" brought together senior civil servants, generals, prefects, senators, and deputies, in addition to members of the government who, seated with the president of the Republic, feasted around a table raised two or five meters (depending on the source of the account) above the ground. Together, they represented "the splendors of the Republic" which henceforth was identified with France itself.[42]

In many respects, the republicans occupied the public sphere. The republican festival was an extension of the revolutionary festival, aimed at "forming the crucible of a citizenship of memory." Unadorned by references to antiquity, and less passionate than the revolutionary festival, the republican festival nonetheless was able, with the cooperation of a great many mayors, to use local networks of sociability to strengthen "the republic in the village" by reactivating the memory of glorious events. In the commune of La Crique, for example, the following notice was posted during the centenary year: "Our fathers of 1789 and of 1792, through their struggles, through their suffering, through their lives and through their deaths, have made us what we are: we would be ungrateful if we did not defend their memory; unworthy if we were to let their heritage perish." Other municipal officials feared that if their grandsons were to lose the memory of the feats of the giants of the Revolution, "the pioneers who painfully cleared the way for us" would be "left in the icy night of eternal oblivion by those who, thanks to them, have reached their goal." The republicans were careful not to obey Renan's advice in seeking to promote a "citizenship of memory" that would unify the public sphere. From the "banquets of the Republic"—sources of a festive republican conviviality where public and private space merged—it was expected that a quasi-organic affective community would emerge through the creation of a single memory shared by all citizens.[43]

Faced with this affirmation of republican unanimity, the episcopate rose up to reject an event that was "at the root of our troubles."[44] Many Lenten pastoral letters condemned the centenary by passing over it in total silence; others openly lashed out against a society that had been "corrupt for a hundred years and [was] dedicated to idolatry of the rights of man." All of them rejected a modernity that attacked Christian society, and all opposed the "war machine" of the republicans as well as liberalism and individualism, which "put souls in the greatest peril." Monsignor Charles-Émile Freppel, the bishop of Angers, took charge of this antirevolutionary crusade: on 5 January 1889 he published the first installment of a work entitled *La Révolution française, à propos du centenaire de 1789*. First serialized in the *Gazette de France*, and then in the monarchist *France nouvelle*, it enjoyed an immediate success. Freppel denounced the rationalist rupture that "eliminat[ed] Christianity altogether" by gradually establishing a "state without God, family without God, marriage without God, school without God."[45] The revolution of 1789 was "one of the direst events in the history of mankind," for it "disrupted the natural course of history"; by liberating the forces of evil, it "unleashed the basest and most selfish instincts of human nature," the "fiercest hatreds."[46]

Reform of the ancien régime surely had been necessary in Freppel's view. For this purpose it would have sufficed to draw inspiration from the books of grievances ordered drawn up by Louis XVI. In 1789, however, in renouncing the notion of a Christian people in order to subject the social order to deist and atheist rationalism [alike], [the Revolution's] representatives presented the world with the sad spectacle of a national apostasy hitherto unmatched in the Catholic countries." As late as 1849, Freppel had described himself as a "Catholic republican"; but with his appointment twenty years later to the bishopric of Angers he came to associate himself with the "ultramontanist party, which is to say with antiliberalism." Elected deputy of Brest in 1880, he became the chief strategist of a group of some forty Catholic deputies who forcefully opposed the secular confiscation of Church property and vigorously defended the monarchy in calling for the maintenance of "the natural alliance between Catholics and royalists." He went on to lead the attack against the celebrations associated with the centenary of the Revolution in 1889, and in November of the following year sought to halt the rallying of Catholics to the Republic before finally adopting a more nuanced position in obedience to the pope.[47]

Along with Charles Maurras, who at just this moment began his career as a polemicist with a furious attack on the republican ideal,[48] social Catholics—disciples of the nineteenth-century engineer and economist Frédéric Le Play, who rejected the individualism of the Enlightenment—also undertook a great movement of counterrevolution, directed by Albert de Mun, against the tide of the events of 1789–93. Eighteen provincial assemblies were held throughout France. In June 1889 their motions were adopted in general assembly in Paris, where grievances against the Republic and economic liberalism were presented. In Brittany, Catholics remained divided into whites and blues, an ideological medley of colors representing revolutionary factions that "reproduc[ed] with a remarkable consistency the lines of force that appeared at the moment of the Revolution, as shown by the maps of constitutional oath-taking and of the insurrections of 1793. The memory of the great clashes of those days survived in the minds of all citizens, who, arms at the ready, remained symbolically either rebels (*chouans*) or patriots (*patauds*)." In this centennial year of 1889, when "traditional religious values encouraged indirect opposition to the official commemoration," Catholics preferred to celebrate the bicentennial of Paray-le-Monial[49] or the ninety-sixth anniversary of the martyrdom of the Children of Nantes.[50] Veneration of the Virgin Mary aroused enthusiasm, while the miracles of Lourdes attracted ever more pilgrims. Lourdes—"tomb of hatred and cradle of love"—crystallized a Catholic countermysticism. In some parts of the country conservative opinion favored a militant clericalism. Thus in the south of France, in certain districts of the Tarn that were "more fanatic than anywhere else," according to the report of one subprefect, some priests openly expressed a desire "to throw the republicans out the window." The outlook of Catholics was generally confident: one provincial journal of the faith predicted that "1889 will inevitably see the collapse of the Third Republic into the gutter, and perhaps [its descent] into bloodshed." Similarly, the *Revue de la Révolution* enjoined its readers to prepare themselves "to witness in 1889 the sudden appearance of barbarians marching behind the banner of Satan."[51]

Once again the apocalyptic vision of Joseph de Maistre made itself felt. One Catholic pamphlet characterized the Revolution as the work of a "sect of vampires" and held it responsible for "institut[ing] revolutionary Satanism." Conservatives loudly and clearly endorsed Maistre's plan for the establishment of a single indivisible Catholic state, accusing the Revolution of widening "divisions" and deepening "hatreds." Édouard Drumont, much listened to in the Catholic world, laid into the Jews with vigor: "The centenary of '89 is their centenary, the centenary of these foreigners who have chased the brave native Frenchmen from their homes, Frenchmen born on [French] soil. They have money and honors." Relentlessly, he hammered away at this theme: "The centenary of 1789 is the centenary of the Jew." During the same year anti-Semitism enjoyed a "strong revival" in the pages of *La Croix*: on Easter 1889, recalling the story of Judas Iscariot receiving money from the chief priests for betraying Jesus, it wrote: "From that day on, Judas, who received the wages of iniquity, traveled the world as did Cain, marked with the sign of the curse. And this sign was the bag of crowns." The whole revolutionary Right, from staunch Catholics to left-leaning Boulangist populists, was united in this demonological vision, consumed with hate for the revolution that Jews and money had made.

The year 1889 thus survives as a landmark in the implacable conflict between clericalism and anticlericalism—a conflict that issued from the French Revolution and that a century later still exercised a preponderant influence upon French political life. Each side sought to impose on the nation a coherent and closed vision of the world that tolerated neither cultural diversity nor differences in beliefs or values. The celebration of the national festival of 14 July, inaugurated in 1880 by the Gambettist Left to mark a radical symbolic rupture with the past,[52] quickly acquired a "strong anticlerical connotation";[53] henceforth, in each village of France, a town hall was built that could be said to be "essentially republican because it is precisely to the Republic that the universality of its presence is due."[54] Marianne, once she had assumed power, imposed her own statues symbolizing the permanence of the republican order: in the period between 1870 and 1914, the year 1889 marked a high point in the erection of monuments to the glory of the Republic on French territory. As Maurice Agulhon observed, "[T]he idea of a monument, the idea of the Revolution as the new faith, the idea of republicanizing the landscape as the Church had Christianized it and, to counterbalance this ancient influence, the idea of a fine public square—all these were very much ideas of their time." It was therefore not surprising that "France would end up one day dressed in the Phrygian cap of the established Republic"—the same Phrygian cap in which nationalist and anti-Semitic forces dressed their disfigured and grotesque version of Marianne as a Masonic prostitute, "the hatred of the Republic deriving in part from that of the French Revolution, which at once carried the baleful display of the feminine symbol to extremes."[55]

Joan of Arc had the same unfortunate experience. The republican camp attempted to claim her as a symbol, as the sans-culottes and then the anticlerical forces had done previously. Thus each year an appeal was made to the people of Rouen to demonstrate in the Place Saint-Ouen: "How could she not be dear to republicans, the great *citoyenne* who was the victim of an incestuous alliance that the separation of church and state will render forever impossible? Joan of Arc and the Republic have therefore served the same cause, the homeland that towers above everything, and [they have] fought the same adversary: clericalism." A nationalist countercult grew up around her as well—and with it a steady rising tide of xenophobia and appeals to violence from Maurice Barrès to Action Française in the 1930s and up through the National Front of the present day. Already in 1878 a pilgrimage to her birthplace in Domrémy, in the Vosges, drew a crowd of some 20,000 people. "In the face of a triumphant Republic," observes the historian Gerd Krumeich, "the perception of Joan of Arc by Catholics was radically transformed. Henceforth Joan rejoined the ranks of the *intégriste* crusade for the 'true France.' "[56] In 1894 Monsignor Gonthe-Soulard, archbishop of Aix, wrote: "Joan belongs to the Church. . . . No one can argue with us about this. . . . Keep your great men. Put them in the Panthéon: we will never argue with you about that. But Joan is ours. . . . One does not secularize saints."[57]

Great nationalist festivals were also organized at Notre-Dame in Paris, and later at the Sacré-Cœur of Montmartre. In the meantime the Congregation for the Causes of Saints proposed Joan's canonization to the pope. When the Dreyfus Affair broke at the beginning of 1894, Drumont, writing in *La Libre Parole*, described Joan as "an Aryan virgin . . . the most admirable embodiment of our race." By March 1898, when tensions between the Dreyfusards and anti-Dreyfusards had reached the boiling point, Joan the earth mother—the very image of a country betrayed by the English and their golden calf, supposedly revered by so many Jews, symbols of the anti-France—had come to embody in the eyes of the nationalists the virtues of the Aryan race. A petition from the "women of France" sent to the Chamber of Deputies led to passage of a law providing for the commemoration of Joan of Arc as the bearer of an "exclusively French ideal."[58]

Where control over symbols was not enough, it was necessary

to control people's perceptions of the world around them. The use of colors aroused profound conflicts between the assembled camps—evidence once more of a genuine "French specificity."[59] Sounds were also of great significance: as Alain Corbin has emphasized, the ringing of village bells—which remained very numerous in the late nineteenth century, and which regulated both Christian time and republican time—was the occasion of bitter and, in the minds of the local authorities, crucial struggles, for they symbolized control over the French countryside itself: hence the ferocity of the clashes. The leaders of the Republic, faithful to the ideals of the Revolution, "attempted to secularize and municipalize the peals, to subordinate [them] to the nation, and to insert [them] into a framework of citizenship. . . . Republican policies in this sphere were designed to curb the expression of everything pertaining to private life" and achieve a "desacralizing of space and time"—without, for all that, managing to extinguish "the desire for bells."[60] By the turn of the twentieth century, the bells seemed old-fashioned, but they continued to function as a prop for collective memory: "Disputes over bells had essentially become conflicts over matters of belief, with anticlericals, freethinkers, and atheists being pitted against clergy, clericals, and zealous Catholics. The most embattled mayors were motivated by an intense desire to desacralize the bells, and by the same token, the rhythms, space, and signals of their communities. They wanted to deprive the clergy of their power to deafen, feeling it to be humiliating and intolerable." Article 101 of the law of 1884 gave mayors the right to possess a key to the bell tower so that they might personally take charge of the ringing of the bells to mark civil occasions. This measure "proved truly traumatic for the clergy"[61] and led to interminable "tauntings" between the republican mayor and the village priest, "miserable rivalries" amounting to a "small war" in which, above and beyond "this business of the bells," the republican secularization of the countryside was at stake.[62] In the event, the republican program was quickly carried out: between 1880 and 1914—truly an "iconoclastic episode" in the history of France—municipal decrees required the removal from public view of crosses, calvaries, and statues in many towns; in others these objects were brutally defaced or destroyed. Throughout the land, schools, courts, hospitals, and cemeteries were secularized, new names were given to streets and squares that evoked the memory of saints, the wearing of the cassock in public was prohibited, and the bell towers of certain churches were painted in the French national colors. Yet the calendar regulating religious festivals resisted modification. In this sense, if freethinkers and anticlerical forces had managed to "impose their mark on space, [they] could not achieve the symbolic victory of time."[63]

The conflict between mutually antagonistic ideals grew more exacerbated year after year, from the Ferry laws of 1881–82 and the Goblet laws of 1886 (which concerned the relationship between church and state) to the law of 1905 ordaining the separation of church and state. In 1889, the year of the Revolution's centenary celebration, new legislation required seminarians to perform three years of military service, provided for the payment only of public school teachers, and, in an act of clear provocation, approved the opening of a crematorium in Paris. Even if certain leaders of the Center-Left joined Ferry in wishing to put an end to the conflict between the rival camps for the sake of religious peace, the Radicals urged action, intent on remaining faithful to the formula uttered by Gambetta in May 1877: "*Le cléricalisme, voilà l'ennemi.*" "As a principle of all education," he stated, "it is necessary to create citizens and not sacristans."[64] The societies of freethinkers that were formed by the hundreds in the early 1880s, which regarded religious feeling as a "cancer of the brain," enthusiastically supported the republicans in their struggle against the influence of the Church. Small wonder, then, that Ferdinand Buisson should have felt moved to exclaim:

There are now only two groups, bloc against bloc. On the one side, all the believers, from the Catholic deploring the collapse of the temporal power of the pope, the establishment of civil marriage, and the dispersal of congregations, to the deist who sees the world as lost if personal faith in God and in personal immortality ever come to be eclipsed. On the other, all the minds emancipated from faith and fear, determined to know the whole truth. . . . One must take up a position in one or the other camp.[65]

The clerical mind was the object of an unlimited and freely acknowledged hatred on the part of republicans. In ridiculing the men of the Church, no holds were barred. On Good Friday, republicans feasted at tables piled high with meats and charcuterie, eating rounds of sausage disguised as hosts and laid out on a crucifix, mocking the stories of the Bible, caricaturing priests as obese and libertine hedonists, and using images of pigs, lice, snakes, owls, and rats to denigrate their enemies—just as the counterrevolutionary nationalist Right had done at the beginning of the nineteenth century and throughout the Dreyfus Affair. The "weight of hatred" was such that even the skulls of the faithful were measured in order to infer their infantilism.[66]

Reaction was not long in coming.[67] In 1888 the public prosecutor of the court of appeals for Limoges observed that "the spirit of the clergy is absolutely the same in [the] three departments [of Limousin]. With very rare exceptions, it is at bottom entirely hostile to our institutions. The priests would ardently do battle against the Republic, from which they expect nothing, . . . if, in this region, they did not feel themselves to be entirely powerless." For *La Croix de Limoges*, "after civil burial, civil marriage and baptism complete the list of civil rights for idiots. . . . Certainly these people are correct in claiming to be the direct descendants of monkeys."[68] In the Tarn, "the determination of the clericalists . . . was matched by anticlerical tenacity" to such a degree that the conflict proved to be "unrelenting," a "dialogue of the deaf" pitting clericalists against anticlericalists, groups that "adhered to two radically opposed visions of the world"; on both sides, "swollen trenchermen" and "fat-bellied warriors" came under attack. In 1889 the *Semaine religieuse* remarked that republicanism "still remain[s] in our region, it needs to be recognized, like an

old leaven of the Albigensian heresy. God would rather that this
leaven had by now entirely disappeared." In Albi, at this same
moment, "it was said that Protestants had one eye in the middle
of their forehead, and so people came out in the street to look at
us." The wishes of the Protestant mayor of Castres, who wrote his
minister that "the future of the country is in the mixing of [Chris-
tian] denominations, in the forgetting of these hatreds, of these
religious divisions that afflict the Midi," were far from being realized.[69] These same divisions were also found in Catholic Brittany,
which was scarcely welcoming to the few Protestants who lived
there, accused of being plotters in the pay of England.[70] During
the same period, in the Tarn and elsewhere, anti-Semitism grew
as well. Plainly the idea of pluralism had still not found its place
in the French political landscape.

Meanwhile, the war in the schools over textbooks and the socialization of French children resumed more fiercely than ever,
each side seeking to eliminate the place allowed the other. For the
republicans, citizenship now had to be detached from all connection with Catholicism—a separation roundly condemned by the
proponents of a wholly Catholic France. Certain books on morality and civic instruction that had been placed on the Index in
1883 were further combated by the bishops, who made strenuous
efforts to urge the parents of pupils to reject them. So great was
the tension between the two camps that a writer in *Le XIXe siècle*
observed, "I defy you to find at the present moment a village, a
single hamlet, where civil war is not about to begin."[71] The
Church issued the threat that children would be prevented from
making their first communion, and their parents would be deprived of the sacraments and endure eternal damnation, if they
persisted in using the textbooks of the Republic—with the result
that, in the Tarn, for example, pupils deserted public schools en
masse.[72]

Here and there attempts were made to seek common ground,
but to no avail. This conflict extended well into the twentieth
century. The Catholic mobilizations of 1909–10 recalled those of
1882–83, both of which were led by parent associations—"bas-

tions of Christianity," that acted in close association with the Church, whose bishops encouraged them to recite the following invocation every day: "Deliver us, Lord, from schools without God and from teachers without Faith!"[73] The public schools were often suspected of being the disguised instruments of domination by Protestants, Jews, and Freemasons who were determined to bring about the de-Christianization of France.

"Catholic France" thus rose up against the notion of republican citizenship. By the same token, as Monsignor Mignot observed, Catholics rejected the state's right to "take possession of children's souls." As the "absolute master of programs, books, and diplomas," commanding "the words and gestures of teachers" and having no regard for divine judgment, "its judgment of doctrines is beyond appeal." France therefore had to be "regenerated" by Christian instruction. As a Catholic publicist enjoined his countryman in 1883, "Be brave! Be French! Be Christians! May Church and Country be the object of our love and our devotion. The Country! It is a cross in the sky, a flag on the ground, a moral and political faith in the heart. God! Church! France!"[74] Accounts by teachers often mentioned the violence directed against them by priests: for one, "since the new priest took over the reins of the parish, it has been war in general and in particular"; another noted having had to "struggle for four years with the local priest, a narrow-minded man, very aggressive, malicious, much feared by his parishioners."[75] The reprisals of the Church particularly affected teachers' mothers who remained practicing Catholics. Between the priest and his enemies, the mayor and the village teacher (now a prominent figure as a representative of the Republic), open warfare had often become obligatory.[76]

The primary school teachers of the Republic,[77] for their part, carried out another program for the regeneration of society, founded on a strict positivist morality consistent with republican ideology. This disciplined army of hussars in black,[78] under the close supervision of an administration intent on enforcing obedience to a code of conduct so austere that they were readily likened to soldier-monks, fought against all forms of particularist attachment that threatened to thwart the active exercise of citizenship. The attempt to uniformly diffuse the Enlightenment by means of a rigid curriculum, though in practice it tended to give way to compromise, often was insensitive to the extreme cultural diversity of the children who were being socialized in the ways of the Republic. The official language that they were expected to speak was in many cases different from their own dialects, which were still commonly used but were frequently combated in the name of French—the language of the Revolution and of national unity—and were suspected of aiding the defense of clericalism.[79] To be sure, the resistance of these patois, especially in the most peripheral regions such as Brittany and the Pyrenees, showed the limits of a policy that had been initiated almost a hundred years earlier by Abbé Grégoire. In many departments instruction was still given in the local language—Flemish, Provençal, Gascon, Breton, the dialects of Picardy and Artois, and many others; which remained the predominant means of local expression not only in outlying areas but also in the very center of the country (in Limousin, for example).[80]

In the 1880s, as a result of the deliberate policy of the Third Republic, whose mistrust of regional autonomy led it (like the Jacobins during the Revolution) to identify the use of patois with clericalism and reaction, "the balance [shifted] in favor of French."[81] The educational legislation of this period had a considerable impact on schooling and the use of French. Regional dialects—bearers of a cultural diversity that, in reality, did not in the least imply hostility toward the Republic—swiftly fell into decline. Though it is true that the process of modernization had begun prior to the Third Republic—indeed, as Maurice Agulhon has pointed out, the Republic "won the day because in whole regions (including rural areas) this acculturation had already taken place"—the gradual disappearance of *patois* and the corresponding rise of French[82]—the language of the community of citizens, considered the unique vehicle of universality and the sole possible agent of Reason—occurred mainly in the last quarter of the century. Eugen Weber has called attention to the decisive role of teachers and the distribution of new textbooks, as well as the stress laid on physical exercise and the circulation of maps of France, which together constituted "a vast program of indoctrination," a "wide-ranging process of standardization that helped create and reinforce French unity, while contributing to the disintegration of rival allegiances."[83]

The historian Claude Nicolet has emphasized the influence of positivism on both the founders of the Third Republic and the officials who were responsible for its educational policy. No matter that the scientistic perspective of positivism may have been far removed from the philosophy of the rights of man and utterly opposed to the control of teaching by the state (even a republican state), it was no less opposed to clericalism. In the name of the religion of progress, positivist doctrine supplied the basis for the policy of secularizing education carried out under the Third Republic by the Protestant politician Paul Bert[84]—this in response to Léon Gambetta's wish, stated in August 1881, that a secular spirit be adopted in constructing "a unified France, everywhere the same, a France that will truly be able, in its peace and in its strength, to gather and reunite all its children."[85] The unification of the country hoped for by Gambetta would inevitably be accompanied, of course, by the unification of minds dreaded by Tocqueville, who denounced the measures of an *État-instituteur* that acted on brains in the same way as "the peoples of the east coast of Africa, [who] have the custom of putting the head of newborn children in a sort of mold that gives all of them the same shape. The top of the head of all the men is therefore either very high or very flattened, depending on the rule adopted at the time of their birth."[86] It ran the risk, too, that public education would turn into the nightmare feared by Benjamin Constant, that other great liberal, who exclaimed:

[W]hat do we not hear of the need to allow the government to take possession of new generations to shape them to its pleasure, and how many erudite quotations are employed to support this theory! The Persians, the Egyptians, Gaul,

Greece and Italy are one after another set out before us. Yet, Gentlemen, we are neither Persians subjected to a despot, nor Egyptians subjugated by priests, nor Gauls who can be sacrificed by their druids, nor finally, Greeks or Romans, whose share in social authority consoled them for their private enslavement. We are modern men, who wish each to enjoy our own rights, each to develop our own faculties as we like best, without harming anyone; to watch over the development of these faculties in the children whom nature entrusts to our affection.[87]

To be sure, Constant's nightmare had not yet quite been reached with the "Republic of the teachers"; neither as a matter of ideological principle nor in actual practice did the Third Republic's plans for standardizing education justify the fears of Constant and Tocqueville. Thus Maurice Agulhon forcefully argues that although "the Third Republic was very pedagogic, very propagandistic, [it was] liberal. Unlike totalitarian dictatorships, it allowed all opposing pedagogies. . . . The danger is that, in taking seriously the metaphor of the 'secular missionary,' today one imagines Jules Ferry's primary school teacher as a sort of political commissar appointed in each village."[88] In the same vein, Mona Ozouf rejects the view of educational policy under the Third Republic held by hard-line republicans, arguing that teachers served chiefly as conduits between two cultures, not least in their eagerness to win recognition for their native regions—the "little homelands" that managed to find a place within the republican framework. Their commitment to encourage diversity was all the stronger as teachers frequently promoted a de facto "bilingualism" through the use of regional patois, which served as a measure of provincial resistance to the Republic's official policy of standardization. In this view, the eradication of regional dialects hoped for by the French Revolution—and also, as a matter of policy, by the Third Republic—failed because ultimately the republicans were wary of authoritarian tendencies.[89] The Republic did indeed show a concern for tolerance: its policy was not one of simple assimilation. Its openness to compromise is all the more impressive since, as Maurice Agulhon has again shown, the Republic found itself faced with growing resistance organized by the Church as well as a hostile workers' movement; "provincial blocs" of Catholic voters waited in the wings, while many other citizens remained allergic to politics, or at least republican politics. Under these circumstances, no genuine unification of society was possible. But even allowing for this de facto pluralism and the fact that "the rites of the state were nowhere imposed,"[90] the Third Republic was not in fact a liberal regime. Nor did its adversaries hide their determination to overturn it at the earliest possible moment.

The ongoing clash between antagonistic unitary visions inherited from the Revolution forced the timid allies of pluralism to retreat further, with the result that all liberal inclinations were swept away. The violence of this conflict was now redoubled with the Dreyfus Affair, which opposed the two Frances in a gigantic confrontation that gave rise to the "Franco-French wars." On the other hand, the nationalist Right mobilized Catholic hostility to the Republic, shamelessly exploiting the ideal opportunity offered by a Jewish officer's betrayal, which by itself testified to the illegitimacy of the republican order; the republicans, for their part, faithful to the principles of 1789, unhesitatingly defended justice and the law.

Catholic Dreyfusards were so few that the republicans long delayed rallying openly to the unfortunate captain's side. To the extent that the affair challenged the legitimacy of the army, whose high command was accused of abusing its authority, the republicans rallied instead to the defense of an institution perceived as sacred to the nation, hoping in this way to forestall accusations from the nationalist and clerical Right of recklessly endangering France's security. The great majority of republicans holding office remained indifferent, if not actually hostile, to the few militant Dreyfusards who continued to fight on in immense solitude. The captain's family was alone in daring to call into question the court's judgment, never doubting for a moment his innocence;

with the isolated support of only a handful of Jews, such as Joseph Reinach (and a bit later Bernard Lazare, Victor Basch, and Grand Rabbi Zadoc-Kahn), it held out against what seemed to be a foregone conclusion until a few years later a cohort of intellectuals and scholars—notably chemists, mathematicians, and historians anxious to enforce respect for the rules of scientific method in an atmosphere of irrationalism—came at last to the captain's rescue. It was not until the Republic found itself endangered by the mobilization of nationalist and populist leagues at the very end of the nineteenth century that its leaders finally pulled themselves together, took up the fight, heard the universalist message of the intellectuals, and—almost against their will—approved review proceedings in the trial of Captain Dreyfus. Still, they dragged their feet—so much so that as late as 1899 Dreyfus was still considered guilty, and he owed his freedom only to a humiliating appeal for clemency from the president of the Republic, when in fact he was quite innocent. Only in 1906 was he actually declared innocent—though the highest authorities of the state had no doubt much earlier been aware of the scope of the plot orchestrated by the army high command, of the illegality of the sentences handed down by military judges serving the republican regime (obtained as a result of forgeries that had remained secret), and of the threats made against Captain Picquart[91] and others within the system who dared to rise up in protest against the injustice done to Dreyfus. Apart from a few dignitaries such as Auguste Scheurer-Kestner, vice president of the Senate and an Alsatian Protestant, the apparatus of the republican state as a whole scarcely budged. A desire to defend the honor of the army, combined with an anti-Semitism that to varying degrees was widely shared, prevented the clear reconstitution of antagonistic camps for a number of years and displaced a pattern of animosity that had endured for more than a century.

At the same time a vast mobilization by nationalist forces had succeeded in bringing together staunch Catholics opposed to the existing order and militant populist groups that were descended from the old Boulangism and linked with various socialist currents by their mutual rejection of the "Jewish Republic." Leagues were organized throughout the country in obedience to the cry, repeated over and over, "France for the French!" Crowds marched in a great many cities shouting slogans hostile to the Republic and to Jews, Protestants, and Freemasons. The Catholic world (in spite of the silence of the Church) entered almost as a bloc into the battle against the Republic, seeing its chance to take revenge on the deeply despised policy of secularization.

In the face of all these things, the republicans could no longer dither:[92] the hour of the defense of the Republic had sounded. But it was scarcely in the name of the virtues appropriate to a liberal society, or in defense of individual rights and the law, or even to protect a minority in a pluralist society, that the Republic finally rallied. In many respects, the Dreyfus Affair testified single-handedly to the impossibility of liberalism ever taking root in France.

Abandoning their prejudices while there was still time, the leaders of the Republic rediscovered the demanding simplicity of the Enlightenment and reformed their ranks. A few judges at last courageously defended the honor of the bench, just as a handful of officers sought to give the army a fresh image of honesty and loyalty. After much hesitation, the Republic took its stand by confronting the mixed coalition of populist elements that had assembled under the banner of fundamentalist Catholicism. Profiting from the rout of the anti-Dreyfusard camp when the truth finally came out, Pierre Waldeck-Rousseau, soon succeeded as premier by Émile Combes, radicalized the earlier secularization measures and in 1905 imposed the very separation of church and state that Catholic France had dreaded—once again promoting, if sometimes heavy-handedly, the cause of standardization. In the face of so much intransigence on both sides, the affair helped bury for several generations a liberalism that was already in a very bad way.[93] One has only to consider the example of the literary critic Ferdinand Brunetière. A member of the Académie Française, fascinated by the United States and apparently a natural candidate to assume the task of adapting the Anglo-American liberal tradition to conditions in France, Brunetière was nonetheless also a member of the Ligue de la Patrie Française [League of the French Fatherland], a group of militant anti-Dreyfusards noted for its nationalist excesses—and this despite his friendships in Dreyfusard circles and his opposition to anti-Semitism.[94]

Now that memories of revolutionary confrontations had been revived on all sides, things were once again clear. Indeed, Action Française was born in precisely this context in 1899. Determined to bring about a restoration of the monarchy, it drew inspiration from the counterutopia of Joseph de Maistre and long thereafter played a dominant role in the nationalist mobilization against the Republic. During the next four decades it directed the campaign against forces of the Left by carefully cultivating memories of the Dreyfus Affair, until an opportunity for vengeance at last presented itself with the "divine surprise" of Vichy. Consumed by a fierce hatred for the Republic and its servants, and ready to resort to armed violence in order to overcome it, Action Française exercised an almost irresistible attraction over French Catholics, who found themselves pushed into a sort of internal exile within their own country. With the entry of the revolutionary Right into the political arena, the extremism of the leagues of the 1890s now intensified as well. The Dreyfus Affair, and particularly the captain's trial at Rennes in September 1899, turned Charles Maurras into a national figure and gave crucial impetus to counterrevolutionary ideas, which helped bring about the splintering and ultimately the collapse of the Third Republic.[95] Conscious of the decisive role of the affair, Maurras later wrote, "All our plans for French order, all our plans for French unity, date back to our thinking before this Chaos."[96]

For Maurras, the Dreyfus Affair was the "turning point of his life," the event that "really brought him before the public eye." It strengthened him in his "hatred" not only of the Jews and the Bible but also of Protestantism, which had "broke[n] up the splendid unity of Catholicism."[97] The message of Maurras's predecessors now assumed an unprecedented urgency. Along with Albert de Mun, who repeated over and over again that "Christian cement"[98] alone held together the French nation, Maurice Barrès, the nationalist republican who insisted that "French nationality is closely linked to Catholicism,"[99] worked to unify the various currents of counterrevolution and Catholicism. Gradually a terrible challenge to the republican order took shape—a countersociety united, in spite of its internal tensions and differences of opinion, against the republican state.

The challenge from the Right was all the more serious since, as we have already noted, Maurras explicitly extended Maistre's counterutopia. Rejecting the Enlightenment in his turn, Maurras loudly and unmistakably proclaimed: "I am not a man of the eighteenth century."[100] In the same spirit, in a famous article that appeared in the 15 October 1899 issue of the movement's newspaper, *L'Action française*, he charged Protestant individualism and its "three Swiss ideas"—liberty, equality, fraternity—with imposing foreign values on the classical order of Catholic France.[101] Devoutly hoping, again very much like Maistre, that they would unleash a violent cataclysm, he had earlier written (in December 1897) to his friend Barrès: "All of Dreyfus's supporters deserve to be shot as rebels. What you have here is an essentially national affair. . . . The idea of seeing Monod [a Protestant scientist] defend a Jewish traitor fills me with enthusiasm. A nation that includes such great diversity will only be unified and reformed through bloodshed. The sword shall have to be drawn."[102] Diversity and pluralism could not have been more clearly rejected. As against the "liberal spirit"—which Maurras saw as generating "atomistic division"—"Catholicism and French order . . . attract each other." The Republic, on the other hand, drew "its real existence and its core support from its Protestant, Masonic, and Jewish [elements], which naturally [are] opposed, historically, morally, and socially, to Catholicism." Again: "Yes, the Republic is evil, yes, evil is inevitable in [the] Republic. . . . To proclaim the Republic is precisely to establish evil permanently."[103]

Accordingly, Maurras harshly attacked Catholics who, in rallying to the cause of republican individualism, had "long caress[ed] the spirit of Revolution," saying that their ideas were of

"Huguenot manufacture" and came from "Geneva or Jerusalem."
As against the "moderate republicans who are moderately French
. . . we, maniacal Frenchmen" must impose Catholic unity upon
"the enemy within"—for "the positive is Catholic and the negative is not."[104] Catholicism was unquestionably the "national
religion" of France[105]—though Maurras himself had lost his
Christian faith and become an agnostic. This did not in the least
alter his conviction that "integral nationalism" implied an osmosis between Catholicism and royalism. In 1906, when the Church
was forced to draw up inventories of its assets, many of which
were subsequently sold off by the state, Action Française was
"initiated into the art of civil rioting" and Maurras became—in
the tradition of Maistre and Veuillot—the uncontested champion
of the Church and of Pope Pius X, the sworn enemy of the expro-
priating Republic, and the resolute adversary of liberalism in all
its forms.[106] It was perhaps inevitable that Maurras's positivism,
his lack of faith, and his quasi-paganism would eventually lead to
his condemnation by Rome and the listing of several of his works
on the Index, along finally with *L'Action française*; even so, he
continued to exercise considerable influence for a good many
years afterward on the political world of French Catholics, most
of whom were openly hostile to the Republic.

The republicans, on the other hand, managed to impose their
convictions with ease from the very beginning. The Constitution
of 1875 made no reference to civil liberties, with the consequence
that the state enjoyed unlimited political, administrative, and judicial powers.[107] The masters of the republican regime were often
newcomers, since systematic purges at all levels of the administrative and judicial apparatus had brought about a "revolution
of jobs" (in the phrase of the historian Daniel Halévy) that
amounted to a veritable spoils system. Conceived by Jules Grévy,
president of the Third Republic from 1879 to 1887, who at the
outset of his first term had emphasized his determination to see
to it "that the Republic be served by officials who are neither its
enemies nor its detractors," this system was extended by his suc-

cessors, notably William Henry Waddington and Charles Frey-
cinet.

With the formation of the *Bloc républicain* at the end of the
century, Pierre Waldeck-Rousseau's cabinet openly confronted its
adversaries: more than during Ferry's time, the Republic now
showed itself to be genuinely "absolute," opposed to all pluralism, fiercely attached to its vision of a unitary society, intent on
drawing logical and practical conclusions from its guiding—
though seldom explicitly formulated—principle: "The Republic
for republicans!" This is what Émile Littré, the great lexicogra-
pher and supporter of the Third Republic, had in mind when he
wrote, "When one speaks of a purge, one uses a word that is not
exact. It is not only reactionary officials that we are after, but also
their jobs: it is a question not merely of making administrative
departments more republican, but also of bringing more republicans into the administration." In a speech at Toulouse on 28 October 1900, Waldeck-Rousseau declared, "The fundamental rule
of a republican policy must be to grant its confidence only to
those from whom it may expect loyal and resolute support." The
famous memorandum of 20 June 1902 addressed by his successor
as prime minister, Émile Combes, to the prefects of the Republic
set the tone even more clearly: "Your duty commands you to reserve the favors you have at your disposal only for those of your
constituents who have given unequivocal evidence of loyalty to
republican institutions. I have reached agreement with my colleagues in the cabinet that no nomination, no promotion of an official belonging to your department shall occur without prior
consultation with you."[108]

Republican loyalism undermined the state's autonomy. The
grading of civil servants, whose advancement was now largely a
matter of political connections, was part of a system of patronage
that curbed individual freedom of opinion and weakened still further the fragile seeds of political pluralism—all the more since
Combes persisted in his anticlerical campaign. A few months
later, on 26 November 1902, in a new memorandum classified,

like the earlier one, as confidential, he addressed the prefects once more:

> I pointed out to you the extreme importance of assuring that jobs and favors are reserved exclusively for those who have given unequivocal evidence of their loyalty to our institutions. I believe I must today confirm these instructions to you. On several occasions I have noted with regret that my recommendations have not always been followed. It has been brought to my attention that, in various local administrations, rewards and promotions have been conferred on officials and agents who openly displayed their preferences for candidates belonging to hostile parties. . . . Such decisions are likely to adversely affect the republican party. It is important to prevent them from being repeated: the government is more resolved than ever to require the unreserved support of civil servants at all levels and of people who solicit favors.[109]

This politicization of public administration, carried out by the republican government and the highest state authorities, was incompatible with a liberal concern for protecting the rights and the freedom of thought of individuals in contexts other than the exercise of their administrative duties. Indeed, as the historian Jean-Pierre Machelon has argued, it amounted to "rejecting the liberal solution."[110] Parliamentary recommendations now flowed to ministries by the tens of thousands every year; one contemporary observer estimated the number of letters received from politicians to be between 50,000 and 100,000. The interior and agriculture ministries were particularly affected by the growth of political clientelism,[111] which established itself all the more readily since the republicans could justify it by pointing to particularly urgent political circumstances. Although it is true that the senior civil service became increasingly professionalized during this period, it grew more politicized as well, and the effectiveness of meritocratic mechanisms, which otherwise might have been expected to counteract a system of widespread favoritism, was diminished.[112]

This system almost justified Charles Maurras, mortal enemy of the Republic, in saying that "Republican heredity is not an empty phrase—nor is republican nobility," and in mocking "the heroic virtue, the stoic virtue, the republican virtue [that] exists only in the dreams of doctrinaire ideologues."[113] The recruitment of government officials was closely monitored, with the result that virtually all of the declared enemies of the Republic were excluded in addition to those whose opinions were regarded as suspect. Foremost among the latter were the Catholics. With the hardening of clerical antirepublicanism, every Catholic came to represent a potential enemy needing to be expelled from the ranks of the state bureaucracy. Anticlericalism was, to be sure, a response to Catholic defiance of the Republic;[114] but when systematically employed as a means of achieving political uniformity in the recruitment of agents of the state, it often encroached on personal values and beliefs. Gambetta, though he had been the first to speak out against clericalism, nonetheless declared: "We are not the enemies of religion, of any religion. On the contrary, we are the servants of freedom of conscience, respectful of all religious and philosophical opinions."[115] But at a time when intensive efforts were being made to mobilize nationalist sentiment among French Catholics, Gambetta's heirs were deaf to his message. The *affaire des fiches* was proof of this: on the orders of General Louis André, Waldeck-Rousseau's minister of war, a large-scale hunt for information on the private lives and beliefs of military officers was undertaken in order to learn whether they went to mass, whether they sent their children to Catholic schools, and so on. Requests for information concerning some 20,000 officers were submitted to the Grand Lodge of France (the Freemasons having become the de facto auxiliary of the republican army in the supervision of military careers). This scandal, which came to light in March 1904 and indirectly led three months later to Combes's resignation,[116] betrayed an extreme mistrust of Catholic officers and a readiness to infer professional disloyalty from personal beliefs. Surveillance of officers was subsequently carried out by the prefects.

Nonetheless, as the historian Maurice Larkin has shown with great originality, even during periods of the most virulent anticlericalism Catholics had little difficulty entering the technical ministries and pursuing careers there. Larkin also makes it clear, contrary to the conventional wisdom, that even in the army under the "Republic of the republicans," between 1881 and 1901, more than 2,000 students at the leading military academies— 1,515 at Saint-Cyr and 572 at the École Polytechnique—came from the Jesuit École Sainte-Geneviève, directed by Albert de Mun. Again, between 1902 and 1913, 568 students from the École Sainte-Geneviève were admitted to Saint-Cyr and 188 to the École Polytechnique. Of these, 219 achieved the rank of brigadier general or higher—indeed, five became marshals of the army. Similarly, the Collège Stanislas, run by the Marians, succeeded in placing each year during the 1890s an average of 36 students at Saint-Cyr and 23 at the École Polytechnique, putting it right after Sainte-Geneviève. The *grandes écoles* preparing students for administrative careers, including the École Normale Supérieure, remained entirely open to Catholics, even devout ones. The École Libre des Sciences Politiques, a private institution preparing students for bureaucratic careers, also remained largely under Catholic influence: 15 percent of its students still came from Stanislas in 1895.

Certain administrative branches of the state traditionally associated with the implementation of government policy were monitored especially closely, and Catholics found themselves for the most part excluded from these. This was especially the case with the prefectural administration.[117] At the turn of the century, though a very few Catholics did manage to become subprefects, none attained the crucial office of prefect. The situation was the same, albeit to a lesser degree, with the Council of State. Surprisingly, however, some graduates of the Collège Stanislas, the École Sainte-Geneviève, and the École de l'Immaculée-Conception (likewise run by the Jesuits) succeeded in becoming judges, even prosecutors, and inspectors of public finance.

This disparity between intransigent ideology and flexible practice explains the failure of the law proposed in November 1899 by Waldeck-Rousseau, which would have required that senior civil servants be recruited from among graduates of the public school system or at least among candidates who had received the last three years of their education in the *grandes écoles*. The plan was intended by its sponsors to guarantee a "compatibility of feelings" between the state and its agents. But in the judgment of Édouard Aymard, leader of the Catholic opposition in the Chamber of Deputies, it violated article 6 of the Declaration of the Rights of Man and of the Citizen, proclaiming equality in employment; in his view, the civil servant must "neither hate nor betray." Aymard pointedly observed that the holders of the most sensitive positions in the prefectural administration, the legal system, and the Council of State were not graduates of the *grandes écoles*—hence the rejection of this plan.[118] Even in such periods of confrontation, the government's vigorous attempts to enforce political obedience remained in many instances closer to the pragmatic policy formulated by Gambetta and Ferry, imposing a public loyalty independent of one's own personal views. Contrary to what many believed at the time, and in spite of a certain rather aggressive spirit of voluntarism, republican practice validated Jules Ferry's last will and testament, as it were. In February 1893, two months before his death, Ferry proudly declared: "Our Republic is open to all; it is not the property of any sect, of any group, not even the group of men who founded it. It welcomes all men of good faith and goodwill; but in order to make room for them, republicans have no need, it seems to me, to declare war on each other."[119]

Nonetheless, the stated policy of the Republic, although it reflected ideology more than reality, rapidly found support within the civil service itself, winning the endorsement of the unions that represented the civil servants in their determined struggle against "the reactionaries and clericalists who still occupy their administrative posts." *La Tribune républicaine des fonctionnaires*, the organ of the Fédération Nationale des Fonctionnaires et Employés d'Administrations Publiques [National Federation of Civil Servants and Public Administration Employees], sought to rally its readers around the slogan *"Les fonctions de la République aux républicains"* ("the offices of the Republic for republicans").[120] Created at the time of the Dreyfus Affair, this union was closely allied with the Ligue des Droits de l'Homme et du Citoyen [League of the Rights of Man and of the Citizen], which defended the right of civil servants (including teachers—the very embodiment of virtuous citizenship) to organize in view of their indispensable role in the battles of the Republic. The league therefore endorsed the removal from the civil service of all those who were indifferent or hostile to the republican order. One of its sections urged that civil servants be recruited only from old republican families; another argued that only graduates of public schools should be allowed to become civil servants; yet another demanded that civil servants be required to send their children to public schools—the essential test for certifying their genuine political loyalty. As the historian H. S. Jones has shown in a remarkable study, controversy rapidly arose within the league and led to many resignations. Some supported the civil servants' right to unionize, as well as the strikes they called, while feeling at the same time (as the syndicalist theoretician Maxime Leroy put it) that "civil servants must be neither republicans, nor atheists, nor monarchists, nor plebiscitarians; they must be civil servants only, as attentive to carrying out their duties where adversaries of the Republic are concerned as where its friends are concerned. . . . If civil servants were to show themselves partial toward adversaries of the Republic, the League of the Rights of Man ought to protest."[121]

On the question of unionization, then, there was a split inside the republican state itself, with many teachers turning toward socialist organizations that sought to deepen the class struggle inside the bureaucracy. Already threatened from without by parties of the nationalist and hard-line Right, the republican state now saw the emergence of a new danger from within—a danger that symbolically was all the less acceptable as it emanated from a group it claimed exclusive authority to represent. Maxime Leroy, for one, supported unionization among civil servants despite his feeling that "behind the impressive fiction of public law, the state, there are a few men, the men who govern, the men who represent a party, an interest, a class."[122] Like the capitalist system itself, "the state formed in the image of the economic regime is not a sort of guardian, a defender of liberties. There is an administrative proletariat that takes orders from the state, its boss, the defender of economic inequality, especially when it covers itself in the formidable purple of emperors."[123] The sociologist Émile Durkheim—another founding member of the league, who came to be identified with the ideals of the Third Republic and whose thinking guided the training of teachers in the *écoles normales*—opposed the unionization of civil servants, which he felt would introduce the idea of class among citizens who were supposed to be concerned solely with the exercise of their administrative duties.[124]

The sudden emergence of the social question divided the old Dreyfusard allies while destroying the unity of the republican camp and arousing a sharp reaction on the part of those in positions of power who were fiercely opposed to pluralism within the state bureaucracy. Paradoxically, the question of unionizing the civil service turned out to be at least as contentious as the continuing religious quarrel. Now that Combes's anticlericalism had triumphed, teachers in many departments of the country no longer went to mass; but here and there Catholic men and women continued to teach,[125] and a few instructors could still play cards with the local priest (outside working hours, of course) without being dismissed from their jobs.[126] In this sense, the social question generated a more acute degree of tension in the state administration than did the issue of secularism, which was firmly dealt with at the level of principle but often with a certain flexibility in practice. Despite a profound commitment to unionization and the socialist struggle, no "secularist tendency" was observable among teachers themselves; instead, as the historians Jacques and Mona Ozouf have emphasized, one finds something nearer to "the antipodes of 'primary' sectarianism." If the state's anticlericalism was the product of a firm conviction, teachers complained of the reprisals to which they were subject in the many "little Vendées" that remained throughout the land, while trying to "repair and conceal the ruptures"—speaking with the priest beyond the party wall, "burying the hatchet around an old bottle of Armagnac." Hence this sensible advice from a priest in the Tarn-et-Garonne to the town's new teacher:

> Castelmayran has two fiercely hostile clans, the republicans and the supporters of the Church; they keep their distance and swear an eternal hatred for each other. The members of the one frequent the Café Bayrou, the members of the other the Café Bouché: the left-wing youth gather in a ballroom that is reserved exclusively for them; the right-wing youth have their own as well. Similarly, each clan has its own grocer, its own butcher. . . . Everyone here is classified, labeled; one associates only with those on one's side, shunning the others. You and I, teacher and priest, are considered to be implacable enemies. You certainly have all my sympathy, but it is in both our interests that we no longer meet. If you were to be caught entering the presbytery, I would lose all my prestige among my congregation; appeals would be made to the bishop to have me transferred. On your side, the republicans would hate you and create difficulties for you until the day when, willingly or unwillingly, you would have to leave as well.[127]

Tolerance, accommodation, and concealment were out of place under such circumstances, for they signaled a determination to oppose the republican state. The sanctions administered, for example, against teachers who dared to advertise their union membership or political affiliation were quite severe. As a police commissioner in the Isère put it: "[T]eachers, one hears it said on all sides, gradually become as troublesome, tiresome, and intolerant as the Catholic priests, against whom energetic and definitive measures have had to be taken. They constitute a secular clergy that likewise will have to be made to see reason if unanimous protests against it among the populace are to be prevented."[128] The state closely monitored the conduct of its servants, as we have seen: teachers were subjected to meticulous police inquiries that violated their privacy; political and union activists who challenged official policy found themselves the subject of police reports and evaluations filed by school inspectors, while letters of denunciation from local notables piled up on ministers' desks. Behavior that introduced a measure of pluralism into the republican public sphere was punished by reprimands, sanctions of various kinds, and even dismissals.

But times soon changed, and the teachers of the Republic began to distance themselves from the positivist dreams of Littré, Bert, and Durkheim. When the government ordered its prefects to surveil union organizations and, if necessary, dissolve them, teachers boldly proclaimed their right to act as individuals enjoying full rights of citizenship, as distinct from the narrower concept of partisan citizenship deriving from the French Revolution that was still influential. For one such teacher, "civil servants are men and citizens before being civil servants. They therefore have a very clear sense of their rights as men and as citizens every time that they are injured in these rights, which must in all cases be respected." The author of a pamphlet published by the Fédération Nationale des Syndicats d'Instituteurs et d'Institutrices de France [National Federation of Teachers Unions of France] remarked with a certain grim humor: "As for our freedom, it is like the freedom to walk, to hear, to see; we will not do our republican Torquemadas the honor of debating how far our freedom to think may extend. This freedom will be defended to the last."[129]

Protest against the republican model of a unified community of citizens slowly but steadily grew. As a result, the dream of an absolute republic—based solely on Enlightenment ideals and established by means of state power—that would easily triumph over its adversaries faded a bit more every day. Nationalist opposition spread from the turn of the century through the interwar period, culminating in the crisis of 6 February 1934. Yet the rules of engagement were now somewhat different: Catholics gradually rallied to the Republic, and republicans, despite a brief secularist revival in 1924 with the coalition of the Left, increasingly abandoned their anticlericalism. The situation became further confused when, two years later, the pope condemned Action Française and, during the course of a "second *ralliement*," some Catholics came to "accept the fact of the secularization of the state, whether for reasons of principle or of opportunity."[130] The "attachment of Catholics to reactionary values" nonetheless explains "the resistance of Catholic opinion" to the condemnation of Maurras, notably by the leadership of General de Castelnau's Fédération Nationale Catholique [National Catholic Federation].[131]

In 1939, during the celebration of the one hundred fiftieth anniversary of the Revolution, Catholic opinion still aligned itself more with the counterrevolutionary editorials of *La Croix* than with *Esprit*, which claimed to carry on the tradition of 1789.[132] As at the end of the nineteenth century, the reactionary and nationalist movements with which a part of the Catholic population had always identified itself continued to mount a vigorous offensive against the Republic. Even as he proclaimed his allegiance to the Republic, the leader of the Croix-de-Feu and subsequently the Parti Social Français [French Social Party (PSF)],[133] François de La Rocque, a graduate of Sainte-Geneviève, acknowledged his debt to the conservative Catholic thinker René de La Tour du Pin: "Our Western civilization is a Christian civilization. . . . Our criterion of Christian civilization is accepted by all the members of the PSF. . . . We are a force deriving from the very nature of our country, 'eldest daughter of the Church.' "[134] An austere officer from an aristocratic Catholic background, La Rocque differed in every respect from the leaders of the extreme Right in Hitler's Germany.[135] His "Christian nationalism,"[136] no less than that of the leaders of the Solidarité Française, was anchored in an authoritarian Catholicism that linked him directly to the anti-Dreyfusard leagues of the turn of the century and often lapsed into the anti-Semitism and anti-Masonic sentiment characteristic of the earlier period.

It hardly matters whether these French organizations of the 1930s may properly be characterized as fascist: unlike comparable movements in Germany and Italy, they belonged to a Catholic counterrevolution that had been peculiar to France since 1789. They were fascist after the fashion of Maistre, as Isaiah Berlin suggested; and they were ready to deploy the same counterrevolutionary violence Maistre had advocated. Far from having its origin in left-wing ideas, the counterrevolution that grew up in France, as opposed to the ones that developed elsewhere, expressed primarily the fears of Catholics who were unalterably attached to a different idea of the nation, to a different history, whose uniqueness they wished to preserve. In many respects, La Rocque and organizers of nationalist movements such as François Coty and Jean Renaud carried on the tradition of Barrès, Déroulède, and Maurras, who once again rallied his troops, as he had at the turn of the century, for an attack on the Republic that would establish at last an organic monarchical society.

Once again the workers' movement, with its unions and political parties, also rose up against the republican order, occasionally supporting populist mobilizations of nationalist feeling. It took up the struggle both within the state and without, with the result that during the Popular Front it "exercised" power without managing to "conquer" it—in the ambiguous formulation of Léon Blum, who turned out to be not at all bent on destroying the state as an institution.[137] The Enlightenment dream of an emancipating state, which with the French Revolution had assumed the form of regenerative utopia, remained intact. Through the establishment of a welfare state that associated unions with the distribution of national wealth, it accommodated new social demands. The workers' movement adapted in its turn to the logic of the strong state; indeed, the popular mobilizations of the 1930s amounted to a petition of state. Weakened and disunited, the workers' movement frequently adopted (albeit reluctantly and in spite of its ideology) a "strategy of patience,"[138] accepting a gradualist perspective incompatible with the immoderate use of revolutionary violence. Little by little it turned away from a view of society that emphasized unanimity and uniformity; and although the will to change the foundations of society persisted, increasingly it was expressed within the context of universal suffrage, which did not, however, imply acceptance of pluralist ideals, let alone endorsement of a liberal conception of the state.[139] With brief exceptions the workers' movement abandoned the populist path opened up by *putschiste* Boulangism—a path that, until the interwar period, lent itself to a variety of alliances. The Matignon agreements of 1936, which put an end to the great strikes of that year, lastingly installed the workers' movement at the heart of republican institutions. Despite harsh and sometimes quasi-insurrectional strikes in the period following the Second World War, and despite the continuing appeal of radicalism, working-class activism developed either within a novel context of multilateral bargaining or in response to it, managing sometimes to take advantage of a neocorporatist framework that gave it access to the state. By contrast—and this is a point to which we shall return—the profound challenge to unions as representative institutions, as well as the genuine upheaval experienced by the "workers' parties," has suddenly given life in our own time to a Boulangist-style populism that once more lends its support to nationalist forces, now directed by Jean-Marie Le Pen and his followers.

In reaction against these developments, an all-out nationalist mobilization aimed at bringing down once and for all the "Jewish Republic" embodied by Léon Blum and the Popular Front[140] threw itself with renewed vigor into violent protest and political maneuvering. The Church was openly hostile to the Popular Front and called upon Catholics to vote against its candidates.[141] The leagues had profited from the experience of the Dreyfus Affair, nibbling away at the state's authority, adapting their slogans to new circumstances, and equipping themselves with new allies, triumphing at last a few years later, unexpectedly, under the singular circumstances of military defeat and Nazi occupation. By the middle of the twentieth century or so, the amnesia praised by Renan had been all but forgotten—French society preferred to recall the antagonisms of the past century rather than finally come to terms with the "great transformation" that had occurred in most Western societies. The turn toward liberalism and pluralism was, in any case, to be indefinitely postponed in France.

Chapter Five

The Retreat from the
Republican State

Then came the storm. Domestic politics, violent but predictable, suddenly became more complicated with the German occupation. For the first time in centuries, France lost its sovereignty. Its legitimate authorities suddenly were transformed into servants of the traditional enemy, Germany, now under Nazi rule. Only a quarter-century earlier, republicans and counterrevolutionaries had joined forces against Germany, forgetting their own mutual antagonism. But memories are short. This time there were many who were willing to accommodate themselves to the Hitlerite presence, thinly disguised by Pétainist legalities; indeed, the purported heirs of the French Revolution and the apostles of reaction virtually fell into each other's arms. It is perhaps not surprising that many veterans of Action Française and the Croix-de-Feu should have immediately felt at ease in the shadow of an authoritarian regime; but there were some who refused to bow down before the enemy, joined by a few republicans who actually had the audacity in the presence of the occupier to openly refuse to rally to a vassalized state. Vague thoughts of carrying on the fight for the survival of the nation quickly gave way, however, to a general willingness to accept the defeat of June 1940. The political and administrative elites of the Third Republic continued to work almost in concert with reactionary leaders and their allies under the watchful eye of the Nazis, who were dumbfounded by so much readiness to oblige. In the face of such widespread and extraordinary loyalty to Marshal Pétain, the famous Franco-French wars of the past suddenly lost all relevance.

The unexpected surrender of the republicans raised hopes within the ranks of social Catholicism, not only among the leaders of the conservative and antirepublican National Catholic Federation but also, and above all, within the Church itself. Rome supported the new order in the expectation it would repeal certain elements of republican legislation, particularly the law mandating the separation of church and state, which the Vatican had never accepted. Leaving to one side Catholic collaborators and Catholic *résistants*, "there remains the bulk of the troop, a third category behind crosses and mitres; until 1943, and sometimes later, it accepted Vichy," as the historian Étienne Pouilloux has pointed out. "A rallying of the Church behind Vichy? This understates the matter; osmosis would be a more accurate way of describing their relationship"—especially considering the "return of well-known Catholics to the corridors of power, after the long republican absence."[1] In July 1940 republican school texts were widely banned, and training colleges for primary school teachers were closed; on 6 December 1940 Jacques Chevalier, the new education minister and a fervent Catholic, reintroduced religious instruction in the public school curriculum, prompting *La Croix* to exclaim: "Godless schools have had their day."[2] The clerical hierarchy made no secret of its enthusiastic support for the government of Marshal Pétain: many bishops rejoiced at his elevation to the nation's highest office, from Cardinals Gerlier and Liénart to Monsignors Feltin, Mesguen, and Costes. In Puy-en-Velay (Haute-Loire), the priests proposed to Monsignor Martin a new version of the *Marseillaise*:

Glorious leader of the Fatherland,
Noble-hearted father, we love you:

Your children's soul is wounded.
But give the order, and we shall follow you.[3]

Seizing upon such a favorable moment, the Church sought to benefit from substantial state support in order to develop its school system and to build new churches; to impose a revision of school texts for the purpose of combating anticlericalism; to bring about as rapidly as possible the formal prohibition of Masonic societies, which it had opposed since the time of the Revolution; to recover the property confiscated by the terms of the 1905 law instituting the separation of church and state; to obtain recognition for orders that had been banned during those troubled times and permission for their members to return to the monasteries; and to reinstall the crucifixes removed from public schools and buildings at the beginning of the century. Despite the reticence of the Vichy authorities in the face of certain of these demands, the crucifix was displayed once more in five hundred schools in the diocese of Verdun alone in November 1942. André Lavagne, recording officer of the Council of State, was expressing a widely held view when at the beginning of 1943 he declared: "I would say that, through the fault of anticlericalism, the Church 'went underground'; it is time that it came back into [public] life."[4]

Pétain himself was hardly a practicing Catholic, even if he now went regularly to mass, where he was greeted by children chanting "Marshal! Here we are!" (Scenes such as this prompted his famous remark "A good mass never did anyone any harm.") While the Church disliked certain aspects of the Vichy regime (such as the oath to Pétain required of civil servants) and carefully avoided becoming directly involved with political institutions, fearing both Pierre Laval, who, as deputy prime minister (1940) and later prime minister (1942–44), was hostile to all signs of clericalism, and Laval's fierce enemy, the right-wing politician and journalist Marcel Déat, its leaders nonetheless remained loyal to the marshal and called for strict obedience from the Catholic population. Most, but not all, Church dignitaries gradually distanced themselves from Pétain; as late as 1944 Monsignor Jean Delay, the bishop of Marseilles, exclaimed: "I passionately wish for all the French to obey him."[5] The end of Vichy—and with it the time for settling accounts and accusations of collaboration—was drawing near. But whereas the leader of the Conseil National de la Résistance, Georges Bidault— one of the most famous Catholics associated with the Resistance— hoped for severe measures against the Church and the resignation of many bishops, General de Gaulle advocated leniency. In the event, only a few priests were forced to resign.

By contrast, the joy felt by Charles Maurras at the advent of the Vichy regime may readily be understood: the hour of revenge, so long awaited, had sounded at last. The "divine surprise" of Vichy had reduced the republican enemy to dust, so that the "real country" (*pays réel*) now finally corresponded to the "legal country" (*pays légal*); and the Jews, Communists, and Freemasons (the ancient anti-Protestant hatred having effectively died out in the interval) were now elevated to the status of major adversaries and swiftly expelled from public life, as Drumont, Maurras, and the turn-of-the-century leagues had so fervently wished. Action Française, the right-wing offspring of the Dreyfus Affair, had finally triumphed and the humiliation of having to acknowledge Dreyfus's innocence was now forgotten. In the judgment of the conservative Catholic historian Pierre Chaunu,

> Action Française came close to exercising power one time and one time only, under Vichy, during the six months of a short winter in 1940–41. It was responsible for what proved in the long term to be the least objectionable part of what the government of defeat achieved, on behalf of the family in particular, and also with regard to professional training. When the long-desired storm came, it was difficult to resist a certain feeling of delight, and difficult to resist expressing it: a brief moment of exhilaration celebrated at the wrong time was apt to be very severely punished.[6]

In detecting an "affinity" between Vichy, Franco's regime in Spain, and that of Salazar in Portugal, Chaunu seems to underestimate both the actual influence of Action Française on Vichy and official approval of the horrors that occurred during that "short winter." The arrests and imprisonment of prominent republican figures and the leaders of the despised Popular Front, which in 1936 had succeeded for the first time in forming a government made up of Radicals and Socialists and supported by the Communist Party; the first Jewish statute; the first camps—all this was done under the paternal, almost tender, regard of the old marshal of Verdun, a phenomenon that seems perplexing even today.

Maurras, for his part, was quite clear what had to be done. In November 1940, after Hitler's meeting with Pétain at Montoire the previous month, he proclaimed his complete confidence in the marshal, whose mission was "to think only of France, of France alone." For Maurras it was obvious by late 1940 that "the Republic in France is the reign of the Foreigner." Thanks to the first Jewish statute, "the French begin again to be at home in France. To be a functionary of the new French state, it will henceforth be necessary to be the son of French parents. The 'international dregs' are in the process of being eliminated. . . . Nationalism should have won the [Dreyfus case]. It lost it." "Not for a moment," Maurras continued, "did the idea of *France for the French* lose the momentum that Drumont had imparted to it. . . . The principle of *France for the French* is now a matter of law. The vicarious pleasure one takes from this is a matter of personal luck. We have won."[7] The logic remained just as clear as it had been at the time of the Dreyfus Affair: the republican state had been in the hands of Jews and Freemasons, and it was essential to eradicate this evil in order that France might belong once again to the French—even if its long-awaited rebirth now occurred under the heel of the detested German occupier.

For Action Française, then, gaining control of the state was the chief imperative. So it was, too, for a variety of movements in the 1930s that favored vigorous reform of the state under the guidance of modernizing economic planners and École Polytechnique–trained engineers, including certain Socialist and union leaders who saw in Vichy a chance to build the corporatist utopia that they had long dreamed of. In view of the fact that a movement such as Action Française enjoyed a permanent "honeymoon" with Vichy; that "even though actual members of the Action Française proper were never very numerous in Vichy, the place was pervaded with a strong, though diffuse, Maurrassism";[8] that the bust of the chief of state now replaced Marianne on postage stamps and in town halls, and the state substituted itself for the Republic in official rulings;[9] that a regime that wholly rejected the values of 1789, that utterly dismissed the promises of Gambetta and Ferry, was determined to settle scores as quickly as possible with the leaders of the Popular Front—in view of all these things, a shocking number of dyed-in-the-wool republicans felt they had no alternative but to make their peace with Vichy. Apart from twenty-four members of parliament who dared to say no to Pétain, along with a few others who decided to carry on the struggle, the leading figures of the Third Republic took up residence in the regime's new palaces without the least inhibition, and legions of former students of the strict "*hussards noirs*"[10] (many of them former teachers themselves[11]) suddenly turned against the Republic. In this battle for power, senior civil servants, the pillars of the state, triumphed over parliamentary deputies by a wide margin.

How are we to explain the fact that most of the servants of the republican state, who had been inculcated with the ideals of the Republic in its primary schools, its best *lycées*, its universities, and even its *grandes écoles*—that these officials, who had steadily pursued their careers within the republican regime, abruptly laid aside their values in order to carry on with their careers undisturbed, in a state that was no longer worthy of the name, now that violence and arbitrary power reigned in it? How are we to interpret the transition—apparently, for these officials, unproblematic—from state to nonstate, to an authoritarian regime dedicated to the cult of the leader, anchored in Frenchness rather than meritocracy?

Starting in July 1940, civil servants could hold office only on the condition that they could prove French paternity. *Le Temps* rejoiced that, from now on, "the humblest and the highest civil servant alike [will] come from the land."[12] No matter that republican principles were treated with contempt, that abuses of civil liberties and tragic expulsions multiplied, and that the traditional basis of the state was undermined; its agents calmly went on with their careers, effortlessly compromising their allegiance to republicanism by unanimously swearing an oath to Marshal Pétain. In doing this they reverted to a kind of personal dependence on an overlord, the like of which had not existed since the formation of the modern state in France. If the embrace of authoritarianism is understandable in the case of the few high-ranking bureaucrats who were disciples of Maurras, it remains more puzzling in the case of those who had previously professed republican loyalties. It is understandable, for example, that Raphaël Alibert, an openly Maurrassian member of the Council of State, should have become minister of justice, and that Henri du Moulin de Labarthète, an inspector of public finances who was openly hostile to the Republic, should have been appointed to Pétain's cabinet. But it is less clear why so many senior officials of the republican civil service should have willingly allowed themselves to become an essential part of the machinery of the Vichyist state.[13] Similarly, judges slipped into the new legal order with ease, ruling that the laws of Vichy constituted legitimate legislation.[14]

There came the moment of being sworn into office. In photographs that have scarcely yellowed, one looks with amazement on these groups of senior officials, turned out with great pomp in their prestigious uniforms identifying them as members of the Council of State, the prefectorial corps, the army, and the magistrature. Upright in bearing and solemn in demeanor, as befits the great servants of the French state, they are seen taking an oath of personal loyalty to the old marshal, now a collaborator with the Nazis. Virtually all officials took part in this ceremony; refusals were few and far between. Even now, this remarkable period of modern French history—before the "ill wind" began to blow two years later, in the late summer of 1942—seems to have an air of quaint legitimacy about it, as though it were a scene from a dazzling court of a bygone age. Indeed, to have been a partisan of the old marshal of Verdun is still today widely regarded as a matter of no particular consequence. To have lent one's active and loyal support to the hero who shook Hitler's hand at Montoire, to have served Pétain in the same way that formerly one had served the Republic that he abominated and ruthlessly combated, still provokes a rather indulgent response among many French people of a certain age. Such service has long been exempt from reproach—so long as it did not continue after the tide had turned in September 1942. In the minds of many, however, this amiable spirit of understanding extends well beyond the late summer, through the end of that year, even into January 1943, after which point collaboration became inexcusable; for it was only in the fall of 1942 that genuine resistance grew up within the civil service, leading by the end of December—and especially the beginning of the next year—to the arrest of certain senior officials, including members of ministerial staffs, directors of central administration, and prefects as well as subprefects.[15]

Here lies the scandal of Vichy: that senior civil servants of the republican state could have, without any great qualms or misgivings, long obeyed a regime under Nazi command; that they could have placed their meritocratic competence, previously certified by competitive examination under the republican regime, in the service of the occupier; and that, after the war, they could have pursued administrative advancement under the reinstated republic—as virtually all of them did, in the aftermath of a purely "symbolic" purging,[16] moving up through the hierarchy grade by grade and receiving the customary honors, not excluding the Légion d'Honneur. The uproar caused by the publication in 1973 of the French translation of Robert Paxton's book, *Vichy France*, was due in part to his insistence on emphasizing the crucial role played by members of the upper echelons of the civil service. What is astounding, as Paxton pointed out, is the "impressive display of continuity across the tormented years between 1939 and 1946."[17] Thus 99 percent of the staff of the National Audit Office in 1942 also figure in its 1949 directory; similarly, 97 percent of the inspectors of public finance working in 1948 had been employed in 1942. In the Council of State, the highest administrative court in France,[18] 80 percent of the section chiefs, 76 percent of the councilors in the civil division (service ordinaire), and 70 percent of the maîtres des requêtes (responsible for reviewing petitions brought before the council) active in 1942 appeared in the yearbook for 1946. Almost two-thirds of the roster of the diplomatic corps in 1942 remained unchanged under the Fourth Republic. Finally, in the prefectorial corps, directly associated with the basest and most repressive activities of Vichy, almost half of the prefects who were in office in 1939 still held their posts in 1946. Paxton's book called attention to the fact that, even if in many cases they did not subscribe to fascist values, with rare exceptions the senior civil servants of the Republic did not resign, but instead swore oaths of loyalty and even worked to improve the performance of central administrative agencies under Vichy. Having helped assure the smooth functioning of institutions that were profoundly opposed to republican values, they went on to discharge their responsibilities under the Fourth Republic (and even later), all the while collecting honors, without troubling themselves too much about questions of legitimacy and ethics. Like dignitaries of the Church who collaborated with the Vichy regime, many senior civil servants came through this traumatic period without great difficulty.[19]

Of course, it might be suggested that, apart from the small number of prefects who resisted and a few crazed collaborators, the majority of prefects under Vichy acted simply out of prudence and not on the basis of deeply held political or moral convictions.[20] The truth is that we do not know; but this hypothesis seems extremely improbable given the profound ideological sympathy that Vichy expected from its favored servants, the prefects, whom it so jealously watched. Cases of voluntary resignation can be counted on the fingers of one hand—which speaks volumes about the capacity for adaptation among these privileged senior officials of the republican order. Four-fifths of the prefects who were in office between 1940 and 1944 had been appointed under the Third Republic on the basis of republican criteria, and they had been trained in the principles of the Republic, often in its public schools. Despite having internalized republican values, and despite their regular apprenticeship in the institutions of the Republic, they remained in place for the most part during Vichy and carried on with their work, only now as servants of a state that in the meantime had been transformed into an authoritarian power.

As against this, it might be argued that the "black hussars" spread the values of the Republic only in primary schools, and not at the secondary level. As a result, unlike a large proportion of the parliamentary deputies of this period, "a significant number of future republican citizens, in particular those who were to be called upon to exercise the Republic's highest responsibilities, largely escaped this moral and political training. . . . Secular morality was therefore never completely the morality of the Republic."[21] It is surprising nonetheless that many men "promoted by Vichy had long been part of the prefectural administration. They made their careers in it in the last years of the Third Republic."[22] Thus 87 percent of the subprefects and prefectural general secretaries in office in 1943 had entered public service before the Occupation.[23] By contrast with the few low-ranking civil servants who risked their lives by failing to comply with the unjust legislation of the state,[24] many prefects, members of the Council of State, and leading academics were content to assure the functioning of the machinery of state, paying strict attention to procedure.

Infamous cases abounded. The career of René Bousquet remains particularly astonishing. A product of Radical-Socialist circles in the southwest, a prefect and ministerial staff member under the Third Republic, he was promoted by Roger Salengro under the Popular Front government of 1936–37 and entrusted with supervision of the central records office of the Sûreté Nationale [National Police], subsequently becoming prefect of the Marne. In April 1942 Laval appointed him secretary general of the Sûreté Nationale, and from then on he closely collaborated with the German police in deporting French Jews. (It was the agreement signed by Bousquet with SS General Karl Oberg that facilitated their deportation in large numbers.) Even if he dele-gated authority—mainly to his deputy, the subprefect Jean Le-guay, who efficiently carried out his orders—it was Bousquet who organized the great roundups of 16–17 September 1942 in Paris. Like Leguay, who quietly resumed his duties in public administra-tion in December 1955, Bousquet survived the war and afterward went on with his career in politics and business as though noth-ing had happened, even assuming the editorship of the Radical-Socialist newspaper of Toulouse, *La Dépêche du Midi*. After the Socialists came to power in 1981, he was welcomed more than once at the Élysée Palace by François Mitterrand, who received this "friend" with "pleasure" and associated with him openly in Paris.[25]

The case of the secretary general of the Gironde prefecture un-der Vichy, Maurice Papon, is remarkable as well. Papon was edu-cated at the Lycée Louis-le-Grand in Paris and then at the École Libre des Sciences Politiques, a breeding ground for leaders of the Third Republic. In his youth he belonged to the Ligue d'Action Universitaire Républicaine et Socialiste [League for Republican and Socialist Student Action], which opposed the Camelots du Roy, the violent paramilitary wing of Action Française, before be-ginning a brilliant career. Assisted by his connections in Radical circles, he obtained a ministerial staff position under the Popular Front. With the advent of Vichy he came to play an important role in applying government policy in the Gironde, particularly in organizing the deportation of the Jews. His superiors described him in their administrative reports as a particularly competent agent. Jean-Pierre Ingrand, the powerful councilor of state who represented the interior minister in the occupied zone, recom-mended him as a high-ranking official "capable of representing a new will." In April 1942, Maurice Sabatier, his superior in Bor-deaux, likewise emphasized that "[we have Papon's] support in the task of national renovation" and the next year stated unre-servedly that "his orientation is that of the government." Simi-larly, in 1944 the *préfet délégué* in the Gironde expressed the view that Papon's "intelligence, his diplomacy, his loyalty, and his authority should lead him to the highest administrative positions."[26] Later, with General de Gaulle's return to power in 1958, Papon became prefect of police in Paris and later, under Valéry Giscard d'Estaing, budget minister. How did the civil service of the republican state tolerate such variation in the values of its highest officials? How was it that members of the highest echelons of the civil service, such as Georges Monier, the rapporteur of the Council of State who served as secretary general for Jewish questions— how was it that these officials, who in many cases did not in the least endorse the anti-Semitic fantasies of the period, lent their support to the implementation of laws that contradicted the very principles on which the republican state rested?

The academy is another example. The most distinguished scientific laboratories calmly went on with their work, notably among them that of Frédéric Joliot-Curie at the prestigious Collège de France,[27] whose professors—with the exception of Jewish faculty members, who had been expelled—disseminated the results of their research no less learnedly than before, sometimes even modifying the direction of their work in order to bring it more into line with the prevailing taste. Thus, during these terrible years, André Siegfried dwelled at length on the shapes of skulls deriving from a specific racial origin.[28] Law professors also went on with their teaching, soberly, sometimes even approvingly, incorporating Vichy legislation into their lectures and commenting on it as it concerned corporalist social reforms, anti-Jewish measures, and other aspects of the new regime.[29] These worthy and erudite representatives of the republican school willingly lent their support to a plan for a new educational system that would be more consistent with present-day values: among the six undersecretaries for education were five *agrégés*,[30] three of them brilliant graduates of the École Normale Supérieure, who in turn surrounded themselves with other graduates of the same school. Again, "the republican administration, at its highest level, collaborated."[31] These senior civil servants unhesitatingly accepted responsibility for the policy of Aryanization, which was put into effect at once and met with little opposition. Virtually all teachers, from primary school through the university level, personally filled out questionnaires certifying that they were not Jewish—some of them repeatedly underlining the word *no*, written in capital letters.[32] The virtually universal indifference shown by secondary school teachers on the day their Jewish colleagues, like them *agrégés* and *capésiens*,[33] taught their last classes before being dismissed from the civil service is altogether remarkable. Like them, they were teachers of long standing at the *lycée* level, having served for many years during the Third Republic. The indifference of gentile teachers was comparable in every respect to that of officials in the senior branches of the civil service who turned away from their Jewish former colleagues, often friends, declining to reply to their urgent and desperate letters. Instead they carried on with their administrative duties, ignoring pleas for help from persons who would soon be headed for the camps and, in more than a few cases, death.[34]

The betrayal by the state, and also by its agents, is undeniable. Again, how are we to explain that the *hussards noirs*, some of them graduates of the École Normale Supérieure, were able to revise their most fundamental values and cast aside their sense of obligation to a state constructed in a universalist spirit? "Remaking the state" was the phrase heard at the time; in reality, as all the evidence goes to show, what was sought was the end of the state. Pierre Laval, a pure product of republicanism, had escaped his working-class background by obtaining a *certificat d'études* at public primary school and passing the *baccalauréat* examination upon finishing the Lycée Saint-Louis; this same Pierre Laval, who went on to become one of the pillars of the political life of the Third Republic, was later to be primarily responsible under Vichy for the application of repressive policies and, in collaboration with the Nazis, the deportation of the Jews.[35] And did not the devoted collaborator Marcel Déat belong to Albert Thibaudet's beloved *république des professeurs*—Déat, whose father was a civil servant and who was himself a scholarship student at the Lycée Henri IV before entering the École Normale Supérieure?[36]

The Ministry of Education supervised a virtual parade of new recruits. During this period, the number of civil servants grew at an extraordinary rate, from 682,000 to 790,000, with new teachers being appointed in accordance with the usual administrative rules and ranked by level of competence. The system functioned smoothly: students continued to prepare for rigorous competitive examinations, including the new entrance examinations instituted by Vichy; others quietly completed their *doctorat d'État* theses and went on to assume professorial posts without concerning themselves with events. And yet in 1943 Abel Bonnard, the education minister, explicitly stated that the neutrality of public service in this domain had to be rejected. (His predecessor, Jérôme Carcopino, had implicitly indicated that in no case were Jewish civil servants to be demoted.) Once it became clear that "the whole of the French administration had slipped into doing almost exactly what the occupier expected of it,"[37] how could the integrity of the state be preserved?

Let us come back for a moment to this "past that doesn't go away"[38]—a past that must not be allowed to go away so long as the mystery remains unsolved of why the Republic for so long allowed itself to wallow in authoritarianism, submission, and exclusion. The remarkable research of Marc Olivier Baruch amply demonstrates, if any further proof were still needed today, the magnitude of our ignorance regarding this sudden shift of allegiance, this wound that remains so raw. For the first time, Baruch expertly takes apart the machinery of the Vichyist state, a topic hitherto neglected by historians more interested in political leaders, ideologues, and the evolution of public opinion. The verdict is damning, undeniable, and unforgiving: almost to a man, the French bureaucracy—proud of its meritocratic system of promotion, the backbone of the strong state from Louis XIV to Gambetta—turned away from its mission of public service. The state, long founded on the rule of law, now gave way to a quasi-feudalism based on servility and bonds of personal loyalty that recalled the medieval system of obligation. The oath taken by Vichy civil servants is only the most symbolic illustration of these bonds: "The high-ranking civil servants who headed the administration of Vichy," Baruch observes, "lacking any particular political viewpoint, placed great willpower and a comparably great capacity for work in the service of a cause that was invalidated from the start." The authorities "had no need to go off in search of men innocent of all administrative experience in order to impose a new order upon the apparatus of the state. Among the members of the three first circles of power—ministers, secretaries general, and directors of central administration—one notes a predominance of the two most prestigious and powerful branches of the French administration, the Inspectorate of Public Finances and the Council of State."[39]

Far from being merely a secondary aspect of the Vichy regime, on which one ought not dwell too long, the way in which the state apparatus was forced to reconfigure almost all of its legal arrangements in order to treat the Jewish question[40] warrants closer examination. It later became clear that no government agency under Vichy had any qualms about managing the funds confiscated from Jews who were arrested and deported—funds that continued to yield income for years afterward. In the past, the republican state had taken moderate and tactful measures to exclude Catholics suspected of counterrevolutionary plotting; but now Jews were actually expelled from public life, stripped of their citizenship. Moreover, the denial of the rights they formerly enjoyed as citizens put them not only outside the state but also outside society, transforming them into involuntary and helpless outlaws. It was not the Republic that did these things, but rather an authoritarian republican state that was no more than a pitiful puppet, all the more strongly attached to its few remaining symbols of sovereignty as it submitted to the Nazi yoke—a state whose absolutism sprang from its disavowal of the Republic's own universal principles. The consequences for French Jews were dramatic: no longer was it a question, as it had been previously, of unjustly losing one's job; now it was a matter of losing one's life. All of this was done coldly, expertly, with respect for proper procedure and for the logic of the law, by high-ranking officials of the former Republic.

The minutes of the meeting on 16 December 1940 to discuss how the Jewish statute of 3 October that year was to be put into effect are worth examining closely.[41] Astonishingly, the discussion was couched in purely technical administrative terms. The participants agreed "to adopt common rules both with regard to the interpretation of arrangements liable to give rise to controversy and to measures of implementation." Maurice Lagrange presided. A typical product of the republican system, since 1929 he had been an extremely able commissioner representing the government on the Council of State, the prestigious institution responsible for declaring the state's legal position. Lagrange's intention was to settle the Jewish question promptly, while showing the fairness and respect for international law for which he was known throughout his career. In April 1945, Lagrange was appointed a councilor of state and thereafter pursued a brilliant career as a member of the European Court of Justice that lasted into the Fifth Republic. Other high officials took part in the debate of December 1940 as well, including Jean Delvolvé, a magistrate formerly attached to Alibert's staff at the Council of State. Delvolvé had been promoted the same month to the position of *maître des requêtes*, with special responsibility for representing the council in its relations with the government and other administrative departments.

The need to implement the law concerning the Jews resulted, as the *Journal officiel* succinctly put it, from an "obligation to rally French forces, whose characteristics have been fixed by a long history." At this decisive meeting, the question was raised at once of determining who counted as a Jew. Lagrange had previously circulated a memorandum addressing the point:

M. Lagrange: Reference is made to memorandum 14.19 SG. I noticed, upon making several telephone calls, that in many [ministerial] departments, you seem to be unware of it. I had it sent at once, and it is most regrettable that this circular should not yet have reached certain departments, for it furnished an interpretation permitting the law to be applied. Since I was worried, I inquired into the matter and found that all the letters had gone out, and I can give you the date and hour at which each of these items was presented to each of your ministerial departments, along with the name of the person who signed for it. Therefore it is solely an internal question needing to be settled in each of your departments. . . . These items were received. It is very unfortunate, since these are questions that require immediate attention. . . . We send our letters to [your] office, and it is up to [your] office to do its job. . . .

M. Delvolvé: In the case of grandparents, [the proposed interpretation] is correct, because they practice the religion in a more assured and consistent way than the present generation, and on the other hand I do not believe that one readily converts to the Jewish religion.

M. Lagrange: Here, obviously, there are a good many assumptions. A strict interpretation of the law is necessary, otherwise half the cases will not be looked into. We need to agree upon a certain number of precise assumptions; this is not strictly legal, and it is a bit arbitrary. [The question of what counts as a Jewish] name must be handled with caution. . . . You now have more and more high-level civil service positions occupied by [Jewish] persons from other sectors of society. It is obvious that these people are aimed at [by the law]. The question becomes trickier as you get to the bottom of the ladder.

M. Delvolvé: The best solution is to adopt a very strict definition [of Jewishness] for the future and, provisionally, to leave each department to take [its own] decision.

It was then noticed that article 3 of the text under discussion allowed an exception to the policy of excluding Jews from public administration to be made on behalf of those who could prove military service in the 1914–18 war, prompting Inspector Albert Mignon, director of general administration in the office of the undersecretary for war, to observe: "This [exception] is all the more dangerous since one might have hoped for a certain measure of sympathy on the part of the Jews, but now this sympathy can no longer be counted on. As a result, if you introduce exceptions, you introduce enemies."

The same desire to exclude Jews from public administration had made itself felt from the time of the Dreyfus Affair up until Vichy. At the end of the nineteenth century, the nationalist Right regularly demanded their removal, and many republicans at first consented (without really admitting it) to Dreyfus's "deportation" to Devil's Island, before changing their minds. With Vichy, the former adversaries seemed to be in virtually complete agreement with regard to the radical policy of excluding all Jews, not only from the state administration, but indeed from public life. One searches in vain for any clear signs of protest from the upper echelons of the civil service, a great many of whom had been promoted by the Popular Front, which in so doing showed its confidence in their attachment to the ideals of the Republic. By a curious irony, at the time of the Dreyfus Affair, many of the high officials who took part in the plot against Dreyfus, such as General Auguste Mercier, had also been selected for their declared republicanism.

If the nationalist Right was openly delighted at this recent turn of events, senior figures in the civil service treated the question of the Jews without apparent emotion, looking only to apply the pertinent legal rules while at the same time, in the course of extensive quibbling that displayed a fine administrative expertise, identifying unacceptable exceptions. Jews, Freemasons, and Communists, consigned to noncitizenship, were to be deliberately handed over to the Nazi occupier. Of the "four confederate estates" abominated by an exultant Maurras, only the Protestants (who, like the Jews and the Freemasons, had been exposed to public contempt since the Revolution) ultimately escaped the condemnation urged by the nationalist Right. With the end of anti-Protestantism,[42] the primary scapegoats became the Jews, whose rejection, authorized and administered by the state, transformed what might perhaps have been a secondary aspect of Vichy into a fundamental moment of its history—a moment when the very nature of French exceptionalism was at stake.

After the Liberation, the need to refound the Republic and to restore a brilliance tarnished by so much dark plotting was widely felt. Members of the wartime bureaucracy were nonetheless kept on whenever possible. Not only was the resistance of the French people to Nazi rule celebrated, state institutions were considered never to have lost their legitimacy. General de Gaulle announced that the government "in no way meant suddenly to make a clean sweep of the great majority of its servants, most of whom, during the terrible years of occupation and usurpation, sought above all to serve the state to the best of their ability." In the same vein, a commission in charge of purging the bureaucratic ranks judged that it was not necessary to "blindly follow" republican legislation since "inflexible justice was detrimental to the higher interests of the civil service."[43] Time was running out. The subject was no longer discussed: one forgot.

What mattered was rebuilding, generating enthusiasm, rolling up one's sleeves. In the French scheme of things, only the state could serve as the engine for mobilizing a reunified citizenry. In order to train a new generation of civil servants, to testify to the scope of the renovation being undertaken, and to respond to the desire of many republicans to see the state's former majesty restored, a national school of public administration, the École Nationale d'Administration (ENA), was created—a new *grande école* intended to revive the republican flame, a sort of École Normale Supérieure dedicated to training the state's elite rather than educating the nation's citizens. To rehabilitate the state without really admitting the need to do so required new blood. The aging bureaucrats of the Third Republic who had remained at their posts under Vichy, and then under the Fourth Republic, were to be allowed to move on quietly, retiring without scandal. For the time being, however, the republican representatives of the major political parties claimed all authority for themselves, as they had done before the cataclysm of Vichy. A party-based regime emerged that was characterized by fragile coalitions and transient majorities composed of notables whose loyalties were rooted in their electoral districts. The renovation of the state was delayed by the resumption of political infighting between Socialist and Communist *frères ennemis*, which briefly benefited the new Mouvement Républicain Populaire (MRP), a Christian Democratic party that now shared power for the first time—proof that Catholics had now, at last and irreversibly, rallied to the Marianne whom they had so recently detested. With the nationalist Right's loss of its natural constituency, the war of the two Frances was profoundly changed. Indeed, it was almost over.

It remained for the Fourth Republic to try to avoid its predecessor's compromises of principle and to prevent the rebirth of clientelisms; to renovate an outmoded parliamentary system; and to rediscover the vocation of a Republic based both on citizen participation and statist control. Support for the values of Joseph de Maistre was negligible under the Fourth Republic, depriving the nationalist Right of any hope of soon imposing its counterutopia. During the 1950s, a period of accelerated economic modernization, social issues came once again to the fore. Unions enjoyed a golden age, orchestrating a wave of harsh strikes whose edge was further sharpened by the Communist unions grouped together in the Confédération Générale du Travail [General Confederation of Labor (CGT)], then in a phase of renewed ascendancy. Finding itself threatened by quasi-insurrectional social movements, the republican state resorted to armed force in order to defend its rule. The violence was commensurate with the frustrations and ephemeral dreams of the period. But the true threat came from a conjunction of domestic protests by special interest groups, particularly small shopkeepers and home distillers attached to their privileges, and the need to take action abroad in defense of French colonies, where independence movements were springing up that rejected the republican values championed by Jules Ferry.

Herein lay the danger that in the end was to carry off the Fourth Republic, which had once again given its support to repressive practices incompatible with its own ideals. Following the war in Indochina, the uprising in Algeria (where the extreme Right and Drumont himself had enjoyed their greatest successes at the turn of the century) caused nationalist and racist values to spread as far as metropolitan France. The government made one compromise after another with the ultraroyalists of Algiers, looking for ways to justify widespread torture and massacres of civilians (in which French soldiers were sometimes involved). Ultimately, the defense of French Algeria cost the Fourth Republic its soul.

The needs of the state, and its determination to rebuild the country, were also forcefully felt. Economic experts and top civil servants invented a distinctively French style of postwar planning that was somewhere between authoritarianism and laissez-faire.[44] Upper-echelon bureaucrats such as Claude Gruson and François Bloch-Lainé, who had served the Vichy government as technical advisers and now assisted the Fourth Republic in its efforts at modernization, worked side by side with officials such as Étienne Hirsch and Jean Serisé who had fought in the Resistance. Gruson and Bloch-Lainé played a crucial role in bringing about the transformation of French society under the direction of the state, inculcating successive classes of ENA graduates (known as énarques) with the values of public service and devotion to public administration. For a brief moment under Pierre Mendès France, whose tenure as prime minister from June 1954 to February 1955 symbolized the resolve to achieve social change through coordinated state action, the modern republic seemed poised to merge with the voluntarist state. But hopes were soon dashed. The same old anti-Semitic rumors reappeared, emanating chiefly from Poujadist circles on the extreme Right[45] but also, as they had from the late nineteenth century through the 1930s, from various parties of the republican Center and from the Left itself. The political situation seemed bound to take a turn for the worse—to the great despair of the civil servants and énarques who were associated with this enterprise of renovation at its highest levels and who were fascinated by the loftiness of the state's view and purpose. They remained loyal to Mendès France, for it was owing to him that allegiance to the state had been renewed through loyalty to the Republic.[46] The Socialist Party—formally known as the Section Française de l'Internationale Ouvrière [French Section of the Workers' Internationale (SFIO)] and led by Guy Mollet, the heir to French socialism à la Jaurès—was now only a shadow of its former self. The fate of the Republic seemed to hang in the balance: rumors of a putsch spread, the extreme Right having infiltrated (albeit to a limited degree) certain sectors of the army, where the tradition of staunch social Catholicism had begun to reassert itself.

The rescue of the Republic was carried out in the name of defending the state: with General de Gaulle's formally proper (but perhaps not altogether legal) return to power in December 1958, the state regained its majesty in a Fifth Republic ruled by a strong executive. This new state did away with government by parties and brought into existence a new class of politicians drawn from the upper levels of the civil service. Meanwhile, if the nationalist Right lost its footing, the revolutionary ideal of a community of citizens also faded with the creation of a self-consciously statist republic. French exceptionalism, though it had managed to survive in the form of the state's claim to control society, was subject to considerable change as a consequence of the retreat not only from the republican utopia but also from the Maistrean and Maurrassian counterutopias. Administrative rationality, bureaucratic guidance, the affluent state, the so-called invention of social issues, the modernization that produced "thirty glorious years" of postwar prosperity[47]—all these things helped push the Franco-French wars back into the past. The state, formerly the instrument of contradictory radical ideals, now held itself aloof, as though governed by a logic of its own. It claimed, first, to incarnate both the nation and the Republic, posing as the custodian of the old nationalist values (which, in fact, it dismissed) while at the same time modernizing republican institutions. With the rehabilitation of national pride under the Gaullist Fifth Republic, it was the state more than the Republic that saw itself as absolute.

With the dissolution of the republic into the state, now the sole bearer of national identity, loyalty to the state as such acquired intrinsic value. A process that had been inaugurated under Vichy, but that was invalidated by the political cause of those years, now assumed its full importance; this time, however, it remained within the republican framework, even if republicanism no longer enjoyed the preeminence it had known during the brief interlude of state-sponsored modernization under Mendès France.

The state, acting more in the name of the rediscovered grandeur of France than of the Republic, took charge of a society that was now called upon to identify itself with its leader. Gambetta and Ferry, along with Jaurès, Waldeck-Rousseau, Blum, and Édouard Herriot, the leader of the Radical Party who had briefly served as prime minister between the wars, were now suddenly out of fashion. What came to be known as the republic of the civil servants stepped between the adversaries of an earlier era. The nationalist Right, despite several grand gestures that cast a certain shadow, was incapable of rising above its petty plotting of the past, while the republicans representing the major political parties were reduced to delegating to the state responsibility for imposing the values they cared about most. More than ten years had gone by since the creation of ENA: the way was now clear for its graduates to converge on the corridors of power. Unceremoniously kicking out the old republican elites—professional politicians who had come up through the major parties and made more or less successful careers for themselves in the Third and Fourth Republics—the ENA-trained bureaucrats set about exercising a genuine "magistracy" by taking advantage of a constitutional system that, in providing for a strong executive branch, strongly favored their interests. It was François Bloch-Lainé, mythical figure of the high bureaucracy of the Fifth Republic, who gave this notion its full meaning while pretending to dismiss it: "I am not sure," he declared, "that 'magistracy' is the most suitable term to define the position of independence in which the state must place, in relation to itself, persons who are appointed rather than elected and whose authority must nonetheless, if they are to carry out their own mission, carry a weight almost equal to that of the executive from whom they proceed. . . . One expects of [the civil servant] an attitude of constant and total independence, a manifest courage, indifferent to threats."[48] To put this magistracy of senior civil servants into effect, it was still necessary to assure the preeminence of the state. Curiously, it fell to Charles de Gaulle, a former pupil of the Jesuits, to solemnly affirm before the general assembly of the Council of State that "France exists thanks to the state alone. Only through it is France able to remain stable. Nothing is crucial except the legitimacy, the institutions, and the functioning of the state."[49]

Henceforth interminable cohorts of *énarques* succeeded one another at its highest levels. Socialized in the ways of the state, they had internalized the values of public service and the paramount importance of the general interest. Thus the "republic of the civil servants" was born.[50] The central place of ENA in this new system was signified by its location within the territory of the state, in the heart of ministerial Paris, the seventh arrondissement. Stiff in bearing, confident of the majesty of their role, distant and often curt, convinced that they embodied the will (even if unexpressed) of the citizenry, the *énarques*—particularly those who had graduated at the top of their class—cultivated a slightly unreal, almost anonymous, personality. The men in their three-piece suits and the women in their severe outfits were determined not to let their personal values interfere with the performance of their duties. Probity, virtue, and the belief that they had been called to public service interposed themselves against all forms of clientelism and corruption. A sense of the grandeur of the state, and of the privileges of public power, guaranteed that policy would be concerned chiefly with questions of equity. High-level civil servants saw themselves as incarnating the power of the state—an active, controlling state, and one that was all the more legitimate because it held itself aloof from politics, from parties, ideologies, and electoral strategies founded on compromise and clientelist relationships that were harmful to the public interest. Scorning interest groups of the sort that were so powerful in England and America, where an economic liberalism favorable to their development reigned unchallenged, they haughtily rejected any suggestion that such groups had a place in France and steadfastly refused to intervene on their behalf.

The most surprising thing about many of these high-ranking servants of the state is the strength of their Catholic convictions. Like General de Gaulle himself, many described themselves as practicing—in some cases very devout—Catholics, attending mass every Sunday in the fashionable districts of Paris, going on retreat at various abbeys, and so on. Not coincidentally, perhaps, a majority of ENA graduates (54 percent) admitted to regular, or at least occasional, observance of the Catholic religion. Members of the *grands corps d'État*—the great departments of government at the apex of the civil service: the Council of State, the National Audit Office, the Inspectorate of Finance, and the Foreign Office[51]—were distinguished by a particularly high degree of regular observance (40 percent). In a striking turn of events, then, the state now drew its most devoted servants from the ranks of those who formerly were the declared enemies of the Republic. The coexistence of religious values, now relegated to the private sphere, with an activist commitment to the public good in itself symbolized not only a rallying to the cause of the state but, still more significant, a dramatic decline in the historic antagonism between the Republic and the Catholic world. The Catholic faith of the chief of state, as well as many senior officials, no longer prevented the Republic from giving its unconditional allegiance to the state.

In the eyes of the *énarques*, concerned with assuring the state's preeminence, politics amounted to little more than a source of problems, of dysfunction and delay. In fact they did give free rein to their prejudices, at least with regard to politicans, looking with disdain upon "Méline's Republic"[52] as well as upon the paternalistic and indulgent governments of the Fourth Republic under Vincent Auriol (president of the Republic from 1947 to 1953) and his successor, René Coty (1953–59), which they thought backward-looking and committed to defending corporatism.[53] Parliamentary deputies seemed to them almost like visitors from another world: persons who still openly sought personal favors, petitioned the state for exemptions or special dispensations overturning this or that ruling, and requested official intervention for the purpose of pushing a case forward, advancing a request blocked at the ministerial level, or improving a politician's image in his district at election time.

Nor were political preferences altogether absent from the world of the *énarques*. Some of them belonged to parties, even to unions that looked to organize students within ENA itself. For a brief moment, in fact, even the Confédération Française Démocratique du Travail [French Democratic Confederation of Labor (CFDT)] exhibited an unusual degree of activism in this hushed universe. Political values nonetheless counted for little next to the administrative and state-centered ideal that served as the backbone of the civil service: attachment to one's role was foremost, encouraging reserve, detachment, and a sense of belonging to a closed community in which a single ethic of public service united a collegial group of like-minded officials. Membership in a senior branch of the civil service deepened this feeling of pride, of ascetic puritanism. Deep down, each member knew that the extreme selectivity of the *grands corps d'État* reflected on his own status and elevated his association with the state above all other relationships. Removed from the worlds of politics and business, with their compromises of principle and reckless risk-taking, and protected against the temptations of money, these high-ranking bureaucrats—often heirs to a family tradition of public service—displayed their loyalty to the state at every opportunity. For them, the state was a genuinely transcendental entity that exercised its influence, now as in the past, by virtue of its majesty, its power, and its legitimacy. In less than a century, these most eminent servants of the state had succeeded in reviving the Jacobin mystique enjoyed by the "black hussars" of the Third Republic.[54]

Within a few years, however, upper-echelon functionaries came to represent a third, and eventually almost half, of the mem-

169

bers of the successive governments of the Fifth Republic, benefiting from the retirement of the lawyers, physicians, and teachers who had populated the governments of the two previous republics as representatives of the major political parties. Many former senior civil servants now assumed ministerial posts directly on leaving their *corps*, without first winning the formal approval of the voters, although most later sought their endorsement at some point. What one finds, then, is a real inversion of career paths that was to be of real significance for the future course of state control. In the past, professional republican politicians—the descendants of Gambetta's "new social strata"—had come from civil society. They entered politics at the local level and then, working within the party apparatus, tried to get themselves elected as deputies, crowning their career, if they were lucky, by becoming ministers. Now, by contrast, a large proportion of ministers came directly from the senior branches of the civil service. Typically, one quit one's post in the bureaucracy to join a ministerial staff (often headed by a former colleague who had likewise left one of the *grands corps* a few years before) and then navigated one's way from one staff to another as changes of government dictated; one might even run a public company if necessary. Once the right opportunity presented itself, depending on the shifting political tides of the moment, a civil servant could realize his deepest ambition, becoming a minister, with the prospect at last of leaving his own mark on the state apparatus. Under the Third and Fourth Republics, the periphery had prevailed over the center, qualifying the preeminence of the state; with the advent of the Fifth Republic, however, the senior bureaucrats of the center steadily extended their influence over the periphery. The hold of the state over the "community of citizens" represented by the Republic was further strengthened since these citizens no longer exercised anything more than a very distant, indeed almost negligible, control over the choice of their leaders, who now covered themselves more in diplomas than in electoral mandates.

From 1962, however, the growing politicization of top civil servants began to gradually weaken the state's authority. Henceforth, from the "UDR state" of de Gaulle and Pompidou through Giscard d'Estaing's "UDF state," and then from Mitterrand's "PS state" through Chirac's "RPR state,"[55] the same accusation rang out: high-level bureaucrats—and especially the *énarques*, who were now the nerve center of a semipresidential system headed by a strong executive—were gradually abandoning their habitual role as pure servants of the state. The more vigorously they took part in politics, the more blurred their image became. The old system that had favored the rise of the state as an autonomous entity run by professional politicians was succeeded by a dramatic politicization of the upper reaches of public administration, with the result that the state's historic mission was undermined from within.[56] François Bloch-Lainé, for one, did not hide his anger: "The *énarques* who have become ministers," he remarked with bitter disappointment more than twenty years ago, "have for the most part always wanted to be ministers, and from the moment they entered the civil service they thought of doing whatever that required. They have, more or less expressly, regarded the civil service as a springboard."[57]

This linkage between the civil service and politics had the effect of erasing the boundaries of the state, transforming certain high-ranking bureaucrats into potential clients of political leaders who themselves had frequently come out of the civil service, perverting the friendships of old classmates, and establishing bonds of personal allegiance in a cold, neutral, and universalist world. Political stability over so long a period worked in its turn to eliminate other possible outcomes, encouraging strategies of dependence and reinforcing the attraction exercised by the regulatory power of a strong interventionist state that was nevertheless controlled by a single party (the Gaullists).

Denied political power in the United States, Great Britain, and Italy, senior civil servants in France literally monopolized it. It is instructive to recall Tocqueville's remark in *Democracy in America*: "American public officials blend with the mass of citizens; they have neither palaces nor guards nor ceremonial clothes. . . . [T]he external pomps of power are by no means essential to the con-

duct of business; the sight of them would offend the public use-
lessly."[58] What a contrast with present-day France, where the servants of the state, having rushed into politics, not only avail
themselves of palaces, guards, and ceremonial clothes, but enjoy
the luxury of noiseless black government limousines that would
have been the envy of Soviet bureaucrats, and even around-the-
clock use of private airplanes. The attractions of power are all the
more seductive as the French state—an immense bureaucracy endowed with considerable financial resources—continues still to
be a powerful machine. The privileged position occupied by ministerial decision-makers confers on them an undeniable aura, a
real celebrity in the public sphere and beyond.[59] Civil servants
who go into politics are constantly in the media spotlight, while
the others—the great majority—carry on with their mission of
public service behind the scenes, often with contempt for their
former colleagues (mixed sometimes with resentment). Within
the *grands corps* itself, particularly the Council of State, the existence of veritable dynasties founded by fathers (and now mothers) and perpetuated by sons and daughters silently testifies to a
commitment to preserve state service in its administrative purity.
These discreet and reserved high-ranking officials—and they are
many—run the state machine in the name of the public interest.
The battalions of civil administrators who graduated from ENA
and now head state agencies hardly ever appear on the front page
of the newspapers. They are also insulated against the unintended
consequences of exercising power, and they help maintain—as do
those relatively few members of the Council of State, the National
Audit Office, and the Inspectorate of Finance who remain irrevocably opposed to partisan engagement—an image of the state as
neutral, cold, responsible, and efficient. Even so, they cannot prevent this image from being degraded, as increasingly it is every
day through the growing politicization of their colleagues.

As early as 1985—four years into Mitterrand's first term—
when the press was celebrating the fortieth anniversary of ENA,
the left-leaning paper *Le Monde* published a cartoon showing an
elegant *énarque* atop a ladder conscientiously painting the walls of

the school a socialist candy pink. *"Allons enfants de la fratrie"*—
thus the slogan around which the *énarques* seemed now to rally.[60]
Like the various clients of the state in years past, both under the
monarchy and under the Republic, who linked their fate to powerful officials, the *énarques* were disinclined to change parties; but
if it was disquieting to think that servants of the state might move
from one position to another in response to changes in political
power, the idea that the administrative elite might adopt the values of the market—that ENA could transform itself into a prestigious business school—seemed so far-fetched that it did not
occur to anyone at the time. Because this possibility was not
taken seriously at the time, the scale of the transformations that
have taken place since is now all the more readily apparent. In the
1980s, the chief danger facing French society was perceived to be
politicization, not the influence of the market or the question of
ethnic and religious identity. Under both Gaullist and Socialist
rule, the state's role was continually reinforced and its legitimacy
increased; the ideological challenge to the state of 1981 lasted
only a moment, whereupon things swiftly reverted to form. The
transfer of power to a Socialist government led to the departure of
certain high officials while benefiting other servants of the state
who had remained in opposition for several decades, but it did
not threaten the preeminence of the state.

The republic of the civil servants that had been born with the
Gaullist Fifth Republic did not undergo a change of character:
other teams of *énarques* took over and went on to occupy the
highest government offices in their turn. The high-level civil servant was not dethroned, and the "pink elite" did not differ notice-
ably in its recruitment style from the Gaullist elites of the 1960s
and 1970s. To be sure, Mitterrand's ministerial appointments did
include a few professional politicians, much like those who a century earlier had served the Third Republic. For a brief period, his
government was more open to participation by lawyers, journalists, and especially teachers, who since Gambetta's time had been
the most militant members of the republican order. It also symbolically welcomed a small number of union leaders and commu-

nity organizers who were supposed to assure, by their mere presence in the government, the preeminence of civil society. Nevertheless, the new elite that flocked to the corridors of power with the Socialist victory of 1981 was composed no less than before of senior civil servants, many of them ENA graduates. Far from transforming the state, the Socialist elite that now occupied it were content to hand over parliament to the professoriat (still a constituency of great importance to the Socialist Party) while reserving real executive power for their fellow *énarques*, champing at the bit from the long years spent in the stables of opposition as expert advisers to the party's various factions—a sort of government-in-waiting modeled after the one it was preparing to replace.[61]

At the governmental level, it is true, the number of members of the *grands corps* and, more generally, of *énarques* dropped significantly after 1981. In the two governments of Pierre Mauroy (1981–83 and 1983–84) and in the one led by Michel Rocard (1988–91), which saw themselves as attentive to civil society, their place had shrunk very considerably, giving way to teachers, members of the liberal professions, technical experts, and so on. The fact remains, however—even under Mauroy, when the ideology of the counterstate was at its height—that four ministers of state were graduates of ENA, along with the foreign minister and the ministers of budget and of industry. More than a half-dozen portfolios were therefore still held by *énarques*, who typically came from the senior branches of the civil service. The same was true at Matignon, the residence and office of the prime minister, where 32 percent of the staff under Mauroy were *énarques* and 39 percent under Laurent Fabius (premier from 1984 to 1986). A fortiori, then, considering Socialist ministerial staffs as a whole, the undeniable decline in the representation of the senior civil service—considerably accentuated under Édith Cresson's government of 1991–92—must not obscure the fact that members of the *grands corps*, all of them products of ENA, still occupied crucial posts in the most important ministries.

Even at the beginning of Rocard's second government, in

June 1988, the publicity value of a new and loudly advertised openness to civil society quickly ran up against its limits: despite Rocard's warning to his government that "[o]ur country finds itself beset by too many difficulties, our state apparatus has become too distant from civil society," the senior civil service was no less fully represented in it than before, counting ministers as well as their staffs. What is more—to the great disappointment of those who had welcomed the Socialist accession to power—more than a third of the ministers who were thought of as representing civil society in fact came from the senior civil service.[62] The Socialists' beloved civil society made itself heard at the summits of the state only in the persons of the historian Alain Decaux, the union leader Jacques Chéréque, the ecologist Brice Lalonde, Bernard Kouchner (the founder of Médecins sans Frontières), and a few others. In reality, the face of political and administrative power had scarcely changed: the Left rapidly abandoned the utopia of civil society, rediscovered the state, and, effortlessly accustoming itself to the trappings of power, gave up the idea of challenging administrative privileges that were now its own.

There was almost nothing new about the first two experiments with *cohabitation*—apart from the entry into government of a fresh round of high-ranking functionaries once more associated with parties of the Right. If, however, the Chirac government in 1986 provided evidence of a significant rebound in the proportion of *énarques*, that of Édouard Balladur in 1993 opened itself up (quite surprisingly, in the light of Gaullist tradition) to lawyers, physicians, university professors, and even professional politicians—provincial notables hoisting the colors of their regions, whose accents they often kept. The influence of senior civil servants had considerably diminished,[63] but *énarques* nonetheless retained control of the ministries of defense, industry, and foreign affairs. Two years later, in an atmosphere marked by the renewed vogue of civil society and ideological protest against the state, to which we will return in a moment, the composition of the neo-Gaullist Alain Juppé's government, appointed in May 1995, testified to another—this time rather sizable—drop in the influence of top bureaucrats. For the first time, both the president of the Republic and the prime minister were ENA graduates who had come out of the *grands corps*, but within the government itself only the ministers of justice and foreign affairs were *énarques*. The other ENA alumni, who for the most part did not come from the *grands corps*, occupied more modest posts, such as undersecretary for the budget or for rural development. What's more—and this in a cabinet that symbolized Gaullism's return to power—physicians and representatives of the health professions were as numerous as senior civil servants (seven), with lawyers and other members of the legal profession (six), teachers (six), and professional politicians (seven) making a similarly impressive showing. Adding to the list two former journalists, one finds a preponderance of political figures comparable to that of the Third and Fourth Republics—quite the opposite of the "republic of the civil servants" that reached its height during the early years of the Fifth Republic. Although the *énarques* remained in charge of ministerial staffs, and preserved their power at the head of state agencies and various commissions exercising decisive authority,[64] their overall proportion in the highest reaches of the state nonetheless had dramatically fallen, and their profile had begun to blur. The president and the prime minister, each one eager to reduce the visibility of the state, promised to substantially diminish the size of ministerial staffs, which three decades earlier had helped assure the preeminent position of the *énarques*.[65] The call for smaller government reflected the mood of the time; indeed, it had already been issued by the Balladur government. Reducing staffs, it was widely assumed, would in turn further reduce the *énarques'* influence over policy. The true situation, however, was more complex.

Despite their ideological differences, both Socialist and new-look Gaullist leaders were faced with the same dilemma: how to present themselves as the spokesmen of civil society, while reducing, even if only symbolically, the visibility of the *énarchie* and at the same time entrusting the real reins of power, as in the past, to the elite of the *grands corps*. As Jacques Chirac was later to argue, "[T]he state does not have to be modest. Its servants are the ones who have a duty of modesty. The state, however, must be great."[66] The solution was to send strong popular signals—approval of social diversity and feminism, modesty in appearance and manner, uninhibited use of regional accents, lively participation in local folk festivals and banquets, and so on—aimed at reducing the distance between state elites and society; to try, on the one hand, to satisfy the popular expectation that the ruling class should reflect the social and cultural diversity of the nation while, on the other, preventing a populist backlash at the very moment when a *"république des grands corps"* was in the process of establishing itself.

The grand return to civil society, in the spirit of May 1968 and of Anglo-American liberalism, posed identical difficulties for the Socialists and the Gaullists, both of whom had been molded by Jacobinism. A hasty reshuffling of political and administrative personnel, marked by a drastic reduction in the size of ministerial staffs (from 408 persons under Bérégovoy [1992–93] to 198 in the Juppé government [1995–97], not counting a very large number of unofficial appointments), enabled the republic of the civil servants—symbolized by a few inspectors of finance (Valéry Giscard d'Estaing, Michel Rocard, Alain Juppé), a few members of the National Audit Office (Jacques Chirac, Pierre Joxe), and a few councillors of state (Édouard Balladur, Laurent Fabius, Martine Aubry)—to give the appearance of gaining in humanity, suddenly seeming closer, more familiar to the people. Curiously, in contrast to the strong personalities of these figures, the competent, austere, rigorous, and reserved *"petit prof"* manner of Lionel Jospin, an ENA-trained civil administrator and future prime minister who taught for many years at a university institute of technology, seemed to testify by its very lack of forcefulness to the unqualified triumph of a technocratic elite in which all political colors merged, without, however, reasserting the preeminence of the state.

The true significance of this new state of affairs, however, lay elsewhere, in the growing influence of the parties over the highest levels of the civil service. By increasing the number of positions reserved for exclusive appointment by the president of the Republic (about 700),[67] the Left (soon followed by the Right) expanded still further the "zone of political discretionality" from which so many members of the *grands corps* had benefited in the past. Not only were high-level positions that traditionally had been filled at the pleasure of the government now exposed to partisan influence; so were many executive positions in public enterprises and in private companies that had been nationalized in 1981. From now on, every change of majority brought with it a sizable rotation of senior civil servants, frequently from the *grands corps*, who were associated with one or another political party. Among those affected almost immediately were the prefects, along with many directors of central administration, ambassadors, superintendents of schools, and heads of nationalized banks and businesses—even television stations and cultural institutions. The considerable increase in discretionary posts aroused the ire of the opposition to such a degree that Jacques Chirac, running for the presidency of the Republic in 1995, promised to repeal a decree of ten years earlier that, more than any other piece of legislation, was responsible for authorizing it. The inclination to push for reform soon faded, however, and the August 1985 decree continued to regulate such nominations, which the new president in any case had great difficulty giving up.[68] The rotation of elites, proportionally more pronounced in France than in the United States, amounted to a gigantic spoils system that threatened the institutional continuity of the state, strengthening a pattern comparable to the one described by C. Wright Mills—with only one fundamental difference: in the French case people from the world of business were—and are—virtually excluded from political and administrative positions. In this sense, France is far from becoming Americanized.

The frequent turnover of officials as a function of party rivalry is nonetheless limited—in contrast, once again, to the American example—by a sort of merit system, based on the *grandes écoles* and competitive civil service examinations, that governs the recruitment of administrative elites. Moreover, the overwhelming majority of ENA graduates reject the prospect of increased politicization: according to a poll of 4,700 graduates,[69] 92 percent are firmly opposed to a system that in their view goes against the values of public service and threatens to delegitimize the state by placing it under the effective control of political parties, as in Germany and Italy—societies in which, for historical reasons, a strong state never developed. Hervé Novelli, deputy (UDF-PR) of Indre-et-Loire, actually introduced a bill intended to force civil servants who were named as members of the government to choose between their ministerial appointment and their administrative duties, on the grounds that "the government has been transformed into a device for assuring the representation [in it] of the civil service." This proposal won the approval of the ENA alumni association, whose last white paper (September 1995) also recommended barring civil servants who enter political life from returning to public administration. After one term of office, agents of the state would have to resign from the civil service if they intended to continue with their political career. An even stronger proposal—that winning a parliamentary seat would entail automatic resignation from the civil service—drew support from 60 percent of ENA graduates.

Evidently the *énarchie* had had a change of heart: most of its members now preferred to cut their ties with the political world, opposing the practice of holding more than one post at a time as harmful to the neutrality of the state. This lively hostility toward a robust and expanding spoils system brought to light an internal split that little by little was dividing the senior civil service into two separate worlds: the one consisting of the vast majority of civil servants who remained committed to a pure administrative ideal, all the more so, in fact, as they seldom benefited from the accelerated career advancement made possible by going into politics; the other, of ENA graduates who belonged to the *grands corps* and who enthusiastically endorsed a form of career mobility that they practiced every day.

The success of the program of decentralization undertaken in 1982 further deepened the divergence in the career paths of political and nonpolitical senior civil servants. In the capital, members of the *grands corps* took steps to broaden their power, moving with ease from one administrative, political, or economic policy position to another. Meanwhile, administrative departments outside Paris were undergoing an upheaval associated with the expansion of the powers of local notables who were now masters of their "fiefs." Staff reductions within the upper levels of the new "smaller" or "modest" state were limited, but symbolically they testified to a genuine transformation of the state. A substantial number of bureaucrats, finding their careers blocked by these changes, were forced to take their expertise, if only temporarily, to the provinces, which is to say to the periphery of the state apparatus. The state now yielded, perhaps for the first time, to a sort of reverse Jacobinism, cannibalizing the state and utterly changing the landscape of local politics. The "monarchization" of the mayor, now the strong man in his domain, further reduced the authority of the state. The presidents of departmental and regional councils also gained in power, with the result that the administrative agencies at these levels, in addition to those at the municipal level, were strengthened, and the size of public administration at all levels increased as well. The provincial bureaucracy suddenly seemed so attractive that it had little trouble hiring away a good many ENA-trained civil servants from Paris—even prefects and subprefects who, in an astonishing turn of events, abandoned the service of the state, bringing to an end a long tradition inaugurated by the intendants of the absolute monarchy, and went over without apparent regret to the opposite camp. (Between 1982 and 1990, 75 members of the prefectorial corps defected to the provinces, where they joined a growing number of *énarques* who had come from the capital to take charge of departmental agencies.) At the town hall in Paris, *énarques* headed almost all seventeen of the imposing departments of municipal administration housed there—miniature ministries that handled everything from finance and education to oversight of architectural planning and restoration.[70]

Though it did not call into question the indivisible character of the state, the transfer of executive authority from the prefect to the council president in the various departments of the country abolished old bonds of mutual self-interest that had previously facilitated rulings of doubtful legality. The complicity that formerly united prefects and notables, which in a roundabout way worked to assure the penetration of the center by the periphery, no longer had any foundation: from now on, prominent local figures who held several posts at once, and who operated for all intents and purposes as professional politicians, had other, more direct means to make themselves heard by the state.

Notables' status now depended less on their privileged relations with the prefect than on their own political skills, personal stature, and roots in a territory over whose resources they exercised predominant control.[71] Henceforth the prefects (who lost even their title for a brief time, being renamed "commissioners of the Republic") could only look grimly upon a situation in which their room for maneuver was sharply curtailed. Even if they were to regain a part of their influence through the exercise of regulatory power and administrative expertise, the change was still considerable. The destabilization of the prefectorial corps—the crucial link in the French system of administration between the *grands corps* and the civil administrators—was such that the ministry of the interior now had difficulty filling even subprefect posts. The prefects, finding their jobs downgraded, thus sometimes neglected the service of the state—an extraordinary reversal, historically, considering that they had once enjoyed access to the highest levels of the administrative machinery of the nation's departments and the power to manage local, even regional, affairs in the name of the *grands notables*. For once, contrary to the sociologist Michel Crozier's famous claim,[72] a mere decree (actually a basic law, approved by the National Assembly) had indeed sufficed to change society and, at the same time, to shatter a whole administrative tradition. Perhaps, on the periphery, the "coronation of the notables" had not quite smashed the civil service to bits; but it nonetheless dealt a serious blow to a coherent and venerable system of administration.

In the senior civil service, it also produced another, more profound sort of rupture. Participation in local political life by members of the prefectorial corps, joined by civil administrators reassigned from Paris to the provinces, led them to adopt the agendas of the leading local figures with whom their careers were now linked. Many examples of the erosion of the state's traditional dominance on the periphery come to mind. The prefect Pierre Costa resigned from the civil service in order to become director of the administrative agencies of the Alpes-Maritimes department, where he implemented the deeply conservative policies of Jacques Médecin, the longtime mayor of Nice. Similarly, the prefect Jean-Charles Marchiani came to unreservedly support the National Front's attempt to instill conservative values among the populace of the Var department. And Philippe de Villiers abandoned the civil service in Paris in order to take up a top political post as president of the departmental council of the Vendée. The growing politicization of provincial administration had the effect of cutting off the state from the rest of the country beyond the capital, where the close relationship between the *grands corps* and the national political elite was now paralleled by that between the regional administration, effectively the domain of provincial notables, and prominent local officials.

It was this unprecedented split between center and periphery—the disruption of central administrative control over the provinces—that finally shattered the integrity of the unitary state. In the wake of the far-reaching laws of 1992 and 1995, which created a complicated web of local administrative agencies, authority now passed to new administrative structures that were related to each other in increasingly complex ways. The partial relocation of ENA from Paris to Strasbourg in the 1990s, and the fierce debates to which it gave rise, dramatized this internal rupture by casting the issue of regionalism in starkly symbolic terms. Moreover, by prompting the great majority of *énarques* to distance themselves from the state center, the seat of real power to which only a very few members of the *grands corps* were to return without difficulty, it testified to a sense of uncertainty that undermined the privileged position of the state and its elites.

The proposal to relocate ENA was announced at the end of 1991 by the Socialist government led by Édith Cresson. Though she was the daughter of an inspector of public finances, Cresson was one of the very few prime ministers of the Fifth Republic not to have come out of the civil service. Instead, on graduating from the École des Hautes Études Commerciales, she entered the business world and went on to hold a number of important posts. The ENA relocation proposal, which few officials wished to question and which was subsequently confirmed by the government of Édouard Balladur (1993–95) and his successor, Alain Juppé (1995–97), was part of a vast program of administrative decentralization that involved the transfer of several thousand public jobs to the provinces. It came from a prime minister who not only was hostile to the upper echelons of the civil service but who was in the habit of making highly disparaging remarks about them. Cresson's ministerial staffs contained the lowest percentage of ENA graduates under the Fifth Republic (19 percent—as compared with 32.4 percent under Jacques Chirac in 1986) and a more limited number of members of the administrative *grands corps*.[73] Cresson's language was colored by a contemptuous populist vocabulary, bordering on the xenophobic, that was particularly insulting to the English and the Japanese. In the eyes of many, her blunt manner of speech and her repeated use of four-letter words helped to create a climate of disrespect for the austere figure of the civil servant, stiffly upholstered in his three-piece suit. Curiously enough, this desacralization of the state received the blessing of the state's highest official: the president of the Republic himself, François Mitterrand, who admired her refusal to indulge in the doubletalk commonly employed in civil service circles ("Cresson," he said, "speaks to the people").

The proposed relocation was fought from the outset by the great majority of *énarques*, who saw it as a shocking betrayal of the centralizing traditions of French exceptionalism. René Lenoir, the director of ENA at the time, expressed regret that "an institution is being wrecked by giving in to a rather facile populism."[74] The almost unanimous outcry from Parisian elites[75] was said by supporters of the measure to express a "Jacobin arrogance." Jacques Chirac felt at the time that the transfer of ENA was "an absurdity, a stupid initiative that will not fly," while three former directors of the school[76] supported a petition from its board of directors asking the government to reconsider its decision. The student representatives of the Condorcet class of 1992[77] expressed the view that "by transferring ENA, the French model for training the supervisory personnel of the state is being destroyed." Anicet Le Pors, the former Communist minister of public administration during the early years of Socialist rule, argued that the move amounted to "substituting a managerial mentality for the spirit of public service. . . . The transfer of ENA involves a denationalization of the state that I, for one, reject."[78] Two RPR deputies representing the gritty suburban department of Seine-Saint-Denis outside Paris, Robert Pandraud and Éric Raoult, came up with a daring solution: why not simply transfer ENA to Montfermeil (where the local immigrant population had been the target of violent attacks) as a way of confronting the elite with the realities of daily life in France? Students contemplated a number of spectacular forms of protest (marches, taking over government offices, and so on), while their representatives undertook a vast lobbying effort to have the decision annulled. The president of the alumni association also intervened, declaring, "To transfer ENA to Strasbourg is to make an abstraction of a historical fact. Paris is the capital of France and the central agencies are located there. . . . One might as well transfer Glénan [site of the famous sailing academy off the coast of Brittany] to Chamonix [in the Alps]."[79] More scornfully still, a student told the TF1 nightly news: "Why not transfer it to a barn in the Larzac [a high plateau of the Massif Central in the Aveyron]?"[80]—a suggestion with which the di-

rector of the tourist office in Millau, the main town of the surrounding district, hastened to agree, praising the area's qualities
in tones that were both caustic and ironic.

The haughtiness of Paris, and by extension that of the state,
thus found itself under attack once more: the clash between Paris
and the provinces, which had been latent for several centuries,[81]
was now being revived by a Jacobin power that turned its back on
its origins and rediscovered the virtues of the market—and of the
land. There was also an antiestablishmentarian aspect to the matter, perfectly expressed early on by Édith Cresson's deputy chief
of staff, Juliette Benzazon, who justified the proposal in almost
populist terms, rejecting the idea that such a school should be located in an upper-middle-class neighborhood of Paris—a legal
country too far removed from the real one: "When one looks at
[the students] who make up a typical class, [one finds] they are
born in the seventh arrondissement, go to nursery school in the
seventh arrondissement, go to college in the seventh arrondissement, manage to perform their military service under the auspices of the VSNE [Volunteers for National Service in Business],
and go on to live their whole professional life in the seventh arrondissement!"[82] It would be only a slight exaggeration to say
that this attack on a Paris cut off from provincial realities evoked
Les Déracinés, Barrès's hymn to Lorraine—right next door, in fact,
to Alsace, which now, in the midst of a vast process of decentralization the like of which the revolutionary tradition had seldom
favored, had caught the attention of the énarques of the rue de
l'Université—unless, of course, it is to be interpreted as nothing
more than a simplistic observation about the social background of
ENA students.

Dramatizing this polemic, but getting things backward, Cresson argued that the transfer of ENA was justified by a desire to
avoid a return to Vichy: "I immediately thought of Vichy," she declared. "I remembered that when one read stories of Bousquet and
so on, and the reports written by the Germans, they said, 'We
would never have obtained such magnificent results if we hadn't
had the help of the French civil service, and its competence'—this

185

was mentioned again and again; and Bousquet himself said he was happy because he didn't want to leave it to others to do. . . . *This was a job for the French civil service!* When you have read this, well, you have understood everything." Reacting violently against statements made by *énarques* who felt as though they had been "deported" to Strasbourg, she added, "I have asked the director of ENA to include as part of the practical work required of students a visit every year to the concentration camp at Struthof, outside Strasbourg—the only concentration camp that the Germans set up during the war in France."[83] In her view, a return to civil society, to the market, and to local realities was the only way to prevent public administration from drifting into authoritarianism.

Cresson's argument is not entirely ridiculous: if the state behaved traitorously under Vichy, it was civil society that resisted, that gave help to the Jews. It is a specious argument nonetheless, to the extent that Vichyist ideology presented itself as an expression of the provinces, rehabilitating folk and local traditions. Nor does the collaboration of high-ranking republican bureaucrats with the Vichy regime imply that every high official of the republican state is a potential Bousquet.[84] In a stunning paradox, local society and provincial life, formerly seen as contrary to ENA's original vocation, were now granted something approaching moral preeminence: in 1945 it had been thought necessary to equip the state with new elites in order to avoid a repetition of the debasement of Vichy; in 1991 the perceived need to remove the temptation of a new Vichy required a return to the provinces, to which were now attributed all manner of virtues—delegitimizing the state in the process.

François Mitterrand, for his part, long before the question of Vichyist allegiance in his own past was openly raised and several years before the decentralization policy had been fully put into effect, declared in 1984:

The temperament of the French inclines them to *étatisme*. From Richelieu and Colbert to Robespierre, from Napoleon

Bonaparte to the brilliant students of ENA. . . . Thus the nation was joined together, its unity forged. I shall not complain about that! . . . The nation was made, with room for the groups that composed it: regions, cultural minorities, associations, a multitude of "*pays*," each with its own history, its own geography, sometimes its own language: I find that all very well. And the omnipresence of the state, the omnipotence of the state, which is expressed in the planning of the ruling classes, must now yield.[85]

Mitterrand's judgment, which contradicted his own government's policy of strengthening the state, foreshadowed the quasi-populist challenge to its elites that would come shortly thereafter with the ENA relocation proposal. The chief of state, a lawyer by training and himself a local notable with roots in the department of Nièvre, was deeply attached to the local, to geography, to the "countries." Seven years later he had still not abandoned this attitude, prejudicial though it was to the traditional preeminence of the French state. In a solemn statement meant to support his prime minister, Édith Cresson, who had come in for rude treatment at the hands of the Parisian elites, François Mitterrand—president of the Republic but also the man born in Jarnac, citizen and deputy of Château-Chinon, who delighted in the most varied forms of local sociability, the solitary lover of the forests of the Landes, known for his walks through Solutré—this man expressed his "full" approval of the transfer of ENA to Strasbourg. Addressing the Prefectorial Corps Association, he remarked ironically: "One is not necessarily exiled when one finds oneself in Orléans, or Reims, or even in Strasbourg. No, ladies and gentlemen, we have not restored exile to Siberia by order of the tsar. There will be neither guard nor watchtower. . . . The provinces are not a foreign land. I am from the country myself, and if I had to go back there, I would not be angry, because I love my land."[86] The graduates of ENA immediately organized a colloquium celebrating the virtues of the "strong state,"[87] and the National Audit Office denounced the "improvisation" and exorbitant cost of the move, which would multiply teaching expenses.[88] At bottom it was a question of turning away, symbolically, from the statist system to which senior civil servants, the servants of the state, had always been attached.

In attempting to rehabilitate the country—the land and local traditions—the Socialists, having converted to a decentralizing Girondinism, turned their backs on a long history of centralization. Coming after the post–May 1968 antiestablishment "back to the country" movement, their carefully considered decision, with its echoes of antistatist populism, was bound to be controversial, so great was ENA's prestige in the popular mind. This bitter episode appears in retrospect as a crucial moment when the symbolic authority of the state—and even the nation—was weakened, since the state and its *grandes écoles* (ENA foremost among them) had long been united in the French imagination with the community of citizens, to which all forms of localism and attempts to extol the virtues of the land had been foreign since the time of the Revolution.

At the time, *Le Monde* published a truly inspired cartoon by Plantu, who is always quick to grasp the scope of an upheaval and the seriousness of the issue that underlies its merely incidental details. It showed a proud father congratulating his son on becoming an *énarque*: "Son, you will be the elite of the nation." To which the son, fresh out of the state's greatest school, replies: "What's the nation?" The whole of ENA's history had unfolded, of course, through its vital link with the nation-state, whose most eminent servants it had supplied for a half-century. But now its image was blurred to the point that it stood as a symbol of the local as against the national—and even, increasingly, a sort of American-style business school. It was as if, beyond the return to civil society, the reign of the market had done away with the state, marginalized its bureaucrats, shrunk the public sphere, and put an end to the idea of citizens devoted to the common interest. It was as if, finally, Americanization had overcome French exceptionalism, right down to the level of everyday speech.

But was this really true? Had the idea of the nation really been so degraded in the minds of the *énarques* that they were prepared to abruptly cast aside their vocation as privileged agents of the supreme state? Had things so much changed that the administrative elite was now ready to desert the public sphere in order to manage private enterprise, from the most prestigious corporations to a diverse array of small- and medium-sized companies? Had ENA, a school of political power, now been transformed into a school of economic power as well, so that the state, paradoxically, was now in charge of the training of the economic elites of the private sector? Had politicization and managerialization converged to turn *énarques* away from the world of public administration, or was managerialization the natural outcome of the career strategies of politicized bureaucrats? Had the concept of a state that advertised its strength, along with its desire to take responsibility for the fate of society as a whole, now been relegated to a distant past, preparing the way for a power elite that would mechanically trigger a formidable populist reaction—one that threatened to sweep away a unified and closed elite that had become foreign to the people, a virtually omnipotent establishment?

In any event, the new establishment gradually took the place of the state in the political imagination of citizens who were excluded from it, giving rise to fresh populisms while at the same time leading to a reexamination of national identity. The old ways of administering the agencies of the state had indeed been stood on their head. The secularization of the public sphere, a long-drawn-out process that had been undertaken by the different Republics out of a desire to create elites devoted to reason and concerned only with the general interest, now found itself abruptly called into question. As a result, the bonds woven over so many years between nation and republic risked being weakened as well. Populist leaders now emerged who were eager to revive the traditional Franco-French wars and to raise once again the nagging question of French identity.

The question remains, however, whether the sudden attacks on the *énarchie* justified a complete change in ENA's mission. As a school of the state, could it really transform itself into a business school, no matter how brilliant? Finding their access to the corridors of state power restricted, could the *énarques* be expected to change their ways and now look for salvation to the very world of business that they had scorned when the state charged them with responsibility for implementing economic plans and regional development? On the other hand, it should perhaps not have come as a surprise that senior civil servants no longer concealed their enthusiasm for the privatization of public companies such as Renault. Promotions, after all, were no longer arranged under the patronage of Saint-Just. Even so, to everyone's amazement, a small notice appeared in *Le Monde* in April 1984 bearing the provocative title "Treat Yourself to an *Énarque*," in which twenty-five ENA graduates—members of the class symbolically named Louise Michel (after the "Red Virgin" of the Commune)—announced to the world their intention to put themselves on the market, like so many ordinary senior managers looking for work. The result was an undeniable "malaise in the *énarchie*" that threatened the majesty of the state and heralded the triumph of the market over the virtues of public service, and the values of private companies over those of the state.[89]

At the beginning of 1986, Roger Fauroux, the newly appointed director of ENA, took note of this development. A graduate of both the École Normale Supérieure and ENA who had left the service of the state thirty years earlier, eventually becoming head of the industrial giant Saint-Gobain-Pont-à-Mousson, he remarked in October 1986 that "the ease of passing back and forth between the public and the private [sectors], between business and civil service," was now evident.[90] In the view of some observers, the transformation of ENA and the career path of its students in the early 1990s was already an accomplished fact: "[E]ven if the majority of its graduates do not go to work for a firm in the private sector, ENA must today be considered as a business school."[91] Typically, the shift to private-sector employment (*pantouflage*) occurs after a stint on a ministerial staff and then involves employment at a major firm (one of perhaps fifty).[92]

So widespread is this tendency, emblematic of French exception-alism, that of the two hundred most important company directors in France, one-third now come from the *grands corps* of the state, having graduated at the top of their class from either ENA or the École Polytechnique.[93] Even if, in the view of the same observers, *pantouflage* affects mainly public companies, which profoundly changes its significance, and even if it currently involves only 17 percent of active *énarques*, it is still on the rise. Even so, it has mostly attracted members of the *grands corps* ("the Inspectorate of Finance having to be considered as a genuine business school"[94]). High-level bureaucrats, especially civil administrators, are for the most part satisfied with their work and reject the idea of moving into the private sector, which they continue to regard with suspicion. Nor does *pantouflage* meet with the approval of all *énarques*, many of whom still pursue their careers within the state and feel that private sector employment is "essentially contrary to [their] code of professional ethics."[95]

The "brain drain" to the private sector was already noticeable at the end of the 1970s. In the years since, it has chiefly involved former inspectors of public finances attached to ministerial staffs who were drawn to high-tech sectors in industry and banking. The old spirit of bureaucratic chivalry that led functionaries to dedicate their bodies and souls to the values of the Republic was a thing of the past. Tempted by the high salaries enjoyed by their former colleagues—the new "golden boys"—a number of promi-nent bureaucrats were now ready to take the plunge. One thinks of a man like Alain Minc, first in his class at ENA and an inspec-tor of public finances, who on his thirtieth birthday left the ser-vice of the state to join the Saint-Gobain group, later going on to work for Carlo de Benedetti's corporate empire. In the public mind, Minc personified this blurring of boundaries and the desire for financial reward. More than a few ex–civil servants now en-joyed great visibility by virtue of their public pronouncements and the prominence of their business activities. Abandoning the reserve and restraint formerly associated with their class, they placed not only their expertise but also their Rolodexes—which is to say, their privileged relations with old school chums still working for the state—in the service of private interests.

But when top bureaucrats suddenly went to work for the private companies over which they had formerly exercised control, doubts irresistibly grew: Were the state's best servants now the captives of vice? When Claude Mouton, a three-star general, quit the ministry of defense to join a firm specializing in military electronics; when Jean-Charles Naouri, chief of staff for the minister of finance, was promoted to associate director of a private bank; when Jean-Marie Messier, an inspector of public finances who handled privatization issues in the Chirac government, joined Lazard Frères, one of several investment banks that greatly benefited from the government's policy in this area; when Jean-Pascal Beaufret, head of the department of monetary affairs at the treasury, became deputy governor of Crédit Foncier (an appointment later annulled, exceptionally, by the Council of State, even though it had been made by the president of the Republic, on the ground that it failed to respect the five-year-waiting-period rule)—in the wake of all these things, *pantouflage*, in the eyes of more than a few observers, had come to constitute a form of corruption.[96]

Measures aimed at limiting this practice were duly adopted in April 1988 and further strengthened in later years. They prohibited senior civil servants, for at least five years following their departure from public administration, from going to work for companies with which they had established professional relations in performing their administrative duties. In 1993 a new enactment by the Balladur government required consultation between the relevant administrative agency and an independent interministerial commission before a civil servant could accept employment with a private firm. The law of 28 June 1994 concerning *pantouflage* was clarified by a decree of February 1995: in the event the commission rendered an unfavorable opinion, the ministry was to make the final decision. In 552 cases submitted to the commission in three years, however, only 6 percent of the opinions it rendered were unfavorable. It is still unclear whether these measures—which are rather timid, really, compared with the wishes of the vast majority of *énarques* themselves, who feel strongly about the need to preserve the "impartiality" of the state—will be effective. Because the distinction—fundamental to the republican tradition—between the public and private spheres is becoming increasingly fuzzy and so many former senior civil servants are now running companies, public and private alike, it may be doubted whether they will succeed in preventing all but the most flagrant abuses.

Though weakened by the outflows of high-level personnel, the state has managed for the most part to preserve the boundary between politics and administration at its various points of entry. Sudden movements between the private and the public sector, so frequent in the circulation of American elites, remain quite unusual in France today, and when they do occur, they elicit sharply negative reactions from the senior branches of the civil service, which are still committed to administrative recruitment based solely on competitive examination. The outer circle of the *grands corps*, which has been enlarged to include new branches such as the Inspection Générale de l'Enseignement [Inspectorate of Education], is reserved for overtly political appointments, which are made perhaps more frequently now than before; nonetheless, the widespread reliance of Socialist governments on such appointments aroused discontent. Thus, in February 1982, diplomatic staff went on strike at the Quai d'Orsay, advising the foreign minister of their "concern" with regard to a "policy that discredits the ministry and . . . works to weaken a branch of the civil service"[97] —a polite way of expressing their anger at the proliferation of political appointments in recent years. In addition to career advancement based on political connections and intrusion by civil servants from other branches, they objected above all to the appointment to prestigious ambassadorial posts of friends of President Mitterrand who came from outside the diplomatic service, such as the journalists Gilles Martinet (posted to Rome) and Éric Rouleau (to Tunis); Pierre Guidoni, the head of CERES, the anticapitalist faction of the Socialist Party (to Madrid), and the industrialist Bernard Vernier-Palliez (to Washington); and the writer François-Régis Bastide (to The Hague). These positions were given almost invariably to persons who were nearing retirement, assuring them of ambassadorial rank and impressive perquisites.[98]

Similarly, in most of the other *corps de l'État*, entry from the outside was restricted almost exclusively to political allies. Still, it did seem surprising when the president's loyalists acceded to the highest positions of state on the eve of decisive legislative elections that the Socialists had given up for lost. Thus, before the Left's defeat in the general election of 1986, Pierre Joxe, the interior minister under Fabius, was named first president of the National Audit Office, while Robert Badinter, the justice minister, became president of the Constitutional Council.[99] These appointments were startling not only in view of their prestige but also with regard to their extent,[100] and led to revolts at both the interior ministry and the Quai d'Orsay that resulted in a series of appeals to the Council of State.[101] Generally speaking, however, this rotation of elites kept members of civil society (particularly business people) out of public administration no less consistently than it had in the past. The vast majority of senior civil servants passed the whole of their careers in the public sector: in 1995, of some 4,200 *énarques* who were then active, 75 percent (about 3,200) remained in the service of the state, 60 percent of them as civil administrators; many held administrative and financial posts in the various inspectorates and decentralized structures. Some 200 ENA graduates worked in public entities, including both municipal bodies and international organizations, and 600 were employed by public companies. Only 200 were employed by private firms, with a final 50 serving as parliamentary deputies and ministers.[102] This hardly looks like the alumni profile of a business school. What these figures do underscore is the attachment of the overwhelming majority of *énarques* to state service, their determination not to step down from their posts, and their opposition to the "modest state." It becomes clear, then, why proponents of economic liberalism such as the sociologist Michel Crozier persist (as did the Socialist and Communist parties before 1981, but for opposite reasons) in urging France to "break out of this administrative straitjacket," to "abolish ENA" in order to "create another training ground for excellence, devoted to [devising] strategies for change and no longer to learning how to acquire power for the sake of acquiring power."[103] The state continues for the most part to be a closed society.

Despite certain destabilizing tendencies, then, the Americanization of the French state is a fiction: a unified, coherent, and manipulative "power elite" à la C. Wright Mills has yet to establish itself in France. Even if the power of the state's political and administrative personnel has diminished somewhat, the French model of the strong state has shown itself to be remarkably resistant to attack. If some of its most prestigious servants display a certain disloyalty by placing their talents at the disposal of the private sector, most of its functionaries, great and small alike, remain irrevocably attached to it and hesitate to adopt purely market-based values that in their view offend against the norms of public service. Senior civil servants occupying the highest administrative positions continue to faithfully serve the government, regardless of its political color, and the vast majority of them condemn the very notion of a spoils system, which, together with the substantial increase since 1981 in the number of posts reserved for appointment by the Council of Ministers, may threaten the neutrality of the state. Public administration remains effectively closed to outsiders from the world of business, in keeping with the statist logic of the system. On the other hand, the line separating the state from political parties has become blurred, eroding its capacity for impartial judgment and diminishing its legitimacy. As a result, the power of state institutions has declined, giving way to more purely political forms of decision-making.

It remains unclear whether ENA will be fantastically transformed into a business school or consigned to oblivion, its meritocratic principles discredited and denied in favor of partisan considerations. But its future is perhaps not brilliant at a moment when commitment to the values of the state as an institution is widely thought to be on the decline in the *énarchie*.[104] The challenge to ENA, although based on sound arguments, nonetheless carries with it a certain element of danger, for it links up with diffuse populisms that likewise rail against a cold technocracy lacking any real sense of national cultural identity, whose values are the sterile products of a despised rationalism. On all sides—curiously, even among the political and administrative elites at the highest levels of the state—cries were heard prior to the 1995 elections against the new "fiefdoms" that hatch their "petty plots" in the shelter of the "national palaces," conspiring to take advantage of honest, ordinary citizens. Although, for the first time in the history of modern France, the field of candidates for the presidency consisted almost exclusively of *énarques* (Jacques Chirac, Lionel Jospin, Édouard Balladur, and Philippe de Villiers), and although in waging their campaigns they relied on the support of a great many other *énarques*,[105] their alma mater found itself endlessly denounced.

Not even those who were most attached to the republican message were above resorting to Maurras's invidious distinction between the legal country and the real country. Jacques Chirac, for example, declared that "the people no longer have confidence in their elites";[106] that "the gap is dangerously widening between the man in the street and a ruling class" that carries on with its "petty plotting," between a liberal and Socialist establishment so distant from "anonymous" French citizens. Talk of the "*jacquerie* against the elites" irresistibly evoked the popular uprisings led against the seigneurs of old.[107] Gaullism, which in the early years of the Fifth Republic had so largely relied on the senior civil service, now curiously participated in this mobilization of opinion against the privileged, including high-level bureaucrats. Thus latter-day Gaullists who had once been high-level bureaucrats themselves, having in the meantime converted to the values of economic liberalism, hastened to add their voices to the chorus calling for a "modest state." Among them was Alain Juppé—a graduate of the École Normale Supérieure, an *énarque*, and a member of one of the senior branches of the civil service—who stood up in the National Assembly to denounce what he saw as an unnecessary surplus of civil service positions ("*la mauvaise graisse*"), which he proposed to curtail by reducing the number of administrative employees.[108]

Almost schizophrenically, following Chirac's example, other *énarques* who had scaled the heights of the state hurried to denounce ENA as well. For Charles Millon, "the elite has become a caste, a nomenklatura; ENA has played an extremely perverse role in this."[109] Jean-Pierre Chevènement decried an "ENA in the service of the established order,"[110] asserting that "the ear of the real elites" is to be found "among the people more than within the Establishment."[111] So loud was this chorus that another *énarque*, Philippe Séguin, seemed out of place in coming to the defense of his old school: "Its imperfections will never be corrected so long as . . . too many leaders in this country stubbornly persist in making this school the scapegoat for our powerlessness. ENA is an essential element in the smooth functioning of the republican state."[112] Similarly, Lionel Jospin refused to yield to what he called a "facile populist rhetoric that is all the less credible as it emanates from these same technocratic elites,"[113] recognizing that in reviving the myth of *les gros*[114]—only now singling out the state and its *énarques* rather than, as in earlier times, the two hundred richest families—critics of ENA risked fueling extremist popular sentiment, whose spokesmen attacked more effectively than anyone else a rationalist and cosmopolitan system of government as foreign to the true people of France.

The state, then, now saw itself transformed into the "establishment"—an almost shameful expression borrowed, ironically, from the American vocabulary of the weak state—while its senior civil servants assumed the features of an ideal scapegoat against which a "populist front" could rise up. The major media fanned the flames, and the leading weeklies, whose front pages were awash with ever more sensational slogans, adopted the most extreme demagogic language, denouncing in an alarmist and irresponsible way the "grand return of the establishment," the "invaders," the "handful of *énarques* who have monopolized the jewels of the Re-

public," the "French nomenklatura," the "caste that has confiscated power," the "people against the elites," "oligarchy *à la
française*," the "Gargantuan manipulation of state elites whose
avowed goal is to pull the people apart." The time had come, they
declared, "to do away with the power of the *énarques*."[115]

The anti-ENA wave rose and fell with the rhythm of the electoral campaigns: it peaked in 1995, partly with the help of ENA
graduates who were having a hard time attracting popular support, and then enjoyed a resurgence again two years later with the
legislative elections of 1997. As resentment grew on the campaign
trail against the *"polytechnarques,"* so competent but so distant,
hopelessly handicapped by their ignorance of local affairs, two
alumni, Alain Juppé and Laurent Fabius, called for the prestigious
school to be abolished.[116] It was now open season on ENA, with
Alain Madelin, the leader of the moderate Right, rashly declaring
that "Ireland has the IRA, Spain has the ETA,[117] Italy has the
Mafia, and France has ENA"; while the slate of Action Citoyenne,
a group devoted to increasing the power of individual citizens in
public affairs, consisted of four candidates whose only platform
was opposition to ENA.[118] With each new round of elections, the
future of ENA was at the center of debate. In the heat of the early
legislative campaign, and in the spirit of Fabius's statement in December 1996 that ENA was "a perverse system," Juppé proposed
in the spring of the following year to replace it "by something
else, closer to reality."[119] This finally upset the applecart: offense
was taken, and emotions rose to such a height that a few days
later Jacques Delors, the former president of the Commission of the
European Community, declared, "No, this is populism through
and through, simply not serious. . . . No, no, I am shocked by
this. It is almost on a level with the National Front, things like
that. Politicians are cowards—it's shameful."[120] With the defeat of
the Right in the 1997 elections, fingers were menacingly pointed
once more: the conservative thinker Denis Tillinac, who had
helped bring many intellectuals into Jacques Chirac's camp, confessed his sadness and distress: "ENA is, like Juppé himself, the
scapegoat for a [sense of malaise] that people do not know how

to put into words, but which they [nonetheless] feel. The style of thinking that was inculcated to manage quasi-military state agencies with a five-percent annual growth rate in budgets is [now] stricken with obsolescence. . . . Our elites are stricken with both sterility and illegitimacy. New ones have to be created."[121]

These rhetorical excesses were forgotten once the elections were over and everything went back to the way it was before, with one *énarque* (Lionel Jospin) succeeding another (Alain Juppé) as prime minister alongside an *énarque* president (Jacques Chirac), the most prestigious government ministries being occupied, as before, by *énarques*.[122] The proportion of *énarques* (33 percent) was one of the highest since 1972, reaching almost unprecedented levels among ministerial chiefs of staff: 20 of 27 were graduates of the celebrated school, half of these coming from the *grands corps*; moreover, the proportion had scarcely fallen among ministerial staffs themselves, where the total number of employees remained undiminished. Lionel Jospin's own office included many *énarques* from the senior branches of the civil service, among them his chief of staff Olivier Schrameck (formerly a member of the Council of State), David Kessler (Council of State), and Jacques Rigaudiat (National Audit Office). The same was true for the office of the interior minister, Jean-Pierre Chevènement. Rather more surprisingly, Dominique Voynet, minister for the environment and a member of the Greens, went against the image of the ecologists as an easygoing bunch by naming an *énarque* as her chief of staff and placing a former inspector of public finances in charge of the ministry's financial section. This return in force of ENA graduates at once aroused criticism on the part of Socialist officials excluded from the new regime: "There are too many *énarques*!" exclaimed Marie-Noëlle Lienemann, head of the left-wing PS faction Gauche Socialiste, echoing a familiar refrain.[123]

Regrettably, the signal that the hunt was on against ENA-trained bureaucrats came at the worst possible moment, a time when scandals followed one after another and tarnished even the bureaucrats themselves. Under the Third Republic, the great fi-

nancial scandals, such as Panama, had almost exclusively involved members of parliament—the *chéquards*, or influence ped-
dlers. Now it was the senior civil servants who found themselves
in the crossfire. The privatizations of 1987, from Suez to Saint-
Gobain and from Paribas to the Société Générale bank and the
UAP insurance group, had dealt a severe blow to the managerial
state by abruptly curtailing its power to intervene in the financial and economic life of the country. These privatizations had
aroused accusations of favoritism, for top bureaucrats with ties to
the RPR had met with no resistance in quitting the service of the
state to join the new private enterprises. Confronted with this
mixing of careers and the blurring of the boundaries between
public and private, the Socialist opposition (itself compromised
by the Pelat affair, a scandal involving an interest-free loan
granted to then–prime minister Pierre Bérégovoy, who was slow
in paying it back) took its revenge. Almost inevitably, the situation gave rise to flights of lyricism. Thus the former interior minister, Pierre Joxe, himself an *énarque*, exclaimed: "Where is the
Zola who will write of the scramble for the spoils in which the
RPR and its wheeler-dealers are taking part before our very eyes?
Where is the Rosi who will make the film *Hands over France*?
Where is the Goya who will paint . . . the pallid and ghostly figures who, behind the scenes, make up both a council of administration and a council of government?"[124]

The old myths were once more pressed into service—most notably that of the two hundred families, fashionable between the
wars—on both the extreme Left and the extreme Right. The "people" rose up against the clandestine power of the "rich" all the
more readily as these figures appeared to be foreigners, outsiders
to French society, evil, diabolically capable of fooling the innocent "little people." François Mitterrand, president of the Republic, thundered against the privatizations carried out by the RPR
state: "It was called the 200 families in 1936. They are many
fewer [today]. Those who see themselves as the new masters will
one day have to be brought to account."[125] *L'Humanité* also
pointed menacingly to the "RPR financiers" who took part in the

"scramble for the spoils,"[126] while *L'Événement du jeudi* saw in it proof of the renaissance of the "feudal system," with its "fiefs" and "cohorts of barons."[127] In the view of many observers, "*L'État et l'ÉNA*" seemed to rhyme with "*copains et coquins*" ("pals and rascals"—an expression coined by the conservative leader and former minister of the interior Michel Poniatowski). This catastrophic scenario was repeated in 1993 with the privatizations approved by the then–prime minister, Édouard Balladur. Some of Balladur's friends were named to head up large, newly private firms (such as Jacques Friedman, who now ran the UAP group), while other ENA graduates took over the reins of BNP and Elf, the nation's largest oil company. The slogan of the "two hundred families" reappeared once more, further eroding the power of the state whose place they were supposed to have taken. It fell this time to Robert Hue, the reformist leader of the French Communist Party (PCF), to summon the shade of Émile Zola and brandish a new *J'accuse* in inveighing against "king money," which he claimed reigned absolutely within the state.[128]

The various slush fund scandals that broke after 1987 affected all the major parties, implicating their leaders (among them a large number of *énarques*, except in the case of the PCF) in dark stories of embezzlement and Swiss bank accounts. In 1995 François Froment-Meurice, a high official of the Centre des Démocrates Sociaux (CDS)—an *énarque*, the son of not one but two *énarque* parents, who moreover was married to an *énarque*—was charged with misappropriation of funds and placed in police custody.[129] Certain ENA-trained senior civil servants who were among the most loyal to the ideals of the Republic were found to have personally enriched themselves, and other ENA-trained ministers and former civil servants were prosecuted for having swimming pools constructed at public expense. That same year, the press mercilessly exposed ENA-trained former ministers who had paid for personal services out of public funds, as well as others who had leased state-owned apartments, located in the best neighborhoods in Paris, at substantially below-market rates to various members of their families, past and present.[130] The *énarque* Didier Schuller played at private detective for a time until, fearing for his life, he fled to the Bahamas, followed by an international warrant for his arrest on charges of influence peddling. Under these circumstances it was difficult for high officials of the senior branches of the civil service to stand tall. Even if public administration as a whole remained untouched by corruption,[131] the integrity of the state was at grave risk of being compromised, opening the way to all manner of excess.

Business leaders, often with close ties to political power, soon found themselves collared by the police, hauled before the courts, and prosecuted for embezzlement, fraud, insider trading, misuse of corporate assets, and use of illicit methods of private surveillance worthy of a tinpot James Bond.[132] Senior civil servants who had crossed over into the world of private enterprise were caught up in affairs from which they sometimes did not personally profit. The chief executive of Saint-Gobain, Jean-Louis Beffa, a graduate of both the École Polytechnique and the École des Mines, was taken in for questioning on suspicion of influence peddling. Similarly, Jean-Louis Haberer—an intimate of powerful political figures on both the Left and the Right, first in his class at ENA, inspector of public finances, "soldier-monk of the state"—was charged with responsibility for the incredible and gigantic "financial hole" into which Crédit Lyonnais had been plunged due to his disastrous strategy for investing public funds. In 1997 the banker Jean-Maxime Lévêque, an inspector of public finances associated with the RPR, was sent to the Prison de la Santé in Paris for "complicity in breach of trust, possession of stolen goods, [and] complicity in submitting inaccurate accounts."[133] Mayors and presidents of regional councils who served also as parliamentary deputies—in Angoulême, Cannes, Grenoble, Nice, Nîmes, and Perpignan, to name only a few cities—were found to have unduly enriched themselves by making personal use of public credit placed at their disposal, in many cases enjoying a luxurious lifestyle. With so many ENA-trained senior civil servants, often former or current ministers, being caught up in corruption scandals and prosecuted by the authorities, each new affair fueled antielitist sloganeering. This time it was the state that found itself in the line of fire.

Corruption thus forced its way into the very heart of state institutions and gave real meaning to Poniatowski's characterization of the age as one of pals and rascals. Though this phrase is inappropriate as a general description of a French spoils system, recent events have given it an indisputable relevance. That so upright and puritanical a bureaucracy, proud of its role, committed to its mission of public service, scornful of money and immune to all forms of temptation, should in so many cases have seen its reputation besmirched came as a surprise. As recently as 1984, François Bloch-Lainé had expressed the opinion that "the French [system of] administration is one of the most honest in the world"; indeed, in his view, the political figures who were entering into the service of the state in growing numbers were thereby protected against corruption.[134] Similarly, Simon Nora, a former director of ENA who symbolizes the devotion of senior civil servants to the state, continued to regard the *grands corps* as "one of the lungs of democracy."[135] But were they not deluding themselves, given what was already known even then about the close ties between the members of the *grands corps* and the managers of the large civil engineering firms?[136] Even if the vast majority of senior civil servants remained proudly attached to the image of the civil service as incorruptible, within the space of a few years a shocking number of them had in fact been proved to be corrupt. What is more, corruption had touched officials at the highest levels of government, destabilizing the foundations of the state itself. In 1996 *Le Monde* harshly criticized this state of affairs, running a cartoon of a high-level bureaucrat depicted as a dog, bowing and offering his leash to anyone who would take it—wads of five-hundred-franc notes sticking out of the pockets of his clothes.[137] This nightmarish image—unbearably belittling the hauteur of the state, which was founded on the civic convictions of servants who were supposed to be impartial and uncorruptible—profoundly upset Parisian sensibilities and provoked a fresh round of indignant protests.

The populist reaction was not long in coming. Bernard Tapie, the wheeler-dealer and ex–Socialist minister for urban affairs whose own career had contributed more than a little to the delegitimization of the state, attacked the members of the political-administrative elite, many of them his old faithful friends: "All of them, or almost all," he wrote in 1994, "graduated from ENA; I received a technical education. All of them, or almost all, are senior civil servants; I run a business. And this is enough [for me] to be forever considered an intruder. It occurs to me, too, that there is less difference between a leader of the Right and a leader of the Left than between the leader of the Left and a voter of the Left." Tapie, a Robin Hood–like figure who as minister had aroused false hopes in the violence-ridden outskirts of Paris before the scope of his corrupt dealings and extravagant spending became known; whose malfeasance had brought him from the heights of the Socialist state to the Prison de la Santé; who had warned the elite that it had "everything to fear from a reaction of the people. . . . One cannot abuse the Third Estate forever"[138]— this man knew what he was talking about. Popular anger was brewing against the privileged *énarques*, who were said to constitute a new "aristocratic class." For a brief moment it seemed poised to sweep away the state, especially since the adversaries of the *État des fonctionnaires* boasted of a limitless energy, a vitality identical to that of the sans-culottes, who had been called upon to regenerate a France hobbled by a king stricken with political impotence. In the eyes of these adversaries, power, cut off from the vital sources of the nation, is there for the taking.

For almost two decades now, the leaders of the National Front have relentlessly advertised themselves as the sole partisans of a "revolutionary program," the sole supporters of another French revolution—on the understanding that this time around, the revolution will be truly French.[139] Like the Jacobin royalist Maistre, Jean-Marie Le Pen, a Jacobin nationalist in the manner of Barrès, posed as the spokesman of the people ready to challenge the monopoly on power exercised by the elite; his every gesture testified to his energy and his strength, theatricalized in a manner reminiscent of the nationalist and fascist parades of the 1930s. In Isaiah Berlin's terms, Le Pen may be said to be a fascist (just as Maistre was a fascist—more so, perhaps, considering Le Pen's friendships, past and present) in the sense that his energy and violence are directed against a state that is perceived as the artificial instrument of a puppet Republic, one that has renounced its distinctively French character. Demogogic attack by mainstream politicians against the state and ENA also helped weaken the institutions of the Republic, already undermined by practices that the "good citizens" of the past would have judged unacceptable. Excessive politicization, *pantouflage*, and corruption all provided grist for the mill of the radical extreme Right. The National Front laid into the "gang of four"[140]—the leftist parties dominated by the *énarchie*—and called for a "clean hands operation" against "the gangrene that afflicts the state":[141] in place of the "decadent and corrupt Fifth Republic a Sixth Republic must be born, national, popular, honest, and responsible."[142] As Bruno Mégret (Le Pen's rival for leadership of the nationalist Right) stressed, it was necessary "to found a new, and once again, national Republic opposed to the politicians of the Establishment."[143]

Philippe de Villiers—the rootless ENA-trained senior civil servant who presented himself as the modern heir to the Vendean revolt against the republican order—hammered away at this theme as well, albeit in the name of staunch Catholicism. In declaring war against the "society of connivance," this "little world that mixes together at the highest levels of the state,"[144] Villiers also helped bring about the sudden rise of a populist camp that fueled its extremist campaign with slogans identifying the state with the establishment, with the rich—which is to say, with the very opposite of what the state stands for: money. This development further destabilized a system of civil administration that on the whole remained faithful to its mission but nonetheless was often denigrated in public opinion,[145] one that remained firmly attached to the ideal of public service but that now, tempted by other sources of power, was in danger of losing its moral bearings. It was shaken, too, by the memory of Vichy, which the Papon trial forcefully and vividly revived, casting doubt retrospectively on its traditional devotion to the values of the Republic—and almost entirely discrediting the many virtues that virtually all servants of the public interest continue to display.

Chapter Six

The Era of Rival Identities

The implications of the retreat from the republican state were all the more difficult to assess now that the Catholic Church was less determined than before to contest the state's power over the minds of its citizens. Moreover, the state's abandonment of its traditional anticlericalism came at a moment when the influence of Catholicism—so pervasive that it described itself "first and foremost as a culture"[1]—had begun to recede. The "leaden cape"[2] long draped over French society—in reaction to which a flourishing free-thought movement emerged in the eighteenth century that provided alternative forms of sociability and encouraged a combative secularism that for much of the nineteenth and twentieth centuries was sustained through the vigorous efforts of the state[3]—had at last been lifted.

For want of combatants, the fundamental conflict that structured French society for almost two hundred years appeared finally to have extinguished itself. Both parties had fed on a struggle that justified utter intransigence, absolute loyalty on the part of their respective armies; now all of a sudden they were talking to each other, meeting with each other, living together with mutual respect. The state reached out to the Church—without, however, renouncing its own preeminence. Bishops were invited to take part in deliberations of state, to give advice on this or that crisis (such as the violent secessionist movement in New Caledonia, where a delegation was sent that included representatives of the Catholic Church and the Protestant Federation, and even a former grand master of the Grand Lodge of France), and to evaluate the ethical consequences of ministerial decisions on questions pertaining to nationality, medical practice (notably in connection with AIDS), and so on.[4]

Now suddenly presidents of the Republic, from Charles de Gaulle to Georges Pompidou and Jacques Chirac, and ministers such as Raymond Barre and Édouard Balladur, openly displayed their Catholic faith, and the media lingered outside the churches where they privately attended mass. Now suddenly François Mitterrand, the Jacobin who Girondized France, revealed himself to be an agnostic who, in his heart of hearts, admitted that "a mass is possible." Now suddenly several ministers of Alain Juppé's government revealed their strong and activist Catholic commitment, one or two even associating themselves with the ideas of Opus Dei.[5] And now suddenly the énarques, the grand servants of the state, let it be known that they too were regular churchgoers. Many prefects and inspectors of public finances acknowledged having received a Catholic education,[6] and one prefect of the Republic, in the Var, even justified his unusually conservative record by the depth of his Catholic faith. Similarly, a deputy public prosecutor in Paris, seeking to remove a movie poster advertising Milos Forman's 1996 film *The People vs. Larry Flynt*, declared: "We are a Christian country, I mean one with Christians at its base, even if the churches are not as full as they used to be. Its roots, its education, its morality are sacrosanct!"[7] The state had yielded, and the Church regained a central place in the life of the nation. The resurgence of religious belief gave all denominations a new vitality, and the cult of a militant, republican citizenry, notwithstanding a few brief fits and starts, gradually faded away. The world of the freethinkers now seemed a distant memory.

The surprising episode of François Mitterrand's funeral in January 1996 is worth dwelling upon for a moment. Memorial services were held not only at Notre-Dame in Paris but also at the parish church in Jarnac—religious services for the man who had reunited the Communists and Socialists; the champion of Enlightenment values, the Revolution, and the Republic; the man whom the wildly enthusiastic people of the Left had cheered at the Place de la Bastille on the day of his election to the presidency in May 1981. Coming on the heels of revelations of Mitterrand's Vichyist sympathies and the friendships he maintained with the likes of Bousquet, this unforeseen return to the bosom of the Church aroused feelings of betrayal in his followers. To be sure, during the course of his first election campaign, the president had plastered on every wall in France a picture of himself and, in the background, a small village with its familiar and reassuring steeple—a picture that provoked widespread comment. But his burial, ostentatiously organized by a willing Republic, seemed suddenly to "bury one of [the Republic's] own founding principles: the separation of church and state"[8] and signaled the emergence of a questioning of identity and cultural belonging. While the Jarnac funeral certainly surprised devout Catholics, it also satisfied the "multicultural France for which avowals of denominational attachment took on, beyond any religious commitment, a new meaning."[9] Thus Mitterrand's successor as president, Jacques Chirac, addressing the nation on television, stated unequivocally, "Catholic commitment has become, beyond the war of the two Frances, one ideological option among others and, at the same time, a choice that personally involves the person who makes it."[10] By this the chief of state meant simply that apart from the exercise of his duties as head of state, he considered himself a man of faith; but the effect of his remarks was to abolish the traditional distance between public service and religious belief—something that de Gaulle, a practicing Catholic, would probably never have done.[11]

If this public act, which declared the cultural identity of the highest official of the state, aroused scarcely any protest, people were nonetheless stunned to learn that the Church would be responsible for organizing the ritual observances of national mourning. This privatization of the executive office, this public unfolding of private beliefs, echoed the publicity surrounding François Mitterrand's final illness. Because the state had made the personal fate of the president of the Republic an occasion for openly addressing matters of death, nothingness, and resurrection, the public display of spiritual anxiety, day after day, affected its secular character as well. Since "in a republic, the chief of state is not seen as personally embodying the nation,"[12] by Mitterrand's funeral ceremony, by erasing the distinction between church and state, abruptly raised the question of national identity.

Additionally, the revelation of a private love life was deliberately projected onto the public stage, prefiguring similar confidences that further privatized the office and desacralized it. The president was revealed to be a man no different than other men, preoccupied with his own identity, his own tastes, his own mortality. Quite unlike the republican funerals of an earlier time, which had been arranged with all the pomp and symbolism of a regime intent on paying homage to its leaders and to its great men, Mitterrand's funeral ceremony assigned to a weakened (indeed, exhausted) Church the role of clarifying a national identity that had become blurred—as though, after two hundred years of dispute, the nature of this identity had suddenly ceased to be a subject of contention. With this ceremony, the boundaries between the Republic and the Church were virtually abolished, allowing the community of believers and the community of citizens to join together: old-style secularists mixed with die-hard *intégriste* Catholics, while Protestants, Jews, and Muslims were left to contemplate a symbolic union that memorialized a singular republican-Catholic identity.

This rapprochement suddenly rendered the antagonisms of the past obsolete. In 1996 a national committee was established to commemorate the fifteen hundredth anniversary of the baptism of Clovis. Introducing the committee, made up mostly of historians and Catholic dignitaries, the prime minister, Alain Juppé, declared that the secular state could neither "obscure the authentically religious dimension of the baptism of Clovis" nor "ignore the essential place that is due to religious faith in the constitution of the national heritage."[13] The Church rejoiced in this celebration, but it did so with prudence and moderation, so much so that Monsignor Bernard Defois, archbishop of Reims, expressed the opinion—to the exasperation of hard-line Catholics, of whom there were now fewer than in the past—that "one cannot say that the day Clovis was baptized all of France became Christian. First, a man was converted to Christ." In Defois's view, "Christianity is one of the seeds of the culture of France." For his part, Jean-Marie Cardinal Lustiger, archbishop of Paris, emphasized that "the idea of a 'Christian nation' is an un-Christian idea. . . . To speak of a Christian nation is a way of referring to a people whose culture and history are marked by the faith of its members. But this is never an established and stable reality. . . . There are no Christian nations, as there are French-speaking nations, for example." Lustiger added: "There is not one France born with the baptism of Clovis [in 496] and another France born with the victory at Valmy [over the foreign coalition of counterrevolutionary armies in 1792]. Clovis and Valmy belong to the memory of everyone."

Far from claiming that this ceremony symbolized the essentially Christian nature of France, the Church's spokesmen unreservedly endorsed the new republican-Catholic identity whose contours had been sketched by the holders of political power. Church and state were now seen as coexisting within the framework of a consensual society open to non-Catholics. Going further still, the secularist Catholic association Chrétiens École Laïque saw "a plural France, where ethnic, regional, philosophical, and cultural differences, open to each other, tend to become integrated," while *Études*, the journal of the Jesuits, expressed the fear that the commemoration of Clovis's baptism would "lead to the exclusion of whole sections of the national community."[14] It was as if, faced with the disarray of the state, the Church had to take responsibility for a multiculturalism *à la française* by renouncing the view of a France unified in Catholicism. All of this was in keeping with the message of the pope, who invited Catholics on this occasion to enter into dialogue with "all the components of the nation."[15]

This conversion to a cultural pluralism that it had resisted ever since the French Revolution[16] gave the Church a new legitimacy; at the same time, its sudden embrace of the rights of man served to eliminate the last remaining traces of its ancient intolerance.[17] This move disarmed its adversaries and legitimized a republican Catholicism—a "republic of Catholics," pacified at last[18]—that, by virtue of its openness to the presence of other faiths, lacked any precise cultural identity. Nor was it entirely free of ambiguity. Even in the more tolerant perspective of Vatican II, as the political theorist Philippe Portier argues, the Catholic Church to some extent "reproduces still today the 'medieval' pattern of temporal dependence in relation to the divine principle. . . . It still refuses to endow the state sphere with the 'fullness of power.' "[19] Similarly, the political values of the bishops seem generally incompatible with political democracy, since a high proportion of them openly prefer a society organized along corporatist lines, in accordance with an organic theory of democracy.[20] In 1972, at Lourdes, the plenary assembly of the French episcopate ratified political pluralism while at the same time taking issue with the "unacceptable dualism" that limited the influence of the Church. It held that the Church "should be one of the places where civic friendship is forged. . . . In a country where Catholicism is [the] majority [faith], the very existence of the Church cannot be without political repercussions, on account of the permanent influence that it exercises. . . . We recognize the ineluctable 'weight' of the Church; [this weight] confers upon it an influence in the struggle waged by men and parties to conserve, exercise, and conquer power."[21]

Fifteen years later, in 1987, the episcopate's plenary assembly reaffirmed this position: while acknowledging the "ever more pronounced pluralism" that was emerging in France, it nonetheless proclaimed that "in this country, [which was] woven out of Christian tradition down to its customs and its laws, professed

and lived Christianity has been, and remains, a precious and in-
alienable part of the identity of our people. . . . The Church must
not be, and does not wish to be, an interest group."[22] In effect,
then, the Church emphasized its openness to other faiths in order
to demand for itself a privileged role due to the quasi-immanence
of Catholicism within French culture. As Cardinal Lustiger put it,
"If the young are not put in possession of what constitutes the secret heart, the center of gravity, the main juncture of French culture, then they will not wholly acquire it later. For me, what gives
French culture its coherence (in its historical, philosophical, literary, and artistic dimensions) is Christian conscience. If therefore
one does not convey to the young [a sense of] the preponderant
place due to Christianity . . . then our civilization will lose the
traits and characteristics that provide it with its identity and its
coherence."[23]

By the same token, the cardinal's support for republican
Catholicism did not prevent him from claiming a Christian origin
for the rights of man, nor from firmly condemning a commemoration of 1789 that minimized the persecutions of Catholics—
priests and believers alike. Nor did he wish to have anything to
do with certain aspects of this celebration of the Revolution, such
as the transfer to the Panthéon of the remains of Abbé Grégoire,
the most famous partisan of the still hated Civil Constitution of
the Clergy. No matter that political circumstances in 1989 were
quite different from a hundred years earlier, when republicans engaged in unrestrained combat with Catholics; Lustiger nonetheless hastened to emphasize that "1789 [is] a date still painfully
engraved in the French consciousness,"[24] and that "Abbé Grégoire's conception of the Church, [his conception] of a national
religion, is contrary to the Catholic religion." In Lustiger's view,
"For the majority of the French, the Revolution is over, but the
work of cleansing [national] memory and mutually facing up to
the past has not been finished. I regret this."[25] Accordingly, the
archbishop pleaded for the complete reintegration of Catholicism
into French public life, on the one hand categorically rejecting
the temptation to assert the autonomy of the French Church in

relation to Rome and, on the other, approving the separation of church and state in a form that owed more to Jules Ferry's style of anticlericalism than to Émile Combes's more extreme version. Just the same, the Church still resisted Clemenceau's formula ("The Revolution is all of a piece"): while accepting the fact of the Revolution, the Church intended to give it a spiritual interpretation compatible with its own message. In the words of one prominent Catholic commentator, "The notions of Christian state and atheist state are henceforth to be banished. We have entered into a world of reciprocal rights that each person must be able to use without abusing them."[26]

By stressing its tolerance of pluralism (while nonetheless claiming a privileged place in the life of the nation) and its respect for the state (to such an extent that the state sometimes demanded its help), the Church moved to settle its differences with a Republic that had retreated from militant anticlericalism. But hard-line Catholics, the heirs of Maistre, were infuriated by the retreat of the Church from reactionary ideals. Grouped around Monsignor Marcel Lefebvre, they denounced "Satan's masterstroke,"[27] which consisted in somehow arranging for "the Church [to] convert to the heretical, Jewish, pagan world," and in this way assuring the triumph of liberalism within it. In Monsignor Lefebvre's view, "the Masonic and anti-Catholic principles of the French Revolution have had two centuries to penetrate the minds of priests and bishops."[28] Echoing the opinions of the antirevolutionary priest Abbé Barruel, he argued that

> Catholic, or so-called Catholic, liberalism served as a Trojan horse enabling its false principles to penetrate inside the Church. It wanted to marry the Church and the Revolution. . . . The most eminent members of the Church have been contaminated by universalist ideas. . . . We find ourselves under the continuing influence of the philosophers of the eighteenth century and of the upheaval that their ideas provoked in the world. Those who have transmitted this poison to the Church admit doing so themselves.[29]

Conservative Catholics, faithful to the Maistrean counterrevolution and to Maurras's program—not troubling to conceal the depth of their anti-Semitism, their hostility toward the Revolution, or their loyalty to the memory of Pétain and the OAS of the Algerian war—proposed to reconstruct a Catholic state in conformity with their concept of French identity. By establishing a network of primary and secondary schools, where new textbooks would teach the "ideal of the crusader" and strict discipline would reign, these Catholics "to the extreme right of God"[30] attempted to repair the rupture between citizenship and identity so that children might feel "completely Catholic" in both the public and private spheres.[31] A similarly radical rejection of a secularized political world appeared within a part of the born-again Christian movement that had not broken its ties with Rome. Urban fundamentalist Catholic groups such as Emmanuel, living in closed utopian communities and professing an absolute and unyielding hatred of the republican political order, prepared to do battle with the Devil: "Our modern Goliath wishes to kill the soul of children. The Holy Ghost mobilizes us for a crusade of love. Truly it is a crusade, for the Devil wishes to kill the faith within us."[32]

These many Catholic traditionalists opposed the commemoration of 1789 with a vehemence worthy of the early stages of the counterrevolution. In January 1989, *Le Chardonnet* (the parish newsletter of Saint-Nicolas-du-Chardonnet in Paris, with a print run of 7,000 but very probably read by almost three times that number) thundered as Maistre had done against the Revolution: "Satan vs. Christ—this is what the France of 1989 is celebrating in full array, all parties united [against Christ]. . . . All against God and war without mercy against what is left of Christianity in France!"[33] This fundamentalist parish devoted much of its energy that year to organizing a

Catholic and national [act] of reparation. On 15 August 1989 France will awaken. It will, if not officially, at least publicly, make reparation for the betrayals, the crimes, the horrors, the sacrileges of the Revolution. At the Place de la

Concorde, the very place where the Very Christian King and so many victims were sacrificed, . . . our fervent throng will offer to God on high the homage of its adoration, its praises, and its reparation.[34]

Abbé Pierre Laguérie, who officiated in this center of Catholic fundamentalism and also ran the Association 15 Août 1989, wrote: "We cannot let this outrage pass without reacting. Together with the Vendeans who gave their blood for their God, we must denounce the grand imposture of 1789 and, setting principle against principle, oppose to the 'rights of man' the social royalty of Our Lord Jesus Christ."[35]

Two conservative journals with close links to the National Front took up the Maistrean anthem. Chrétienté-Solidarité accused the Revolution of "eradicating the faith of our forefathers," while L'Anti-89 proclaimed that "France begot revolution. The counterrevolution will be the light of Christian Europe. It cannot wait. There is no time to lose. God wills it." In the view of the extreme right-wing pamphleteer François Brigneau, "L'Anti-89 prevented the conciliar Church from fully participating in the commemorations. It made [the Church] cautious and ashamed. The only Catholic movement was a counterrevolutionary movement."[36] Another journal of the Catholic far Right, Présent, tirelessly repeated the slogan "Catholic laws for Catholic people." Éléments, not to be outdone, went back to Burke, Bonald, and Maistre in order to denounce 1789 and the "new masters," the Socialists who had gotten rich by wheeling and dealing, protected by "abstract reason" until the moment when Providence would come at last to give back to Catholicism its rightful place.[37]

Conservative Catholics distanced themselves still further from the Church by militantly supporting the commemoration of Clovis, calling upon France to use the occasion to renew its "alliance," to become once again the "apostle of Christ" and the "eldest daughter of the Church." For the Association du XVe Centenaire de la France, the "baptism of Clovis was also [the baptism] of France." France's true identity was to be found in Catholicism, not in the French Revolution or the strong state. Addressing himself to those who "miss no opportunity to caricature the history of France and to glorify the French Revolution," Father Jean-Paul Argouac'h, an ally of Action Française, asked that "it be permitted to us to show how bright a beacon in the darkness is the cathedral of Reims." Echoing him, Alain Griotteray, an RPR deputy, wrote in the *Journal du XVᵉ centenaire*: "The rupture of 1789 is unbearable because it denied the prior secular accomplishments [of the Church]." In the same issue, Patrice de Plunket, a journalist formerly associated with the right-wing Groupement de Recherche et d'Études pour la Civilisation Européenne [Research and Study Group for European Civilization (GRECE)] and now the editor of *Figaro-Magazine*, attacked the bishops of France who "snub the bishops of Gaul," the roots of French identity being found there rather than anywhere else, as "the *énarques* believe"—in spite, one might add, of their avowed Catholic beliefs.[38]

Writing in the pages of *L'Action française*, Clovis's eulogists sought to protect the Christian uniformity of French society by inviting "the immigrants to be baptized."[39] Other integrist Catholics waged a violent campaign against the Church's reconciliation with the Republic, which they saw as subverted by Protestant ideas, indeed as de-Christianized—Judaized. Hurling abuse in the spirit of Maurras against the supporters of "doctrinal relativism," Abbé Aulagnier, the strict overseer of the province of France for the Society of Saint Pius X (the largest fundamentalist organization in the world, which calls for a return to "Catholic monarchy"), made it clear that neither Muslims—adherents of an utterly "fanatical" religion—nor the "deicidal Hebrew people" had any place in the "Catholic heritage of France."[40]

Far from approving the Church's acceptance (however ambivalent) of cultural diversity, the various hard-line Catholic tendencies carried on the battle in favor of a unified France, rejecting all forms of pluralism contrary to revealed truth. For Monsignor Lefebvre, to give the impression that the Catholic Church defends the freedom of all religions is not possible, for it cannot defend the freedom of error. To demand the freedom of all religions to be able, like the Catholic religion, to express themselves outwardly, to have their [own] press, their institutions, their schools, their temples, is to tread on very dangerous ground. Because then one day we are going to see temples and mosques everywhere, and Catholics will be able to say nothing because they will themselves have agreed to grant freedom to error. . . . Those popes who were not liberals, who remained firm in their faith, always expressly distinguished the true [religion] from false religions. . . . False religions were invented by the Devil.[41]

While it is "relatively easy" to convert Protestants, Lefebvre remarked, it is "virtually impossible to convert Muslims" and "one never knows whether Jews truly convert. . . . It is very difficult to tell."[42]

Fiercely attached to Maistre's dream, this movement mobilized thousands of the faithful during the great traditional pilgrimages to Chartres and Lourdes,[43] ran churches, convents, monasteries, and schools in almost all the departments of France, sponsored petitions that were widely circulated, and exercised influence over various political organizations. Even so, fundamentalist Catholics were still a long way from constituting a force comparable to the one that, a century earlier, was able to do battle on almost equal terms with the Third Republic. Theirs was a rearguard action in a society in which conventional religious belief had resolutely turned away from the uncompromising ideals of Maistre and the propagandist and reactionary bishops—notably Veuillot, Dupanloup, Freppel, and Lefebvre—who followed in his footsteps. It seemed all the more out of place in a Catholic landscape where, as Jean-Marie Cardinal Lustiger put it, "history teaches Christians modesty. . . . Purely religious confrontation is one of the fields where it is necessary to work together, so that crucial points may be addressed without fear and in truth. Christians, Jews, and

Muslims are brothers who must enlighten and help each other on the paths of peace."[44] French Catholicism had turned its back on fundamentalism, admitting the truth of other faiths and accepting their presence within an open and multifaceted society. Thus the catechism—still taught to 40 percent of French children by more than 200,000 parochial school teachers who continued to transmit a powerful message—now attached vital importance to the rights of man and respect for cultural differences in the political socialization of these future citizens.[45]

The *intégriste* reaction appeared all the more out of step with the times since, within the very heart of Catholicism, a religious pluralism had grown up that engendered increasingly diverse ways of believing. An "à la carte" Catholicism involving the most varied "modalities of belief"[46] was gradually replacing the uniform Catholic belief of the past. As if to confirm official Church teaching that even a small dose of relativism fatally undermines belief in a unique truth,[47] a majority of the French population (52 percent in 1990) felt that fundamental truths and significance could be found in all religions. (In 1994, 72 percent said they did not believe that "there is a single true religion.") A growing proportion considered that no religion offered truth and that, accordingly, "in our day each person must define his religion for himself independently of the churches" (71 percent in 1994). Certainty in the existence of God fell from 51 percent in 1952 to 31 percent in 1986; belief in hell fell to 16 percent in 1990, and in the Devil to 19 percent, while doctrines of resurrection and reincarnation merged in an ever vaster syncretism that accommodated "parallel beliefs" such as telepathy, spiritualism, and astrology. By 1995 only 75 out of 100 people in France called themselves Catholics.

All indicators of participation in institutional rites pointed downward. The rate of baptism, still high in 1958 at 92 percent, had dropped to 64 percent in 1987; by 1992 no more than about 40 percent of children aged 8 to 14 received catechetical instruction. During the same period only 50 percent of couples had official marriages; over the course of thirty years, weekly attendance fell from 25 percent to about 15 percent, and monthly attendance from 33 percent to about 20 percent. In 1994, only 8 percent of French Catholics said they had gone to confession that year.[48] Similarly, the firm stance taken by the Church on abortion, divorce, and sexuality (despite some gradual modifications) proved to be far removed from the more liberal sentiments expressed by the population.[49] The upheaval in French Catholicism and the turning away from religion particularly affected young people: in the 18 to 34 age group, a feeling of Catholic attachment was now shared by only 37 percent; weekly observance stood at 3 percent, and monthly observance at 7 percent. Only 11 percent were convinced that Catholicism is the sole religion anchored in truth, while belief in the parasciences and astrology showed signs of growth among young and old Catholics as well.[50] In a society that was one of the most secularized in Europe, the dogmas professed by the Church met with greater resistance than in the past.

At the same time, a wholly spiritual sort of religiosity was blossoming. Religious belief was now widely experienced as a vital force detached from Catholic culture, and religion itself had become an essentially private affair, remote from the Church as an institution, associated with a personal reading of the Bible, disconnected from historical tradition. Indeed, it was almost foreign to the Catholic holism that, as late as the end of the nineteenth century, still claimed to govern French identity. A profound crisis of vocations for the priesthood further assisted this crucial transformation. The traditional figure of the local priest slowly disappeared from the large cities as well as from certain rural areas, weakening the life of parishes, which were now left to their own devices. Ordinations fell sharply (from about a thousand a year in 1950 to a hundred or so in 1995 and 1996); seminaries failed, with the result that in 1997 the number of monks and nuns was half what it was twenty years earlier (when there were about 100,000); and the number of diocesan priests dropped from 41,000 in 1979 to 25,700.[51] All these upheavals led to a decline in the authority of the Church, which now permitted lay Catholics greater autonomy outside its structures in counseling the young, preparing for marriage, and filling the chaplaincies of prisons and hospitals. At the same time, charismatic communities such as Charismatic Revival and Emmanuel attracted vocations and passionate commitments, and pilgrimages enjoyed an unprecedented popularity. The conversion of many Catholics to religious pluralism and an increasingly individual conception of religious faith had the effect of blurring denominational boundaries while, at the same time, undermining the institutional identity of the Church and affecting the way it operated within society. Now that "extramural" Catholicism had wholly given way to an individualization of belief, religious identifications henceforth appeared partial and religious identities plural.[52]

The sudden and dramatic diversification of belief among French Catholics dealt a severe blow to the old monism—the dream of a society uniformly devoted to a single faith—and relegated great clashes of principle to the past, eroding the very strong bonds that had linked religious practice and political behavior. The particularly close relation between religious belief and support for the Right that once characterized the Catholic electorate began to subside, disrupting a pattern long taken for granted. Regular observance among Catholic voters was no longer customarily associated with an automatic preference for right-wing parties, in part because of the waning influence of Catholicism—a univocal bloc shaped by its opposition to the French Revolution and its rejection of liberalism—in reinforcing politically conservative tendencies among its adherents. Despite the Catholic world's abiding rejection of the society produced by the revolutionary dream,[53] the appearance of internal divisions and multiple sensibilities during the course of the twentieth century worked to undermine the old quasi-uniformity of political belief.

In our own day, the internal transformation of Catholicism testifies to the scope of an event that, as the political scientist Jean-Marie Donegani points out, "truly marks the turning point of recent years: the penetration of Catholicism, via religious avenues, by principles it [had] officially repudiated on the political level," with liberalism "silently imposing the terms of debate."[54]

Pluralism had at last managed to establish itself, shattering the old unity. As a result, in the 1997 legislative elections the share of votes cast for the Right by people who called themselves Catholics fell substantially by comparison with the same elections eleven years earlier, from 54 percent in February 1986 to 42 percent today. To be sure, the Right preserved its privileged position among the Catholic electorate—the Socialists attracted only 26 percent of ballots cast by Catholics; nonetheless, it is important to note the vigorous role played by Catholics in transforming the Socialist Party during the Mitterrand years.[55] Practicing Catholics broke ranks more and more frequently with the official intransigence of years past, declaring their preference for the moderate Right especially forcefully and rejecting the ideas of the National Front. Indeed, the more regular the rate of religious observance, the stronger the hostility expressed toward Le Pen's movement.[56] In the 1997 elections, only 12 percent of Catholics cast their ballot for the National Front.[57]

The declericalization of French Catholicism led in turn to a more frank acceptance of secularism. While conservatives remained true to their proud tradition of radical opposition, accusing "secular fundamentalists" of hosting "a carnival of Satan" inspired by "hatred of God,"[58] the Church moved to inaugurate a dialogue with republicans, most of whom had pulled back from their former anticlericalism and renounced their old "crusading spirit."[59] While the spiritual children of *petit père* Combes resolved to close ranks and answer all attacks on secularism—organizing lively banquets mocking believers on the occasion of " 'Good' Friday"[60]—traditionally anticlerical organizations such as the Ligue Française de l'Enseignement, a teachers' association, recognized that "the clergy and, still more, the faithful have accepted, at least within the framework of the French nation, the principle of the separation of church and state." The association, for its part, solemnly agreed to admit,

> as against the dominant opinion of lay people in the nineteenth and early twentieth centuries, that diversity and plu-

ralism are no longer contrary to the unity of the Republic and that religions—among other things—are no longer a divisive factor in secularized French society; to recognize, as a consequence, that unity cannot be confused with uniformity, which is the totalitarian perversion of it; to recognize that the "right to roots"—religious [roots] included—must be combined with the right to options. . . . We have accepted religions as enduring cultural facts out of which France has been made.[61]

The battle between the anticlerical and secular traditions had therefore reached a critical turning point.[62] Even if "extreme minorities were still to be found on both sides,"[63] secularism had finally lost its demonic dimension; and a rapprochement between freethinkers and Catholics, unimaginable only a short while ago, was now at last coming to pass. Indeed, from now on, as Claude Nicolet has argued, "the true criterion is not whether one is a secularist but whether one is republican."[64]

If French secularism remained exceptional by comparison with the rest of Europe,[65] the Church gradually was to adapt to the emergence of a "new secularism." The first step was to reject its former image as a countersociety that threatened the Republic. Monsignor Jean Vilnet, in his address to the plenary conference of the episcopate in 1987, expressed the view that "the hour seems to have come to work with others to redefine the institutional framework of secularism. . . . The churches, and religions in general, can work together to educate the public. . . . We should stand ready to identify the common values that are capable of providing a basis for 'living together.' "[66] The following year, before the same assembly, Monsignor Albert Decoutray, chairman of the conference, envisioned the possibility "of freeing secularism from secularist ideology, from anticlerical and clerical suspicion," and asked, "How can the institutional framework of secularism be given a content that will make it possible to bring forth, to the benefit of the nation as a whole, the resources, the dynamism, and the hopes of all its members?"[67] In the opinion of the bishops,

"[T]here has in fact been a sudden shift from a secular state that possesses a common morality, to a view of society as pluralist. . . . The raison d'être of secularism is to make possible democratic co-operation within democratic society. The Christian churches live alongside Judaism, Freemasonry, free thought, and indeed Marxist thought as well."[68] The bishops then concluded their work by forcefully declaring that "the Church has no privilege to demand, only the social space necessary to its own existence and its own affirmation. And this, of course, with respect for all other faiths and spiritual families."[69] In 1991 the social commission of the episcopate recognized that "the principle of secularism is an important and necessary achievement: it cannot be called into question. But it must enrich public life rather than empty it, serve it rather than enslave it."[70]

Just when prospects for reconciliation seemed bright, a controversy erupted over the wearing of headscarves in public schools by Muslim girls. Republican secularist ideals abruptly regained incendiary dimensions, arousing passions on all sides and imparting fresh impetus to the nationalist campaign against an alleged "North African invasion." Just as the Dreyfus Affair had done a century earlier, the *affaire des foulards* unexpectedly dramatized the question of French identity while blurring exactly what was at issue. In mid-October 1989, the principal of the Collège de Creil in Oise, firmly supported by the school's teachers, expelled three girls for refusing to remove their veils in class. Although similar incidents had occurred elsewhere, it was the Creil case that put the issue of secularism back at the heart of public debate. The principal, Ernest Chénière, who later became the parliamentary deputy for Oise and carried on his campaign against the "insidious jihad" in the National Assembly, was now seen as the chief spokesman for secularism: "The school is French," he said, "it is in the town of Creil, and it is secular. We will not let ourselves be plagued by religious problems."[71]

His ejection of the girls immediately drew sharp protests. The Mouvement contre le Racisme et pour l'Amitié entre les Peuples [Movement Against Racism and for Friendship Among Peoples

(MRAP)] objected that other communities displayed their religious attachments without fear of punishment. Another left-wing organization that had converted to the new secularism—a secularism attentive to religion—advocated by the Church, SOS-Racisme, came to the defense of community identities within the public sphere, arguing that no sanction should be imposed on pupils on account of their faith. Lionel Jospin, then minister of education, stalled, adopting a tolerant and pragmatic attitude before finally referring the matter to the Council of State. In the meantime the polemic intensified between partisans of Jacobin "leveling" and intellectuals from quite varied (indeed, sometimes opposite) backgrounds who joined the Church in supporting the recognition of differences in public schools. This alignment represented a considerable change: no longer was the Church alone in its desire to give republican ideals a new basis. Not only did its position resonate among Socialist and Communist organizations concerned with defending immigrant identities; now Protestant pastors and rabbis—who had been sympathetic to hard-line republican secularism at the turn of the century, when combating staunch Catholicism was the order of the day—joined with the Catholic Church in supporting the Muslim girls.

Beyond the issue of the veil, all these parties felt the necessity of defending the visibility of religious symbols. Cardinal Lustiger exclaimed, "Let us not make war on teen-aged *beurs*—cease fire!" Claudette Marquet, spokeswoman of the Protestant Federation, stated that "Protestants do not think there is any reason to prohibit the wearing of the veil at school," and warned: "France now shakes off its drowsiness to go to war against a religion—an old story that ought to be a reminder for Protestants."[72] By working on behalf of religious visibility for all, did the Protestants hope to regain visibility for themselves? It did not escape notice that the Protestant triumvirate of Michel Rocard, Lionel Jospin, and Pierre Joxe played a decisive role in defending the girls.[73] Whereas at the turn of the century Protestant secularizers such as Jules Steeg and Ferdinand Buisson had laid stress on the radical character of secularism, challenging the preeminent position of the Catholic

Church in public life, these three advocated adapting secularism to modern realities by adopting an attitude of tolerance toward all faiths, recommending pluralism as a more wholesome alternative to the old obsession with uniformity. Similarly, whereas the Jewish deputy Camille Dreyfus and the Jewish senior civil servants Ernest Hendlé and Paul Grunebaum-Ballin had earlier made every effort to give effect to republican legislation,[74] Jewish consistorial officials promptly came to the aid of the young Muslims. Thus the grand rabbi of Paris declared: "Those who refuse Muslim children the right to wear the chador or Jewish children the right to wear the kippah are intolerant. Today it is not religious persons who display intolerance, as they are so often reproached for doing, but lay people. The secular school must set an example of tolerance."[75] And the grand rabbi of France, Joseph Sitruk, wondered: "Must a pupil be forced to renounce his religious convictions in order to attend a public school, which constitutes an attack on the free exercise of worship, or can this pupil be permitted, in the name of freedom of worship, to be excused on Saturdays while assuming full responsibility for this choice (catching up with course work and so on), thus showing that the French are allowed to be responsible citizens while remaining faithful to their religious convictions?"[76]

On the other side, an equally mixed coalition formed in support of the principal, Chénière, that included representatives of the feminist movement as well as of certain groups within the Socialist Party led by Jean-Pierre Chevènement, who complained about these "damned shawls."[77] (In a highly provocative gesture, two Socialist deputies, former schoolteachers, took up their places on the benches of the National Assembly wearing Muslim headscarves.)[78] The teachers' unions also supported Chénière. Yannick Simbron, secretary general of the Fédération de l'Éducation Nationale [Federation of National Education (FEN)], argued that "the right to education must take precedence over the right of religious beliefs and customs to respect," while Michel Boullier, secretary general of the Syndicat Générale de l'Éducation Nationale [General Union for National Education (SGEN)], exclaimed: "The rise of fundamentalism now uses students to reach the schools. Down with headscarves!"[79] Also joining in were the secular old guard—Socialists and Radicals—of the southwest, along with the Communists (*L'Humanité*, for example, denounced Lionel Jospin's "capitulation" before "disturbing fanaticisms");[80] the Gaullists, who intervened in the name of the nation; and the moderate Catholic Right, which did not hide its hostility to Islam.

Chénière's supporters also included the extreme Right, which presented itself as the sole movement capable of preserving the homogeneity of French identity. But it seemed to be of two minds, sometimes converting the battle against the veil into a war against the Islamic world as the enemy of national identity (Jean-Marie Le Pen asserted that the veils illustrated "the colonization of France"),[81] sometimes attaching a positive value to the same veils out of respect for ethnic differences (which, to Le Pen's mind, logically implied the expulsion of foreigners from France and their return to faraway homelands). To everyone's astonishment, these various wholesale rejections of Muslim identity enabled the National Front to triumph in the legislative by-election in Dreux in December 1989—a veritable thunderclap over the French political landscape that heralded the *lepéniste* explosion at the national level. In the ensuing fracas, all the old arguments were hauled out again and stood on their heads, contradicting each other in an inextricable confusion since the strategies of the various parties, in both camps, were not merely diverse but often incompatible. The press fanned the flames, running cartoons of Marianne cloaked in a veil that was variously called a *tchador*, a *hidjeb*, or a *khiemar*, the better to emphasize its foreign aspect; sometimes simply a shawl or headcovering or headscarf, when the media wished to downplay the issue, in support of those calling for assimilation rather than exclusion.[82]

Many hastily conducted polls seemed to suggest that the French people felt a real hostility toward the wearing of the veil in school.[83] Opening a Pandora's box that would long stay unshut, the weekly magazine *Le Nouvel Observateur* sternly lectured SOS-Racisme:

Democracy is not a contentless form on which each person is free to impose his prejudices. It is not a bring-your-own-sectarianism resort, a Club Méditerranée where nice leaders organize activities for nice citizens. It, too, has certain shrines where one must remove one's hat, one's kippah, and one's headscarf. . . . For once, it is the prohibition that liberates. Without it, [religious] believers would never believe that we believe in something as well.[84]

In the same issue, a group of five vehemently secular intellectuals (including Régis Debray and Alain Finkielkraut) harshly criticized Lionel Jospin's handling of the matter in an open letter to the minister of education[85] that distilled the essence of the Jacobin position:

The future will decide if the year of the bicentennial will have seen the Munich of the republican school. . . . It is necessary that pupils have the leisure to forget their community of origin. . . . If one wants teachers to be able to help them and the school to remain what it is, a place of emancipation, [religious] attachments must not dictate the law to schools. . . . The right to difference that is so dear to you is a freedom only if it is matched by the right to be different from one's difference. In the contrary case, it is a trap, indeed an enslavement. . . . The partisans of the "new secularism," in whose ranks you place yourself, advocate a vague tolerance. They want a school open to community and religious pressures . . . in which each student is constantly identified with his parents, reminded of his condition, tied to his "roots": this is a school of social predestination.[86]

Echoing the doctrines of the Comte de Clermont-Tonnerre, the deputy of the National Constituent Assembly who proposed the emancipation of the Jews in 1789—but also, and especially, the (not altogether ambivalent) position of Abbé Grégoire—these defenders of an emancipating universalism went to the heart of the matter: secularism remained incompatible with a multiplicity of communities. They rejected the discussion of differences supported by the churches and by SOS-Racisme, the post-1968 Left, and—albeit for opposite reasons—the followers of GRECE and the National Front. If the Republic intends to remain faithful to the revolutionary message that grounds French exceptionalism, they argued, it must preserve citizenship, work toward the elimination of differences, resist the temptations of multiculturalism, promote assimilation and adherence to reason, and defend a militant and liberating secularism.

Their philippic aroused a good deal of protest. The historian Jacques Le Goff weighed in against the "secularism of resistance, . . . this Maginot line of secularism"[87]—not a very formidable line of defense, perhaps, considering how ineffective the original Maginot line was. The letter's uncompromising stance on behalf of a doctrine peculiar to French intellectuals, refusing the least concession to the spirit of the times, recalled the campaign that one of the authors, Régis Debray, had enthusiastically mounted against the "Republic of the Center." Debray now associated the abandonment of radical secularism with the replacement of the Republic by a democracy open to every sort of pluralism and therefore, to his mind, to every sort of compromise, in which the spirit of 1789 would inevitably be lost: "In a republic, each person is defined as a citizen. . . . In a democracy, each person is defined by his 'community.' . . . A republic has no black mayors, yellow senators, Jewish ministers, or atheist school principals. A democracy has black governors, white mayors, and Mormon senators. Fellow citizen does not mean coreligionist."[88] A few months before, Debray had exclaimed: "*Vivement les jacobins!* . . . The return of ethnic groups announces the grand return of religion. . . . Each person brings his faith, his grandmother, his money. Gangs—take your marks. War of all against all. Saint Bartholomew's Day massacres are the result of devalued and domesticated central powers."[89]

Alain Finkielkraut, employing similar rhetoric, maintained that "class is an abstract place that must not be transformed into juxtapositions of communities. . . . The French version of democracy is the republic. It is not the Anglo-American model. It is necessary to defend this version because [the French] model of integration is superior, I believe, to the one that prevails in America and in England."[90] The end of universalism, of the republican ideal, of Marxism, would encourage cultural pluralism and raise the specter of America—the antimodel simplistically identified with the growing power of ethnic and religious communities, ignoring its fundamental civic dimension.[91] It would destroy secularism, the pedestal of the republic of citizens freed from particularist attachments; abolish French exceptionalism; and, in time, assure both the ultimate triumph of the Maistrean counterutopia and a return to the wars of religion that preceded the triumph of the state.

Having called for the elimination of distinct cultural identities, the five musketeers of secularism found themselves accused of playing the National Front's game—unfairly, since Jean-Marie Le Pen's party rejected differences on behalf of an exclusionist national identity, whereas the musketeers rejected them in the name of an assimilationist Republic. Still, they had gone off to war a bit late. "To accept fundamentalist displays," they wrote, "no matter whether the fundamentalism is Catholic, Jewish, or Muslim, in school—the only public space common to all that survives today—is to unleash chain reactions of the worst xenophobia. In rejecting differentialist arguments, we signal our solidarity with all those who are opposed to their own community's fundamentalism. Racism cannot be conquered without denouncing fundamentalism."[92]

The 27 November 1989 opinion of the Council of State attempted—with some difficulty—to stake out a middle ground that would reconcile secularism and respect for religious beliefs. In this essential document, which was to leave its mark on the whole of contemporary French jurisprudence, the council argued that "the freedom recognized on the part of children comprises the right to express and to manifest their religious beliefs inside the school, displaying respect for pluralism and the freedom of

The Era of Rival Identities

others and without adversely affecting the activity of teaching, the content of course syllabuses, or the obligation of diligence." Having thus pronounced itself in favor of an open secularism that respects obligations falling upon all pupils, the council came to the crux of the matter: how was the public school system to be made compatible with the expression of religious beliefs without calling into question the French tradition of secularism?

> The wearing by students of symbols by which they mean to manifest their religious attachment is not in and of itself incompatible with the principle of secularism to the extent that it represents the exercise of freedom of expression and a manifestation of religious beliefs. But this freedom cannot permit students to sport emblems of religious affiliation that by their nature, by the conditions in which they are worn, individually or collectively, or by their ostentatious and assertive character constitute an act of intimidation, provocation, proselytizing, or propaganda; threaten the dignity and freedom of students or other members of the educational community; compromise their health or security; disrupt the usual course of instruction and the educational activities of teachers; or, finally, disturb order within the school and interfere with the normal functioning of public education.[93]

Implementation of the Council of State's opinion was left to the judgment of school principals. This was an unsatisfactory state of affairs, however, since it is a matter of opinion whether a symbol of religious conviction has an "ostentatious character," and since there are no clear and simple criteria for deciding whether an attitude "intimidates," or risks compromising the health of students, or threatens to disrupt the life of the school. Despite the plain rules laid down by the Council of State, the problem of how they were to be applied in practice exposed the new doctrine to considerable skepticism. Most commentators felt the council's ruling was unlikely to prevent the personal opinions of school officials from weighing heavily upon their view not only of the wearing of the Islamic headscarf but also of the wearing of the Christian cross and the Jewish kippah—all the more as other issues inevitably came into play as well, such as the question of civil rights of Muslim women subject to the authority of fathers and brothers in their own households. It seemed more probable that the new doctrine would produce disparate local judgments, in some cases licensing an extreme severity contrary to the spirit of the Council of State's ruling, in others a vast laxity at variance with the principle of neutrality. If teachers as well as syllabuses have a duty to respect neutrality, it might be asked, why should the same duty not fall upon students? If freedom of conscience is not considered to be incompatible with the obligations of confidentiality and neutrality incumbent upon teachers, then, out of respect for European Union agreements regarding freedom of religious expression, must not a still greater neutrality be imposed on students as well? But in that case, how far can the display of religious symbols in school be limited without emptying the principle of freedom of conscience of all substance?[94]

The Council of State's opinion, produced by its general assembly, was followed in December 1989 by a memorandum from Lionel Jospin, who adopted the conclusions of the council while adding that

> students' clothes must in no case prevent the normal completion of exercises required in connection with physical education and sports, lab work, and shop . . . ; attempts to avoid medical checkups and vaccinations scheduled in the interest of the health of students and the educational community cannot be accepted. . . . It is only by strictly obeying these regulations that all students can acquire a general education and recognized qualification, regardless of their social, cultural, or geographical origin.[95]

Jospin went out of his way to harshly criticize "ideologues who have reaffirmed an ideal secularism with icy intransigence. . . . It is very important, in this kind of situation, to be careful not to start out on the side of Robespierre and Saint-Just and wind up on the side of Robert Lacoste and Max Lejeune."[96] Implicitly, he accused the advocates of an aggressive secularism of lending their support to the revanchists of the Algerian war, still determined to do battle with Islam. In vigorously attacking the upholders of "abstract universalism" and distancing himself from the "fixed and sometimes pretentious character of the French model," the education minister, while remaining opposed to Anglo-American multiculturalism, challenged the leveling and destructive character of attempts to assimilate cultural attachments.[97]

The council's opinion, together with the ministerial memorandum, led to changes in the internal regulations of many schools. Muslim girls were ordered to stop wearing the headscarf; their parents went to court to challenge the order, unsuccessfully; this judgment was appealed in turn to the Council of State, acting now as a judge of the system of public administration rather than as an adviser to the government. In November 1992 the council clarified its earlier ruling with reference to a case involving the Collège de Montfermeil (Seine-Saint-Denis), where female students had been expelled for continuing to wear the headscarf in defiance of the ban. The school's rule "prohibiting . . . the wearing of any religious symbol in school" was considered too absolute, especially since the students were not found guilty of proselytizing or refusing to attend classes. The council thus annulled the girls' expulsion and required that the school's rule be modified. In the view of the government's commissioner, David Kessler, who proposed this solution to the general assembly of the Council of State, the obligation of neutrality falls above all on teachers in their capacity as agents of the public interest; so far as students are concerned,

> the public sphere is neutral, a sphere that must be able to accommodate differences in beliefs. . . . The leading idea that must guide the authorities is that their role ends where that which is private begins. It is clear that to wear a headscarf in school is to introduce the private into the public sphere. But

so long as its display is not of an aggressive or proselytizing nature, it remains private in character, and the state has no right to object to this custom in the name of any rule that it might lay down in interpreting the custom.[98]

Recognizing that "the content given to the notion of secularism was not the same twenty years ago or fifty years ago,"[99] the government, with the endorsement of the council, thus implicitly gave its strong approval to the notion of a "new secularism" forged by the Church and other parties. Not the least part of the episode's interest was that it revealed the willingness of Jewish members of the Council of State,[100] along with their Protestant colleagues in the *grands corps*, to distance themselves from the doctrinaire secularism that their predecessors had adopted in reaction to the intransigence of the Catholic Church and to lend their support to a different notion of secularism that now met with the approval of the Church as well. The Church, for its part, "rushed to [their] aid,"[101] in a general rapprochement that altered the image of French exceptionalism and paved the way—to the great displeasure of those who remained intent on perpetuating the rivalry of church and state—for the introduction of cultures and beliefs into the public sphere, thus nullifying the Homeric combats of the past.

The council's solution represented a major turning point in French institutional opinion. It satisfied the various religious groups without alienating a secular camp that had rejected systematic anticlericalism. Nonetheless, it was pregnant with possibilities for misunderstanding, suspicion, and conflict, for when the old rivalry between secularism and Catholicism had collapsed, a whole tradition of informal understandings and ways of adapting to changing circumstances—all of which had been careful to respect the preponderant influence of the Catholic imagination—disappeared as well. Under the old dispensation, of course, unexpected developments could always occur, which is why the issue of secularism enjoyed a permanent topicality. Thus, for example, in June 1984, when the education minister, Alain Savary, proposed that a unified, secular government agency be put in charge of national education, and that private schools be placed under its jurisdiction as well, an immense crowd gathered in Versailles, and then in Paris, to defend the special character of private schools.

Ten years later the tables were turned. In December 1993 the education minister of the day, François Bayrou, announced the government's plan to revise the Falloux law[102] with a view to allowing local authorities to contribute to the financing of private schools—mostly Catholic—out of public funds. At that point massive demonstrations led by republicans broke out in Paris and in the provinces, reviving the school wars of the past.[103] In January 1994 the Left marched from the Place de la République in Paris to the Place de la Nation, shouting punning slogans in defense of the state primary school system with the same cheek and derision as in the old days.[104] A long, placid river of almost a million people (estimates ranged between 600,000 and 900,000), stoically enduring the rain and cold, spontaneously rediscovered its anticlerical eloquence: "Come back, Jules!" it implored, reliving one last time the great moments of the Third Republic.[105]

The emotion, however, was only momentary. Conflict was no longer appropriate. If the school quarrel still retained symbolic force, the issue had changed: for those on the Right it was not so much a question of defending Catholic schools as of defending secular private schools, to which 45 percent of French families send their children at one point or another;[106] for those on the Left the paradoxical defense of the Falloux law (paradoxical because the Left had formerly opposed it) implied something like acceptance of a compromise in the spirit of open secularism.[107] In a society that had become pluralist with respect to beliefs, the "breakdown of secularism"[108] could be surmounted only by forging a new relationship between universalism and pluralism that would redraw the line dividing the public sphere from the private.[109] Whence the question: Is openness to ethnic and religious identities fatal to republican universalism?

David Kessler, the government's commissioner on the Council

of State who had encouraged its general assembly to take an open view of religious symbols in schools without ruling out the possibility of sanctions, in 1993 addressed the issue of the relation between the new secularism and communitarianism;[110] "Secularism no longer appears to justify the prohibition of all religious display," he wrote. "Education is secular not because it prohibits the expression of different faiths but, to the contrary, because it tolerates all of them. This reversal of perspective, which makes freedom the rule and prohibition the exception, seems to us particularly important as well." Citing Jules Ferry, Kessler expressed the opinion that "if the symbol thus challenged is not in and of itself contrary to the principles that the school must protect, its display is lawful so long as provocation and incitement to proselytizing are absent from it."[111] In an article published several years later he suggested that "France loses some of its uniqueness" with the return of religion to the public sphere, which in the past had shown tolerance for the demands of the Church (for example, in the scheduling of its school holidays); a "Catholic public sphere" is therefore similarly obligated to open itself to other faiths rather than reject them.[112]

The doctrine of the Council of State, which refused to see the wearing of the headscarf as ipso facto an act of proselytizing and which refused judicial intervention unless behavior led to disturbances of public order, now seemed established.[113] It was, in effect, a gamble: in order to avoid fundamentalist excess, curb the explosive growth of parochial school education, and at the same time maintain the secular republican tradition, the council hoped that by keeping a certain distance from the hussars of strict secularism, it might be possible to coax the various denominations into limiting themselves to a more personal faith—one that would be compatible with the strengthening of schools as sources of a robust and full conception of citizenship, unencumbered by narrow cultural identifications. Given this modest ambition, was it really reasonable to suggest (as Juppé's education minister, Claude Allègre, did in 1997) that "today the school of Jules Ferry is outmoded"?[114]

The crisis of the headscarves continued long after the Creil affair of October 1989. A year after the November 1992 ruling in favor of the girls at Montfermeil, in which the Council of State ruled that the wearing of headscarves was legitimate so long as was neither ostentatious nor motivated by an intent to proselytize, a similar controversy broke out at a school in Nantua (Ain). The council subsequently found (in a March 1995 ruling) that in this case the girls had in fact engaged in proselytizing, and therefore upheld their expulsion. In the meantime some teachers refused to hold class in the presence of girls wearing veils. As growing numbers of Muslim girls were expelled from public schools, controversy escalated. A memorandum drawn up in September 1994 by the education minister, François Bayrou, in order to clarify the government's position, stated that "the French idea of the nation and of the republic . . . excludes the splitting up of the nation into separate communities indifferent to each other."[115] This triggered a further wave of expulsions. In response to the Bayrou memorandum, the Council of State issued an opinion that was widely considered to be antisecularist for failing to endorse a systematic prohibition; nonetheless, it concurred in holding that "the nation is a community of destiny. This ideal is constructed first at school."[116] At the same time, the opinion also symbolized the rejection of a French Islam and signaled a new chapter in the history of a melting pot that since the nineteenth century had received Italian, Belgian, and Polish Catholic immigrants eager to blend in and become assimilated, while preserving only a memory of traditions whose observance was limited to the private sphere.

The sudden emergence of multiculturalism—associated with the Islamic faith and culture professed by immigrants from North Africa, some of whom had become French citizens—was complicated by nostalgic longing, disappointments, and prejudices that were comparable in many ways to the traumatic recollections of those on the Right who still mourned the loss of French Algeria. At the height of the *affaire des foulards* in the fall of 1989, certain statements made by Jean-Marie Le Pen foreshadowed the exclusionist campaign later mounted by the National Front. Thus, for example, Le Pen remarked: "Once again one encounters the complicities of the Algerian war, only now the people carrying suitcases have become ministers"[117]—officials who, in his view, were working to legitimize an Islam that threatened to destroy French identity. Cast in these terms, multiculturalism, connected mainly with the Muslim presence in France, was felt as a cultural—but also political—betrayal, and its rejection followed symbolically upon a long series of rejections of the foreigner, emanating from both the revolutionary and counterrevolutionary traditions.

For the revolutionaries of 1789, from Barère to Robespierre, it was England that threatened the French spirit; for their official heirs today, it is the America "in [our] minds"[118] that works to impose an unwanted communitarianism by destroying republican values. In the view of those who oppose the presence of the Muslim veil in French schools, "multiculturalism in the United States is an ideology of the humiliated and the frustrated who have not been 'integrated' that must be avoided at all costs in France. . . . The multiculturalist discourse is close to that of Muslim fundamentalism"; a "generalized [freedom to wear the] veil" would thus lead to a communitarianism analogous to the one familiar in "American society, which has done a very poor job of integrating its minorities."[119] Alain Finkielkraut, one of the most outspoken leaders of the fight against the veil, likewise called for resistance to open secularism and American-style multiculturalism, warning that if this model were to "cross the ocean, the secular teacher will not be at the bottom of its list of concerns."[120] Those who joined Finkielkraut in upholding a Jacobinism that takes little or no account of current realities maintain that the adversary remains the proponent of the federalist countermodel, the Girondin, the Anglo-Saxon, the American—the foreigner par excellence—even if in reality, as Denis Lacorne rightly emphasizes, "the American multiculturalism denounced in France is every bit as mythical as the Jacobin and republican wonder that is ceaselessly praised."[121]

Opposition to multiculturalism is found not only on the Left, where it is seen as contradicting French exceptionalism by its rejection of a homogeneous community of citizens produced by the French "melting pot,"[122] but also on the Right, which clings to its vision of a homogeneous Catholic people having no need of political instruction from the institutions of a strong secular state. Opposition is fueled also among intellectuals by the critique of the philosophical foundations of multiculturalism developed by the political theorists Charles Taylor and Michael Sandel, who anchor the self in a deep sense of rootedness in a larger community that, by virtue of its traditions and its shared ways of doing and believing, is alone capable of assuring its equilibrium.[123] Fears of multiculturalism based on the extreme and oversimplified interpretation of American society that has gained currency in France are plainly groundless. Indeed, this interpretation has few supporters in the United States, contrary to what many French intellectuals believe. But another model merits serious consideration: an open and liberal multiculturalism, similar to the one imagined by the political theorist Michael Walzer, that avoids closed communitarianism while at the same time recognizing the legitimacy of particular cultural attachments; and that, in respecting citizens' choices, is compatible with the new secularism that has been so strenuously debated in France in recent years. As Alain Touraine (a signatory of the countermanifesto in support of the new secularism authorizing the wearing of the headscarf) has argued, the "multiculturalist specter" ought not to unduly frighten anyone.[124]

This moderate form of multiculturalism is ultimately the one that was endorsed by the National Commission on Social Integration, which also condemned "communitarian groupings constituted on an ethnic or national basis, negotiating their own areas and specific rights." Looking to go beyond partisan disputes, the Commission calmly observed: "Secularism is identified today with the republic and democracy. . . . Therefore a return to the original sense of secularism makes it possible today to propose [a] pluralism"[125] resistant to all narrow forms of communitarianism within the public arena—a formula accepted, according to the Commission, by French Muslims, who nonetheless frequently encounter discrimination in the name of a quasi-ethnic conception of the nation.[126] This plural secularism perfectly expresses the idea of a public arena in which citizens preserve the "thin" identities—as distinct from "thick" identities—described by Walzer.[127] Thin identities, limited in scope and embodying a universalist conception of humanity, a common "minimal morality," remain mutually compatible within a public (indeed, republican) sphere, whereas thick identities imprison individuals in particular communitarian cultures that are incompatible both with the Anglo-American model of democracy and, a fortiori, with the French notion of republicanism. Still, it must be admitted that the course of modern history in France has hardly favored such a plural conception of secularism.

When all is said and done, for staunch secularists as well as for those who, since the time of Maurice Barrès, have soldiered on behalf of a wholly Christian France, multiculturalism represents a new weapon in the arsenal of the foreigner. The heterogeneous coalition that took up arms against the new secularism fought against the least concession to "tribalism" (Alain Finkielkraut's word) with the same zeal that it combated the intrusion of American ideas into French life, and with them the ghettos, "the communitarian plague, . . . the slide of the unitary state into a state that is a federation of 'communities.' "[128] In a 1990 Senate debate, Charles Pasqua, the once and future Gaullist minister of the interior, gave a clear explication of conservative assimilationist logic (the counterpart of which may be found among the hard-line defenders of the Republic), arguing that "it is not reasonable to advocate the organization of a pluricultural or multicultural France. . . . It leads ineluctably to discrimination and ghettos. . . . The French respect all the ethical and spiritual values of France, they recognize the principle of secularism. It is necessary not to belittle the nation but, to the contrary, to make it more sure of itself."[129]

For the leading spokesmen of the counterrevolutionary Right, from Abbé Barruel to Édouard Drumont, Charles Maurras, and now Jean-Marie Le Pen, England eternally remains the Devil, guilty of having smuggled into France (with the subversive assistance of its Protestant and Jewish agents) a spirit of capitalism and individualism ruinous to French Catholic identity. England, they believe, has always sought to destroy France through the introduction of a multiculturalism contrary to its nature. Just as Barrès formerly denied Jews the status of Frenchmen, whatever their degree of assimilation, Monsignor Lefebvre, echoing Le Pen's platform, now claimed that "Muslims cannot be Catholics, they cannot really be French."[130] For conservative Catholics, as for the theoreticians of the National Front, multiculturalism constitutes absolute evil. Le Pen's journal *Identité* applauded secularist attacks against the "tribes," citing in its turn Alain Finkielkraut and Régis Debray, who now found themselves in the awkward position of being cited as authorities by the extreme Right. The editors of this journal likewise called for a return to the nation, except that for the National Front this was the ethnic nation—thus standing on their head the arguments made by defenders of a republican nation who were openly hostile to a conception of ethnicity based on blood rather than on soil.[131]

The National Front appealed to Fernand Braudel as well as Pierre Chaunu in order to justify the rejection of an "extra-European immigration incompatible with the permanence of the French ethnic group, whose blood and culture is distinct from that of any other ethnic group."[132] Bruno Mégret, for his part, denied any value to Anglo-American democracy or to the coexistence of multiple cultures, not by proclaiming the necessity of adhering to the republican paradigm but by presenting himself as the herald of a nation sharing only "a common identity, language, and religion," within which the "young *beurs*" (second-generation North Africans) remained irreducibly different from those who were "French born and bred."[133] Jean-Marie Le Pen, introducing the first issue of *Identité*, frankly stated his opinion: "I believe that the white man of Europe is characterized by an alchemy of nuances. . . . We are of the same race and of the same spirit. . . . We also respect the foreigner as part of that universality of humanity that makes each man, each group and nation, a

241

distinct being."[134] In other words, the foreigner, the nonwhite, has his rightful place in his own nation—as far away as possible from France. Under no circumstances can he pretend to have been assimilated into the homeland of Clovis; nor can he maintain his own identity in a nation that has become multicultural—especially since "races" are not only different but also, as Le Pen unambiguously declared, "unequal." All the more reason, then, to challenge any and all forms of multiculturalism threatening a purely French society.

Like the debate over secularism, the debate over multiculturalism gave new life to the nineteenth-century quarrel between contrary ideals of homogeneous societies. But by the 1990s things had changed: republicans, like the Church, were now open to difference, admitting the plural character of society, contesting—in the name of democracy—the assimilationist and reductive revolutionary model of loyalties symbolized by Abbé Grégoire. Thus Cardinal Lustiger, a supporter of the new secularism, harshly criticized the argument made long ago by the Comte de Clermont-Tonnerre: "I am not very satisfied," he wrote, "with the status accorded the Jews by the Revolution, for example, if this is summed up by Clermont-Tonnerre's famous formula: 'Everything must be refused to the Jews as a nation and everything granted to them as citizens.' . . . Does it follow that the individual has an identity only insofar as he is defined as a citizen? For French democracy in the 1990s, such an approach is of no help in facing up to a phenomenon like Islam."[135] In the event, far from disappearing, Jewish identity managed to find other ways to survive. But the surprising thing about the cardinal's statement was its unexpected call, in the name of democracy, for a degree of tolerance that would encourage the development of Islam in France by renouncing the revolutionary discourse of 1789 that was supposed to have destroyed Jewish identity.

Opposed on all sides by latter-day Jacobins, a mobilization of nationalist sentiment with deep roots in the political landscape gathered momentum, reviving the intransigence of the old days by forcefully, and with conviction, emphasizing an underlying racial dimension to French identity—a claim that was now vehemently disputed by the Church. Thanks to the National Front, the multiculturalism associated with Anglo-American democracy found itself suddenly transformed. The end of the conflict between the republican state and the Church gave free rein to fantasies about national identity—which from now on were couched more in biological than in religious terms, resurrecting the doctrines of the late-nineteenth-century racial theorist Jules Soury—with the result that multiculturalism became still more illegitimate in the eyes of those who rejected the presence of "inferior races" in French society. Under the circumstances, the corresponding intransigence of old-style secularists in defending the republican assimilationist ideal at all costs only made the search for common ground more difficult.

The new elites that had emerged from the North African immigration were keenly aware of the hostile ideological atmosphere surrounding this debate. They joined devout Muslims in denouncing the rejection of the veil as an irrational and racist refusal of ethnic difference while at the same time, in demanding a full and complete recognition of their culture, showing that they were capable advocates of the new secularism. Salem Kacet, the deputy mayor of Roubaix, a representative of the moderate Catholic CDS party and a former member of the commission appointed to advise the government in revising the regulations governing nationality (the Code de la Nationalité, first formulated in 1889), wholeheartedly applauded the position adopted by Lionel Jospin. Kacet wrote: "And so the Republic is in danger! Traitors have capitulated and betrayed France. . . . Resistance is organized—against headscarves." He went on to praise secularism as a "vital necessity" and public schools as an emancipating institution for second-generation North Africans, concluding with the words: "France must anchor in the nation those French men and women whose memories are not short." Secularism, yes; loss of memory, no. Emancipating assimilation thanks to public schools, yes; the "suspicion that attaches to Muslims who have assumed their responsibilities, all the responsibilities associated with their status as French [citizens], no."[136] Jamal-Eddine Bencheikh, a professor at Université de Paris–VIII, spoke in similar terms: "I learned French at public school, where I was forced to do nothing other than be myself, think correctly, reason freely. . . . With all due respect to those who are enraged by the expulsions and to those who defend a prickly authenticity, I have never felt torn between my two cultures, neither one of which seeks to seize the rights of the other. I cast a friendly but vigilant glance from each one to the other; the two occupy my imagination and my soul."[137] Another university professor, Amr Helmy Ibrahim, observed:

> I [used to] think of myself first and foremost as a Frenchman, . . . but gradually things took a different turn. I became more and more annoyed by the French-Muslim distinction. . . . [The French] haven't recovered from the Dreyfus Affair. . . . I would go further than the archbishop of Paris: each community, because it collectively manifests a form of consciousness, ought to be represented or at the very least consulted. . . . The Anglo-American democracies do a good job of adapting themselves to a communitarian situation, to cultural plurality, without therefore giving up trying to achieve a consensus about citizenship.[138]

Unlike the assimilationists but also, and especially, unlike supporters of the National Front, most French of North African origin accept secularism, the predominance of the common law over ethnic or religious traditions, and integration into the public sphere without assuming that this implies an abandonment of multiple loyalties. Abdelatif Benazzi, the captain of the French national rugby team who in 1997 was appointed to the National Commission on Social Integration, criticized those who "change their first name or dye their hair. . . . I am true to my convictions," he wrote, "to my faith, to my religion. To do otherwise is to show one's weakness—even to betray [one's heritage]. . . . Nationality wins by respecting the laws of the Republic. . . . Quite simply, by being a citizen."[139] A decade earlier Rémy Leveau, a scholar of contemporary Islam, and Dominique Schnapper, a historian of modern French Judaism, had commented:

> Dreyfusard Jews defended Captain Dreyfus not because he was Jewish, but in the name of the rights of man, because he was innocent. It is with reference to the universal values of democracy, equality for all persons, [and] respect for individual convictions that young North Africans defend the building of mosques and places of prayer that they do not themselves frequent. . . . They have internalized the idea that religious convictions and practices come within the domain of private life: for Jews and for North Africans, Judaism and Islam belong to the religious—and therefore private—sphere. . . . French Muslims, including proselytes, accept the political order of France. . . . They challenge group solidarities.[140]

It needs to be pointed out, however, as against a purely assimilationist interpretation of the Dreyfus Affair, that Jews at that time were far from indifferent to the fact that Captain Dreyfus was a Jew, for they ran up against the same vigorous anti-Semitism he did: they, too, were concerned to defend a shared culture.[141] Many second-generation North Africans, infuriated by the growth of racism and anxious, as Jews were a century ago, to protect their dignity as citizens, have taken part in group protests that reinforce their beleaguered sense of ethnic identity.[142]

Nonetheless, few second-generation North Africans today wish to resign themselves to a purely communitarian logic. The multiculturalism they fervently advocate, again like the Jews of a century ago, is nearer the kind imagined by Walzer than by Taylor: open to society as a whole while concerned with protecting the right of personal choice, and opposed to the identification of individuals with the language, religion, or customs peculiar to a given group. Contradicting many of the prejudices of the racist extreme Right, and as many recent studies have confirmed, *beurs* have often made progress in assimilating, although it is also true that they are apt to encounter considerable resistance from the state itself (in particular from the army). Nonetheless, their secularization has made great strides, so much so that 95 percent of second-generation North Africans feel that "one can be perfectly integrated in French society and practice the Muslim religion privately."[143] Moreover, the "lack of interest in religion seems huge among young people of Algerian origin": while many *beurs* observe Ramadan and dietary restrictions, respect for such ritualized practices has declined with the increase of exogamous marriages.[144] Unlike the Turks and Kurds, for example, who are strongly committed to preserving their collective identity, young people of Algerian origin are gradually becoming acculturated within French society, even if their sociability is still influenced by racist prejudice and resentment—memories of which remain fresh—and even if the confining atmosphere of neighborhood communities continues to hinder their entry into public life and aggravates the curiosity felt toward them by a class of French citizens who sense their difference from others.[145]

The tragic and much-publicized odyssey of Khaled Kelkal, a young Frenchman of North African extraction from Vaulx-en-Velin, an eastern suburb of Lyons, eloquently testifies to the troubling ambivalence that often accompanies rapid assimilation. Attracted to an insurgent Muslim movement that had grown up in metropolitan France as a consequence of the fundamentalist uprising in Algeria, Kelkal joined in the underground armed struggle in the name of Islam, taking part in terrorist attacks. On 29 September 1995 he was tracked down by the police and killed. In death he became the symbol of the radical Islamicism emerging in French society. Many young Muslims in France interpreted Kelkal's saga as an urgent call to revolt, rejecting assimilation, even integration, and repudiating all participation in secular society. Within the space of only a few months, the particularly violent manner of his death made him a hero in immigrant neighborhoods. Filled with outrage over his fate, they exploded in violence. At the time, observers drew attention only to the personal difficulties that Kelkal—like all young *beurs*—had encountered in integrating himself into French society, portraying him as the sacrificial victim of a racist and intolerant system.

A sensational interview with Kelkal, published a week after his death, seemed to confirm the view that social discrimination had turned him into a religious radical. Yet a careful reading of Kelkal's responses reveals the effectiveness of a process of integration that, despite grave defects, still managed to function in his case, albeit with difficulty. His passage through primary and middle schools, where he showed himself to be a good student, was normal enough; but everything changed drastically when he entered the *lycée*. In middle school, he recalled, his "French [schoolmates] did not have the same principles, but, even so, they adapted, and we adapted too—one didn't notice the difference too much." Teachers recognized the immigrant pupils' abilities. In the *lycée*, however, teachers "came in and started teaching and didn't stop until the end. Good-bye! . . . I couldn't find my place. . . . I said to myself that total integration is impossible—to forget my culture, to eat pork, I couldn't do it." Against the wishes of his parents, Kelkal left school. One of his sisters continued her medical studies, and both of his brothers obtained their vocational training qualification. After several thefts and repeated acts of violence, he was arrested and sentenced to prison, where he rediscovered Islam and met instructors who encouraged him to pursue training in electronics; after a short time he gave up, wishing to study biology and chemistry instead. His frequent experiences of racism and unjust treatment by various institutions caused him to want nothing more than to leave France and return to Algeria. In the meantime he predicted the arrival of American-style violence in the *banlieues*, the gritty neighborhoods on the outskirts of French cities, and attacked Christianity (a "false religion") and Jews.[146]

Despite the stress that Khaled Kelkal laid upon all the obstacles he had encountered, the racist contempt and the social injustice, his distressing testimony nonetheless suggested that integration was actually possible from an early age—thus the experience of his sister and brothers, and indeed his own in primary and middle school. It also suggested that even prison could offer a belated opportunity to embark upon a professional career. The new secularism no longer insists that French Muslims forget their culture, nor obliges them to eat pork; it does not require a "total integration" that denies ethnic and religious identities; it is tolerant of differences, without therefore imposing a narrow communitarian ideal. In light of all this, one wonders whether Kelkal's tragic flight might have been avoided—whether he might not just as readily have carried on with his schooling, as did the other members of his family as well as tens of thousands of young people like himself, in spite of unfavorable social circumstances, and finally have entered society without betraying his heritage in the process, achieving in the end of the same success enjoyed by generations of immigrants before him.

Notwithstanding the persistence of hostility toward the entry of immigrants into French society and, more rarely, outright rejection of them, the public sphere had undeniably become more open. But the urge to rebel against French tradition remained strong among young people of North African origin. Some, inspired by Khaled Kelkal, discovered with delight the extreme multiculturalism that was then flowering in Great Britain and tried to import to France the forms of Islamic community organization found there, especially to *banlieues* that in the name of ethnic and religious difference were becoming virtual Muslim enclaves.[147] Even among adult professionals, men such as Abdel Salmani, a chemical engineer from Roubaix (the same city where Salem Kacet was deputy mayor), looked for inspiration to Islamic fundamentalists across the Channel, where Muslim immigrants enjoyed a substantial degree of political and cultural autonomy within a public sphere explicitly founded on the recognition of ethnic and religious differences.[148]

In Great Britain, the courts in recent years have extended the legal protection of cultural traditions practiced in the public sphere much further than their counterparts in the United States have been willing to do, even going so far as to approve mechanisms for assuring specific representation for immigrants from the West Indies and the Indian subcontinent. A proportional system of quotas, based on a deliberately ethnic census, has been set up for the appointment of municipal administrative staff according to the relative size of each immigrant community, while within the Labour Party a dual system of representation permits West Indians to be grouped together in specific political sections, leading to the election of "ethnic" members of parliament whose main responsibility is to the communities that elect them.[149] Despite a real risk of racial segregation—the opposite case to that of a nation such as France, with its strong state—Great Britain has remained true to its grand decentralizing traditions and an age-old desire to ensure the representation of diverse social and cultural groups in parliament. Its administrative and electoral arrangements push to an extreme a democratic logic that in France, and justly so perhaps, deeply frightens strict republicans who oppose any political or cultural expression of ethnic difference within the school system and, a fortiori, the political system.

French political parties reject such a system of dual representation as unimaginable in a nation-state whose citizenry remains passionately committed to the existence of a universalist public sphere. Indeed, many elected officials today who originally came to France as part of the postwar wave of immigration from North Africa entered public life in order to represent all of their fellow citizens. One sign of the growing ethnicization of French politics, however, is that political parties are now willing to make use of immigrant elites in order to win the votes of ethnic groups. Thus, in 1990, the Conférence Nationale des Élus Socialistes Originaires du Maghreb [National Conference of North African–Born Elected Socialist Representatives (CNESOM)] was created, bringing together a hundred Socialist representatives who sought to affirm a North African sensibility within the party. Unlike the West Indian sections of the Labour Party in Great Britain, however, this ethnic structure rapidly collapsed. More generally, the attempt to create a mediating body between the state authorities and the immigrant population from North Africa failed, and this even though it was supported as much by party activists, who wished to become the spokesmen for their respective cultural groups, as by the parties themselves, which sought intermediaries through which they might reach this population.[150]

In the municipal elections of 1989, and again in those of 1995, about 150 candidates of North African descent made good showings both in the Paris and Lyons suburbs and in the north, heading the lists not only of the Socialists and Communists but also of the Gaullists (and thus becoming eligible to stand in the second ballot in the event their list was one of the top two vote-getters in the first). Other young *maghrébins* who formed lists in the Pas-de-Calais and in Nanterre boasted of their "instinctive Frenchness."[151] Still, in the recent legislative elections of 1997, no candidate of Arab or African origin figured on either the RPR, UDF, or Communist lists, while the Socialist Party contented itself with proposing a former minister, Kofi Yamgnane, in Finistère, where he was elected. A new party, the Parti des Musulmans de France [French Muslim Party], sought for the first time to appeal to the electorate with a platform frankly based on ethnic identity— though without any real hope of making itself heard, despite the fact that young North Africans were likelier to register to vote as the *lepéniste* threat became clearer.[152] But the new party found its initiative condemned by the Fédération Nationale des Musulmans de France [National Federation of French Muslims].[153] Such a narrow communitarian strategy, pursued by elected representatives who had broken away from major national parties, was doomed to failure because it challenged the traditional French understanding of citizenship, which remained fundamentally unchanged.

As it turns out, the political behavior of French Muslims is no more uniform than that of other citizens. The Gulf War, for example, though it disturbed a sense of national identity among French Muslims by arousing conflicting loyalties, did not lead them to stand together as a single community united in support of Saddam Hussein. Paradoxically, Salem Kacet—the deputy mayor of Roubaix who, as a medical doctor and elected official, was the very embodiment of successful social integration—was among a minority calling for Islamic solidarity. A few members of the Cercle Socialiste de Culture Musulmane [Socialist Society of Muslim Culture] resigned from the Socialist Party in protest of the government's support of the Gulf War, frustrated by the party's refusal to take greater account of the group identity of its Muslim members. Indeed, Muslim opinion was out of line with French public opinion as a whole, which overwhelmingly approved the military intervention in Iraq; even so, most French Muslims managed to preserve their sense of integration as citizens of the nation. Apart from a minority who have been unsparing in their criticism of the West and Israel, French Muslims have so far avoided openly challenging government policy from a particularist point of view, taking care not to cast their political attitudes in exclusively ethnic terms.[154]

Allegiance to the state therefore has not been placed in doubt, despite the fact that more than a million French citizens of Algerian extraction are constrained to honor a dual allegiance.[155] Given the disfavor with which France looks upon multiple and partial allegiances, the acceptance by these immigrants of full and complete French citizenship, carrying with it all the attributes of nationality, remains the only alternative consistent with traditional French conceptions. Just as the community of citizens cannot allow a closed communitarianism, so it must rule out variable forms of citizenship; and yet just as it allows the loyalties, traditions, and memories of various social groups to flourish, so active republican citizenship cannot be understood as requiring citizens to renounce their personal values.

In this sense, a British-style conception of citizenship that permits nonnationals to enjoy the rights associated with it and even to vote in national elections[156] is scarcely imaginable in France, where the new secularism authorizes only the controlled expression of identities in the public sphere. The first stage of the reform of the Code de la Nationalité carried out by the Chirac government in 1986, according to which the determination of nationality was now to be made partly on the basis of parentage (*jus sanguinis*), in addition to the traditional criterion of residence (*jus soli*), was a consequence of growing official impatience with claims of dual allegiance. Among persons between sixteen and twenty-one years of age, only those who had immigrated to France had to swear allegiance to their country of residence; those born of French parents were exempted from this solemn oath-taking. The oath itself was rapidly abandoned, but the general approach adopted by the government had the effect of muting the sharp contrast between the French and German traditions, the former resting on an inclusionist *jus soli*, the latter on an ethnic *jus sanguinis*. In fact, each society had incorporated certain aspects of the other's conception of nationality while remaining true to its own heritage.[157] The French nation—at bottom, a political community—had always assimilated foreigners, and ever since the law of 1889 it had considered as French, on reaching his or her majority, every individual born on French soil, even persons born of foreign parents. Cultural communities such as Germany and Switzerland, by contrast, grant naturalization to foreigners only very sparingly; lacking German or Swiss blood, such persons are considered unqualified to participate in the life of the nation on equal terms. It is a measure of the extreme distance separating France from these two neighboring societies that a Turk born in either Germany or Switzerland of Turkish parents who were themselves born there has difficulty obtaining citizenship.[158]

The 1986 reform of the nationality code, undertaken in the face of pressure from the National Front and aimed at limiting automatic acquisition of French nationality, seemed to confirm Jean-Marie Le Pen's contention that "Being French is something that has to be earned"; at the same time, it won support among hard-line republicans, on both the Right and the Left, who invoked the shade of Renan in regarding the expression of an avowed desire to acquire nationality as a legitimate consideration. Just as in the case of the *affaire des foulards*, profoundly heterogeneous camps emerged. Whereas the parties of the Right sought to prevent the bearers of another culture from becoming French and appeared to call for an elective conception of nationality, many forces on the Left, in defending the acquisition of nationality at birth, seemed to endorse a passive, deterministic version even as they appealed to a unique and integral *jus soli* that fully belonged to the republican tradition. The reform of the code aroused strong opposition not only from the Council of State but also from the League of the Rights of Man, while high dignitaries of the Church and prominent lay Catholics denounced its "fundamentally anti-Christian" aspect. To be sure, the reform was symbolically important; but it did not call into question in any basic way the French assimilationist tradition founded on a *jus soli*, nor did it have the effect of limiting access to nationality. Some suspicion still attached to the requirement that only children of immigrants take the oath—a requirement that seemed to suggest that "the feeling of national belonging would be transmitted more surely through genes than through the schools of the Republic."[159]

In a striking reversal of positions, Alain Finkielkraut, that strict secularist and fierce adversary of multiculturalism, passionately endorsed the proposed reform on the condition that its repressive elements (forcing people to register, provide names and addresses, and the like) be eliminated. In his view, precisely because young *maghrébins* brought up in a foreign culture can nonetheless understand "a verse of Racine"—just like young Jews before them (contrary to the allegations of the extreme Right at the turn of the century), who were also accused of indifference to Racine's poetry despite their brilliant record at school—the elective theory of the nation was justified: the simple statement of intention, he argued, far from calling the theory into question, signaled a rejection of an ethnic vision of France.[160] Despite the symbolically crucial change embodied by the new law, potentially threatening since certain restrictive conditions limited its application (persons convicted of an offense, for example, were ineligible), 126,300 people acquired French nationality in 1994. At no point since the war had so many citizens been created so quickly. The young, in particular, supported an approach that singled them out: in 1994 three age groups (sixteen, seventeen, and twenty-one), representing about 80,000 persons, were affected by this reform. More than half this number decided to seek citizenship several years before the law required them formally to apply; what's more—and this is the essential point—the courts rejected only 2 percent of the applications submitted. Considering that the children of Algerians were not required to apply in this way (because their parents had been born in French Algeria), and that 30 percent of those who followed this procedure were Moroccan and 11 percent Tunisian, the force of the integrationist model and its continuing attraction for persons born in North Africa is clear.[161]

The consequences rapidly made themselves felt at the level of collective action. In 1983 young immigrants from the Maghreb had mobilized en masse for a March for Equality, which (under the banner "Living together with our differences") marked the entry of the *beurs* into the public sphere. The following year a march on Paris ("Living as equals who share many similarities, whatever our differences may be") was organized by Convergence 84. During this same period, SOS-Racisme was born. In the spring of 1985, great festivals were sponsored by these organizations, together with a new march. In 1985–86, massive protests were mounted against the plan to reform the nationality code and concerts were organized along with various demonstrations that enjoyed the support of President Mitterrand and Socialist leaders. By the 1990s, however, none of these ways of taking a public stand in the name of an identity any longer seemed appropriate.[162]

In June 1997, on the eve of its return to power, the Socialist Party announced its intention to revert to the strict application of the *jus soli*. This amounted to a veritable "refounding of the Republic," implying integration and equal treatment of all citizens, reaffirmation of the concept of a "people of citizens," and rejection of any model based on an ethnic or cultural nation.[163] The proposed law sent by the government on 15 September 1997 to the Council of State nonetheless did not entirely restore the legislation in force prior to July 1993 (prior, that is, to the second stage of reforms, carried out by the Balladur government and following upon the initial proposals of 1986). Instead, it held to an intermediate position that once again permitted automatic acquisition of citizenship at the age of eighteen by children born in France of foreign parents (assuming a continuous period of residence), but that also allowed minors to "ask for French citizenship by declaration" at the age of sixteen (an option that was later made available at the age of thirteen). The failure to wholly reinstated *jus soli* aroused sharp protests from a fragmented Left and from various groups already outraged by certain repressive aspects of the new legislation regarding immigration.[164] But now that the new secularism had been joined to a new cultural pluralism that rejected strict communitarianism and permitted young immigrants to accede to full citizenship, collective action lost its old ethnic-based character. From now on, French citizens of North African birth who took part in the great demonstrations organized by the major political parties were simply swallowed up within larger crowds protesting, for example, the assassination of young *beurs* or the many racist attacks that had accompanied the strong upsurge of support for the National Front.[165] The ethnically mixed crowds that turned out to demonstrate against murderous racism did so not in order to demand the preservation of a particular cultural identity or to assure the permanence of an ethnic community, but rather in the name of the justice due to each citizen and to each foreigner.

A number of questions arise. Is a new France gradually emerging, one that stands midway between communitarianism (wrongly dreaded as an inevitable source of ethnic isolation) and republicanism (mistakenly considered to be purely assimilationist)? Beyond the rhetoric and the prejudice on all sides, have the new secularism and the recent debates over citizenship actually helped to end the sterile confrontations of the past? If so, have they abolished French exceptionalism in the process (as the fierce and relentless adversaries of America so deeply fear—though in reality American society is more open than anyone in France dares acknowledge)? Is America now able to enter into the minds of the French without filling them up with fantasies and revulsion?[166] Do second-generation North Africans, like Protestants and Jews before them, now inhabit a Republic that is more respectful of "little countries," of foreign ways and customs, foreign languages, identities, and loyalties?[167] And finally, without singing the praises of ethnic difference (so easily exploited by the National Front for exclusionist purposes), is there ground for believing that a moderate de facto form of multiculturalism is taking shape at last, a plural memory that may yet find favor in the eyes of the Jacobins of our day now that they have rid themselves of their blinders?

Paradoxically, it was Cardinal Lustiger who contemplated such a middle course when he asked: "Is there a republican religion that prohibits one from being a Catholic, a Protestant, a Jew, a Muslim—even a skeptic? The republican ideal of citizenship does not claim to be a substitute for religion."[168] It fell to this man, the archbishop of Paris, a converted Jew speaking in the name of the Church, to state the terms of a genuine civil peace acceptable to all, apart from defenders of fierce irredentisms who assert the primacy of closed, uniform, and constraining cultural and ethnic identities. Nonetheless, it remains to be seen whether the Church, in trying to define the contours of a new secularism with the support of many Jews, Protestants, and Muslims, will in fact succeed in winning acceptance for a moderate pluralism that until now Jacobins of every stripe have considered unacceptable.

Faced with such a reconfiguration of the public sphere, the Jews of today seem more divided than they were a hundred years ago. Those in the service of the state who have played a part in rethinking secularism, breaking with the strict ideals championed by their predecessors at the end of the last century, find themselves openly and vigorously opposed by other Jews hostile to all forms, even the most moderate, of multiculturalism. Has French Judaism remained faithful to its alliance with the Republic, or does it now lean toward an uncompromising communitarianism of its own? Will it be able to create a place for itself alongside other cultural minorities in a newly plural society?

Things have changed a great deal since the late nineteenth century, when Jews overwhelmingly accepted the republican contract, enthusiastically endorsing the formula of active citizenship, yielding without undue protest to the separation of church and state, and even helping to put official policies into effect. A century ago they joined together to represent Jewish interests before the state, while at the same time ardently taking part in the battles of the Republic. In doing so they became the faithful servants of the state, swiftly integrating themselves (without, however, disappearing through assimilation) and moving up in the social hierarchy (thanks to the advantages of a meritocratic system) while preserving their innermost religious loyalties (even if this meant restricting the public expression of their faith). Along with Protestants, they managed to enter the political and administrative ranks of the Republic against the categorical objections of conservative Catholics. In linking their destiny with that of the Republic, they were also exposed to the full force of the nationalist reaction, whose antirepublican leagues were eager to do battle with the Republic's Protestant and Jewish allies.[169]

In our own time, the end of the conflict between church and state has reshuffled the deck. Consider, for example, the Church's abandonment of its historic practice of teaching contempt for the Jews. Gradually the Church rid itself of all traces of its traditional anti-Semitism; little by little it came officially to recognize Jewish identity. The new catechism adopted in 1993 characterizes Jesus as a rabbi "born a Jew of a daughter of Israel" and rejects the charge of deicide. This recognition of the Jewish faith was reaffirmed in October 1997, with the solemn renunciation of Christian anti-Judaism—"the soil in which the poisonous plant of Jew hatred flowered"—which was responsible for the Church's "silence" when Vichy imposed the Jewish statute of October 1940 and for the "deadly spiral" that followed. For this "error," of which it is still "ashamed," the Church asked the Jews "to hear these words of repentance" that definitively legitimized their full and complete place within a not-wholly Catholic nation. The unnatural and, for so many years, traditional alliance between the Church and militant Catholic movements now came to an end, preparing the way for an open society to emerge.[170]

The virtual extinction of the Maistrean counterutopia, now

pushed back to the edges of society, beyond the boundaries of the Church itself, eased Jewish fears and prompted the return of Jews to public life while making official protection of their civil rights seem less urgent than before—even if anti-Semitism, whether avowed or latent, continued to be a constant feature of Jewish experience. Despite appearances to the contrary, very nearly half the French people (49 percent) reckoned anti-Semitism to be either very much or fairly widespread still in 1995. The fact that a quarter of the population put the number of French Jews at more than five million (the average figure given was three million) also revealed the force of prejudice and fantasy.[171] In fact, the number of Jews in France is considerably smaller (between 600,000 and 700,000), their political attitudes are increasingly divergent, and if they tend more often than their fellow citizens not to vote for the National Front, their traditional ties with the Left have weakened. Apart from a very few microsocieties such as Sarcelles, a suburb north of Paris—where, contrary again to the usual view, rival community structures have indeed emerged—they have hardly any specific political force.[172]

The gradual rise of cultural pluralism has considerably changed the place of Jews in French society. Once a fragile minority symbolically associated with the development of the strong state, they have become one minority among others; moreover, their place is officially recognized by the architects of the new secularism. The controversy over headscarves directly concerned them, all the more as it began (though this is seldom acknowledged) with a refusal on the part of the authorities to continue to agree tacitly to the absence of Jewish students from school on Saturday mornings. At Creil, where the scandal first broke, the principal, Chénière, had announced (with the approval of the local school board) that the absence of Jewish students for religious reasons on Saturday mornings would no longer be tolerated. It was then that certain teachers raised the case of students wearing veils, arguing that it was necessary to treat them in the same way if educational secularism were to be preserved.[173]

Once it had become a national issue, the *affaire des foulards* immediately raised a parallel set of questions about the wearing of the kippah by Jewish boys. To be sure, one does not find in this case evidence of a tendency to strengthen inequality comparable to the experience of young Muslim women who were forced, in effect, to advertise their submission to the law of their father and their brothers. To be sure, too, the Jewish children never refused to attend certain classes, meeting physical education requirements like all the other students. The kippah did not represent the same prohibitions: it was not a factor of segregation; its proselytizing aspect remained extremely limited; its public effects were less pronounced. Nonetheless, the wearing of the kippah wound up being associated by many with that of the veil: the rabbis, it will be recalled, were not slow to perceive this and came at once to the defense of the young Muslim women, to the great displeasure of Jews attached to the old Jacobin style of secularism. Whereas the grand rabbi, Joseph Sitruk, gave teachers one kind of advice ("Be open to the religious diversity of young people: if a student wears in your presence a cross, a scarf, a kippah, accept him as he is"), Alain Finkielkraut argued by contrast that "the secular school has been an instrument of emancipation and Jews are greatly indebted to it. Now, in defending the Islamic veil and the kippah in a single gesture, religious dignitaries have behaved as though they were union leaders or corporate executives. They have shown irresponsibility and indifference toward the girls involved and toward the future of [public] school[s]. Once again identity has taken precedence over the message [that needs to be sent]."[174] Others, while strongly opposed to fundamentalism, identified themselves more closely with the perspective of a plural secularism.[175] Like Muslims, Jews thus found themselves caught up in a general debate over the larger question of tolerance of symbols of religious attachment within the public school system: does the kippah, like the veil, have an inherently prosletyzing character that is unacceptable in the eyes of other children, whereas the cross, or even the Star of David, worn in a nonaggressive manner, remains within the limits of civility?

This new and not altogether unambiguous Franco-French

quarrel prompted another decisive intervention by the state. An administrative court in Nice had set a precedent by ruling against Jewish students who had claimed an exemption on religious grounds from regular school attendance on Saturday mornings and recommended the expulsion of one pupil, Yonathan Koen. Brought before the Council of State for review, the case aroused less of an outcry than that of the headscarves, but it nonetheless reaffirmed the council's crucial role in the interpretation of secularism. This time, however, the final opinion of the council diverged from the conclusions of the government's commissioner, Yann Aguila. In the government's view, "the law of the Republic imposes itself on religious precepts. . . . If one chooses to take part in the educational community, one must respect its constraints." Taking issue with the Jewish students' claim of respect for the Sabbath, Aguila argued that it revealed the existence of the manifestation of "a new and real problem, namely the attitude of the state toward communities whose national identity tends to be affirmed more strongly through a strengthening of religious feeling." Accordingly, "to set out on the path of school à la carte, in which each [student] chooses his courses and his hours of attendance, according to his convictions" was unacceptable; such students were advised instead to seek education "in the private denominational schools, [which are] better adapted to religious convictions."[176]

The Council of State rejected this strict interpretation and expressed its continuing support for an open and plural secularism: in April 1995 it ruled that practicing Jewish students need not attend Saturday morning classes so long as such absences did not interfere either with their education or the life of their school. As in the case of the headscarves, the council left it up to secondary school and *lycée* administrators to decide on a case-by-case basis whether such requests posed a problem. Still, it upheld the expulsion of the student at the Lycée Masséna in Nice, ruling that Saturday morning attendance was required of all students who were taking courses in higher mathematics because examinations were frequently scheduled at this time.[177] This decision drew ironic comment from *Le Monde*, which usually took the side of doctrinaire secularism but now sounded a note of urgency in rallying to its defense:

> The debates over the "Islamic headscarf" seem to have had the unanticipated consequence of awakening the ardor of pious Jews. Certain observers have noted a sprouting of skullcaps on the heads of *collégiens* and *lycéens*. . . . [Public] school[s] once appeared as the instrument and symbol of the emancipation and integration of Protestant and Jewish minorities. Today . . . the threat emerges of a self-service school. How can the proliferation of special educational demands be avoided without encouraging the multiplication of community schools?[178]

The Council of State nonetheless held to its course of plural secularism, seeking to avoid both proselytizing within the public school system and the emergence of a private denominational school system catering to particular communities. But once again fears of communitarian isolation and withdrawal from society were exaggerated. If France is far from having entered into the "age of tribalism" feared by Alain Finkielkraut, signs of religious revival are nonetheless indisputable: the trend toward at least occasional observance has become more marked in recent years, and a majority of Jews—who are all the more determined to remember Vichy as the National Front's gains prompt them to exercise vigilance—are concerned with affirming personal loyalty and memory. Even so, the risks of communitarianization, amplified though they may be by the extravagant statements of this or that rabbi and by the spectacular growth of Lubavitch groups, ought not to be overestimated. Jews approve an open secularism while remaining firmly committed republicans. As Jean Kahn, president of the consistory—the institution most insistent upon a strict and demanding respect for faith—recently declared, "[T]he law of my country is my law, as our texts say. The Jewish community will not infringe this rule. It remains very attached to the principle of secularism and republican schools. This is one of the foundations of French society, to which we totally subscribe."[179]

Contrary to the sensational reports that appear on the front pages of certain major national newspapers, expressing alarm at a "religious crisis" in the "Jewish community," which is said to be attracted to a militant fundamentalism, French Jews hardly constitute a uniform and closed group. Indeed, under the influence of republican secularism, their beliefs and values have become ever more varied. Yet when Grand Rabbi Sitruk requested in 1995 that the cantonal elections that year—scheduled for the first day of the Jewish Passover (commemorating the exodus from Egypt)—be pushed back, the reaction was sharp. Jews and other readers of *Le Monde* were learnedly advised that "Judaism is increasingly distressed by the assaults of modernity and secularism. . . . The most radical religious [Jewish] tendencies have not laid down their arms." This question, they were told, "may seem exotic," but "the *halakhah* [Jewish religious law] prohibits all travel on feast days and on the Sabbath days; it does not allow writing, or indeed speaking, to a non-Jew."[180] But surely, one might think, it is altogether unreasonable to ask a religious community to break with the Republic on election day, thus ostracizing itself from the life of the nation. Not at all, replied *Libération*: "populist Judaism" even demands "a sort of cultural exception" that takes the form of being excused from class, since "the new school year and examination periods often fall during the feasts of Yom Kippur and Rosh Hashanah"—proof, if any more were needed, of "a rejudaization of the community that has been manifest since the massive arrival of Sephardi from North Africa in the early 1960s. . . . This hyperreligiosity is limited for the most part to its disciplinary aspect, to the strict observance of rules known here as *mitzvot*."[181]

This vision of Jews as a backward—almost threatening—race, couched in a language full of mystery, is staggering: one can scarcely imagine such a strange, sectarian indictment being brought against another denomination. But more striking still is the fiercely hostile response to a request that, within the framework of an open secularism, one should have thought would be granted without discussion; a request that neighboring societies, such as Italy, grant without a murmur of protest. It was as though rescheduling an election threatened the foundations of the Republic—which nonetheless has never chosen Easter Monday as a day for elections. No one will deny that clerical pressures are present in the Jewish world, just as they are in the Catholic, Protestant, and Islamic worlds; nor that intolerance, dogmatism, and the rejection of pluralism and diversity may be found among Jews, as they are among Muslims and Christians. Still, the communitarianization of French Jews is more fantasy than reality; indeed, in many respects they still form an "imaginary community." Though microsocieties do form here and there, they in no way transform French Jews into a homogeneous group, for the simple reason that their unshakable commitment to republican citizenship works to prevent self-imposed isolation or withdrawal from the larger society. French Jews have joined their fellow citizens in subscribing to the new secularism—a secularism that is plural, hostile to proselytizing, respectful of the public sphere, but respectful also of the survival, deep in people's hearts, of private beliefs and loyalties. Curiously, it is the state and, to a lesser extent, the media that treat French Jews as an undifferentiated whole,[182] assigning them a place within symbolic boundaries. The absurdity of regarding citizens who hold to a particular creed as constituting a single community (thereby separating them, as in the past, from their fellow citizens) needs hardly be pointed out: daily experience alone refutes such nonsense. No less than that of citizens of other faiths, Jewish life within contemporary French society is characterized by a high degree of pluralism.

Protestantism stands out as perhaps the most individualized of the major faiths in France, having freed itself from the temptation to imagine itself as a community while rejecting externally imposed communitarian conceptions. The disappearance of anti-Protestantism, which was still virulent at the turn of the century, led to the decline of a demeaning and stereotyped perception of Protestants, while among them the memory of persecution faded as well. Like Catholics, Jews, and, increasingly, Muslims—probably still more so, in fact—Protestants have opposed all attempts to institutionalize their identity. Their collective visibility remains weak, even if their presence in the highest offices of the state since the Left's return to power in 1981 cannot be ignored: in the persons of Michel Rocard, Lionel Jospin, and many others,[183] Protestants have played a considerable role in government. Lionel Jospin, it will be recalled, exercised a decisive influence in the adoption and implementation of an open secularism. On becoming prime minister in July 1997, his government made a decision that was highly charged with symbolic significance. Within days of taking office, the new prime minister, who had previously shown great tolerance in the matter of the headscarves, met with spokesmen for undocumented immigrants—persons who, along with their families, were being harassed by the police, hunted from church to church, and rudely kicked out of one disused shelter after another. He promised rapid naturalization for those who were spouses of French men or women, regularization of the status of parents of children born in France, protection for political refugees, and so on.[184]

The values of Protestantism (notably individualism, tolerance, secularism) seem actually to have become those of society as a whole—so much so that the notion of the Protestantization of French society has practically become a cliché. Hence the question whether Protestantism is doomed to die out, having lost its special character. The funeral of Gaston Deferre, the interior minister (1981–84) and then minister of planning (1984–86) under Mitterrand—conducted with great pomp at the Cathédrale de la Major in Marseilles at the request of Deferre's wife, a Catholic—caused much gnashing of teeth among Protestants, who considered it a "suicidal" expression of goodwill. Eight young people (a black African, an Armenian, an Asian, a North African, a Christian, a Jew, a Muslim, and a Provençal) wearing white shirts decorated with the socialist rose marched inside, symbolizing the communities of Marseilles and of *la France plurielle*. At the end, the archbishop pronounced absolutions, thus "Catholiciz[ing] the ceremony."[185]

There have been signs of Protestant renewal, particularly the success enjoyed each September by the Gathering in the Desert, a festival commemorating the Edict of Nantes (1598)—the paramount symbol of the integration of Protestants into the nation and *lieu de mémoire* of French Protestantism.[186] Nevertheless, Protestant identity has seemed in recent years to be suffering from "a loss of visibility."[187] Far from embodying a Walzerian "thick" communitarianism, it has become increasingly diluted. In 1995 only 39 percent of Protestants said they continued to believe in salvation "by grace alone." Fifty-three percent did not believe in it at all; 15 percent never went to church, even on major religious holidays; 26 percent never prayed, and 34 percent never read the Bible. If Protestants remain faithful to a certain moral strictness, being more apt than their fellow citizens to feel that cheating on taxes, driving too fast, and shoplifting are morally wrong, their opinions about marital infidelity, abortion, and homosexuality do not in any way set them apart from their compatriots.[188]

And while Protestants remain sympathetic to the Left, they have moved closer politically to the electorate as a whole; indeed, as their voting behavior less and less resembles that of a community, it has become increasingly hard to distinguish them from Catholics.[189] Even if they are not indifferent to the born-again Christian movement, with the Alliance Évangélique Française [French Evangelical Alliance] organizing rallies that display the same passionate sense of identity as their counterparts in the English-speaking world;[190] if in 1998 they celebrated with great fanfare the four hundredth anniversary of the signing of the Edict of Nantes by Henry IV; and if they also protested the pope's coming to Paris on 23 August 1997 to celebrate the closing mass of the World Youth Conference, the eve of the four hundred and twenty-fifth anniversary of the Saint Bartholomew's Day Massacre,[191] still the profound integration of Protestants into French life prevents them from defining themselves any longer by contrast with a hostile Catholic majority. All of this makes the character of their collective identity still more uncertain.[192]

Some religious minorities do show a tendency, on the other hand, to form closed, homogenous, institutionalized communities, endowed with a strong emotional dimension and organized around a ceaselessly reimagined past. The Armenians, for example, though they too have experienced integration on an individual level, preserve a communitarian belief that is consolidated by their apostolic church and shaped by a tragic history that they continue to recall every day. Whereas the first generations of Armenians in France were rapidly integrated, since the 1970s they have collectively felt a need to maintain a sense of ethnic identity.[193] Still others, such as the Asian minority in Paris, are concentrated in specific neighborhoods and have their own ethnic networks and community organizations. They nonetheless consider themselves to be French citizens and do not wish to be seen as constituting a separate community. They are strongly opposed to any form of ethnic representation, and the fact that they continue to seek integration within the larger society suggests that they will eventually disperse into other arrondissements of the capital.[194]

All this goes to show the extreme diversity of ethnic and religious identities in France today. To be sure, advocates of radical communitarianism are at work almost everywhere: from the fundamentalists of Saint-Nicolas-du-Chardonnet and their ilk to the Lubavitch; from Protestants influenced by American evangelism to upholders of the shari'a, or traditional Islamic law; from Armenian irredentists to Vietnamese who devote themselves to the preservation of traditional native culture—not omitting the many members of millenarian religious sects, who, like the born-again Christians, are the prisoners of their own certitudes. But if the supporters of a "thick" ethnic and religious communitarianism enjoy great visibility, the irreversible advance of secularization assures that they will remain a very marginal presence. French society is hardly threatened by a fatal "ghettoization" signaling withdrawal into communities whose private forms of association are inimical to a shared public life. With the rise of a moderate communitarianism, which is establishing itself despite misunderstandings, prejudices, and tensions—even occasional conflicts—among members of different communities, and with the gradual demise of intermediate institutions between the state and the various churches, the way toward a nuanced form of cultural pluralism channeled by an open secularism, under the vigilant supervision of the Council of State, slowly begins to open up.

There is still a tendency to think of French identity, as exemplified by the nation's great public works, its monuments and its architecture, as a uniform whole.[195] But the explosion of identities in recent years—including the new voice found by women, who had long been relegated to the home and private life,[196] and the sudden emergence of the gay community[197]—has had the effect of breaking up the old monolithic picture. The process of decentralization, whose political consequences we noted earlier, in its turn has encouraged the emergence of dormant local and regional identities, which are now reimagined with the ebbing away of Jacobin centralism and, like other forms of specific identity, are gradually finding formal expression within the framework of public law.[198] The time when Barère angrily inveighed against a "Tower of Babel" in France, arguing that "the language of a free people must be one and the same for all," and when Grégoire vowed to "utterly destroy dialects,"[199] now seems very far away indeed.[200] It is with a mixture of astonishment and misgiving that one looks back today on Jacobin plans for geometrically carving out new departments, shattering cultures and traditions in the name of Reason;[201] but how familiar, by contrast, Mirabeau's objection now seems: "I would like a physical division directly related to localities and circumstances, not an almost ideal mathematical division whose execution seems to me impracticable. I would like a division whose objective is not only to establish proportional representation but also to draw together the administration of men and things and to encourage greater participation on the part of citizens."[202]

Mirabeau's program would have been better adapted to con-

temporary France, and to the current atmosphere of profound political and cultural decentralization, than to revolutionary France.
To be sure, as article 2 of the Constitution of 1958 stipulates,
"France is an indivisible Republic." But the recent decentralizing
measures come at a moment when the nation is celebrating the
official birth of "countries" (defined by the Pasqua law of 1993 as
"coherent spaces . . . that express a community of interests," constituting an actual "biological memory of the Hexagon" that com-
prehends more than 250 entities characterized by "geographic,
cultural, economic, and social cohesiveness")[203]—in the Béarn
and the Catharist lands of the southwest, for example, Protestant
regions that once were the site of violent clashes with Catholics;
at a moment when regions blossom with reborn identities, when
ancient languages once again flourish, and even a certain political
irredentism asserts itself, both in Alsace and in the Basque country. Under these circumstances, a purely Jacobin conception of
the national territory no longer seems appropriate. The Giordan
report, commissioned by the Mauroy government in 1982, forcefully argued that "the recognition and promotion of minority
languages are at the heart of the elaboration of a new policy concerning the linguistic practices of France."[204] The report advocated the rehabilitation not only of Occitan (of which Provençal
is a dialect) in the south and southwest but also of the linguistic
cultures of Normandy, Picardy, Poitou, Corsica, the Flemish-
speaking north, Alsace, Brittany, and the Basque country; expressed eagerness to assist minority languages such as Yiddish;
and favored the publication and use of such languages on television as well as in a regional context (on road signs, for example,
with administrative officials being trained in the language of the
region, and so on).

This renaissance of regional identities—which would have
made Abbé Grégoire turn over in his grave—developed to such a
point that bilingual schools emerged in Brittany and the Basque
country, partially financed by parents and recognized by the municipalities,[205] while in 1986 a formal qualification for teaching
Breton at the secondary level was created. The *langue d'oc*, like

other regional languages, was now offered as an elective at all levels, the government justifying such instruction on the grounds that it "does not challenge national unity, but opens up to families who desire it a new dimension in the education of their children."[206] In September 1997, going a step further, the first bilingual French-Occitan secondary school opened outside Montpellier.[207] This respect for differences, relying on cultural policies put into effect by municipalities,[208] has aroused uneasiness among supporters of a unified and indivisible France, but lacking any "thick" communitarian aspect, it cannot plausibly be seen as undermining the coherence of the nation.

Events in Corsica, however, were more troubling. In 1982 Gaston Deferre declared before the regional assembly of Corsica that the legislation proposed by the government pursuant to the Giordan Report, "while taking into account the special circumstances of Corsica, while granting Corsicans the possibility of affirming their cultural identity and their distinctive place in French life, . . . of freely administering their own affairs," was meant to guarantee civil order. In October 1988 the Corsican assembly recognized "the existence of the Corsican people as a historic community" whose "cultural identity" must be defended. In May 1990 Pierre Joxe proposed to "search for lasting solutions to the Corsican problem" by recognizing "the original character of the interests of the region of Corsica" and by refusing to "disregard its cultural and social identity." He found that Corsica's special character made necessary "a new definition of local institutions outside the common law governing regions created since 1982," which is to say the election of members of the regional assembly on an island-wide rather than departmental basis, with local ministerial agencies, local control over cultural policy, a "plan for the Corsican language," and so on.

For defenders of French unity this was too much, for it laid the groundwork for Corsica to exit the French nation. Corsican representatives to the National Assembly, by contrast, as well as local leaders committed to challenging the island's traditional clientelist elites, welcomed the recognition of the Corsican people and its language, its identity, and the possibility of creating a place for Corsican nationalism.[209] The Constitutional Council was quick to order an abrupt halt to the "separatism"[210] to which it feared regionalism might lead "if the state were to be absent,"[211] and in its decision of 9 May 1991 refused to validate an essential part of the government's plan. Reaffirming the unity of the nation, it cited the fact that

> France is, as article 2 of the Constitution of 1958 proclaims, an indivisible, secular, democratic, and social Republic that assures the equality before the law of all citizens, whatever their origin; moreover, the mention made by one legislator of the "Corsican people," as a component of the French people, is contrary to the Constitution, which recognizes only the French people, composed of all French [who are] citizens, without distinctions as to origin, race, or religion.[212]

The council therefore moved to set limits to Corsican claims of separate identity, whose potential "thickness" it saw as an alarming sign of the disintegration of national unity, especially since such claims were founded on a "community of blood" that was incompatible with the "community of citizens," official recognition of which would constitute a "genuine failure of the Republic."[213]

Extending its call to order in Corsica, the council went on to challenge certain aspects of a proposed statute concerning French Polynesia that would have deprived the state of its prerogatives, to the advantage of local authorities.[214] Regional identities could not be allowed to compete with allegiance to the nation. For this reason, France refused to sign the European accord on regional and minority languages. Indeed, of all the countries in the European community, only France refers in its Constitution to an official language without mentioning the other languages spoken on its territory.[215] In the wake of the Constitutional Council's veto, identity-based regionalism met with a certain indifference on the part of the population as well: in 1993 only one pupil in five elected to take regional language courses.

Apart perhaps from the Corsican example, where a "thicker" identity expresses itself, regional identities typically are "thin," volatile, and irresolute, and therefore unlikely to serve as a framework for an imprisoning communitarianism. Like religious and cultural identities, with but rare exceptions, regional identities aim to establish themselves in the public sphere without, however, claiming to represent "nations within a nation." As mutual rivals, they highlight the pluralist dimension of French society, and because they are partial perspectives, devoid of conquering pretentions, none of them has the ambition of reimagining France in some new and different way. The difficulty of the present situation, then, consists in exactly this: peace between the old fraternal enemies, the Catholic Church and the republican state, has favored the emergence of plural identities and cultures, but the void has not been filled, with the result that France's future as a nation is no clearer than it was before, perhaps less so. This void is precisely the one that the National Front wishes to fill.

For the first time in the history of France, a party has been able to attract roughly 15 percent of the vote by openly declaring itself to be racist. Even in the legislative elections of May 1997, where circumstances were unfavorable to it, the FN managed to conserve this share. Its leader, Jean-Marie Le Pen, had provoked an immense brouhaha a few months earlier by calmly remarking, "I observe that races are unequal."[216] Not to be outdone, Bruno Mégret, writing in the official program of the Front National, *L'Alternative nationale*, asserted that an authentic people constitutes "a community of men and women who mutually recognize themselves as united to each other by language, culture, blood, and history."[217] In his view, French identity could not support any rival identities whatsoever. Blood and race constitute its cultural foundation, which tolerates no pluralism, no difference. Le Pen, for his part, called not only for an electoral "war" but also for a "civil war,"[218] exhorting the young people of the movement in the following terms: "Now only the National Front can snatch the

271

country from decadence.[219] . . . There will come a moment when everything will stop and this will be the revolution.[220] . . . You must prepare your hearts and minds for it."[221]

Le Pen adopted the fascist slogan of the 1930s, "Neither Left nor Right—French!"; opened the ranks of the FN to radical organizations such as L'Œuvre Française (whose name refers to the work needing to be carried out in order to renew France) and Nouvelle Résistance [New Resistance]; objected to the characterization of his movement as extreme right wing, claiming to speak in the name of the real people, beyond the false cleavages of political life; and renewed the populist agitation of the interwar period, only this time on behalf of a powerful party with solid local seats, durably established in the French political landscape thanks to its many electoral successes. Reviling the "anti-French racism" that makes "native-born French . . . an inferior race,"[222] he sought to salvage antiracism by posing as the defender of the French race, the only race, in his view, that no longer preserved its uniqueness, its "superiority."[223] In the opinion of Pierre Vial, a member of the FN political bureau, "We are headed straight for an ethnic war, and this war will be total"[224]—so great is "the anger of the people,"[225] who are once again ready to rise up, as they did at the turn of the century, against the "swine," the "politician-dogs" (*politichiens*), the technocrats insensitive to the values and expectations of the real France.[226] As the direct heir to the counterrevolutionary Right, the National Front endorsed the Catholic violence of Maistre, whose "brutal lucidity"[227] it continued to venerate while putting it in the service of the populism earlier embodied by Drumont and Barrès, mixing xenophobic and racist chauvinism with the cult of the soil. In many respects, the *lepéniste* movement exploited the bellicose chauvinism that for centuries had sworn an implacable hatred of the English, Muslims, and Jews,[228] only now this chauvinism was transposed from the rural to the urban world, where it flourished all the more. "Will we still be French in thirty years?"—thus the anguished cry of the National Front.[229]

Rejecting both the church—at once Protestantized and Judaized—and the state—which, in the hands of the "Establish-ment," had become the captive of "globalism"—the National Front rushed into the void created by the ideological retreat of the old fraternal enemies. At a moment when the creation of a society open to "thin" rival identities remained in doubt, it offered itself as the yeast for reconstituting a "thick" national community pos-sessed of a strong identity. The image of France that it success-fully peddled to a segment of the population vehemently opposed to multiculturalism, secular openness, and cultural pluralism was not a new one. The FN pursued a deliberate strategy, aimed well beyond its own voters, of conquering the minds of the people in order then to conquer power. Denouncing "the school of the cos-mopolitan republic," Le Pen paid tribute to Charles Martel, who had repelled an earlier "Muslim invasion" (at Poitiers in 732), while hedging his bets with a skillful syncretism that blended race, blood, and faith.

Le Pen cast his net wide: claiming descent from the Celts, Vikings, and the Aryans, he broadcast the message of a New Right in search of Indo-European roots; organized expeditions in the forest of Brocéliande, known for its evil spells; venerated pagan Saxon warriors; and, brandishing the solar wheel, claimed to draw inspiration from an ancient Hellenic-Celtic civilization. At the same time he presented himself as the heir of Catholic France. Surrounded by loyal supporters from Chrétien-Solidarité [Chris-tian Solidarity] and fundamentalist Catholics who embraced the ideas of Monsignor Lefebvre (as well as all those who nursed nos-talgic memories of Vichy and the OAS), Le Pen took every oppor-tunity to make his religious devotion known. He took part in pilgrimages, worshiped the Virgin Mary, celebrated the memory of Clovis and Joan of Arc, denounced the "forces of evil" at every turn, attended every mass publicized in the media, and joined the Crusaders of the Sacred Heart in their struggle against abortion, which was alleged to pervert the soul of Christian France—all the while propagating a vitalist, organic, and racial ethnonation-alism.[230] As the spokesman of a hybrid tradition that crossed fundamentalist Catholicism[231] with Poujadism, he assiduously cultivated an anti-Semitism whose insidious formulas relied on malignant metaphors. In his speeches, which borrowed directly from revisionist interpretations of the Holocaust, he dismissed the genocide of the Jews as a mere historical "detail." Referring in 1988 to the "Durafour-crématoire," he combined contempt for the crematoriums (*fours crématoires*) of the Nazi concentration camps with mockery of Michel Durafour, then the minister of public administration. He tirelessly assailed the "Jewish [and Masonic] internationals," whose power was supposed to be such that they controlled the press, politicians, and even Jacques Chirac, who was "kept" by Jewish organizations, as François Mitterrand had been before him—a "pact" that "turned out well for him: as you can see, he's president."[232]

But with the rise of Le Pen, a genuine fissure appeared for the first time between Catholicism and the extreme nationalist Right. Catholic support for the Republic was now unmistakable: the counterrevolutionary model had broken apart. Despite its dramatic gestures and ostentatious shows of solidarity with the remnants of the old staunch and revanchist Catholicism, the National Front no longer enjoyed the support of a part of the population on which the leagues of the late nineteenth century and the interwar period had always been able to count. Catholics whose sense of religious identity was unambiguous, and profoundly felt, now turned away from Le Pen.[233] Although the self-proclaimed standard-bearer of Christian France declared with conviction, "I am proud of being Christian as I am proud of being French,"[234] Jean-Marie Le Pen had become the bête noire of the Church.[235] Observant Catholics kept their distance, preferring the traditional parties of the Right. From now on, a "left-wing *lepénisme*"[236] drew its followers more from the traditionally Communist and Socialist working class. It prospered in departments of the north and east that were hard hit by deindustrialization: Seine-Saint-Denis outside Paris, the Haut-Rhin and Bas-Rhin of Alsace, and Moselle in Lorraine. In these districts the old unions had lost a substantial part of their membership: of those that remained, 5 percent of the Socialist CFDT, 7 percent of the Communist CGT, 16 percent of the moderate FO [the result of a split within the CGT], and 17 percent of the Socialist teachers' union FEN said they voted for Le Pen in the 1995 presidential election.[237] The Communist Party, for its part, had seen its rank-and-file membership greatly reduced: the working class was split and fragmented, crippled by wave after wave of dismissals and redeployments of industrial capacity that transformed the "workers' fortresses" of Lorraine, the Nord–Pas-de-Calais region, and the Paris basin into so many dreary ecomuseums designed to attract tourists in search of a faded past, so many *lieux de mémoire*—places of memory rather than of life or action. Many disappointed labor activists now turned to Le Pen,[238] who assumed the role of tribune, claiming to represent the interests, as well as the confusions, of a working class that had lost its sense of collective identity and now found itself left to its own devices.[239]

The mythic landmarks of the working-class past were suddenly collapsing: the Renault plants in Boulogne-Billancourt, coveted by real estate developers, had been dismantled; the glassworks at Carmaux, which Jaurès had represented a century ago, were now closed. Strikes were now rare, as were the great marches of the past from the Place de la Nation to the Place de la Bastille in Paris, and from the Place de la République to the Place de la Nation. The working class was coming apart, to the point that the transmission of its culture to the next generation was now a matter of some doubt. Workers were abandoning collective action, and the CGT lost its long-uncontested primacy in elections to worker-management committees. In such a world, anything was possible. The National Front sought to appeal to workers by proposing a new form of imaginary community, one detached from social cleavages and indifferent to social issues. Among this splintered segment of the population, the FN suddenly became the leading party: in the 1995 presidential election, 30 percent of employed workers declared themselves in favor of the FN. The party subsequently maintained its standing among workers, achieving unheard-of electoral successes in areas where large-scale industries had once ruled. The FN was now the leading party among the unemployed as well. In this respect, it was quite unlike Action Française in the early decades of the century, which had recruited its members from the ranks of the wealthy rural French society of the Catholic counterrevolution; quite unlike, too, the Poujadism of the 1950s, which appealed to the small shopkeepers of provincial France.

In a certain sense the FN might be said to have revived the xenophobic socialism of the populist Boulangism of the late 1880s, bringing together workers, artisans, shopkeepers, various elements of the middle class, and supporters of the Catholic counterrevolution in a broad-based common front, an "alliance of shop and workshop."[240] Unlike its predecessor, however, the FN enjoyed a firm electoral foothold, with deep-rooted long-term support among local politicians and an entirely novel institutional infrastructure. This unprecedented alliance was all the more impressive as it asserted itself through the ballot box rather than through the volatile demonstrations either of *putschiste* Boulangism or of the fascist movements of the prewar period—movements that were similarly hostile to church and state and that, like the National Front, were anxious to do away with both in order to impose an imagined community founded on blood and race rather than citizenship or faith.

Le Pen found that he was able to exploit fictive and reinvented identity-based demands to his advantage, such as the ones now being heard in Alsace—prosperous, peaceful, yet uneasy;[241] and to give voice to the sort of particularist fears shared along the coast of Brittany.[242] In this way the National Front succeeded in challenging the growing appeal of individualistic morality, given life to visions of a communitarian utopia beyond republican dreams and reactionary counterdreams, and reimagined a strong collective identity—all this before an alternative model of economic liberalism combined with cultural pluralism managed to establish itself. It seeks its own models where fortress identities survive and where difference is openly rejected; where the last closed social systems successfully resist the great liberal transformation of the late twentieth century.

Though the FN enviously contemplates an eternally homogeneous Japan, where no foreigner, or almost none, can become Japanese,[243] it is above all to Switzerland that it turns a jealous eye—curiously, or so it would appear at first, considering the National Front's dreams of power and virile domination. The FN has little to say about Swiss democracy, or about the Swiss tradition of social and cultural pluralism. Nonetheless, it sees in Switzerland a society that is admirably attached to its roots, accepting foreigners only on the condition (with very few exceptions) that they remain foreigners. It sees a society hostile to European institutions that dissolve national identity; a society that gives itself over wholeheartedly to the mechanism of popular referendum, through which the real society expresses itself—determined, unlike the legal society (which is to say the state), to preserve its traditions, its culture, its identity. The National Front's unrivaled admiration for the former canton of Appenzell recalls the very favorable opinion of it formed by Solzhenitsyn, who was impressed by its practice of a community-based democracy untainted by individualist assumptions inimical to collective identity—as if to say: here you are, then, an example to follow instead of the pernicious American multiculturalism!

Yvan Blot, the founder and principal spokesman of the extreme right-wing Club de l'Horloge, sings the praises of the Helvetian model in his turn. The Swiss cantons were "not created with the stroke of a pen by the central administration" but rather were the "product of an organic historical evolution." The national assembly, composed of citizens who put on "ceremonial dress and respect rites that give them a feeling for what is sacred, . . . rooted in common values," seems to him obviously "related to the assemblies of the ancient Teutons," translating the values of the people into reality. "Having witnessed," he adds, "sessions of the National Assembly in Paris and the *Landsgemeinde* of Appenzell, I can testify that the behavior of the citizens of this small canton tucked away in the mountains is much more dignified than that of many of my colleagues, notably during the hectic televised Wednesday afternoon sessions."[244] Blot is inexhaustible when it comes to boasting of the authenticity of the cantons of Vaud, Uri, Schwyz, and Unterwalden, whose citizens represent so many "companions united by oath"; he is reassured that "the Swiss people have proved to be very cautious in the matter of naturalization," noting that ultimate authority resides with the commune of residence, which is careful to think twice before issuing its approval. Freedom, in his view, is well defended only "by citizens having roots [where they live and] who are sure of their identity. . . . Consequently, to see what suits France, we need first to find our own national roots."[245] The Club de l'Horloge, for its part, misses no opportunity to pay tribute to Switzerland in its newsletters.[246]

Jean-Marie Le Pen shows a particular fondness for the Swiss model as well, holding it out to his countrymen as an ideal paradigm for France. In this he stands in sharp contrast to Maurras, who harshly attacked France's neighbor to the southeast as the source of individualist Protestant ideas. "Switzerland," Le Pen notes approvingly, "does not hesitate to protect the jobs of its nationals. . . . It thus furnishes proof that democracy is perfectly compatible with a national[ist] employment policy."[247] As against the importation of multiculturalism à l'américaine, with its variable identities; as against "these colonies of people that no longer intend to live in accordance with the norms of the French system but according to their own customs";[248] and as against the prospect of "a multicommunity France . . . , a tribal France" and the "formation of foreign enclaves on French territory,"[249] the National Front points to examples of strong state control that promise to defend a common and organic collective identity while ensuring that the outsider remains a stranger, forever locked up in his difference, barred from a native community that is securely rooted in a "thick" culture. It is not a coincidence that the FN's success continues to grow at a time when rival identities flourish—identities that nonetheless for the most part show respect for each other. What the National Front proposes to the French people, who are increasingly captivated by the prospect of a uniform national identity closed to immigrants,[250] is a magical solution to their distress, to their loss of confidence in grand political visions of the nation and in the legacy of the Enlightenment, now in disarray, as well as an alternative to the growing de-Christianization of France: in short, another means of believing.

Conclusion

The image of France begins to blur. What was once a triangle narrowing toward the south,[1] barely recognizable, then became a square, a circle, an octagon; next, an irregular quadrilateral; and finally, a hexagon—a France "symmetrical, proportionate, and regular" (in Ferdinand Buisson's phrase). The nation's contours have varied over the course of its history, giving rise to opposed views of France and what it means to be French.[2] The boundaries that formerly divided the country from its neighbors so effectively now begin to fade; absorbed into a larger European territory, they have lost both their sureness and their distinctness. Now the Rhine no more protects France than do the Pyrenees. The defense of France, no longer left to the blue line of the Vosges or the Maginot line, but to a professional army (or even a multinational force whose common language is as likely to be German or English as French), slowly recedes in the imagination of its citizens. The enemy is no longer within view, so ranks cannot be closed against it. Unlike the old French passport, the passport of the European Union does not unambiguously testify either to a sharp separation of one country from another or a clear belonging to one country rather than another. As this new community nears the moment of its full and final Constitution, the law of France begins to lose its majesty, and the currency of France its independence.

It is no longer obvious how France is to be imagined. Rival identities have emerged, and local allegiances to particular memories and cultures have come into conflict—at the very moment when those two old warriors, the republican state and the Catholic Church, each of which had modeled its ambitions on the other's for so many years, have finally laid down their arms and abandoned their claims to unify the minds of the people. The Republic has renounced utopian dreams, and Catholicism has forsaken its ancient intransigence; immutable cleavages have been repaired; the local has become central; and "thin" community allegiances have enabled individuals to freely choose their values, just as a new habit of overlapping consensus permits them to make a passionate commitment to public life. Political and administrative elites, obedient to their vocation of serving the public interest, have given up their arrogant claim to govern the nation, learning the virtues of dialogue, coexistence, and cohabitation, while also discovering the road that leads to the private sector—and to money. Belligerent rhetoric has suddenly become outmoded: talk of lopping off heads and taking down names is no longer acceptable. Voters have come to be aware of the value of their personal decisions without thereby becoming pure "strategists," selfish traitors to the common good. Intellectuals and political parties are less able than they once were to dictate the meaning of history, which now suddenly seems to be within the comprehension of the ordinary citizen. Boulogne-Billancourt has been transformed into a luxurious green expanse filled with businessmen rushing about. Scotch whiskey has supplanted Ricard in the bars.

France hesitates today between apprenticeship to a foreign pluralism and a leap into the unknown; between renovating the public sphere and continuing to tolerate an impotent state, corrupt elites, attacks on the ideal of inclusive citizenship, and clashes among its constituent communities. The country's foundations may seem to be threatened by the *lepéniste* menace, which imagines a France that is neither truly republican nor essentially Catholic—an ethnic France that has been cobbled together out of heterogeneous elements, a France that is unified not by citizenship or faith but by blood. Nonetheless, the country's foundations are sound. Now that French society has been stripped of its old absolutes, which encouraged exclusion and expulsion; now that it has been freed from its interminable civil wars, from its ancestral hatreds and anxieties, France—and the uniqueness of France—have a bright future. *"Vive la France! quand même!"* exclaimed Heinrich Heine, overcome with admiration for "this persevering Penelope who each day makes and unmakes her web."[3] Only now it is a France released from the tyranny of utopian myths, determined to show respect for the cultural memories of all its citizens and to give them a sense of shared civic values—determined, too, to encourage all its citizens to work on behalf of the public good.

List of Abbreviations

BNP   Banque Nationale de Paris [National Bank of Paris]
CDS   Centre des Démocrates Sociaux [Center of Social Democrats]
CERES   Centre d'Études, de Recherches et d'Éducation Socialistes [Center for Socialist Study, Research, and Education]
CEVIPOF   Centre d'Études de la Vie Politique Française [Center for the Study of French Political Life]
CFDT   Confédération Française Démocratique du Travail [French Democratic Confederation of Labor]
CGT   Confédération Générale du Travail [General Confederation of Labor]
CNESOM   Conférence Nationale des Élus Socialistes Originaires du Maghreb [National Conference of North African–Born Elected Socialist Representatives]
ENA   École Nationale d'Administration [National School of Administration]
FEN   Fédération de l'Éducation Nationale [Federation of National Education]
FN   Front National [National Front]
FO   Confédération Générale du Travail–Force Ouvrière [General Confederation of Labor–Workers' Force]

GRECE	Groupement de Recherche et d'Études pour la Civilisation Européenne [Research and Study Group for European Civilization]
IFOP	Institut Français d'Opinion Publique [French Institute of Public Opinion]
MRAP	Mouvement contre le Racisme and pour l'Amitié entre les Peuples [Movement Against Racism and for Friendship Among Peoples]
MRP	Mouvement Républicain Populaire [People's Republican Movement]
OAS	Organisation de l'Armée Secrète [Organization of the Secret Army]
PR	Parti Républicain [Republican Party]
PCF	Parti Communiste Français [French Communist Party]
PS	Parti Socialiste [Socialist Party]
PSF	Parti Social Français [French Social Party]
RPR	Rassemblement pour la République [Rally for the Republic]
SFIO	Section Française de l'Internationale Ouvrière [French Section of the Workers' International]
SGEN	Syndicat Générale de l'Éducation Nationale [General Union for National Education]
UAP	Union des Assurances de Paris [Union of Insurance Companies of Paris]
UDCA	Union de Défense des Commerçants et des Artisans [Union for the Defense of Shopkeepers and Artisans]
UDF	Union pour la Démocratie Française [Union for French Democracy]
UDR	Union des Démocrates pour la République [Union of Democrats for the Republic]
VSNE	Volontariat pour le Service National en Entreprise [Volunteers for National Service in Business]

Notes

Introduction: Solzhenitsyn in the Vendée

1. In late winter of 1793, peasants in the Vendée rose up in violent revolt against the French Revolution when it turned against the Catholic Church. They were brutally defeated by the republican armies under Jean-Baptiste Kléber at Cholet on 17 October of the same year, though guerrilla resistance continued until 1796. —TRANS.
2. *Le Monde* (26 September 1993).
3. *Le Monde* (28 September 1993).
4. Jean-Claude Martin and Claude Suaud, *Le Puy-du-Fou, en Vendée: L'Histoire mise en scène* (Paris: L'Harmattan, 1996).
5. The reference is to the Nazi massacre of 10 June 1944 in Oradour-sur-Glane (Haute-Vienne).—TRANS.
6. *Le Figaro-Magazine* (24 April 1993). In the opinion of *Le Quotidien de Paris*, "a spiritual solidarity has been exercised these past three days, from one Vendée to the other, from that of Catholic France to that of Orthodox Russia" (27 September 1993); see also *La Croix* (28 September 1993). Philippe de Villiers has long made such quasi-"revisionist" comparisons: in his view, the Convention used the procedures of the "Final Solution" against the people of the Vendée and, in committing itself to "regeneration," foreshadowed "the Nazi hell, Stalinism, and Pol Pot"; see *Le Nouvel Obser-*

vateur (4 May 1989). Villiers therefore adopts the terminology of Reynald Secher in *Le Génocide franco-français: La Vendée-Vengée* (Paris: Presses Universitaires de France, 1986), originally a thesis defended at the Sorbonne before a jury that included the conservative Catholic historian Pierre Chaunu, who in various writings has himself adopted the expression "genocide." See too the critical review of this book by Jean-Clément Martin, in *Annales*, no. 5 (1986). Like many historians, François Lebrun challenges the use of the term "genocide" in connection with the massacres of the inhabitants of the Vendée: see "La Guerre de Vendée: Massacre ou génocide?" *L'Histoire* (May 1985), as well as his article "Terreur bleue en Vendée?" *Le Monde* (27 April 1986).

7. *Le Parisien* (24 September 1993).
8. *Le Figaro* (24 May 1993); *Le Monde* (25 May 1993).
9. *Le Monde* (7 April 1995).
10. *Le Figaro* (22 September 1993).
11. See Pierre Nora, ed., *Les Lieux de mémoire*, 7 vols. (Paris: Gallimard, 1984–92). In Nora's use of the term, *lieux* refers to a vast range of events and ideas, far beyond the literal sense of "places" or "sites": see his preface to the three-volume English-language edition, *The Realms of Memory*, trans. Arthur Goldhammer (New York: Columbia University Press, 1998). The original French edition was published in three parts: a single volume, *La République*, appeared in 1984, followed by three volumes under the title *La Nation* in 1986 and finally in 1992 another three volumes under the title *Les France*. In citing the French edition, reference will be made to the volumes sequentially. Thus, for example, the first volume of the third part is cited as the fifth of the seven volumes.—TRANS.
12. Alexander Solzhenitsyn, *Rebuilding Russia: Reflections and Tentative Proposals*, trans. Alexis Klimoff (New York: Farrar, Straus and Giroux, 1991), 21.
13. Ibid., 61.
14. Ibid., 66–67.
15. See Andrzej Walicki, *A History of Russian Thought from the Enlightenment to Marxism*, trans. Hilda Andrews-Rusiecka (Stanford: Stanford University Press, 1979), chap. 6.
16. See Yves Hamant, "L'Idéologie soviétique et l'idée nationale russe (soviétisme et russité)," in Michel Niqueux, ed., *La Question russe: Essais sur le nationalisme russe* (Caen: Centre de Recherche sur l'Évolution de l'URSS de l'Université de Caen, 1992). The author

explicitly associates Solzhenitsyn's recent writings with another patriotic and spiritual tendency that is chiefly concerned with facilitating the resurgence of the Church but that nonetheless rejects any backsliding into Bolshevist nationalism (94–95). See also Paul Latawski, ed., *Contemporary Nationalism in East Central Europe* (New York: St. Martin's Press, 1995).

17. Ernest Gellner quite particularly insists on this relationship between cultural resurgence, nationalist explosion, and challenge to the state in post-Soviet societies: see his "Nationalism and the Vacuum," in Alexandre Motyl, ed., *Thinking Theoretically About Soviet Nationalities: History and Comparison in the Study of the USSR* (New York: Columbia University Press, 1992). In the same vein, see Jack Snyder, "Nationalism and the Crisis of the Post-Soviet State," *Survival* (Summer 1993).

18. Krzytof Wolicki, "Une Pologne toute catholique?" *Le Débat* 67 (1991). See also Paul Zawadzki, "Entre histoire et politique: La Constitution du 3 mai et la construction étatique en Pologne," *La Nouvelle Alternative* (October 1991).

19. Denis Paillard, "Russie/URSS: Le Discours national russe comme mémoire et refus," *Langages* (June 1994), 100–101. On the explosion of anti-Semitism in the countries of Eastern Europe, something that had not gone away during the Soviet period, see André Gerrits, "Paradox of Freedom: The 'Jewish Question' in Post-Communist East Central Europe," in Ian Cuthbertson and Jane Leibowitz, eds., *Minorities: The New Europe's Old Issue* (Prague: Institute for EastWest Studies, 1993). See also Neil Landsnen, "Anti-Semitism in Eastern Europe," *Journal of Area Studies*, no. 4 (1994); and Paul Zawadzki, "Transition, nationalisme et antisémitisme: L'Exemple polonais," in Pierre Birnbaum, ed., *Sociologie des nationalismes* (Paris: Presses Universitaires de France, 1997).

20. See Todoritchka Gotovska-Popova, "Nationalism in Post-Communist Eastern Europe," *East European Quarterly* (June 1993), 173. On the resurgence of nationalist sentiment in the countries of the former Communist bloc, see the various articles in *Journal of Area Studies*, no. 4 (1994).

21. Isaiah Berlin, *Russian Thinkers*, eds. Henry Hardy and Aileen Kelly (New York: Viking, 1978), 64–65, 67.

22. Ramin Jahanbegloo, *Conversations with Isaiah Berlin* (London: Peter Halban, 1992), 172, 185–86.

23. Colette Beaune, *Naissance de la nation France* (Paris: Gallimard, 1985).

24. In her fine book on nationalism, Leah Greenfeld holds that France, having borrowed neither the Anglo-Saxon model oriented toward individualism and civic nationalism nor that of nations farther to the east, from Germany to Russia, committed to ethnic nationalism, constitutes an "ambivalent" case; in her view, the clash between the ethnic and civic dimensions of French nationalism has historically been so strong that *la Grande Nation*—the most national of nations—exhibits a split personality marked by extreme devotion to radically opposed ideals. See *Nationalism: Five Roads to Modernity* (Cambridge, Mass.: Harvard University Press, 1992), 14, 187.

25. From Maurice Agulhon's preface to Jacqueline Lalouette, *La Libre-Pensée en France, 1848–1940* (Paris: Albin Michel, 1997), 12.

26. Jacques Le Goff, *Saint Louis* (Paris: Gallimard, 1996), 292, 795–96, 800, 802. See also Jean Richard, *Histoire des croisades* (Paris: Fayard, 1996), 51ff.

27. Bernhard Blumenkranz, *Les Juifs en France: Écrits dispersés* (Paris: Les Belles Lettres, 1989), 126.

28. Francisco Bethencourt, *L'Inquisition à l'époque moderne: Espagne, Portugal, Italie, XVe–XIXe siècle* (Paris: Fayard, 1995), 299–300.

29. Robert Mandrou, *Introduction à la France moderne, 1500–1640: Essai de psychologie historique* (Paris: Albin Michel, 1961), 361. On the complex interaction of historical figures who downplayed the responsibility of the monarchy, see Mary Sutherland, "Le Massacre de la Saint-Barthélemy: La Valeur des témoignages et leur interprétation," *Revue d'histoire moderne et contemporaine* (October–December 1991). Denis Crouzet, choosing to stress the unforeseeability of decisions and sequences of events in an international context that favored every kind of rumor, writes that "the inhuman and barbarous night of 24 August 1572 deserves to be considered the most significant event of a long sixteenth century, as it concentrated all the anxiety and elation, all the resentments and aspirations [of the period], becoming for a long while one of the major issues of French memory." In Crouzet's view, the massacre resulted from a dominant "exclusivist imagination" that challenged any notion of religious pluralism; see *La Nuit de la Saint-Barthélemy* (Paris: Fayard, 1994), 26, 537.

30. See Natalie Zemon Davis, *Society and Culture in Early Modern France: Eight Essays* (Stanford: Stanford University Press, 1975); also Élisabeth Labrousse, "Calvinism in France, 1598–1685," in Michael Prestwich, ed., *International Calvinism, 1541–1715* (Oxford: Oxford University Press, 1986); and the conference proceed-

ings edited by Roger Zuber and Laurent Theis, *La Révocation de l'édit de Nantes et le protestantisme français en 1685: Actes du colloque de Paris (15–19 octobre 1985)* (Paris: Société d'Histoire du Protestantisme Français, 1986). In his article "La Décision royale," Pierre Chaunu compares the people of the Vendée with the Protestants of Cévennes, the Camisards, with this formula: "Camisards and *Vendéens*: Same cause, same fight"—both fighting, in his view, for freedom and against the state (that of Louis XIV and the French Revolution, respectively). For highly critical commentary on this style of analysis, according to which the French Revolution was guilty of "genocide," pure and simple, see Steven Kaplan, *Adieu 89* (Paris: Fayard, 1993), pt. 4, chap. 1.

31. The Edict of Nantes, defining the rights of French Protestants, had been promulgated by Henry IV in 1598 to restore internal peace in France, disrupted by the Wars of Religion since 1562.—TRANS.

32. Warren Scoville, *The Persecution of Huguenots and French Economic Development, 1680 to 1720* (Berkeley: University of California Press, 1960). See also Sanche de Gramont, *Epitaph for Kings* (New York: Putnam's, 1967), and Abraham Lavender, *French Huguenots* (New York: Peter Lang, 1990).

33. François Lebrun, "L'Enracinement (1677–1770)," in François Lebrun, ed., *Histoire des catholiques en France* (Paris: Hachette, 1985), 231.

34. See Élisabeth Labrousse and Robert Sauzet, "La Lente mise en place de la réforme tridentine, 1598–1661" and "Au Temps du Roi-Soleil (1661–1720)," in Jacques Le Goff and René Rémond, eds., *Histoire de la France religieuse, XIVᵉ–XVIIIᵉ siècle* (Paris: Seuil, 1988).

35. Élisabeth Labrousse, *Une Foi, une loi, un roi? La Révocation de l'édit de Nantes* (Paris and Geneva: Labor et Fidès, 1985). See also Nancy Lyman Roelker, *One King, One Faith: The Parlement of Paris and the Religious Reformations of the Sixteenth Century* (Berkeley: University of California Press, 1996). Olivier Christin analyzes "the failure of the peaceful coexistence of denominations" in France and Germany, and the recourse to an impartial state as a form of protection, although in France the state "chose its camp and betrayed its word"; see *La Paix de religion: L'Autonomisation de la raison politique au XVIᵉ siècle* (Paris: Seuil, 1997), 78ff., 176, 201.

36. Janine Garrisson, *L'Édit de Nantes et sa révocation: Histoire d'une intolérance* (Paris: Seuil, 1987), 101, 275. This war of religions was also a war of propaganda: satirical drawings were widespread

during the period, as Catholics used the cruelty of Protestants to justify their own atrocities. On the war of images waged on the Catholic side, see the example of Richard Verstegen, whose *Le Théâtre des cruautés* (1587) has recently been reprinted (Paris: Éditions Chandeigne, 1995).

37. "Et réunis enfin sous une même foi/N'ayons qu'un Dieu, qu'un cœur, qu'une Église, qu'un Roi." Charles du Périer, *Poème*, in *Pièces de poésies qui ont remporté le prix de l'Académie française depuis 1671 jusqu'à 1747* (Paris, 1747), 67; cited by Geoffrey Adams, *The Huguenots and French Opinion, 1685–1787: The Enlightenment Debate on Toleration* (Waterloo, Ont.: Editions SR, 1991), 19.

38. Cited by Joseph de Maistre in *Réflexions sur le protestantisme*, in *Œuvres complètes*, 14 vols. (Lyons, 1884–86), 8:80.

39. Bertrand Badie and Pierre Birnbaum, *Sociologie de l'État* (Paris: Hachette, 1982).

40. Jacques-Bénigne Bossuet, *Politique tirée des propres paroles de l'Écriture sainte* (1709), cited by Philippe Boutry, "Dieu," in Jean-François Sirinelli, ed., *Histoire des droites en France*, 3 vols. (Paris: Gallimard, 1992), 3:230.

41. Quoted in Michel Vovelle, "C'est la faute à la Révolution," in Le Goff and Rémond, eds., *Histoire de la France religieuse*, 262. See also, in the same volume, Vovelle's article "Cultes révolutionnaires et religions laïques," 510–11.

42. Éric Conan and Henry Rousso, *Vichy: Un Passé qui ne passe pas* (Paris: Fayard, 1994).

43. Marie-Claire Lavabre, "L'Identité française est-elle en crise?" *French Politics and Society* (Winter 1996).

44. François Furet, Jacques Julliard, and Pierre Rosanvallon, *La République du centre: La Fin de l'exception française* (Paris: Calmann-Lévy, 1986), 18.

45. Régis Debray, *Modeste Contribution aux discours et cérémonies officielles du dixième anniversaire* (Paris: Maspero, 1978), 39–40.

46. Michel Crozier, *La Société bloquée* (Paris: Seuil, 1970), 179.

47. See Pierre Birnbaum, *La Fin du politique* (Paris: Hachette, 1995).

48. Furet, Julliard, and Rosanvallon, *La République du centre*, 11, 54–55, 66, 106, 138, 144–45. Serge July likewise feels that France is becoming "normalized" and writes in the same vein, "A common economic culture has been imposed, making possible a cohabitation of ideas that until recently was unthinkable. . . . France is discovering the politics of consensus"; see *Les Années Mitterrand: Histoire baroque d'une normalisation inachevée* (Paris: Gras-

set, 1986), 16–17. See also Mark Kesselman, "La Nouvelle Cuisine en politique: La Fin de l'exceptionnalité française," in Yves Mény, ed., *Idéologies, partis politiques et groupes sociaux* (Paris: Presses de la Fondation Nationale des Sciences Politiques, 1989); and Jill Lovecy, "Comparative Politics and the Fifth French Republic: La Fin de l'exception française," *European Journal of Political Research* (1992), 21. Lovecy sees recent changes in the nature of political power as the most striking symbol of the end of French exceptionalism. The recent Anglo-American literature concerning the questioning of French exceptionalism is quite extensive: see, for example, Gregory Flynn, ed., *Remaking the Hexagon: The New France in the New Europe* (Boulder: Westview, 1995), and John Keeler and Martin Schain, eds., *Chirac's Challenge: Liberalization, Europeanization, and Malaise in France* (New York: St. Martin's Press, 1996).

49. François Furet, "L'Énigme français," *Le Monde* (23 September 1997).

50. André Malraux, *La Politique, la culture*, ed. Janine Mossuz-Lavau (Paris: Gallimard, 1996), 348.

51. Pierre Nora, "Comment écrire l'histoire de la France?" in Nora, ed., *Les Lieux de mémoire*, 5:29–30.

52. Maurice Agulhon, *The French Republic: 1879–1992*, trans. Antonia Nevill (Oxford: Blackwell, 1993), 472.

53. André Burguière and Jacques Revel, eds., *Histoire de la France: L'Espace français* (Paris: Seuil, 1989), 17.

54. Régis Debray, *Que vive la République* (Paris: Odile Jacob, 1989), 13.

55. Ibid., 72, 76, 79, 84.

56. Jean-Marie Benoist, quoted in Denis Lacorne, Jacques Rupnick, and Marie-France Toinet, eds., *L'Amérique dans les têtes: Un Siècle de fascinations et d'aversions* (Paris: Hachette, 1986), 30.

57. Anicet Le Pors, quoted in Lacorne et al., 34.

58. The phrase comes from the right-wing Groupement de Recherche et d'Études pour la Civilisation Européenne [Research and Study Group for European Civilization (GRECE)], quoted in Lacorne et al.

59. Régis Debray, "Républicain ou démocrate?" *Le Nouvel Observateur* (30 November 1989). From a similar perspective, Jean-Pierre Chevènement also intends to "come back to French exceptionalism"; see *Le Temps des citoyens* (Monaco: Éditions du Rocher, 1993), 82. On this debate see Paul Thibaud and Alain Touraine, "Républicains ou démocrates?" *Projet* 233 (1993).

60. See Kaplan, *Adieu 89*, pt. 4, chap. 5.

61. The Girondins were the moderate republican party during the Revolution; the Jacobins, a more radical group, advocated egalitarian democracy.—TRANS.

62. *Le Monde* (11 July 1989).

63. *Le Nouvel Observateur* (30 November 1989).

64. *Le Monde* (7 November 1996).

65. See Pierre-André Taguieff, "Un Programme 'révolutionnaire'?" in Nona Mayer and Pascal Perrineau, eds., *Le Front national à decouvert* (Paris: Presses de la Fondation Nationale des Sciences Politiques, 1989).

66. Jacques Ion, "L'Évolution des formes d'engagement public," in Pascal Perrineau, ed., *L'Engagement politique: Déclin ou mutation?* (Paris: Presses de la Fondation Nationale des Sciences Politiques, 1994), 37. See also, by the same author, *La Fin des militants?* (Paris: Éditions de l'Atelier, 1997). Janine Mossuz-Lavau analyzes the depoliticization, disenchantment with politics, and "weariness" of the French in *Les Français et la politique* (Paris: Odile Jacob, 1994), 354.

67. Daniel Boy and Nonna Mayer, eds., *L'Électeur français en question* (Paris: Presses de la Fondation Nationale des Sciences Politiques, 1990), 12, 206.

68. Guy Michelat, "À la recherche de la gauche et de la droite," in Boy and Mayer, eds., *L'Électeur français en question*. See also Jean Charlot, "Recomposition du système de partis français ou rééquilibrage limité?" in *Le Vote sanction: Les Élections législatives des 21 et 28 mars 1993* (Paris: Presses de la Fondation Nationale des Sciences Politiques, 1993), 274; and the more nuanced article by Étienne Schweisguth, "L'Affaiblissement du clivage gauche-droite," in Perrineau, ed., *L'Engagement politique*.

69. See *Le Vote de crise: L'Élection présidentielle de 1995* (Paris: Presses de la Fondation Nationale des Sciences Politiques, 1995).

70. See, for example, Yves Mény, "La Faiblesse des partis politiques français: Une Persistante Exceptionnalité," and François d'Arcy, "L'Administration territoriale de la République ou le maintien de la spécificité française," in François d'Arcy and Luc Rouban, eds., *De la Vᵉ République à l'Europe: Hommage à Jean-Louis Quermonne* (Paris: Presses de la Fondation Nationale des Sciences Politiques, 1996); also Emmanuel Godin, "Le Néo-libéralisme à la française: Une Exception?" *Modern and Contemporary France*, no. 1 (1996).

71. Pierre Birnbaum, "L'Impossible Américanisation de l'État," in *L'État de la France* (Paris: La Découverte, 1992); and Birnbaum,

"La Déchirure du lien étatique," in Noëlle Burgi, ed., *Fractures de l'État-nation*, 2d ed., revised and corrected (Paris: Kimé, 1994).

72. Mario Vargas Llosa, "De l'Exception culturelle française," *Libération* (19 October 1993); see also Llosa, "Cher Régis, tu sais aussi bien que moi," *Libération* (12 December 1993).

73. Maurice Agulhon, *Histoire vagabonde: La Politique en France d'hier à aujourd'hui* (Paris: Gallimard, 1996), 9–10, 284.

Chapter 1. The Innermost Thoughts of Alexis de Tocqueville

1. Alexis de Tocqueville, *Correspondance d'Alexis de Tocqueville et de Francisque de Corcelle et Correspondance d'Alexis de Tocqueville et de Madame Swetchine*, ed. Pierre Gibert, 2 vols. [constituting vol. 15 of *Œuvres complètes*, ed. J.-P. Mayer (Paris: Gallimard, 1951–89)], 1:174.

2. George Armstrong Kelly, *The Human Comedy: Constant, Tocqueville, and French Liberalism* (Cambridge: Cambridge University Press, 1992), 227ff.

3. Alexis de Tocqueville, *Democracy in America*, ed. J.-P. Mayer and trans. George Lawrence (New York: Harper & Row, 1966), 47.

4. See Robert Bellah, "Civil Religion in America," *Daedalus* (Winter 1967), and Seymour M. Lipset, *The First New Nation: The United States in Historical and Comparative Perspective* (New York: Basic Books, 1963).

5. Alexis de Tocqueville, "Les Desseins d'une nouvelle revue," in *Œuvres complètes*, vol. 3, *Écrits et discours politiques*, ed. André Jardin (Paris: Gallimard, 1962–90), 2:37–38.

6. Alexis de Tocqueville, *The Old Regime and the Revolution*, ed. François Furet and Françoise Mélonio, trans. A. S. Kahan, 2 vols. (Chicago: University of Chicago Press, 1998–), 1:97. On the same page, Tocqueville further describes the "hatreds" that the ruling classes inspired.

7. Tocqueville, *Democracy in America*, 288–89.

8. Ibid., 289.

9. Alexis de Tocqueville, *De la démocratie en Amérique*, ed. Eduardo Nolla, 2 vols. (Paris: Vrin, 1990), 1:225.

10. Tocqueville, *Democracy in America*, 300–301.

11. Unpublished manuscript, quoted in Tocqueville, *De la démocratie en Amérique*, 1:233.

Notes

12. Tocqueville, *Democracy in America*, 450.
13. Unpublished manuscript, quoted in Tocqueville, *De la démocratie en Amérique*, 2:38.
14. Catherine Zuckert, "The Role of Religion in Preserving American Liberty—Tocqueville's Analysis 150 Years Later," in Eduardo Nolla, ed., *Liberty, Equality, Democracy* (New York: New York University Press, 1992).
15. Doris Goldstein, *Trial of Faith: Religion and Politics in Tocqueville's Thought* (New York: Elsevier, 1975), 102.
16. Alexis de Tocqueville, *Correspondance anglaise*, ed. J.-P. Mayer and Gustave Rudler, 2 vols. [constituting vol. 6 of *Œuvres complètes*], 1:38.
17. Alexis de Tocqueville, *Correspondance et écrits locaux*, ed. Lise Queffelec-Dumasy (Paris: Gallimard, 1995), 85, 191, 197, 205.
18. Tocqueville, *Correspondance anglaise*, 2:515. Gustave de Beaumont accompanied Tocqueville on his travels in America and later wrote a famous novel drawing on this experience, *Marie; or, Slavery in the United States* (1835). Senior himself conducted a long correspondence with Tocqueville.
19. Tocqueville, *Correspondance et écrits locaux*, 245, 252, 258, 260, 274, 299, 353, 380, 395, 397, 411. Tocqueville repeatedly uses this image to describe local political life.
20. Alexis de Tocqueville, *Correspondance d'Alexis de Tocqueville avec P.-P. Royer-Collard et avec J.-J. Ampère* (Paris: Gallimard, 1970), 374.
21. Tocqueville, *Correspondance et écrits locaux*, 322, 356.
22. Tocqueville, *Democracy in America*, 177, 97, 285.
23. Ibid., 311, 315.
24. Ibid., 315.
25. Ibid., 299.
26. Unpublished manuscript, quoted in Tocqueville, *De la démocratie en Amérique*, 1:263.
27. Tocqueville, *Democracy in America*, 363.
28. Alexis de Tocqueville, *Recollections*, ed. J.-P. Mayer and A. P. Kerr, trans. George Lawrence (Garden City, N.Y.: Doubleday, 1970), 62.
29. Alexis de Tocqueville, "Mon instinct, mes opinions," in *Écrits et discours politiques*, 87.
30. Tocqueville, *De la démocratie en Amérique*, 2:15.
31. Alexis de Tocqueville, "Lettre à Édouard de Tocqueville," quoted in *De la démocratie en Amérique*, 2:119.

32. Alexis de Tocqueville, *L'Ancien Régime et la Révolution*, ed. J.-P. Mayer, 2 vols. [constituting vol. 2 of *Œuvres complètes*], 1:36.
33. Ibid., 1:39, 1:41, 1:53, 1:62, 1:90, 1:85. Tocqueville's essay, *L'État social et politique de la France*, laying out his main ideas on the subject, appeared several years before the publication of *L'Ancien Régime et la Révolution*. In the 1952 edition of the latter work, it is included as a preface.
34. Tocqueville, *The Old Regime and the Revolution*, 1:98.
35. Tocqueville, *Democracy in America*, 674.
36. Tocqueville, *De la démocratie en Amérique*, 1:208.
37. Tocqueville, *Democracy in America*, 632–33.
38. This preparatory note was published in the Nolla edition of *De la démocratie en Amérique*, 1:208.
39. Tocqueville, *The Old Regime and the Revolution*, 1:139.
40. Preparatory note, cited in Tocqueville, *De la démocratie en Amérique*, 2:253.
41. Tocqueville, *Democracy in America*, 72, 74, 203, 207.
42. Tocqueville, *The Old Regime and the Revolution*, 1:131.
43. Tocqueville, *Écrits et discours politiques*, 107.
44. See James Schleifer, *The Making of Tocqueville's "Democracy in America"* (Chapel Hill: University of North Carolina Press, 1980).
45. Tocqueville, *Democracy in America*, 675.
46. Tocqueville, *L'Ancien Régime et la Révolution*, 2:287.
47. Ibid., 2:48. Just before this Tocqueville writes: "Why is it that the hatred of despotism came first?" (2:47). Later he once again emphasizes the decisive character of this "hatred of despotism" (2:150).
48. Ibid., 2:238, 2:240, 2:241.
49. Tocqueville, *L'Ancien Régime et la Révolution*, 1:180.
50. Tocqueville, *Correspondance anglaise*, 2:280.
51. Tocqueville, *L'Ancien Régime et la Révolution*, 2:239.
52. Tocqueville, *The Old Regime and the Revolution*, 1:244.
53. Tocqueville, *L'Ancien Régime et la Révolution*, 2:115. A bit further on, he emphasizes how the "old hatreds" that divided classes had been allowed to ripen.
54. Ibid., 2:118, 2:127.
55. Tocqueville, *The Old Regime and the Revolution*, 1:221, 1:229, 1:241.
56. Ibid., 1:229.
57. Ibid., 1:241.
58. Tocqueville, *L'Ancien Régime et la Révolution*, 2:136, 2:139, 2:142.

Conversely, Burke was consumed by "hatred" for the French Revolution (ibid., 1:80).

59. Tocqueville, *L'Ancien Régime et la Révolution*, 2:147; see also 2:149, where Tocqueville writes that "the aristocracy was faltering as well as hated."

60. Ibid., 2:153; see also 2:154.

61. Ibid., 2:160; on "hatred" of the nobility, see also 2:336.

62. Ibid., 2:194, 1:41.

63. Ibid., 2:103. In the space of a single page (2:102), Tocqueville repeats on two occasions that "hatred" was felt toward the institutions that parliament represented.

64. Ibid., 2:230; see also 2:233.

65. Ibid., 2:274.

66. Tocqueville, *The Old Regime and the Revolution*, 1:170–71.

67. Tocqueville, *L'Ancien Régime et la Révolution*, 2:282, 2:134, 2:227. When Tocqueville was defeated in the 1837 elections, he stressed how far he had come into conflict "with the hatred of the nobility" allied with "the power of money"; see *Correspondance d'Alexis de Tocqueville et de Gustave Beaumont*, ed. André Jardin, 3 vols. (Paris: Gallimard, 1967), 1:262. In 1852, welcoming an old friend to his home, Tocqueville regretted that his friend had preserved "his old hatreds." Later, in 1857, commenting on a work by Maréchal de Marmont, Tocqueville observed "his great hatred of freedom" (3:63 and 3:463).

68. Tocqueville, "Notes politiques" (1845) and "Notes politiques," in *Écrits et discours politiques*, 213, 217; see also page 489, where Tocqueville, in a speech delivered to the Chamber of Deputies, reverts to this theme: France, temporarily, "is bored."

69. Tocqueville, "Notes: 1847," in *Écrits et discours politiques*, 719, 721, 727.

70. Tocqueville, *Correspondance et écrits locaux*, 449.

71. Tocqueville, *Recollections*, 87, 74.

72. Alexis de Tocqueville, *Souvenirs* (Paris: Gallimard, 1964), 210.

73. Tocqueville, "Projet de discours sur les affaires religieuses," in *Écrits et discours politiques*, 588–89.

74. Tocqueville, "Sur la liberté religieuse," ibid., 599–600.

75. Tocqueville, "Sur les jésuites," ibid., 698.

76. Tocqueville, *Souvenirs*, 171.

77. Tocqueville, *Correspondance anglaise*, 2:102, 2:108, 2:134, 2:134–35.

78. Tocqueville, *The Old Regime and the Revolution*, 1:246.

79. Ibid., 1:247.

Chapter 2. The Body of the Nation

1. See George L. Mosse, *Nationalism and Sexuality: Respectability and Abnormal Sexuality in Modern Europe* (New York: H. Fertig, 1985); Eugen Weber, *France, Fin de Siècle* (Cambridge, Mass.: Belknap Press of Harvard University Press, 1986); Zeev Sternhell, ed., *L'Éternel Retour: Contre la démocratie, l'idéologie de la décadence* (Paris: Presses de la Fondation Nationale des Sciences Politiques, 1994).
2. Camille Desmoulins, *Les Révolutions de France et de Brabant* (Paris, 1789–91).
3. Cited by Antoine de Baecque, "L'Homme nouveau est arrivé: La 'Régénération' du Français en 1789," *Dix-Huitième Siècle* 20 (1988), 204. See the discussion of this theme by Mona Ozouf, "La Révolution française et la formation de l'Homme nouveau," in *L'Homme régénéré: Essais sur la Révolution française* (Paris: Gallimard, 1989).
4. Jacques-Guillaume Thouret, "Premier Discours sur la nouvelle division du royaume," in François Furet and Ran Halévi, eds., *Orateurs de la Révolution française* (Paris: Gallimard, 1989), 1099.
5. Emmanuel-Joseph Sieyès, *What Is the Third Estate?* trans. M. Blondel (New York: Praeger, 1964), 160.
6. As Lucien Jaume remarked, "[I]n the intolerance unleashed by the Terror, Jacobinism rediscovered the condemnation of differences in opinion that Bossuet's Catholicism had issued against the Protestants. . . . Once in power, Jacobinism rejected the very premises of democratic give-and-take of opinion. It imposed and defended a single and indivisible legitimacy, invariable and unalterable." *Échec au libéralisme: Les Jacobins et l'État* (Paris: Kimé, 1990), 52. See also Olivier Le Cour Grandmaison, *Les Citoyennetés en révolution (1789–1794)* (Paris: Presses Universitaires de France, 1992).
7. Henri-Baptiste Grégoire, *Essai sur la régénération physique, morale et politique des juifs* (Paris: Flammarion, 1989), 160–61.
8. Henri-Baptiste Grégoire, "Rapport sur la nécessité et les moyens d'anéantir les patois et d'universaliser l'usage de la langue française," reprinted in Michel de Certeau, Dominique Julia, and Jacques Revel, *Une Politique de la langue: La Révolution française et les patois: L'Enquête de Grégoire* (Paris: Gallimard, 1975), 302–3, 317.
9. Ibid., 52, 16–17, 161–69.

10. Bertrand Barère de Vieuzac, "Rapport du Comité de salut public sur les idiomes," 8 Pluviôse, Year II (27 January 1794), in Certeau et al., 294–97.
11. Sieyès, *What Is the Third Estate?* 162.
12. Emmanuel-Joseph Sieyès, "Essai sur les privilèges," in *Écrits politiques*, ed. Roberto Zapperi (Paris: Éditions des Archives Contemporains, 1985), 95, 104. [Note that the "Essay on Privileges," originally a separate pamphlet that likewise figured in the debate over the forms of convocation of the Estates General, was customarily reprinted as a preface to *What Is the Third Estate?* in subsequent editions.—TRANS.]
13. Emmanuel-Joseph Sieyès, "Reconnaissance et exposition raisonnée des droits de l'homme et du citoyen," in Furet and Halévi, eds., *Orateurs de la Révolution française*, 1012.
14. Sieyès, "Qu'est-ce que le tiers état?" in *Écrits politiques*, 181.
15. Sieyès, "Essai sur les privilèges," 104.
16. The lesson of Saint-Simon's parable was that if all the aristocrats and their circle were suddenly to disappear, no one would notice; but that if the best carpenters, cabinetmakers, and engineers vanished, French society would grind to a halt. See William H. Sewell, Jr., *A Rhetoric of Bourgeois Revolution: The Abbé Sieyès and "What Is the Third Estate?"* (Durham: Duke University Press, 1994), 201.
17. Murray Forsythe, *Reason and Revolution: The Political Thought of the Abbé Sieyès* (Leicester: Leicester University Press, 1987), 3.
18. On these scurrilous accounts of life at court and among the leading figures of government, which flourished during the 1770s and 1780s, see Robert Darnton, *The Forbidden Bestsellers of Prerevolutionary France* (New York: Norton, 1995).
19. See Sewell, *A Rhetoric of Bourgeois Revolution*, 141.
20. Ibid., 60–65, 139ff., and 185ff.
21. Greenfeld, *Nationalism*, 172.
22. See Sewell, *A Rhetoric of Bourgeois Revolution*, 134–38.
23. Ibid., 139.
24. Lucien Jaume emphasizes that "despite [Sieyès's] liberal intentions (protection of civil society, freedom to the private sector), his approach engendered the absolute unity of the 'general will'—whether this unity was real or fictive, and in this case imposed on society." See *Le Discours jacobin et la démocratie* (Paris: Fayard, 1989), 164; also Jaume, "Constitution, intérêts et vertu civique," in Michel Troper and Lucien Jaume, eds., *1789 et l'invention de la Constitution* (Paris: Librairie Générale de Droit et de Jurispru-

dence, 1994). In the same vein, Pasquale Pasquino remarks that "the success and extraordinary diffusion of his text on the Third Estate to a certain degree disfigured or, at least, deformed Sieyès's contribution, for they caused to be forgotten, and almost to disappear from the collective memory, his writings on political and constitutional theory, which contained one of the most significant contributions to public law and political science of contemporary Europe"; see "Emmanuel Sieyès, Benjamin Constant et le 'gouvernement des modernes,'" *Revue française de science politique* (April 1987), 218. Pasquino cites the great French liberal Benjamin Constant, who observed that "Sieyès is one of the men who did the most good for France in '89 and who, since, on two or three occasions, has done it the most harm" (214). It is indeed a paradox that Sieyès should have also been a source of inspiration to Constant, whose outlook was utterly opposed to that of Sieyès the radical.

25. See Sewell, *A Rhetoric of Bourgeois Revolution*, 34–35, 94ff.
26. Baecque, *Le Corps de l'histoire*, 123.
27. Colette Clavreuil rigorously analyzes this notion of adunation in "L'Influence de la théorie d'Emmanuel Sieyès sur les origines de la représentation en droit public" (Ph.D. diss., Université de Paris–I, 1982), 2:358ff.
28. Charles-Augustin Sainte-Beuve, *Causeries du lundi*, 15 vols. (4th ed., Paris: Garnier, 1882?–85), 10:165. Marc Lelandais also observes that Sieyès showed himself to be "disconcerted that things could have reached that point"; see "L'Abbé Sieyès sous la Convention nationale" (master's thesis in history, Université de Paris–I, 1989), 70.
29. Pasquale Pasquino, "Le Concept de nation et les fondements du droit public de la Révolution: Sieyès," in François Furet, ed., *L'Héritage de la Révolution française* (Paris: Hachette, 1989), 320. This metaphor is also used by Marcel Gauchet, according to whom Sieyès "opened a Pandora's box of 'metaphysical discussions'"; see *La Révolution des droits de l'homme* (Paris: Gallimard, 1989), 68. The metaphor also implies the unleashing of consequences beyond what Sieyès had intended or could have foreseen, confirming Sewell's conclusion.
30. On the Terror, see François Furet, "Terror," in François Furet and Mona Ozouf, eds., *A Critical Dictionary of the French Revolution*, trans. Arthur Goldhammer (Cambridge, Mass.: Belknap Press of Harvard University Press, 1989), 137–50. See also Mona Ozouf, "The Terror After the Terror: An Immediate History," in Keith M.

Baker, ed., *The Terror*, vol. 4 of *The French Revolution and the Creation of Modern Political Culture* (Oxford: Pergamon, 1994). In the same volume, Bronislaw Baczko argues that the Terror could not have existed without the language of the Terror, which was not something extraneous to the system but an essential feature of it. While granting the Terror's centralizing and unifying purpose, Baczko seeks to draw attention to the unintended consequences of such a concentration of power ("The Terror Before the Terror? Conditions of Possibility, Logic of Realization," 33–34).

31. Quoted in Serge Bianchi, "Grégoire et le concept de vandalisme," in Equipe "18ème et révolution," ed., *Langages de la Révolution (1770–1815)* (Paris: Klincksieck, 1995), 593, 594.

32. Henri-Baptiste Grégoire, "Mémoires ecclésiastiques, politiques et littéraires," in *Mémoires de Grégoire* (Paris: Éditions de Santé, 1989), 79, 109.

33. Sieyès, *What Is the Third Estate?* 56, 177 (note e).

34. Sieyès, "Essai sur les privilèges," 95.

35. Sieyès, *What Is the Third Estate?* 60, 57, 60, 66, 165.

36. Ibid., 174.

37. Sieyès, "Dire de l'abbé Sieyès sur la question du veto royal," in *Écrits politiques*, 232, 234, 237.

38. Ernst-Wolfgang Böckenförde, cited in Claude Klein, *Théorie et pratique du pouvoir constituant* (Paris: Presses Universitaires de France, 1996), 4; on the magical dimension of this interpretation of constituent power in Sieyès, see pages 16, 67ff. On the internal contradictions in Sieyès's thought, see Olivier Beaud, *La Puissance de l'État* (Paris: Presses Universitaires de France, 1994), 229.

39. Sieyès, "Qu'est-ce que le tiers état?" 171.

40. Gauchet, *La Révolution des droits de l'homme*, 81.

41. Sieyès, *What Is the Third Estate?* 143.

42. Baecque, *Le Corps de l'histoire*, 12.

43. See Mona Ozouf, *La Fête révolutionnaire, 1789–1799* (Paris: Gallimard, 1988).

44. See Maurice Angulhon, *Marianne into Battle: Republican Imagery and Symbolism in France, 1789–1880*, trans. Janet Lloyd (Cambridge: Cambridge University Press, 1981); and Maurice Agulhon and Pierre Bonte, *Marianne: Les Visages de la République* (Paris: Gallimard, 1992).

45. Sewell, *A Rhetoric of Bourgeois Revolution*, 53. Sewell adopts here a notion used by Keith Baker in connection with Abbé Mably.

46. See Antoine de Baecque, "De la Dignité royale à la sévérité républicaine: Le Rituel des venues de Louis XVI devant l'Assemblée na-

tionale française, 1789–1792," in Michel Vovelle, ed., *Révolution et République: L'Exception française* (Paris: Kimé, 1994), 350.

47. See Serge Bianchi, *La Révolution culturelle de l'an II: Élites et peuples, 1789–1799* (Paris: Aubier, 1982).

48. See Antoine de Baecque, *La Caricature révolutionnaire* (Paris: Presses du Centre National de la Recherche Scientifique, 1988), 15.

49. From the preface by Claude Langlois to Annie Duprat, *Le Roi décapité: Essai sur les imaginaires politiques* (Paris: Cerf, 1989), 9. See also Langlois, *Les Septs Morts du roi* (Paris: Anthropos, 1993).

50. Joël Cornette, *Le Roi de guerre: Essai sur la sourveraineté dans la France du Grand Siècle* (Paris: Payot and Rivages, 1996).

51. Baecque, *La Caricature révolutionnaire*, 94, 75.

52. Ibid., 94.

53. Antoine de Baecque, "Le Sang des héros: Figure du corps dans l'imaginaire politique de la Révolution française," *Revue d'histoire moderne et contemporaine* 62 (1987), 34. In this connection, see also Baecque, *La Caricature révolutionnaire*, 130ff. On revolutionary caricatures of the *"gros abbés,"* see Arundhati Virmani, "Ils sont passés ces jours de fête: L'Anticléricalisme dans la caricature révolutionnaire," in Michel Vovelle, ed., *L'Image de la Révolution française*, 4 vols. (Paris and New York: Pergamon, 1990), 1:437–51.

54. See Pierre Birnbaum, *Le Peuple et les gros: Histoire d'un mythe*, 3d ed. (Paris: Hachette, 1995).

55. Cited by Gérard de Puymège, *Chauvin, le soldat-laboureur: Contribution à l'étude des nationalismes* (Paris: Gallimard, 1993), 127. Similarly, Barère wished that "national hatred declare itself" against the English and that "young republicans suck hatred of the English name with their nurses' milk"; see Sophie Wahnich, *L'Impossible Citoyen: L'Étranger dans le discours de la Révolution française* (Paris: Albin Michel, 1996), 276.

56. Jean Starobinski, *1789: The Emblems of Reason*, trans. Barbara Bray (Charlottesville: University of Virginia Press, 1982), 60–62.

57. Bronislaw Baczko, *Les Imaginaires sociaux: Mémoires et espoirs collectifs* (Paris: Payot, 1984), 52–53.

58. Mona Ozouf, *L'École de la France: Essais sur la Révolution, l'utopie et l'enseignement* (Paris: Gallimard, 1984), 83.

59. Ozouf, *L'Homme régénéré*, 52, 172.

60. Jaume, *Le Discours jacobin et la démocratie*, 13.

61. Ibid., 322.

62. Ibid., 131, 145.

Notes

63. Furet, *Interpreting the French Revolution*, 39.
64. Jaume, *Le Discours jacobin et la démocratie*, 322.
65. Cited by Ozouf, *La Fête révolutionnaire*, 191.
66. Cited by Lucien Jaume, "Le Public et le privé chez les Jacobins, 1789–1794," *Revue française de science politique* (April 1987), 246.
67. Ozouf, *L'Homme régénéré*, 9.
68. See Nathalie Goedert, "La Révolution et l'école," in Francis Hamon and Jacques Lelièvre, eds., *L'Héritage politique de la Révolution française* (Lille: Presses Universitaires de Lille, 1993).
69. See chapter 3 of Lynn Hunt, *The Family Romance of the French Revolution* (Berkeley: University of California Press, 1992); and her article "Male Virtue and Republican Motherhood," in Baker, ed., *The Terror*.
70. See Hunt, *The Family Romance of the French Revolution*, 69–70. In this connection, see particularly Hunt's *Politics, Culture, and Class in the French Revolution* (Berkeley: University of California Press, 1984), 94–119.
71. Cited by Michel Baridon, "Les Formes colossales dans l'imaginaire de la Révolution," in Vovelle, ed., *L'Image de la Révolution française*, 3:263.
72. Ibid.
73. Judith E. Schlanger, *L'Enjeu et le débat: Les Passés intellectuels* (Paris: Denoël-Gonthier, 1979), 159.
74. Hunt, *Politics, Culture, and Class in the French Revolution*, 98.
75. Ibid., 100–105.
76. Schlanger, *L'Enjeu et le débat*, 157, 163–64.
77. See, for example, James Leith, "Le Symbolism montagnard en l'An II," in Vovelle, ed., *L'Image de la Révolution française*, 1:270.
78. Thus, for example, Annie Duprat contests the interpretation that Antoine de Baecque gives of a famous caricature entitled "My Constitution," adopting a reading proposed by Claude Langlois in *La Caricature contre-révolutionnaire* (Paris: Presses du Centre National de la Recherche Scientifique, 1988); on this view, it was not a revolutionary caricature but actually a caricature emanating from the royalist camp. See Duprat, *Le Roi décapité*, 30.
79. See Élisabeth Liris, "De la République officieuse aux Républiques officielles," in Vovelle, ed., *Révolution et République*, 366–77.
80. This argument is made by Lynn Hunt in her article, "Pourquoi la République est-elle une femme?" in Vovelle, 361.
81. Hunt, *The Family Romance of the French Revolution*, 197–200.

Chapter 3. The Counterutopia of Joseph de Maistre

1. Joseph de Maistre, *Considerations on France*, trans. Richard A. Le-Brun (New York: Cambridge University Press, 1994), 48.
2. Joseph de Maistre, "Bienfaits de la Révolution française," in *Œuvres complètes*, 7:488.
3. Isaiah Berlin, *The Crooked Timber of Humanity: Chapters in the History of Ideas*, ed. Henry Hardy (New York: Knopf, 1991), 109.
4. Ibid. [The reference is to Carl L. Becker's *The Heavenly City of the Eighteenth-Century Philosophers* (New Haven: Yale University Press, 1932).—TRANS.]
5. Ibid., 150, 113, 170.
6. A movement that sprang up in the late 1880s, taking its name from General Georges Boulanger (1837–91), whose program of "political radicalism and anti-German nationalism united left- and right-wing enemies of the Opportunist Republic in a populist movement prefiguring fascism while also recalling the popular Bonapartism of the late 1840s"; see Robert Tombs's article in David Bell, Douglas Johnson, and Peter Morris, eds., *A Biographical Dictionary of French Political Leaders Since 1870* (New York: Simon and Schuster, 1990), 44–46.—TRANS.
7. Émile Faguet, *Politiques et moralistes du XIXe siècle*, 3 vols. (Paris: Lecène and Oudin, 1891–1900), 1:27.
8. Berlin, *The Crooked Timber of Humanity*, 37, 245.
9. Isaiah Berlin, *Against the Current: Essays in the History of Ideas*, ed. Henry Hardy (New York: Viking, 1980), 12–13. See also *Conversations with Isaiah Berlin*, 95ff.
10. See Jean Boissel's preface to Maistre's *Considérations sur la France* (Geneva: Slatkine, 1980), 11.
11. See Berlin, *Russian Thinkers*, 58–62. Berlin also mentions a surprising lecture delivered by Albert Sorel on 7 April 1888 at the École Libre des Sciences Politiques in Paris, in the course of which Sorel associated Maistre with Tolstoy, declaring: "The distance from the theocrat to the mystic, and from the mystic to the nihilist, is smaller than that from the butterfly to the larva, from the larva to the chrysalis, from the chrysalis to the butterfly" (62); Sorel's lecture was subsequently printed as "Tolstoï historien," *Revue bleue* (1888), 460–599.
12. Quoted by Robert Triomphe, *Joseph de Maistre: Étude sur la vie et sur la doctrine d'un matérialiste mystique* (Geneva: Droz, 1968), 21.
13. Berlin, *Russian Thinkers*, 77.

N o t e s

14. Ibid., 64–65.
15. Ibid., 22. For Berlin, "Tolstoy was by nature a fox, but believed in being a hedgehog" (24); the "emotional cause [of Tolstoy's outlook] is a passionate desire for a monistic vision of life on the part of a fox bitterly intent upon seeing in the manner of a hedgehog" (76). Though Berlin does not say so explicitly, it may be supposed that for him Maistre was a hedgehog pure and simple.
16. See Stephen Holmes, *The Anatomy of Antiliberalism* (Cambridge, Mass.: Harvard University Press, 1993), chap. 1.
17. See Carl Schmitt, *Political Romanticism*, trans. Guy Oakes (Cambridge, Mass.: MIT Press, 1986).
18. Richard Allen LeBrun, *Throne and Altar: The Political and Religious Thought of Joseph de Maistre* (Ottawa: University of Ottawa Press, 1965), 91.
19. Faguet, *Politiques et moralistes du XIXᵉ siècle*, 1:67.
20. Albert O. Hirschman, *The Rhetoric of Reaction: Perversity, Futility, Jealousy* (Cambridge, Mass.: Belknap Press of Harvard University Press, 1991), 18–19.
21. Ibid., 32. Hirschman repeats the same comparison further on: "The perversity argument of Maistre with regard to the French Revolution was compared to that of [William] Forrester with regard to the Welfare State" (144).
22. Ibid., chap. 1. Hirschman applies the analysis of reactionary rhetoric to left-wing arguments in chapter 6.
23. Ibid., 48. Raymond Boudon also discusses this comparison between Maistre and Tocqueville in "La Rhétorique est-elle réactionnaire?" *Le Débat* (March–April 1992), 94, 100; see too, in the same issue, Hirschman's reply as well as his more general response in *A Propensity to Self-Subversion* (Cambridge, Mass.: Harvard University Press, 1995).
24. See the introduction by Jack Lively to his translation of *The Works of Joseph de Maistre* (London: Allen and Unwin, 1965), 42, 45.
25. Maistre, *Considerations on France*, 21, 9.
26. Joseph de Maistre, *Du pape*, in *Œuvres complètes*, 2:xxiv, 2:xxvi.
27. Joseph de Maistre, "Fragments sur la France," in *Œuvres complètes*, 1:488–89.
28. Ibid., 1:205, 1:215. On this theme, see too Jean-Yves Le Borgne, *Joseph de Maistre et la Révolution* (Brest: Université de Bretagne Occidentale, 1976), 176ff.
29. Maistre, *Considerations on France*, 7–8.
30. Joseph de Maistre, "Lettre au comte de Blacas," in Ernest Daudet, ed., *Joseph de Maistre et Blacas: Leur correspondance inédite et l'his-*

toire de leur amitié, 1804–1820 (Paris: Plon-Nourrit, 1908), 39, 69.

31. Joseph de Maistre, "Lettre à la baronne du Pont," in *Œuvres complètes*, 9:400.
32. Maistre "Lettre au comte de Blacas," 6.
33. Maistre, "Fragments sur la France," 1:219.
34. Joseph de Maistre, *St. Petersburg Dialogues, or, Conversations on the Temporal Government of Providence*, ed. and trans. Richard A. LeBrun (Montreal and Kingston: McGill–Queen's University Press, 1993), 109, 111.
35. Joseph de Maistre, *Essai sur le principe générateur des constitutions politiques et des autres institutions humaines*, in *Œuvres complètes*, 1:235.
36. Joseph de Maistre, *De l'église gallicane dans son rapport avec le souverain pontife*, in *Œuvres complètes*, 3:81, 3:86.
37. Joseph de Maistre, *Réflexions sur le protestantisme dans ses rapports avec le souveraineté*, in *Œuvres complètes*, 8:70, 8:78, 8:84.
38. Joseph de Maistre, "Lettres à M. le marquis . . . sur la fête séculaire des protestants," in *Œuvres complètes*, 8:473. See also *Du pape*, in *Œuvres complètes*, 2:531. George Cogordan notes that Maistre "had two great hatreds: Jansenism and Gallicanism"; see his *Joseph de Maistre* (Paris: Hachette, 1922), 203.
39. Maistre, *Réflexions sur le protestantisme*, 8:70. [The Chouans were Catholic royalists who waged guerrilla warfare in Brittany during the Revolution.—TRANS.]
40. Ibid., 8:84, 8:86, 8:94, 8:97.
41. Maistre, *Du pape*, 2:xxviii–xxix, 2:xxviii, 2:524.
42. Joseph de Maistre, *Letters on the Spanish Inquisition: A Rare Work, and the Best Which Has Ever Appeared on the Subject*, trans. T. J. O'Flaherty (Boston: P. Donahoe, 1843), 22.
43. Joseph de Maistre, *Lettres à un gentilhomme russe sur l'Inquisition espagnole*, in *Œuvres complètes*, 3:292.
44. Maistre, *Letters on the Spanish Inquisition*, 24.
45. Maistre, *Lettres à un gentilhomme russe sur l'Inquisition espagnole*, 3:320, 3:397.
46. Joseph de Maistre, *Éclaircissements sur les sacrifices* (Paris: Pocket, 1994), 65–67.
47. Maistre, *St. Petersburg Dialogues*, 19–20.
48. Ibid., 3–4.
49. Ibid., 14, 18, 188–89, 193, 272.
50. Maistre, "Bienfaits de la Révolution française," 7:486.
51. Joseph de Maistre, "Discours à la marquise de Costa," in *Œuvres complètes*, 7:248–49.

52. Joseph de Maistre, "Troisième lettre d'un royaliste savoisien," in *Œuvres complètes*, 7:152.

53. Maistre, *Considérations sur la France*, 160.

54. Maistre, *Considerations on France*, 84.

55. Maistre, *Du pape*, 2:xxxii–xxxiii. On the theme of the regeneration of all of Europe in Maistre's writings, see chapter 5 of Bruno Brunello, *Joseph de Maistre: Politico e filosofo* (Bologna: Riccardo Patron, 1967).

56. Maistre, *Considerations on France*, 13. Gérard Gengembre observes, "[D]ivine law is legible in the circulation of the blood. . . . Whence the profound truth of Christianity, founded on Christ's bloody sacrifice. The Passion was regeneration. . . . De Maistre's God allows the course of events to be apprehended, placing every revolution and every restoration in a tragic perspective. History is purified through redemption made universal by spilled blood. . . . The monarchy must emerge regenerated from the counterrevolutionary struggle." *La Contre-Révolution ou l'histoire désespérante* (Paris: Imago, 1989), 125. Hence Maistre's "complete rejection": see also Gérard Gengembre, "La Contre-Révolution et le refus de la Constitution," in Troper and Jaume, eds., *1789 et l'invention de la Constitution*, 68ff.

57. Roger Dupuy, "Esquisse d'un bilan provisoire," in François Lebrun and Roger Dupuy, eds., *Les Résistances à la Révolution* (Paris: Imago, 1987), 474.

58. Jean-Clément Martin, *La Vendée et la France* (Paris: Seuil, 1987), 82, 188–98, 204, 240, 316. See also Jean-Clément Martin, "La Vendée, région-mémoire," in Nora, ed., *Les Lieux de mémoire*, 1:595–617.

59. Maistre, "Lettre au comte de Blacas," 68. [Robert Damien tried to assassinate King Louis XV, and was brutally tortured and executed as a result.—TRANS.]

60. Ibid. In a letter to Vignet des Étoles, dated 28 October 1794, Maistre also wrote: "It is natural that you should desire the successes of the coalition [against] France because you see the general good in them. It is natural that I desire these successes only against Jacobinism because I see in the destruction of France the seed of two centuries of massacres, sanctioning maxims of the most odious Machiavellianism, the irrevocable debasement of the human species, and even, what will greatly surprise you, a mortal wound to religion."

61. Maistre, *Considerations on France*, 16. See F. Vermale, "Joseph de Maistre et Robespierre," *Annales révolutionnaires* 12 (1920), and

"Joseph de Maistre et la Terreur," *Annales historiques de la Révolution française* (July 1930).

62. Maistre, *Considerations on France*, 14, 16.
63. Langlois, *La Caricature contre-révolutionnaire*, 25.
64. Ibid., 55, 71, 81.
65. Ibid., 207.
66. Ibid., 142, 151, 164, 185, 191.
67. Charles de Rémusat, "Du traditionalisme," *Revue des deux mondes* (15 May 1857), 244.
68. Joseph de Maistre, *On the Sovereignty of the People*, in Richard A. LeBrun, ed. and trans., *Against Rousseau: "On the State of Nature" and "On the Sovereignty of the People"* (Montreal and Kingston: McGill–Queen's University Press, 1996), 115, 117.
69. Joseph de Maistre, *Étude sur la souveraineté*, in *Œuvres complètes*, 1:553.
70. Maistre, *Considerations on France*, 78, 85.
71. Ibid., 56.
72. Maistre, *Considérations sur la France*, 128, 129.
73. Maistre, *Considerations on France*, 56, 87.
74. Maistre, "Bienfaits de la Révolution française," 7:443.
75. E. Villard, *Le Droit de punir et Joseph de Maistre* (Nancy: Vagner, 1886), 9, 19.
76. Ibid., 34.
77. Charles Maurras, *Enquête sur la monarchie* (Paris: Nouvelle Librairie Nationale, 1924), 349; see also 311. Maurice Barrès, searching for a passage in Maistre's writings, turned to Maurras for assistance, prefacing his query with the words, "You who read a great deal of Joseph de Maistre . . ."; see Maurice Barrès and Charles Maurras, *La République ou le Roi: Correspondance inédite (1888–1923)*, ed. Guy Dupré (Paris: Plon, 1970), 409.
78. Quoted by Victor Nguyen, *Aux origines de l'Action française: Intelligence et politique vers 1900* (Paris: Fayard, 1991), 713.
79. Charles Maurras, *Après dix ans* (Paris: Librairie de l'Action Française, 1927), 179, 943.
80. Charles Maurras, *Mes idées politiques*, ed. Pierre Chardon (Paris: Fayard, 1937), 71.
81. Lazare de Gérin-Ricard, *Les Idées politiques de Joseph de Maistre et la doctrine de Maurras* (La Rochelle: Éditions Rupella, 1929), 12, 15, 18, 56. See also Achille Segard, *Charles Maurras et les idées royalistes* (Paris: Fayard, 1919), 117ff.
82. Jacques Maritain, *L'Antimoderne*, 2d ed., revised and expanded (Paris: Éditions de la Revue des Jeunes, 1922), 174, 176, 178, 194.

83. Jacques Maritain, *Une Opinion sur Charles Maurras et le devoir des catholiques* (Paris: Plon, 1926), 13, 36–37.

84. Francis Bayle, *Les Idées politiques de Joseph de Maistre* (Lyons: Imprimerie des Beaux-Arts, 1944), 138.

85. Charles Maurras, *La Seule France* (Lyons: Lardanchet, 1941), 241.

86. Puymège, *Chauvin, le soldat-laboureur*, 279.

87. Joseph de Maistre, *Une Politique expérimentale*, ed. Bernard de Vaulx (Paris: Fayard, 1940), 19, 43, 47.

88. René Connard, *Histoire des doctrines économiques* (Paris: Librairie Générale de Droit et Jurisprudence, 1943), 600.

89. André Delay, *Vers l'union par-delà les sanglantes horreurs: Étude sur la philosophie de Joseph de Maistre, considérée au point de vue de l'organisation des relations sociales* (Paris: Institut d'Études Politiques et Sociales, 1943), 4, 218, 220, 248, 249.

90. Joseph Barthélemy, *Ministre de la justice: Vichy, 1941–1943* (Paris: Pygmalion/G. Watelet, 1989), 449, 577.

91. Baron Michaud, "En relisant Joseph de Maistre," *Revue des deux mondes* (15 September 1943).

92. See, for example, Jean Lacroix, *Vocation personnelle et tradition nationale* (Paris: Bloud et Gay, 1942); Robert Vallery-Radot, "Source d'une doctrine nationale," *Sequana* (1942); François Perroux and Yves Urvoy, *Renaître*, fascicle no. 2 (Paris: Librairie de Médicis, 1943); Henry Bordeaux, "J. de Maistre avant la Révolution," *La Revue universelle* 69 (November 1943); Charles Maignial, "J. de Maistre, vrai ou faux ancêtre de la Révolution nationale?" *Métier du Chef* 22 (March 1943); Raoul Raguenau, "Plaisant Monsieur de Maistre," *Au Travail* 142 (20 November 1943). Francis Bayle, in his law thesis (defended in November 1943 and published the following year), proposed to show that the work of Maistre "still contains valuable lessons for our epoch"; see his *Les Idées politiques de Joseph de Maistre*, 9.

93. See, for example, Emmanuel Beau de Loménie, *Maurras et son temps* (Bourg-en-Bresse: ETL, 1953), 21–31. C.-J. Gignoux published a study, *Joseph de Maistre: Prophète du passé, historien de l'avenir* (Paris: Nouvelles Éditions Latines, 1963), in a series edited by Jean Madiran, longtime spokesman of the extreme Right and, later, reliable propagandist for Jean-Marie Le Pen, that continued to link the defense of "Christian Europe" with Maistre's thought. Maistre, he wrote, deserves "our recognition," for "it is difficult to dispute that the essential phenomenon of our time is precisely the intense denunciation of the principles" of 1789 attacked by Maistre (10–11). "It may be wondered," Gignoux adds,

"if our country is not sick from skepticism and poisoned by heresy, with the result that, by reaction, in the strict sense of the word, an absolute cure becomes tempting. . . . After the Stalinist tyranny, one cannot say that absolute power definitively belongs to the past[;] and de Maistre's executioner appears as a rather small figure next to the technicians of the Cheka" (217). Jacques Alibert has noted that the upholders of a muscular Catholicism still see themselves in Maistre, so much so that, for them, John Paul II, "the enlightened pope," could without difficulty "adopt as his own" whole sections of Maistre's thought: "In the eyes of the Christian, Joseph de Maistre is still current"; see *Joseph de Maistre: État et religion* (Paris: Téqui, 1990), 224.

Chapter 4. The Difficult Career of Liberalism

1. Françoise Mélonio, *Tocqueville et les Français* (Paris: Aubier, 1993), 112, 115, 118, 163.
2. On Tocqueville's influence on the École Libre des Sciences Politiques, see Pierre Birnbaum, *Sociologie de Tocqueville* (Paris: Presses Universitaires de France, 1969), chap. 7; also Pierre Favre, *Naissance de la science politique* (Paris: Fayard, 1989).
3. Stephen Holmes judiciously observes, very much in the manner of Hirschman, that Constant "lauded citizen withdrawal and indifference in situations of civil war when participation was largely a vehicle for partisan hatred and revenge"; see *Benjamin Constant and the Making of Modern Liberalism* (New Haven: Yale University Press, 1984), 34.
4. See Biancamaria Fontana, *Benjamin Constant and the Postrevolutionary Mind* (New Haven: Yale University Press, 1991), 105.
5. Quoted in Holmes, *Benjamin Constant and the Making of Modern Liberalism*, 105. Holmes adds: "Constant was pulled toward relativism, despite his philosophical convictions about progress and decrepitude, because relativism was also an effective position for someone striving to dampen the mutual fears and hatreds that marked French political life" (197).
6. See Benjamin Constant, *De l'esprit de conquête et de l'usurpation* (Paris: Flammarion, 1986), 118–25, 181, 270, 275.
7. Lucien Jaume, "Morale publique et morale privée dans le libéralisme," *Pouvoirs* (April 1993), 38–40.
8. Lucien Jaume, *Échec au libéralisme: Les Jacobins et l'État* (Paris:

Kimé, 1990), 73. George Armstrong Kelly stresses the influence of the religious factor in the different types of liberalism that appeared in France: see *The Human Comedy*, 35, 69ff.; also Jean-Claude Lamberti, *Tocqueville et les deux démocraties* (Paris: Presses Universitaires de France, 1983), 82.

9. Thus Georges Weill emphasizes the "failure" of liberal Catholicism: see *Histoire du catholicisme libéral* (Geneva: Slatkine, 1979), 171. On these distinctions, the classic article remains that of Jean-Marie Mayeur, "Catholicisme intransigeant, catholicisme social, démocratie chrétienne," *Annales* (March–April, 1972), which lays particular emphasis on the close links between the two branches of Catholicism mentioned in the title. More generally, it is difficult to understand how André Jardin can write that "from 1814–1875, liberalism dominated French political life"; see his *Histoire du libéralisme politique de la crise de l'absolutisme à la Constitution de 1875* (Paris: Hachette, 1985), 211.

10. See Claude Willard, *Le Mouvement socialiste en France (1893–1906): Les Quesdistes* (Paris: Éditions Ouvrières, 1965); Michelle Perrot and Annie Kriegel, *Le Socialisme français et le pouvoir* (Paris: Études et Documentation Internationales, 1966); Birnbaum, *Le Peuple et les gros*; Jacques Julliard, "Le Peuple," in Nora, ed., *Les Lieux de mémoire*, 5:185–229; Yves Lequin, "La Classe ouvrière," in Jean-François Sirinelli, ed., *Histoire des droites en France*, 3 vols. (Paris: Gallimard, 1992), 3:473–508.

11. See Jacques Rougerie, *Paris insurgé: La Commune de 1871* (Paris: Gallimard, 1995).

12. Ernest Renan, "Qu'est-ce qu'une nation?" in *Qu'est-ce qu'une nation? et autres écrits* (Paris: Agora, 1992), 41–42.

13. Benedict Anderson, *Imagined Communities: Reflections on the Origin and Spread of Nationalism*, rev. ed. (London: Verso, 1991), 200–201.

14. Ernest Gellner, "Le Nationalisme et les deux formes de la cohésion dans les sociétés complexes," in G. Delannoi and P.-A. Taguieff, eds., *Théories de nationalisme* (Paris: Kimé, 1991), 224.

15. Renan, "Qu'est-ce qu'une nation?" 42, 52.

16. See Ernest Gellner, *Encounters with Nationalism* (Oxford: Blackwell, 1994), 192.

17. Ernest Renan, *Histoire générale et système comparé des langues sémitiques*, in *Œuvres complètes*, ed. Henriette Psichari, 10 vols. (Paris: Calmann-Lévy, 1949), 8:145.

18. Renan, "Qu'est-ce qu'une nation?" in *Œuvres complètes*, 1:904.

19. See Tzvetan Todorov, *Nous et les autres: La Réflexion française sur la diversité humaine* (Paris: Seuil, 1989); also Pierre Birnbaum, *"La France aux français": Histoire des haines nationalistes* (Paris: Seuil, 1993), chap. 4.

20. See, for example, *Identité* (July–August, 1991).

21. See Philip Nord, *The Republican Moment: The Struggle for Democracy in Nineteenth-Century France* (Cambridge, Mass.: Harvard University Press, 1995).

22. Odile Rudelle, *La République absolue: Aux origines de l'instabilité constitutionnelle de la France républicaine, 1870–1889* (Paris: Publications de la Sorbonne, 1986), 289–90.

23. Émile Faguet, *Le Libéralisme* (Paris: Société Française d'Imprimerie et de Librairie, 1903), 113.

24. Tony Judt, *Past Imperfect: French Intellectuals, 1944–1956* (Berkeley: University of California Press, 1992), 238.

25. Pierre Rosanvallon, *Le Sacre du citoyen: Histoire du suffrage universel en France* (Paris: Gallimard, 1992), 292–93.

26. On the conflicting reinterpretations of the past during the nineteenth century, see Robert Gildea, *The Past in French History* (New Haven: Yale University Press, 1994), chaps. 1 and 4.

27. Maurice Agulhon, *Histoire vagabonde*, 3 vols. (Paris: Gallimard, 1988–96), 3:18–19.

28. Quoted in Pierre Barral, ed., *Les Fondateurs de la troisième République* (Paris: Armand Colin, 1968), 8, 164.

29. Ibid., 110, 115.

30. Ibid., 131, 148.

31. Ibid., 131.

32. In Jacques Godechot, ed., *Les Constitutions de la France depuis 1789* (Paris: Flammarion, 1993), 37.

33. See Ozouf, *La Fête révolutionnaire*, and Olivier Ihl, *La Fête républicaine* (Paris: Gallimard, 1996).

34. See, for example, Jean-Clément Martin, *La Vendée et la France*; also his *Blancs et Bleus dans la Vendée déchirée* (Paris: Gallimard, 1987).

35. Renan uttered his warning on 22 February 1889 in the course of a welcoming speech at the Académie Française; quoted in Pascal Ory, *Une Nation pour mémoire, 1889, 1939, 1989: Trois jubilés révolutionnaires* (Paris: Presses de la Fondation Nationale des Sciences Politiques, 1992), 142.

36. Each department of France is headed by a prefect, with responsibility for the smaller units of which it is composed residing with

subprefects. The system of prefectural administration, created by Napoleon, symbolizes the centralization of French government. —TRANS.

37. See the contributions of Robert Chagny, Patrick Garcia and Brigitte Marin, Jean-Clément Martin, and Philippe Dujardin in Jean Davallon, Philippe Dujardin, and Gérard Sabatier, eds., *Politique de la mémoire: Commémorer la Révolution* (Lyons: Presses Universitaires de Lyon, 1993).

38. Quoted in Henri Loyrette, "La Tour Eiffel," in Nora, ed., *Les Lieux de mémoire*, 3:483. In the same volume of *Les France*, see François Loyer, "Le Sacré-Cœur de Montmartre," 3:457ff.

39. More generally, with regard to the links between construction of monuments and nationalism, see Avner Ben-Amos, "Monuments and Memory in French Nationalism," *History and Memory* 2 (Winter 1993).

40. Céline Monier, "Le Sacré-Cœur en lutte pour la domination du ciel de Paris" (DEA, Université de Paris–I, 1993), 47, 56, 89–90.

41. Ory, *Une Nation pour mémoire*, 104ff.

42. The preceding quotations are reproduced in Jocelyne George, "1889: La République entre mystique et politique: Les Réponses des maires à l'invitation au banquet organisé par le conseil municipal de Paris," *Revue d'histoire moderne et contemporaine* (July–September 1991). See also Jocelyne George, "Le Banquet des maires ou la fête de la Concorde républicaine," in Alain Corbin, Noëlle Gérôme, and Danielle Tartakowsky, eds., *Les Usages politiques des fêtes aux XIXᵉ–XXᵉ siècles* (Paris: Publications de la Sorbonne, 1994); and Jean-Yves Mollier and Jocelyne George, *La Plus Longue des Républiques* (Paris: Fayard, 1994), 187–89.

43. The preceding quotations are taken from Ihl, *La Fête républicaine*, 126–33, and from Ihl's "Convivialité et citoyenneté: Les Banquets commémoratifs dans les campagnes républicaines à la fin du XIXᵉ siècle," in Corbin et al., eds., *Les Usages politiques des fêtes aux XIXᵉ–XXᵉ siècles*.

44. This and the three extracts that follow are from Monsignor Charles-Émile Freppel, quoted in Yves Déloye, "Gouverner les citoyens: Normes civiques et mentalités en France," *L'Année sociologique* 46, no. 1 (1996), 94–98.

45. Monsignor Charles-Émile Freppel, *La Révolution française, à propos du centenaire de 1789* (Paris: Le Trident, 1987), 15–22.

46. These remarks and the ones that follow in the next paragraph are from Freppel, 37–62.

47. See also the articles by Jacques-Olivier Boudon, "Le Parcours de

Mgr Freppel avant son élection au siège d'Angers," Jean-Clément Martin, "Monseigneur Freppel et la Révolution française," J. Cadot, "La Doctrine sociale de Mgr Freppel: Moyen de lutte contre la République," and Jacques Gadille, "Théologies et projets politiques des évêques français de la seconde République au Ralliement (1848–1892)," in Bernard Plongeron, ed., *Catholiques entre monarchie et république: Monseigneur Freppel en son temps* (Paris: Letouzey et Ané, 1995).

48. See Nguyen, *Aux origines de l'Action française*, chap. 4 ("1889 ou le centenaire contesté").

49. Paray-le-Monial is a town in the Saône-et-Loire, in central France, famous as the destination of conservative Catholic pilgrimages. The bicentennial celebration was organized by the Catholic right to commemorate the founding of Paray-le-Monial's famous monastery.—TRANS.

50. The *"enfants nantais"* were Catholic children killed in 1793 by the Jacobins, who threw their bodies into the Loire.—TRANS.

51. The preceding quotations, as well as those in the following paragraphs, are taken from articles by Brigitte Basdevant-Gaudemet, "L'Épiscopat français et le centenaire de la Révolution," Michel Lagrée, "Les Catholiques bretons en 1889," and Pierre Pierrard, "Les Catholiques sociaux et le centenaire de la Révolution," in Pierre Colin, ed., *Les Catholiques français et l'héritage de 1789: D'un centenaire à l'autre, 1889–1989* (Paris: Beauchesne, 1989). On the centenary in Brittany, see C. Brunel, "Le Premier Centenaire de la Révolution à contre-courant: La Restauration des droits de Dieu," in Hervé Le Goff, ed., *La Révolution dans le Trégor, les bleus, les blancs et les autres: Analyses, portraits, documents* (Tréguier: Trégor 89, 1989), and Michel Lagrée, *Religion et culture en Bretagne* (Paris: Fayard, 1992); on the Tarn, see Jean Faury, *Cléricalisme et anticléricalism dans le Tarn* (Toulouse: Publications de l'Université Toulouse–Le Mirail, 1980), 167ff. See also Marc Angenot, *1889: Un État du discours social* (Montreal: Le Préambule, 1989).

52. See Rosemonde Sanson, *Les 14 Juillet: Fête et conscience nationale* (Paris: Flammarion, 1976), 35.

53. Christian Amalvi, "Le 14 Juillet," in Nora, ed., *Les Lieux de mémoire*, 1:431.

54. Maurice Agulhon, "La Mairie: Liberté, Égalité, Fraternité," in Nora, 1:168.

55. Maurice Agulhon, *Marianne au pouvoir: L'Imagerie et la symbolique républicaines de 1800 à 1914* (Paris: Flammarion, 1989), 136, 224, 279, 324.

56. Gerd Krumeich, *Jeanne d'Arc à travers l'histoire*, trans. Josie Mély, Marie-Hélène Pateau, and Lisette Rosenfeld (Paris: Albin Michel, 1993), 206, 219, 205.

57. Michel Winock, "Jeanne d'Arc," in Nora, ed., *Les Lieux de mémoire*, 7:698.

58. Krumeich, *Jeanne d'Arc à travers l'histoire*, 241, 225.

59. Agulhon, *Histoire vagabonde*, 3:173.

60. Alain Corbin, *Village Bells: Sound and Meaning in the Nineteenth-Century French Countryside*, trans. Martin Thom (New York: Columbia University Press, 1998), 3, 23, 30.

61. Ibid., 191 (emphasis in original deleted), 244.

62. Barnett Singer, *Village Notables in Nineteenth-Century France: Priests, Mayors, Schoolmasters* (Albany: State University of New York Press, 1983), 68–69. [These phrases are quoted by Singer from the French and translated here.—TRANS.]

63. Lalouette, *La Libre-Pensée en France, 1848–1940*, 331.

64. Quoted in Pierre Barral, "La Citoyenneté chez les fondateurs de la troisième République," in Dominique Colas, ed., *L'État de droit: Travaux de la Mission sur la modernisation de l'État* (Paris: Presses Universitaires de France), 16. Gambetta, good strategist that he was, rapidly moderated his anticlericalism. On 17 January 1878, for example, he wrote: "Tomorrow, I will go to mass, despite my anticlerical loathings: I whisper to myself, by way of apology and without wishing to plagiarize the *Béarnais* [Henri IV]: Rome is worth a mass"; letter to Léonie Léon quoted by Jérôme Grévy, "Les Opportunistes: Milieu et cultures politiques, 1871–1889" (Ph.D. diss., Institut d'Études Politiques de Paris, 1996), 53.

65. Quoted in Lalouette, *La Libre-Pensée en France, 1848–1940*, 166ff. and chap. 2.

66. Ibid., 186–87 and chap. 6. See also Jacqueline Lalouette, *Libre-Pensée et religion laïque en France de la fin du second Empire à la fin de la troisième République* (Strasbourg: Cerdic-Publications, 1980).

67. See Anatole Leroy-Beaulieu, *Les Doctrines de la haine: L'Antisémitisme, l'antiprotestantisme, l'anticléricalisme* (Paris: Calmann-Lévy, 1902); also René Rémond, *L'Anticléricalisme en France: De 1815 à nos jours* (Paris: Fayard, 1976).

68. Quoted in Louis Pérouas, *Refus d'une religion, religion d'un refus en Limousin rural, 1880–1940* (Paris: Éditions de l'École des Hautes Études en Sciences Sociales, 1985), 120, 128.

69. Faury, *Cléricalisme et anticléricalism dans le Tarn*, 211, 226, 237, 241, 257, 360, 493.

70. This was especially true, according to Michel Lagrée, "during the years 1890–1900 when Catholicism, including Breton [Catholicism], was overcome by patriotic, indeed nationalist, ideology [emphasizing] the theme of 'British gold,' [which was] supposed to fuel thriving missions"; see *Religion et culture en Bretagne*, 138.

71. Quoted in Yves Déloye, *École et citoyenneté: L'Individualisme républicain de Jules Ferry à Vichy: Controverses* (Paris: Presses de la Fondation Nationale des Sciences Politiques, 1994), 218.

72. Faury, *Cléricalisme et anticléricalism dans le Tarn*, 147–48.

73. See Déloye, *École et citoyenneté*, 77–86.

74. Ibid., 268, 287, 294.

75. Jacques Ozouf and Mona Ozouf, with Véronique Aubert and Claire Steindecker, *La République des instituteurs* (Paris: Gallimard/Seuil, 1992), 189, 197.

76. See Singer, *Village Notables in Nineteenth-Century France*, 86ff.; also chaps. 5 and 6.

77. See Jacques Ozouf, *Nous, les maîtres d'école: Autobiographies d'instituteurs de la Belle Époque* (Paris: Gallimard/Julliard, 1973).

78. The famous description of primary school teachers as "*les hussards noirs de la république*" is due to Ferdinand Buisson, quoted in Antoine Prost, *Histoire de l'enseignement en France, 1800–1967* (Paris: A. Colin, 1968), 397.

79. See Faury, *Cléricalisme et anticléricalism dans le Tarn*, 251–53; and Lagrée, *Religion et culture en Bretagne*, 233ff.

80. See Eugen Weber, *Peasants into Frenchmen: The Modernization of Modern France, 1870–1914* (Stanford: Stanford University Press, 1976), chap. 6.

81. Ibid., 312.

82. Maurice Agulhon, "Quelques problèmes socioculturels . . . (À propos d'Eugen Weber et de l'acculturation républicaine)," *Bulletin de la Société d'histoire moderne*, no. 1 (1986), 18. In Agulhon's view, "to say that the French rural countryside experienced national integration and modernity between 1870 and 1914 is to assign somewhat too early a date: certain remote mountain cantons were scarcely opened up before 1930. Moreover, many of the rural regions of the Paris basin, the northeast, and the east were 'nationalized' around either 1830 or 1848"; see "Compte rendu du livre d'Eugen Weber," *Annales* 31 (1978), 844. See also Eugen Weber, "Comment la politique vint aux paysans: A Second Look at Peasant Politicization," *American Historical Review* (April 1982), as well as Melvin Edelstein's article arguing for a position

nearer that of Agulhon, "Integrating the French Peasants into the Nation-State: The Transformations of Electoral Participation (1789–1870)," *History of European Ideas* 15 (1992).

83. Weber, *Peasants into Frenchmen*, 334, 338.
84. See Claude Nicolet, *L'Idée républicaine en France, 1789–1924: Essai d'histoire critique* (Paris: Gallimard, 1982), 188ff., 231ff.
85. Quoted in Déloye, *École et citoyenneté*, 20.
86. Tocqueville, *Écrits et discours politiques*, 2:586.
87. Benjamin Constant, "The Liberty of the Ancients Compared with That of the Moderns," in *Benjamin Constant: Political Writings*, trans. Biancamaria Fontana (Cambridge: Cambridge University Press, 1988), 322–23.
88. Agulhon, "Quelques problèmes socioculturels . . . ," 19–20.
89. See Mona Ozouf's preface to Jean-François Chanet, *L'École républicaine et les petites patries* (Paris: Aubier, 1996), 14–15. Chanet insists on this sense of rootedness among teachers in chapters 2 and 3; see also part III, "Les Arpenteurs des petites patries."
90. Agulhon, "Quelques problèmes socioculturels . . . ," 20.
91. Georges Picquart was a Catholic army officer who became convinced of Dreyfus's innocence and fought on his behalf, for which he was sentenced to prison by a military court.—TRANS.
92. See Stephen Wilson, *Ideology and Experience: Antisemitism in France at the Time of the Dreyfus Affair* (London: Associated University Presses, 1982), and Michel Winock, *Nationalisme, antisémitisme et fascisme en France* (Paris: Seuil, 1990), chap. 6, as well as my article "La Mobilisation des ligues: Affaire Dreyfus, culture catholique et antisémitisme," in Michel Winock, ed., *Histoire de l'extrême droite en France* (Paris: Seuil, 1993), and my book *L'Affaire Dreyfus: La République en péril* (Paris: Gallimard, 1994). See also Pierre Birnbaum, ed., *La France de l'affaire Dreyfus* (Paris: Gallimard, 1994), and Vincent Duclert, *L'Affaire Dreyfus* (Paris: La Découverte, 1994).
93. See Robert Tombs, ed., *Nationhood and Nationalism in France: From Boulangism to the Great War, 1889–1918* (London: HarperCollins Academic, 1991); and René Rémond, "Liberal Models in France, 1900–1930," in Joseph Klaits and Michael H. Haltzel, eds., *Liberty-Liberté: The American and French Experiences* (Washington, D.C.: Woodrow Wilson Center Press and Baltimore: Johns Hopkins University Press, 1991).
94. See Antoine Compagnon, *Connaissez-vous Brunetière? Enquête sur un antidreyfusard et ses amis* (Paris: Seuil, 1997).
95. See Charles Maurras, *Au signe de Flore: Souvenirs de vie politique,*

l'affaire Dreyfus, la fondation d'Action française, 1898–1900 (Paris: Les Œuvres Représentatives, 1931).

96. Maurras, *Après dix ans*, 202.

97. Albert Thibaudet, *Les Idées de Charles Maurras* (Paris: Éditions de la Nouvelle Revue Française, 1920), 86, 88, 99, 102, 108.

98. Albert de Mun, *Discours et écrits divers*, 6 vols. (Paris: Plon-Nourrit, 1905), 6:149.

99. Maurice Barrès, in *Bulletin officiel de la Ligue de la patrie française* (1 January 1907).

100. Charles Maurras, *Réflexions sur la Révolution de 1789* (Paris: Les Îles d'or, 1948), 29. See also the informed but sometimes doubtful analysis by Maurice Weyembergh, *Charles Maurras et la Révolution française* (Paris: Vrin, 1992).

101. This crucial article by Maurras, "Idées françaises ou idées suisses," is reprinted in *Réflexions sur la Révolution française*.

102. Maurice Barrès and Charles Maurras, *La République ou le Roi* (Paris: Plon, 1922), 154–55.

103. Maurras, *Mes idées politiques*, 283, 286.

104. Charles Maurras, *La Démocratie religieuse: Le Dilemme de Marc Sangnier, la politique religieuse, l'Action française et la religion catholique* (Paris: Nouvelle Librairie Nationale, 1921), 28, 196, 198, 205, 248.

105. See Nguyen, *Aux origines de l'Action française*, 857.

106. See the remarkable work by Michael Sutton, *Nationalism, Positivism, and Catholicism: The Politics of Charles Maurras and French Catholics* (Cambridge: Cambridge University Press, 1982), 92, 100ff. As Eugen Weber notes, "If the areas of Action Française recruitment were socially heterogeneous, they were almost uniformly Catholic"; see *Action Française: Royalism and Reaction in Twentieth-Century France* (Stanford: Stanford University Press, 1962), 65.

107. See Odile Rudelle, "De Jules Ferry à Raymond Poincaré ou l'échec du constitutionnalisme républicain," in Serge Berstein and Odile Rudelle, eds., *Le Modèle républicain* (Paris: Presses Universitaires de France, 1992).

108. The preceding quotations are found in Jean-Pierre Machelon, *La République contre les libertés?: Les Restrictions aux libertés publiques de 1879 à 1914* (Paris: Presses de la Fondation Nationale des Sciences Politiques, 1976), 286–90, 335, 340.

109. From the appendix to Anne Loïs, "Les Instituteurs et la République: Le Loyalisme contre la citoyenneté (1880–1930)" (Ph.D. diss., Université de Paris–I, 1997).

110. Machelon, *La République contre les libertés?* 291, 300. As Mache-

lon says further on, "[T]he liberalism of the Third Republic was at once ill-assured in its motivation, poorly adapted to its ends, and 'poorly tempered' in its implementation" (451).

111. See Jean-François Médard, "Political Clientelism in France: The Center-Periphery Nexus Reexamined," in S. N. Eisenstadt and René Lemarchand, eds., *Political Clientelism, Patronage, and Development* (London: Sage, 1981).

112. See Christophe Charle, *Les Hauts Fonctionnaires en France au XIXe siècle* (Paris: Gallimard/Julliard, 1980), 230ff.

113. Maurras, *Mes idées politiques*, 173, 293–94. In his *Enquête sur la monarchie*, Maurras also denounced the "money-grubbing republicans" (xxi).

114. On the extreme anticlericalism of the republicans, see René Rémond, *L'Anticléricalisme en France*. Claude Nicolet, citing Rémond's book as well as that of Louis Capéran, *Histoire contemporaine de la laïcité française* (Paris: Bibliothèque des Sciences Politiques et Sociales, 1957), judges it "scandalous" that "the history of anticlericalism has been written without first recalling the oppressive atmosphere created by clericalism between 1850 and 1906"; see *L'Idée républicaine en France, 1789–1924*, 271.

115. Quoted by Barral, *Les Fondateurs de la troisième République*, 179.

116. See François Vindé, *L'Affaire des fiches, 1900–1904: Chronique d'un scandale* (Paris: Éditions Universitaires, 1989).

117. See note 36 above.

118. Here I follow Maurice Larkin's analysis in *Religion, Politics, and Preferment in France Since 1890: La Belle Époque and Its Legacy* (Cambridge: Cambridge University Press, 1995); see pages 37–39, 81–82, 94–98, 101–5, 109. See also Larkin, *Church and State After the Dreyfus Affair: The Separation Issue in France* (London: Macmillan, 1974), chap. 8.

119. Jules Ferry, *La République des citoyens*, ed. Odile Rudelle, 2 vols. (Paris: Imprimerie Nationale, 1996), 2:456.

120. Quoted by H. S. Jones, *The French State in Question: Public Law and Political Argument in the Third Republic* (Cambridge: Cambridge University Press, 1993), 115. I am indebted to his analysis on this point.

121. Maxime Leroy, *Bulletin officiel de la Ligue des droits de l'homme* 7 (1907), 1542–43; the original French text is quoted in Jones, *The French State in Question*, 119.

122. Maxim Leroy, *Les Transformations de la puissance publique: Les Syndicats de fonctionnaires* (Paris: V. Giard and E. Brière, 1907), 158–59; quoted in Jones, *The French State in Question*, 136.

123. Maxim Leroy, *La Loi: Essai sur la théorie de l'autorité dans la démocratie* (Paris: V. Giard and E. Brière, 1908), 222–23; quoted in Jones, *The French State in Question*, 135; see also Jeanne Siwek-Pouydessau, *Le Syndicalisme des fonctionnaires jusqu'à la guerre froide: 1848–1948* (Lille: Presses Universitaires de Lille, 1989).

124. See Pierre Birnbaum, "La Conception durkheimienne de l'État: L'Apolitisme des fonctionnaires," *Revue française de sociologie* 17 (1976), 247–59.

125. See Françoise Mayeur, *L'Enseignement secondaire des jeune filles sous la troisième République* (Paris: Armand Colin, 1977), 370.

126. See Larkin, *Religion, Politics, and Preferment in France Since 1890*, 139.

127. This quotation, and the ones preceding it, are taken from Ozouf et al., *La République des instituteurs*, 176, 200–205.

128. Quoted in Loïs, "Les Instituteurs et la République," 111. I am indebted to her argument here and in what follows.

129. Ibid., 396, 399.

130. Jean-Marie Mayeur, "La Laïcité de l'État: Du conflit à l'apaisement, de Ferry à Poincaré," in Colin, ed., *Les Catholiques français et l'héritage de 1789*, 91.

131. Philippe Boutry and Alain-René Michel, "La Religion," in Sirinelli, ed., *Histoire des droites en France*, 3:668. According to Gérard Gengembre, with Maurras "nationalism became the sole absolute, a substitute for religion. But this profound and irremediable divergence did not entirely succeed in detaching Action Française from the ultramontaine and authoritarian branch of Catholicism, the ancestor of contemporary fundamentalism"; see *La Contre-Révolution ou l'histoire désespérante*, 321. Eugen Weber, for his part, argues that "[p]erhaps the most significant effect of the condemnation was the freeing of the Church and Catholic organizations from the influence of the Action Française, which had been so strong in the early 'twenties. For better or for worse, the future lay with the champions of social Catholicism of one kind or another" (*Action Française*, 255).

132. See Claude Langlois, "Les Catholiques français et l'héritage de 1789: 1889–1989," in Colin, ed., *Les Catholiques français et l'héritage de 1789*.

133. The Croix-de-Feu, a nationalist group of World War I veterans founded in 1927, was dissolved by the Popular Front eleven years later and replaced by the PSF, a group that was likewise heavily influenced by Catholicism, opposed to democracy, and hostile to the Jews. The PSF encouraged anti-Semitic movements in the late

1930s, particularly in Alsace and Algeria, and subsequently supported Vichy.—TRANS.

134. Quoted in Jacques Nobécourt, *Le Colonel de La Rocque, 1885–1946, ou les pièges du nationalisme chrétien* (Paris: Fayard, 1996), 347.

135. The blind obedience required of his shock troops, "permanently" available to take action against the Republic, along with the Croix-de-Feu's view of the world have nonetheless led Robert Soucy to dissent from the dominant historiographical opinion in regarding La Rocque as a fascist, even while admitting that he had nothing in common with Himmler, Eichmann, Valois, Taittinger, Doriot, or Déat; see *French Fascism: The Second Wave, 1933–1939* (New Haven: Yale University Press, 1995), chaps. 3 and 4. See also Michael Curtis, *Three Against the Republic: Sorel, Barrès, and Maurras* (Princeton: Princeton University Press, 1959), a now somewhat outdated work notable for its claim that these three writers "made remarkable prophetic predictions of national socialism" (49). To the contrary, as Philippe Burrin has argued more recently, "the reactionary Right, or, more accurately, the restorationist Right, criticized fascism for prolonging, in spite of its wishes to the contrary, the despised aftermath of 1789. The mobilization of the masses and plebeian elites in place of the hierarchy of natural authorities, . . . the civic cult in place of religion: in all these respects fascism seemed, to the Maurrassians, for example, to constitute the ultimate incarnation of the democratic principle, even if they recognized that it contradicted all of the essential values of [democracy]"; see "Le Fascisme: La Révolution sans révolutionnaires," *Débat* (January–March, 1986), 165.

136. See Nobécourt, *Le Colonel de La Rocque, 1885–1946*, 808ff., which strongly questions the anti-Semitic orientation of La Rocque's thought, particularly during the drafting of the Jewish Statutes by Vichy. Some have seen the Parti Social Français (PSF) not as a fascist party but instead as a Christian patriotic movement: see, for example, Philippe Machefer, "Sur quelques aspects de l'activité du colonel de La Rocque et du 'Progrès social français' pendant la Seconde Guerre mondiale," *Revue d'histoire de la deuxième guerre mondiale* (1963), 58.

137. See Guy Bordé, *La Défaite du Front populaire* (Paris: Maspero, 1977); also Jean-Charles Asselain et al., *La France en Mouvement, 1934–1938* (Seyssel: Champ Vallon, 1986), and Jacques Kergoat, *La France du Front populaire* (Paris: La Découverte, 1986).

138. Alain Bergounioux and Bernard Manin, *Le Régime social-*

démocrate (Paris: Presses Universitaires de France, 1989), 35. See also the discussion of the French example in Adam Przeworski and John Prague, *Paper Stones: A History of Electoral Socialism* (Chicago: University of Chicago Press, 1986).

139. See Perrot and Kriegel, *Le Socialisme français et le pouvoir*; also Hugues Portelli, *Le Socialisme français tel qu'il est* (Paris: Presses Universitaires de France, 1980), and Marc Sadoun, *De la démocratie française: Essai sur le socialisme* (Paris: Gallimard, 1993).

140. See Ralph Schor, *L'Antisémitisme en France pendant les années trente: Prélude à Vichy* (Brussels: Éditions Complexe, 1992), and Birnbaum, *Un Mythe politique*.

141. See Paul Christophe, *1936: Les Catholiques et le Front populaire* (Paris: Desclée, 1979).

Chapter 5. The Retreat from the Republican State

1. Étienne Fouilloux, *Les Chrétiens français entre crise et libération, 1937–1947* (Paris: Seuil, 1997), 100, 128. Fouilloux goes on to say that although the presence of Catholics in positions of power was a "sign of the indubitable improvement in church-state relations under Vichy," it was nonetheless "for the most part an indirect and still cautious presence: the [automotive] image of a political driveline therefore seems unwarranted" (128–29).

2. Déloye, *École et citoyenneté*, 344–45.

3. *Chef glorieux de la Patrie,*
   Père au grand cœur, nous t'aimons:
   Tes enfants ont l'âme meurtrie.
   Mais, commande, et nous te suivrons.
   The original French is quoted in W. D. Halls's remarkable book, from whose analysis I draw here, *Politics, Society, and Christianity in Vichy France* (Oxford: Berg, 1995), 52.

4. Ibid., 91. See also Halls's article "Catholicism Under Vichy: A Study in Diversity and Ambiguity," in Roderick Kedward and Roger Austin, eds., *Vichy France and the Resistance: Culture and Ideology* (London: Croom Helm, 1985).

5. Jacques Duquesne, *Les Catholiques français sous l'Occupation* (Paris: Grasset, 1966), 17, 84, 267.

6. Quoted by Nguyen, *Aux origines de l'Action française*, 21.

7. Charles Maurras, *La Seule France: Chronique des jours d'épreuve* (Lyons: Lardanchet, 1941), 136, 182–87, 288.

8. Weber, *Action Française*, 493.

9. See Marc Olivier Baruch, "Servir l'État français: L'Administration en France de 1940 à 1944," 3 vols. (Ph.D. diss., Institut d'Études Politiques de Paris, 1995), 1:83. A revised version of this dissertation was subsequently published by Fayard in 1997.

10. The famous hussars of the Republic: see chap. 4, n. 78.

11. See François Grèzes-Rueff, *La Culture des députés français (1910–1958): Essai de typologie* (Toulouse: Presses Universitaires de Mirail, 1994).

12. Baruch, "Servir l'État français," 1:126.

13. Thus Pétain's cabinet included not only a commissioner of audit in the Cour des Comptes, Pierre Gentil, but also several members of the Council of State, among them Georges Dayras and Jean Delvolvé. Two inspectors of public finance, Paul Baudouin and Yves Bouthillier, were named respectively to the Ministry of Foreign Affairs and the Ministry of Finance. Similarly, Jean-Pierre Ingrand, rapporteur of the Council of State, was named the representative of the minister of the interior in the occupied territories. André Lavagne, also a member of the Council of State, played an important role close to Pétain; other members of the Council of State headed the staffs of most of the ministries, just as they had under the Third Republic, working closely with inspectors of public finance and graduates of the École Normale Supérieure. Several members of the Council of State even became prefects, playing a particularly decisive role in carrying out a repressive policy. See Jean Marcou, "Le Conseil d'État sous Vichy" (thesis, Université de Grenoble–II, 1984).

14. See Jean-Pierre Dubois, "La Jurisprudence administrative," in "Le Discours antisémite de Vichy," a special issue issue of *Le Genre humain*, nos. 30–31 (May 1996) devoted to the anti-Semitic law of Vichy.

15. See the first volume of Baruch, "Servir l'État français," chap. 9.

16. See François Rouquet, *L'Épuration dans l'administration française* (Paris: Éditions du Centre National de la Recherche Scientifique, 1993).

17. Here and below the reader is referred to Robert O. Paxton, *Vichy France: Old Guard, New Order, 1940–1944* (New York: Knopf, 1972), 335–43; see too the discussion of the role of experts in French public administration, 259–68.

18. Under Vichy, the Council of State served both "as a court of law for private persons seeking redress of administrative grievances" and, reviving a Bonapartist tradition neglected under the Third

Republic, as a consultative body passing on the constitutionality of proposed legislation: see Paxton, 338.

19. See François Bloch-Lainé and Claude Gruson, *Hauts Fonction- naires sous l'Occupation* (Paris: Odile Jacob, 1996). Of administra- tive officials in 1940, they write: "As for the special character of Nazism, they attached no importance to it" (18); and they go on to say, "At the outset, for virtually all of us, as its servants, the state was there, in place, whether we regretted or not that it had not emigrated. The fact that its nature had changed the day after the vote in Parliament, the fact that its legality did not suffice to assure its legitimacy, appeared to most of us only gradually" (50).

20. See Sonia Mazay and Vincent Wright, "Les Préfets," in Jean-Pierre Azéma and François Bédarida, eds., *Le Régime de Vichy et les Français* (Paris: Fayard, 1992).

21. Mireille Gueissaz, "Jules Barni (1818–1878) ou l'entreprise dém- opédique d'un philosophe républicain moraliste et libre-penseur," in Jacques Chevallier, ed., *Les Bonnes Mœurs* (Paris: Presses Uni- versitaires de France, 1994), 244.

22. Bloch, "Servir l'État français," 1:194.

23. See Larkin, *Religion, Politics, and Preferment in France Since 1890*, 183.

24. See, for example, Jean-Marie Muller, *Désobéir à Vichy: La Résis- tance civil de fonctionnaires de police* (Nancy: Presses Universi- taires de Nancy, 1994).

25. Pierre Péan, *Une Jeunesse française: François Mitterrand, 1934– 1947* (Paris: Fayard, 1994), 314, 318. See also Jean-Pierre Husson, "L'Itinéraire d'un haut fonctionnaire: René Bousquet," in Azéma and Bédarida, eds., *Vichy et les Français*; Jean-Pierre Husson, "Un Préfet de la région de Champagne à l'époque de Vichy: René Bous- quet, 1941–1942," in Georges Clause, Sylvette Guilbert, and Mau- rice Vaïsse, *La Champagne et ses administrations à travers le temps* (Paris: La Manufacture, 1990); and *Le Monde* (10 June 1993, 9 and 14 September 1994).

26. See Gérard Boulanger, *Maurice Papon: Un Technocrate français dans la collaboration* (Paris: Seuil, 1994), 202, 245–46.

27. See Philippe Burin, *La France à l'heure allemande, 1940–1944* (Paris: Seuil, 1995), 315ff.

28. See Birnbaum, *La France aux Français*, chap. 5.

29. See Dominique Gros, "Le 'Statut des juifs' et les manuels en usage dans les faculté de droit (1940–1944)," in Philippe Braud, ed., *La Violence politique dans les démocraties européennes occidentales*

(Paris: L'Harmattan, 1993); also two articles by Danièle Lochak, "La Doctrine de Vichy ou les mésaventures du positivisme," in Centre Universitaire de Recherches Administratives et Politiques du Picardie, ed., *Les Usages sociaux du droit* (Paris: Presses Universitaires de France, 1989), and "Écrire, se taire. . . : Réflexions sur l'attitude de la doctrine française," in *Le Genre humain*, nos. 30–31 (May 1996), and Anne-Françoise Ropert-Précloux, "Qu'enseignait-on à la faculté de droit de Paris?" in the same issue of *Le Genre humain*.

30. Members of the *agrégation*, the class of successful candidates in the competitive examinations administered each year for the recruitment of university-level teachers in literature, philosophy, law, medicine, and so on.—TRANS.

31. These three were Georges Ripert (private and criminal law), Jacques Chevalier (philosophy), and Jérôme Carcopino (history); among their subordinates were Édouard Galletier, director of higher education, and Pierre Clarac, inspector general. See Denis Brousolle, "L'Élaboration du statut des Juifs de 1940," in *Le Genre humain* (see note 14), 126.

32. I am indebted here to Claude Singer's fine work, *Vichy, l'université et les juifs: Les Silences et la mémoire* (Paris: Les Belles Lettres, 1992).

33. Holders of the secondary school teaching qualification, the CAPES (*certificat d'aptitude professionnelle à l'enseignement secondaire*).—TRANS.

34. See chapter 22 of my book *Les Fous de la République: Histoire des Juifs d'etat de Gambetta à Vichy* (Paris: Seuil, 1995), published in English as *The Jews of the Republic: A Political History of State Jews in France from Gambetta to Vichy*, trans. Jane Marie Todd (Stanford: Stanford University Press, 1996).

35. See Jean-Paul Cointet, *Pierre Laval* (Paris: Fayard, 1993).

36. See Philippe Burrin, *La Dérive fasciste: Doriot, Déat, Bergery, 1933–1945* (Paris: Seuil, 1986).

37. Marc Olivier Baruch, "L'Administration française sous Vichy: L'Exemple du ministère de l'éducation nationale" (D.E.A., Institut d'Études Politiques de Paris, 1992), 28.

38. See Conan and Rousso, *Vichy, un passé qui ne passe pas*.

39. Baruch, "Servir l'État français," 3:1026, 3:1028.

40. The special issue of *Le Genre humain* on Vichy (see note 14) strikingly demonstrates the extent to which not only administrative law but criminal and commercial law were revised.

41. Here and in what follows, see the whole of chapter 3, as well as

appendix E-1, of the first volume of Baruch, "Servir l'État français."

42. See Jean Bauberot, "L'Antiprotestantisme à la fin du XIXe siècle," *Revue d'histoire et de philosophie religieuse*, no. 4 (1972) and no. 2 (1973).

43. Baruch, "Servir l'État français," 3:527, 3:985; see also Olivier Wieviorka, *Nous entrerons dans la carrière: De la Résistance à l'exercise du pouvoir* (Paris: Seuil, 1994), 28.

44. See François Bloch-Lainé and Jean Bouvier, *La France restaurée, 1944–1954: Dialogues sur les choix de modernisation* (Paris: Fayard, 1986); on French society during this period, see Jean-Daniel Reynaud, ed., *Tendances et volontés de la société française: Études sociologigues* (Paris: SEDEIS, 1966).

45. The Union de Défense des Commerçants et des Artisans [Union for the Defense of Shopkeepers and Artisans (UDCA)], a movement founded in the Lot in July 1953 by a bookseller named Pierre Poujade protesting tax increases at a time of economic recession, symbolized the violent rejection of the state by nationalist elements of the middle class; see the article on Poujade by Roger Eatwell in Douglas Bell et al., eds., *A Biographical Dictionary of French Political Leaders Since 1870*, 351–53.—TRANS.

46. See François Bédarida and Jean-Pierre Rioux, eds., *Pierre Mendès France et le mendésisme: L'Expérience gouvernementale (1954–1955) et sa postérité* (Paris: Fayard, 1985).

47. See Jean Fourastié, *Les Trente glorieuses ou la révolution invisible* (Paris: Fayard, 1979).

48. François Bloch-Lainé, *Profession, fonctionnaire: Entretiens avec Françoise Carrière* (Paris: Seuil, 1976), 237–38.

49. Quoted in André Passeron, ed., *De Gaulle parle des institutions, de l'Algérie, de l'Armée, des affaires étrangères, de la communauté, de l'économie et des questions sociales* (Paris: Plon, 1962), 71.

50. See Pierre Birnbaum, *Les Sommets de l'État*, 2d rev. ed. (Paris: Seuil, 1993).

51. Respectively, the Conseil d'État, charged with advising the government on matters of administrative law; the Cour des Comptes, responsible for auditing public accounts; the Inspection Générale des Finances, responsible for supervising the management of public revenues and expenditures; and the Quai d'Orsay, as the Ministry of Foreign Affairs is commonly referred to.—TRANS.

52. The phrase refers to Jules Méline, prime minister between 1896 and 1898, whose socially conservative republicanism was concerned primarily with defending vested economic (especially agri-

cultural) interests and the values of provincial France.—TRANS.

53. See John T. S. Keeler, *The Politics of Neo-Corporatism in France: Farmers, the State, and Agricultural Policy-Making in the Fifth Republic* (New York: Oxford University Press, 1987); also Patrick Hassenteufel, "Les Groupes d'intérêts dans l'action publique: L'État en interaction," *Pouvoir* (1995), 74.
54. See Alain Darbel and Dominique Schnapper, *Morphologie de la haute administration française*, rev. ed. (The Hague: Mouton, 1972); also Ezra Suleiman, *Politics, Power, and Bureaucracy in France: The Administrative Elite* (Princeton: Princeton University Press, 1974), Jean-François Kessler, *L'ÉNA, la Société, l'État* (Paris: Berger-Levraut, 1985), Jean-Luc Bodiguel, "La Socialisation des hauts fonctionnaires," in Danièle Lochak et al., eds., *La Haute Administration et la politique* (Paris: Presses Universitaires de France, 1986), and Marie-Christine Kessler, *Les Grands Corps de l'État* (Paris: Presses de la Fondation Nationale des Sciences Politiques, 1986). On the culture of ENA specifically, see Irène Bellier, "Regard d'une ethnologue sur les énarques," *L'Homme* 121 (1992), and by the same author, *L'ÉNA comme si vous y étiez* (Paris: Seuil, 1993); and Jean-Michel Gaillard, *L'ÉNA, miroir de l'État: De 1945 à nos jours* (Brussels: Complexe, 1995).
55. Between 1971 and 1976, the Gaullist party, previously called the Union pour la Défense de la République, was known as the Union des Démocrates pour la République (UDR). The Union pour la Démocratie Française (UDF), an alliance of non-Gaullist center and right-wing parties, was formed in 1978. The Parti Socialiste (PS) was the successor to the old Section Française de l'Internationale Ouvrière (SFIO). The neo-Gaullist Rassemblement pour la République (RPR) was formed in 1976 by Jacques Chirac to revitalize the Gaullist movement.—TRANS.
56. See Jean-Luc Bodiguel and Jean-Louis Quermonne, *La Haute Fonction publique sous la Ve République* (Paris: Presses Universitaires de France, 1983).
57. Bloch-Lainé, *Profession, fonctionnaire*, 231.
58. Tocqueville, *Democracy in America*, 203.
59. For a comparison of the role and values of high-ranking bureaucrats in France and the United States, see John Rohr, "Ethical Issues in French Public Administration: A Comparative Study," *Public Administration Review* (July–August 1991), and Marie-France Toinet, "La Morale bureaucratique: Perspectives transatlantiques et franco-américaines," *International Political Science Review* 9, no. 3 (1988).

60. "Arise children of the brotherhood"—a play on the first line of *La Marseillaise* ("Allons enfants de la patrie . . .").—Trans.

61. See Benjamin Angel, "Les Transformations des élites politiques dans la décennie 80, 1981–1991" (D.E.A, Université de Paris–II, 1992); also Jean-Luc Bodiguel and Luc Rouban, *Le Fonctionnaire détrôné?: L'État au risque de la modernisation* (Paris: Presses de la Fondation Nationale des Sciences Politiques, 1991); Philippe Dhennin, "Regards sur la composition sociologique du gouvernement Rocard et des ses cabinets ministériels" (D.E.A., Université de Paris–I, 1989); Monique Dagnaud and Dominique Mehl, *L'Élite rose*, revised and expanded (Paris: Éditions Ramsay, 1988); Jacques Chevallier, "La Gauche et la haute administration sous la cinquième République," in Lochak et al., eds., *La Haute Administration et la politique*; and Pierre Birnbaum, ed., *Les Élites socialistes au pouvoir* (Paris: Presses Universitaires de France, 1985).

62. Among these were Roger Faroux, Pierre Arpaillange, Hubert Curien, and even the energetic professor Léon Schwartzenberg.

63. Notably among them Alain Juppé, François Léotard, Jacques Toubon, Alain Lamassoure, Dominique Perben, and Hervé de Charette, who had been been superseded by political heavyweights such as Charles Pasqua, Simone Veil, and Pierre Méhaignerie—not to mention Michel Giraud, André Rossinot, Alain Carignon, François Bayrou, Daniel Hoeffel, and Philippe Douste-Blazy, whose power almost without exception was anchored in the political control of whole regions.

64. A good example is the Commission on Privatization, which included several inspectors of finance in addition to members of the Cour des Comptes and the Conseil d'État. See Frédéric Lassagne, "État privatiseur: La Privatisation des entreprises publiques en France de 1986 à 1988" (D.E.A., Université de Paris–I, 1990), 75; as its president, Pierre Chatenet, remarked, "[T]hese relations between senior civil servants belonging either to the same agency or to neighboring agencies such as the Conseil d'État, the Cour des Comptes, and the Inspection des Finances are entirely natural. We have all known each other since [our days together on] the rue Saint-Guillaume [i.e., as classmates at the Institut d'Études Politiques de Paris, which supplies ENA with most of its students]" (76).

65. A directive issued by the Juppé government limited the number of persons officially attached to ministerial offices to 198. Official staff under the Bérégovoy government, by contrast, numbered 408. See *Le Monde* (1 July 1995) and *Libération* (31 May 1995).

66. *Le Monde* (5 January 1996). In the same vein, see the book by Jean Picq, a member of the Cour des Comptes and author of several reports on reforming the state, *Il faut aimer l'État: Essai sur l'État en France à l'aube du XXIᵉ siècle* (Paris: Flammarion, 1995).

67. This increase was authorized by an ordinance of 28 November 1958, a decree of 22 February 1967, and, above all, a decree of 8 August 1985.

68. See *Le Monde* (9 January 1997).

69. See "Les Anciens Élèves de l'ÉNA aspirent à une éthique renforcée du service publique," *Le Monde* (23 September 1995).

70. See *Le Monde* (12 October 1993).

71. On the period prior to 1982, see Jean-Pierre Worms, "Le Préfet et ses notables," *Sociologie du travail* (July–September 1966); also Pierre Grémion, *Le Pouvoir périphérique: Bureaucrates et notables dans le système politique français* (Paris: Seuil, 1976), and Douglas E. Ashford, *British Dogmatism and French Pragmatism: Central-Local Policymaking in the Welfare State* (London: Allen and Unwin, 1982). On changes since then, see Jacques Rondin, *Le Sacre des notables: La France en décentralisation* (Paris: Fayard, 1985); François Dupuy and Jean-Claude Theonig, *L'Administration en miettes* (Paris: Fayard, 1985), and, by the same authors, "La Fonction préfectorale après la décentralisation: Entretien avec Olivier Philip, préfet,"*ÉNA mensuel* (April 1985); Stéphane Dion, *La Politisation des maires* (Paris: Economica, 1986); Philippe Garaud, *Profession, homme politique: La Carrière politique des maires urbains* (Paris: L'Harmattan, 1989); Jean-Michel Linfort and Jean-Claude Closset, "Élus locaux: Origine socioprofessionnelle et fonctionnarisation croissante," *Revue politique et parlementaire* (June 1989); Vivien A. Schmidt, *Democratizing France: The Political and Administrative History of Decentralization* (Cambridge: Cambridge University Press, 1990); Yves Mény, "La République des fiefs," *Pouvoirs* 60 (1992), and by the same author, *La Corruption de la République* (Paris: Fayard, 1992); Michel Crozier and Sylvie Trosa, eds., *La Décentralisation: Réforme de l'État* (Paris: Éditions Pouvoirs Locaux, 1992); I. Tobin, "L'Administration de l'État face à la décentralisation: L'Évolution du système d'action des préfectures" (Ph.D. diss., Institut d'Études Politiques de Paris, 1993); Albert Mabileau, "De la monarchie municipale á la française," *Pouvoirs* 73 (1995); and Patrice Duran and Jean-Claude Theonig, "L'État et la gestion publique territoriale," *Revue française de science politique* (August 1996). Finally, see the very complete article by Albert Mabileau, "Les Génies invisibles du lo-

cal: Faux-semblants et dynamiques de la décentralisation," *Revue française de science politique* (June–August 1997).

72. Michel Crozier, *On ne change pas la société par décret* (Paris: Grasset, 1979).

73. See "Cabinets ministériels: Plus de femmes, moins d'énarques," *Le Guide du pouvoir* (1991).

74. *Le Quotidien de Paris* (20 November 1991).

75. "Tapie à l'ÉNA" was the derisive crack frequently heard at the time, referring to the scandal-plagued businessman Bernard Tapie—a sign that bureaucratic circles saw even modest decentralizing measures as proof of scandal and the reign of business in France.

76. The three were Pierre Racine, Roger Fauroux, and Simon Nora.

77. This class took its symbolic name from the Marquis de Condorcet (1743–94), mathematician, economist, philosopher, and politician, who sought to introduce a comprehensive system of public education in France and who "embodied the convergence between the values and interests of organized science and those of the reforming state" and the "rationalization of social and political life"; see Keith M. Baker's essay in Furet and Ozouf, eds., *A Critical Dictionary of the French Revolution*, 204–12. Condorcet's ashes had recently been transfered to the Panthéon, in 1989.—TRANS.

78. *ÉNA mensuel* (January–February 1992).

79. *Le Figaro* (25 November 1991).

80. *Politis* (28 November 1991).

81. See Pierre Deyon, *L'État face au pouvoir local: Un Autre Regard sur l'histoire de France* (Paris: Éditions locales de France, 1996).

82. Quoted in Anne Wuilleumier, "L'ÉNA: De Versailles à Strasbourg" (D.E.A, Université de Paris–I, 1993), 90.

83. Quoted in Wuilleumier, 105, 106. As if echoing the latter remark, at the trial in Bordeaux of the senior civil servant Maurice Papon for crimes against humanity in connection with his role in the deportation of the Jews, Juliette Benzazon, one of the plaintiffs, said to Papon, "I received my education in the marketplace, not at ÉNA"; see *Le Monde* (17 December 1997).

84. René Bousquet, the senior civil servant who collaborated with the Nazis; see pages 153–54 above.

85. Quoted in *L'Expansion* (6 December 1984).

86. Quoted in *Le Monde* (29 November 1991). For *Le Point*, "ÉNA is the state. To transfer the one to the provinces obviously affects the other symbolically. . . . Neither strictly Marxist nor Proudhonian, but rather [a] nationalizing [doctrine], the socialism of 1981

was a form of statism. [The socialism] of 1991, lacking either doctrine or soul, destroyed the administrative Bastille with its own hands in order to win the applause of the people" (16 November 1991).

87. *Libération* (18 January 1992).
88. *Le Monde* (1 September 1997).
89. *Le Monde* (21 April 1984).
90. Quoted by Gaillard, *L'ÉNA, miroir de l'État*, 188.
91. Michel Bauer and Bénédicte Bertin-Mourot, *Les Énarques en entreprise de 1960 à 1990: Trente Ans de pantouflage* (Paris: Centre National de la Recherche Scientifique/Boyden, 1994), 11.
92. These firms included Elf-Aquitaine, CNCA, Suez, Paribas, Thomson, Saint-Gobain, Havas, and Pechiney: see Bauer and Bertin-Mourot, 20. In 1990, according to the authors, 1,003 *énarques* occupied high executive positions in business, 42 percent of them being employed in companies that had always been private. On these questions, see Ezra Suleiman, "Les Élites de l'administration et de la politique dans la France de la Vᵉ République: Homogénéité, puissance, permanence," in Ezra Suleiman and Henri Mendras, eds., *Le Recrutement des élites en Europe* (Paris: La Découverte, 1995). For his part, Jean-Marie Duffau, the director of studies at ÉNA, described the idea of transforming this *grande école* into a business school as "stupid"; see "Les Études à l'ÉNA," *Revue administrative*, special issue (1996), 17.
93. See Michel Bauer and Bénédicte Bertin-Mourot, *Vers un modèle européen de dirigeants? Comparaison Allemagne/France/Grande-Bretagne* (Paris: Centre National de la Recherche Scientifique/Boyden, 1996), 69, 137. On the relations between state elites and business, see Vivien Schmidt, *From State to Market? The Transformation of French Business and Government* (Cambridge: Cambridge University Press, 1996).
94. *Le Monde* (19 May 1991).
95. "Les Anciens Élèves de l'ÉNA aspirent à une éthique renforcée du service public," *Le Monde* (23 September 1995).
96. Nor was this all. Bernard Ratat, a senior engineer at the ministry of defense, where he was in charge of arms sales, left to join Dassault. Benoît Jolivet, former head of the insurance division at the ministry of finance, suddenly became an official of the Union des Assurances de Paris. Jacques Bombal, supervisor of agribusiness at the ministry of agriculture, joined the Caves de Roquefort Société. Philippe Jaffré was appointed président–directeur général of Elf-

Aquitaine, and Michel Pébereau chief executive officer of the Banque Nationale de Paris. The *énarque* Robert Lion went from the interministerial committee on industrial restructuring to the Arnaud group. See *Le Canard enchaîné* (24 November 1993), *Libération* (11 November 1993), and *Le Monde* (6 May 1994 and 10 December 1996).

97. *Le Monde* (7 October 1982 and 20 February 1986).

98. See Bernard Destremeau, *Le Quai d'Orsay: Derrière la façade* (Paris: Plon, 1994), 386, 440.

99. Despite the 5 to 4 majority of conservatives on the Constitutional Council (created by the Constitution of 1958 and charged with reviewing the constitutionality of statutes enacted by parliament), Badinter thus found himself in a position to cast the deciding vote on behalf of the Socialists in cases where a member's absence produced a tie vote. On the use of this body (formerly thought by conservatives to be "a guardian of legislative rectitude") for political purposes by both the Left and the Right to thwart unwanted reform programs after 1981, see Larkin, *France Since the Popular Front*, 387–89.

100. See *Le Point* (22 December 1986); also Danièle Lochak, "Les Hauts Fonctionnaires et l'alternance: Quelle politisation?" in Pierre Muller, ed., *L'Administration française est-elle en crise?* (Paris: L'Harmattan, 1992).

101. See *Libération* (11 March 1993) and *Le Monde* (9 April 1995).

102. See *Le Monde* (23 September 1995).

103. Michel Crozier, *La Crise de l'intelligence: Essai sur l'impuissance des élites à se reformer* (Paris: InterÉdition, 1995), 186. Others, more numerous today, wish only to see ÉNA's monopoly abolished so that greater diversity may be introduced in the recruitment of senior civil servants, with the various branches of the civil service taking charge of recruitment themselves, as in the nineteenth century; see, for example, Yves Cannac, "Faut-il maintenir le monopole de l'ÉNA?" *Pouvoirs* 80 (1997).

104. Kessler, *L'ÉNA, la société, l'État*, 238.

105. Among them Philippe Séguin, Jacques Toubon, Jean-Pierre Chevènement, Michel Rocard, Laurent Fabius, Martine Aubry, Élisabeth Guigou, Nicolas Sarkozy, and Alain Lamassoure.

106. Jacques Chirac, *La France pour tous* (Paris: Nil Éditions, 1994), 12.

107. See *L'Express* (10 June 1993), *Le Point* (11 June 1994), *Le Figaro* (13 June 1994), and *L'Express* (16 June 1994), respectively.

108. *Le Monde* (18 December 1994).
109. *Le Monde* (10 January 1995).
110. *Libération* (8 February 1995).
111. *Libération* (23 May 1996).
112. *Le Monde* (18 March 1997).
113. *La Croix* (19 April 1995).
114. The myth that France is ruled by the wealthy, whose fat bank accounts are matched by the size of their stomachs (and who stand in contrast to the innocent, patriotic *petits français*), has been a recurring theme of political life in France since the Revolution of 1789. See pages 61–62 above and Birnbaum, *Le Peuple et les gros.* —TRANS.
115. Ibid., 230ff.
116. *Le Monde* (29 April 1997).
117. The Basque separatist movement Euzkadi Ta Askatasuna. —TRANS.
118. *Le Monde* (15 May and 24 May 1997).
119. *Le Monde* (29 April 1997).
120. *Le Monde* (2 May 1997). See also the feature "La France malade de ses élites?" in *Le Monde* (9 September 1997), emphasizing the "divorce" between French society and its administrative elites.
121. *Le Monde* (5 June 1997). This analysis is shared by Ezra Suleiman, who wrote in the 16 June 1997 issue of *Le Monde* that "France refuses, more or less, to admit that the era of a monochrome and all-powerful elite is over. It remains the only country where this notion still preoccupies political analysts. Henceforth it must be accepted that in a world characterized by openness and competition there is little room for an elite that is sure of itself and domineering. . . . Only France persists in relying on the vestiges of a state aristocracy."
122. These included Martine Aubry, in charge of both labor and national solidarity (the latter now a major portfolio), Jean-Pierre Chevènement at interior, Élisabeth Guigou at justice, Hubert Védrine at foreign affairs, and Alain Richard at defense—not to mention a number of secretaries of state, among them Ségolène Royal (primary education), Pierre Moscovici (European affairs), and Christian Pierret (industry).
123. See *Le Monde* (6 June, 7 June, 27 June, and 20 August 1997) and *Libération* (15 June 1997); also Luc Rouban, "Les Énarques en cabinets, 1984–1996," *Les Cahiers du CEVIPOF* 17.
124. *Le Monde* (7 October 1987).

125. *Le Monde* (22 April 1988).
126. *L'Humanité* (2 October 1987).
127. *L'Événement du jeudi* (17 September 1987).
128. *L'Humanité* (8 November 1994). On the privatizations, see Charles Kaduschin, "Friendship Among the French Financial Elite," *American Sociological Review* (April 1995), and Franck Baucel, "Le Processus de privatisations: La Spécificité française," in Fabrice Dion, ed., "Les Privatisations en France, en Allemagne, en Grande-Bretagne et en Italie," *Notes et études documentaires*, no. 5024 (Paris: La Documentation Française, 1995).
129. *Le Monde* (24 June 1995).
130. The most famous case of state-owned property being used for personal advantage was that of Alain Juppé, the product of a strict *grand corps*; but there were others as well. See *Libération* (23 June 1995) for an impressive list of senior civil servants and politicians who benefited from such real estate deals; also *Le Monde* (29 June 1995).
131. The problem of corruption had already attracted attention in the media before the wave of scandals broke in the late 1980s; see the series of articles that appeared under the title "La Corruption en France à travers" in *Le Monde* (January 1980–June 1984); also *Pouvoirs* 31 (1984), 119.
132. These included Pierre Bergé, Martin Bouygues, and Bernard Tapie; but also, and especially, Didier Pineau-Valencienne (the head of Schneider), Pierre Suard (Alcatel), André Lévy-Lang (Paribas), and Françoise Sampermans (Générale Occidentale), to mention only a few. See *Le Monde* (30 December 1995).
133. *Le Monde* (31 May 1997).
134. See Philippe Ardant, François Bloch-Lainé, Albin Chalandon, and Yann Gaillard, "Débat: L'Administration française est-elle corrompue?" *Pouvoirs* 31 (1984); also Yves Mény, *La Corruption de la République* (Paris: Fayard, 1992).
135. "Entretien Simon Nora-Marcel Gauchet," *Le Débat* 40 (1984), 105.
136. Jean-Pierre Worms, Jean-Claude Thoenig, and Pierre Grémion, "Administration et pouvoir économique," *La Table ronde*, special issue (January 1973).
137. *Le Monde* (27 November 1996).
138. Bernard Tapie, *De l'énergie pour l'Europe* (Paris: Éditions Radicales, 1994), 96, 100–101.
139. See Pierre-André Taguieff, "Un Programme 'révolutionnaire'?" in

Nonna Mayer and Pascal Perrineau, eds., *Le Front à découvert*, 2d revised and expanded edition (Paris: Presses de la Fondation Nationale des Sciences Politiques, 1996).

140. *Le Monde* (18 October 1994).
141. *Le Monde* (14 March 1995).
142. *National-Hebdo* (14 March 1995).
143. *National-Hebdo* (20 October 1994); see also *Le Figaro* (19 December 1994) and *Le Français* (13 January 1995).
144. Philippe de Villiers, *La Société de connivence ou comment faire avaler des serpents à sonnettes* (Paris: Albin Michel, 1994), 92.
145. According to polls conducted by Sondage Sofres–*Le Nouvel Observateur*, senior civil servants rank second in incompetence, just behind parliamentary deputies. Ranked according to usefulness, they hold second-to-last place, just ahead of prostitutes and deputies, who once again win the prize for distrust. Everything considered, the French show greater confidence in the president of the Republic and mayors than they do in civil servants and deputies. See "La Hiérarchie sociale vue par les Français," *Le Nouvel Observateur* (26 September 1990), and "Les Institutions et la politique," *Le Nouvel Observateur* (11 March 1991).

Chapter 6. The Era of Rival Identities

1. See Alphonse Dupront, *Puissances et latences de la religion catholique* (Paris: Gallimard, 1993).
2. Nicolet, *L'Idée républicaine en France*, 271.
3. Lalouette, *La Libre-Pensée en France, 1848–1940*, 401.
4. See Claude-Albert Colliard and Gérard Timsitt, eds., *Les Autorités administratives indépendantes* (Paris: Presses Universitaires de France, 1988); Évelyne Pisier, "Vous avez dit indépendantes? Réflexions sur les AAI," *Pouvoirs*, no. 45 (1989); and Jean-Paul Willaime, "État, éthique et religion," *Cahiers internationaux de sociologie* 88 (1990).
5. Opus Dei, a conservative society devoted to bringing lessons of the Gospel to bear on professional life, was founded in 1928 and approved by Pius XII in 1947. See *Le Monde* (16 August 1996); also Anouck Michel, "Les Ultra-catholiques et les droites radicales en France," *Cahiers politiques* (1996), 97ff.
6. See Larkin, *Religion, Politics and Preferment in France Since 1890*, 194ff.

7. *Le Monde* (20 February 1997).
8. Danielle Sallenave, "L'Autre Enterrement," *Le Monde* (19 January 1996).
9. Danièle Hervieu-Léger, "Une Messe est possible," *Le Débat* (September–October 1996), 25.
10. Quoted in Hervieu-Léger, "Une Messe est possible," 26; see also Robert Solé, "La République à Notre-Dame," *Le Monde* (13 January 1996).
11. See Émile Poulat, "Le Président, la République et Dieu," *Esprit* (May 1996).
12. Jean-François Bouthors, "Le Président, la France et la mort," *Esprit* (November 1994), 102.
13. *Le Monde* (4 April 1996).
14. These quotations from ecclesiastical figures and organs are taken from Yves Déloye, "Commémoration et imaginaire national en France (1896–1996): 'France, fille aînée de l'Église, es-tu fidèle aux promesses de ton baptême?' " in Birnbaum, ed., *Sociologie des nationalismes*, 70–72.
15. *Le Monde* (20 September 1996); see also the feature in the previous day's edition entitled "Clovis, l'Église et la République."
16. See Claude Langlois, "Religion, culte ou opinion religieuse: La Politique des révolutionnaires," *Revue française de sociologie* (July–September 1989), 478–79.
17. On this topic, see the proceedings of the 1989 conference organized by the Société Français d'Histoire des Idées et d'Histoire Religieuse, *L'Église catholique et la Déclaration des droits de l'homme* (Angers: Presses de l'Université d'Angers, 1990).
18. See Michel Winock, "La République des catholiques," *L'Histoire* (May 1996), and by the same author, *Parlez-moi de la France* (Paris: Plon, 1995), particularly chap. 4 ("La Fille aînée de l'Église est-elle une fille perdue?"). In this connection, Jean-Paul Willaime writes: "We have gone from the political-patriotic *civisme* of a conquering Republic to the political-ethical *civisme* of a managerial Republic responsible for supervising a pluralist democracy in which the spiritual and moral forces of the nation are invited to take their place"; see "Le Religieux dans l'espace public," *Projet* (January–March 1991), 79.
19. Philippe Portier, "La Philosophie politique de l'Église catholique: Changement ou permanence?" *Revue française de science politique* (June 1986), 326, 340. Portier argues that the strategy of the Church, which has "restor[ed] the norms it posits to a central place among [its] social [concerns]," consists, as in the case of the

other faiths, in "putting the spiritual back into the very heart of public debate" and "is accompanied by a considerable restructuring of [its] missionary activity"; see his book *Église et politique en France au XXe siècle* (Paris: Montchrétien, 1993), 144–46.

20. Brigitte Vassort-Rousset, *Les Évêques de France en politique* (Paris: Cerf, 1986), 90.

21. Assemblée Plénière de l'Épiscopat Français, *Politique, Église et foi* (Paris: Le Centurion, 1972), 64, 109.

22. Statement of the Assemblée Plénière de l'Épiscopat Français (Lourdes, 1987), 4.

23. *Le Monde* (5 October 1988).

24. Ibid.

25. *Le Monde* (8 December 1989).

26. Henri Madelin, "Conflits et accords entre laïcité et christianisme," in Colin, ed., *Les Catholiques français et l'héritage de 1789*, 110. Madelin wishes for "neither a Christian state, nor an atheist state, nor a neutral state, but a constitutional and pluralist state"; see his remarks in *La Croix* (2 May 1989), the whole of which is devoted to a discussion between Catholic leaders and union representatives of public school teachers.

27. Monsignor Marcel Lefebvre, *Le Coup de maître de Satan* (Paris: Éditions Saint-Gabriel, 1977), 7; see also, by the same author, *Ils l'ont découronné: Du libéralisme à l'apostasie, la tragédie conciliaire*, 2d ed. (Escurolles: Éditions Fideliter, 1987). On this movement, see Jean-Yves Camus, "Intégrisme catholique et extrême droite en France: Le Parti de la countre-révolution," *Lignes*, no. 4 (October 1988), and Émile Poulat, "L'Intégrisme, de sa forme catholique à sa forme savante," in Jacques Lemaire and Jacques Marx, *Les Intégrismes* (Brussels: Éditions de l'Université de Bruxelles, 1986).

28. Monsignor Marcel Lefebvre, *Lettre ouverte aux catholiques perplexes* (Paris: Albin Michel, 1985), 28. In the same vein, see Jean Madiran, *L'Hérésie du XXe siècle* (Paris: Nouvelles Éditions Latines, 1968); in Madiran's view, the Church became Lutheran under the influence of Satan.

29. Monsignor Marcel Lefebvre, *Un Évêque parle: Écrits et allocutions, 1963–1974*, 2d ed., 2 vols. (Paris: Éditions Dominique Martin Morin, 1974), 1:257. For evidence of the diversity that characterizes the "integrist" movement, certain of whose members nonetheless remain faithful to Rome, see Grégoire Celier, *L'Église déchirée: Appel aux "catholiques Ecclesia Dei"* (Eguelshardt: Éditions Fideliter, 1994).

30. See the remarkable issue of *Golias* (Fall 1991).

31. See Martial Berne, "La Reconstitution d'une citoyenneté catholique: L'Enseignement catholique en France en 1993" (D.E.A., Université de Paris–I, 1993).

32. Quoted in Gautier Willaume, "Catholicisme et citoyenneté: Étude comparative de deux mouvements d'action catholique, la Jeunesse indépendante chrétienne et la Jeunesse ouvrière chrétienne, et deux communautés du Renouveau charismatique, le Chemin neuf et l'Emmanuel" (D.E.A., Université de Paris–I, 1991), 201. See also Danièle Hervieu-Léger, "Charismatiques catholiques et institution," in Paul Ladrière and René Luneau, eds., *Le Retour des certitudes: Événements et orthodoxie depuis Vatican II* (Paris: Centurion, 1987), and Françoise Champion and Danièle Hervieu-Léger, eds., *De l'émotion en religion: Renouveaux et traditions* (Paris: Centurion, 1990).

33. Quoted in Michel Anglade and Thierry Costerg, "Monographie de Saint-Nicolas-du-Chardonnet" (Paris: Institut d'Études Politiques de Paris, 1989).

34. Quoted in Anglade and Costerg.

35. Quoted in Anglade and Costerg.

36. See *Chrétienté-Solidarité* (January 1989) and *L'Anti-89* (November 1989).

37. See, for example, *Éléments* (Spring 1989); also the Christmas issue from the year before, "La France n'a pas commençée en 1789."

38. This and the other passages quoted previously in this paragraph are taken from Déloye, "Commémoration et imaginaire national en France (1896–1996)," 76–78.

39. Quoted in Déloye, 78.

40. See "Le Retour des croisés," *Golias* (Fall 1991), 57–58, and, in the same issue, "Le Cadavre de Maurras bouge encore." See also part 3 of Christophe Bourseiller, *Extrême Droite, l'enquête* (Paris: François Bourin, 1991).

41. Monsignor Marcel Lefebvre, *C'est moi, l'accusé, qui devrais vous juger* (Eguelshardt: Éditions Fideliter, 1994), 182.

42. Ibid., 207–9.

43. See Jean-Claude Manet, "Pèlerinages de tradition," *Le Mouvement social* (April–June 1991).

44. Jean-Marie Cardinal Lustiger, *Devenez dignes de la condition humaine* (Paris: Flammarion, 1995), 156.

45. See Michel Fruton-Letard, "Enjeux politiques de la catéchèse: Les Nouveaux Visages du militant chrétien" (D.E.A, Université de Paris–I, 1993).

46. See Hervieu-Léger, "Charismatiques catholiques et institution."
47. In this connection, see Yves Lambert, "La Religion: Un Paysage en profonde évolution," in Hélène Riffault, ed., *Les Valeurs des Français* (Paris: Presses Universitaires de France, 1994), as well as Guy Michelat, Julien Potel, Jacques Sutter, and Jacques Maitre, *Les Français sont-ils encore catholiques?: Analyse d'un sondage d'opinion* (Paris: Cerf, 1991), and Sophie Sahakian-Marcellin and Franck Frégosi, *Être catholique en France aujourd'hui* (Paris: Hachette, 1997).
48. These figures are from the *Le Figaro*–Sofres poll published in *Le Figaro* (20 December 1994); see also *L'Actualité religieuse dans le monde* (15 May 1994).
49. See Martine Sevegrand, *Les Enfants du Bon Dieu: Les Catholiques français et la procréation au XXe siècle* (Paris: Alin Michel, 1995).
50. See Daniel Boy and Guy Michelat, "Croyances aux parasciences: Dimensions sociales et culturelles," *Revue française de sociologie* 27, no. 2 (January–March 1996), and Yves Lambert, "Âges, générations et christianisme en France et en Europe," *Revue française de sociologie* (October–December 1993).
51. See *Le Monde* (8 May 1997).
52. In this connection, see Jean-Marie Donegani, *La Liberté de choisir: Pluralisme religieux et pluralisme politique dans le catholicisme français contemporain* (Paris: Presses de la Fondation Nationale des Science Politiques, 1993), and by the same author, "L'Individu et ses crédos," *Projet* 240 (1994), 52.
53. See Guy Michelat and Michel Simon, *Classe, religion et comportement politique* (Paris: Presses de la Fondation Nationale des Sciences Politiques, 1977); Émile Poulat, *Église contre bourgeoisie: Introduction au devenir du catholicisme actuel* (Tournai: Casterman, 1977); Christel Peyrefitte, "Religion et politique," in the Sofres volume *L'Opinion française en 1977* (Paris: Presses de la Fondation Nationale des Sciences Politiques, 1978); Philippe Braud, "Les Élections législatives de mars 1978 en Bretagne," *Revue française de science politique* (December 1978); Pierre Brechon and Bernard Denni, "L'Univers politique des catholiques pratiquants," *Revue française de sociologie* (July–September 1983); and Guy Michelat and Michel Simon, "Religion, classe sociale, patrimoine et comportement politique," in Daniel Gaxie, ed., *Explication du vote: Un Bilan des études électorales en France* (Paris: Presses de la Fondation Nationale des Sciences Politiques, 1985). See, too, three articles in a series entitled "Le Pluralisme

catholique" in *La Croix* (19 March 1993, 28 April 1994, and 13 May 1997), and Hugues Portelli, "L'Évolution politique des catholiques," in the Sofres volume *L'État de l'opinion* (Paris: Seuil, 1994).

54. Donegani, *La Liberté de choisir*, 471–72.

55. See Henri Rey and Françoise Subileau, *Les Militants socialistes à l'épreuve du pouvoir* (Paris: Presses de la Fondation Nationale des Sciences Politiques, 1991).

56. See *La Croix* (13 May 1997).

57. See the CSA–*La Vie* poll published in the 12 June 1997 issue of *La Vie*: 64 percent of practicing Catholics said that they had voted for the mainstream Right in the first round of these elections.

58. See, for example, André Guès, "Les Preuves de l'imposture laïque," *Intinéraire* (April 1982), and by the same author, "Les Intégristes de la laïcité," *Permanences* (June–July 1996).

59. See Henri Madelin, "Catholiques dans la France laïque," *Études* (October 1996), 321.

60. See *Le Monde* (11 April 1995).

61. This statement is found in Michel Morineau, ed., *Une Laïcité pour l'an 2000*, Proceedings of the 1989 Congress of the Ligue Française de l'Enseignement (Toulouse: Ligue Française de l'Enseignement, 1989), 26–27. See also the various contributions to the league's January 1989 publication, *Laïcité 2000: Nouvelles attitudes—pour un débat sans concession*.

62. For an analysis of secularism from the nineteenth century until the present period, see Émile Poulat, *Liberté, laïcité: La Guerre des deux France et le principe de la modernité* (Paris: Cerf, 1988).

63. René Rémond, *Le Catholicisme français et la société politique* (Paris: Éditions Ouvrières, 1995), 189. Note, however, that for Rémond, "today the battle has been won" (196).

64. Claude Nicolet, "L'Idée républicaine, plus que la laïcité," *Projet* (September–October 1988).

65. See Françoise Champion, "Entre laïcisation et sécularisation: Des rapports Église-État dans l'Europe communautaire," *Le Débat* (December 1993), 70; also William Genieys, "Le Devenir de la laïcité: La Laïcité ouverte?" (D.E.A., Université de Paris–I, 1989).

66. From the record of the plenary assembly of the episcopate at Lourdes in 1987.

67. Quoted in *La Croix* (18 December 1987).

68. "Vers une expression nouvelle de la laïcité," *Documents Épiscopat*, no. 1 (January 1989).

69. Quoted in *Le Monde* (27–28 October 1989).
70. Commission Sociale de l'Épiscopat, "Politique: Affaire de tous," *La Documentation catholique* (1 December 1991).
71. *Libération* (4 October and 6 November 1989); see also *Le Monde* (7 October 1989). On the Creil affair, see *Hommes et migrations* (February–March 1990).
72. *Réforme* (4 November 1989).
73. See the statement signed by Mithridate Dupont, "L'Éthique protestante et l'esprit du multiconfessionnalisme," *Esprit* (December 1989), 122.
74. See my book *The Jews of the Republic*, chap. 7.
75. *Le Monde* (21 October 1990).
76. Joseph Sitruk, "La Communauté juive de France et ses rapports avec l'État," *Administration* (December 1993).
77. A piece of wordplay in French ("*fichus fichus*"); see *Le Monde* (9 November 1989).
78. A photograph of this event appeared in *Libération* (26 October 1989) and at once attracted comment.
79. *Le Monde* (22 October 1989); see also "Le Défi à la laïque," *Libération* (22 October 1989).
80. *L'Humanité* (27 October 1989).
81. *Le Monde* (28 October 1989).
82. See Paul Siblot, "Ah! qu'en termes voilés ces choses-là sont dites," *Mots* (March 1992); also Camille Lacoste Dujardin, "Les Fichus islamistes: Approche ethnologue," *Hérodote* (January–March 1990).
83. See the polls published in *La Vie* (26 October 1989) and *Le Monde* (30 November 1989). The IFOP's 22 November 1989 report, "L'Islam en France," indicated that 75 percent of those polled were opposed to the wearing of the veil in school, 38 percent were against the construction of mosques, and 86 percent objected to a call to prayer broadcast over loudspeakers. Sixty-eight percent rejected the idea that a Muslim might be elected president of the Republic, and 56 percent disapproved of the two principal Islamic religious festivals being made official holidays for Muslims (73 percent were against their being made national holidays for the country as a whole). Other polls were more nuanced: 44 percent of those polled by BVA–*Le Parisien libéré*, for example, felt that the wearing of the veil called secularism in the schools into question; see *Le Parisien libéré* (23 October 1989).
84. *Le Nouvel Observateur* (27 October 1989). See the counterappeal signed by Harlem Désir, Alain Touraine, René Dumont, Joëlle

Notes

Kaufmann, Jean Lacouture, and Gilles Perrault, opposed to French-style secularism, in *Politis* (9 November 1989). "The rejection of the headscarf," they pointed out, "is already felt to be a humiliation by a part of the North African community."

85. The other signers of this letter were Élisabeth Badinter, Élisabeth de Fontenay, and Catherine Kintzler. Along with Debray and Finkielkraut, I refer to them collectively below as "the five musketeers of secularism."

86. *Le Nouvel Observateur* (27 October 1989).

87. Jacques Le Goff, "Derrière le foulard, l'histoire," *Le Débat* (January–February 1990), 28. [The Maginot line consisted of a series of fortifications built along the eastern and northeastern borders of France between 1929 and 1936 for the purpose of repelling a German attack; in May–June 1940, the Nazi armies swept around it with ease, passing through the Ardennes.—TRANS.]

88. Régis Debray, "République ou démocratie," *Le Nouvel Observateur* (30 November 1989); see also, by the same author, "La Laïcité, une exception française," in Hubert Bost, ed., *Genèse et enjeux de la laïcité: Christianismes et laïcité* (Geneva: Labor and Fides, 1990). Jacques Le Goff was among those who criticized Debray's reasoning and, addressing himself to Debray directly, implored him to avoid extremism: "Pluralism is not [the same as] dissipation and mess. . . . Haven't you heard the cries of all those who have rebelled in Eastern Europe, raised in the name of democracy and pluralism? . . . Do not be the Bonald and the Joseph de Maistre of secularism and its theoretical foundations"; see "Derrière le foulard, l'histoire," 32–33. For Claude Nicolet, writing in *Le Monde* (22 December 1989), if one does not wish the Republic to become a "museum," if one intends to maintain the "republican form of the French state" by refusing to join with the Anglo-American tradition in privileging civil society, it is important that secularism accept the headscarf in the school while rejecting the creation of places of prayer and religious instruction within its walls.

89. *Le Monde* (11 July 1989).

90. *Libération* (7 November 1989).

91. Denis Lacorne sets the record straight in this connection, severely criticizing caricatures of American society that ignore its civic basis and consider only its ethnic dimension; see *La Crise de l'identité américaine: Du melting-pot au multiculturalisme* (Paris: Fayard, 1997).

92. *Libération* (13 November 1989).

93. *Journal officiel* (27 November 1989).
94. See *L'Actualité juridique* (20 January 1990) and Jean Rivéro, "L'Avis de l'assemblée générale du Conseil d'État en date du 27 novembre 1989," *Revue française de droit administratif* (January–February 1990); also Jean-Claude William, "Le Conseil d'État et la laïcité: Propos sur l'avis du 27 novembre 1989," *Revue française de science politique* (February 1990). On the introduction of the idea of cultural pluralism in the jurisprudence of the Conseil d'État, see its 1996 public report, *Sur le principe de l'égalité* (Paris: La Documentation Française, 1997), 65ff.
95. *Journal officiel* (15 December 1989). On this memorandum, see Claude Durand-Prinborgne, "La Circulaire Jospin du 12 décembre 1989, *Revue française de droit administratif* (January 1990).
96. Lacoste and Lejeune were leading Socialist figures under the Fourth Republic who became persuaded of the need to use armed force against the insurgents in Algeria, the former as minister for Algerian affairs between 1956 and 1958.—TRANS.
97. See "Le Moment ou jamais: Entretien avec Lionel Jospin," *Le Débat* (January–February 1990), 16–19. As prime minister, Jospin continued to uphold this open secularism in the face of the large Catholic rally held in Paris during the Journées Mondiales de la Jeunesse, in August 1997, in which more than a million faithful took part. In the presence of the pope, he reaffirmed the "French conception of secularism, respectful of religious freedom"; see *Le Monde* (26 August 1997).
98. Quoted in "Laïcité—du combat au droit: Entretien avec David Kessler," *Le Débat* (November–December 1993), 98–99.
99. Ibid., 100.
100. It should be noted that Martine Laroque, a member of the Conseil d'État, is the daughter of Pierre Laroque, who was himself an important member of this institution and who played a decisive role in the establishment of the social security system. Vichy forced him into retirement under the terms of the Jewish statute of October 1940, although he did not consider himself as being of the Jewish religion. David Kessler, also a member of the Conseil d'État, takes part in the activities of liberal Jewish circles. Both Laroque and Kessler subscribe to the new secularism, as does Roger Errera, a councilor of state who edits the "Diaspora" series for Calmann-Lévy.
101. "Les Catholiques au secours de la laïcité," *Le Figaro* (14 November 1989).
102. The Falloux law (enacted in 1850 and amended in the 1880s) es-

tablished a system of private education while limiting the amount of funding that local authorities could set aside for private schools.—TRANS.

103. See the 28 June, 18 December, and 22 December 1993 issues of *Libération* as well as the 29 June and 19 December 1993 issues of *Le Monde*.

104. Thus, for example, *"Du fric pour les laïques, des gnons pour les curetons"* ("Money for the people, punishment for the priests"); *"Pour une école sans calotte et sans-culotte"* ("For clergyless republican schools"); *"Laïques dans la rue, grenouilles dans le bénitier"* ("People in the street, frogs [Catholics] in the font [church]"); *"Coupez les bourses aux curés"* ("Cut budgets for priests"); *"Falloux, hiboux, genoux, cailloux, Bayrou dans les choux"* ("Falloux, owls, knees, pebbles, Bayrou bringing up the rear"—a play on the children's spelling rhyme "Bijoux, cailloux, choux, genoux, hiboux"); *"Dieu s'est fait Marie, il ne se fera pas Marianne"* ("God had Mary, but he won't have Marianne"); *"Savez-vous planter les choux à la mode de Bayrou?"* ("Do you know how to live in the country in the Bayrou style?"); and *"De Villiers, Bayrou, au fond du Puy-du-Fou"* ("De Villiers and Bayrou at the bottom of Puy-du-Fou").

105. See the 14 January and 18 January 1994 issues of *Le Monde*; the 7 January, 15 January, and 18 January 1994 issues of *Libération*; and the 17 January 1994 issue of *L'Humanité*.

106. In November 1983, a few months before the great demonstrations of June 1984, 70 percent of the French declared themselves in favor of the existence of private education, including 45 percent who claimed no religious attachment; see the Sofres poll of that month, "Les Français et l'enseignement privé." Conversely, 26 percent of those who attended mass every week felt that public school suited the needs of Catholic families rather well; see the 16 February 1984 *La Vie*–Louis Harris poll.

107. See Jean-Marie Mayeur, "La Guerre scolaire: Ancienne ou nouvelle histoire?" *Vingtième Siècle* (January–March 1985); "Les Libertés et la querelle scolaire," in Sofres, *Opinion publique, 1985* (Paris: Gallimard, 1985); and Jean Baubérot, "Les Avatars de la culture laïque," *Vingtième Siècle*, no. 44 (1994).

108. Joël Roman, "La Laïcité comme religion civile," *Esprit* (October 1991), 113.

109. See, for example, *Le Monde de l'éducation* (July–August 1991). While favorably disposed to the introduction of religious education in school, the French approve the separation of church and

state and firmly reject all control by the Catholic Church over their private life; see the CSA–*La Croix* poll in René Rémond, ed., *Nouveaux Enjeux de la laïcité* (Paris: Centurion, 1990).

110. The term *conduct* is used here and in what follows to refer to the notion that the expression of private beliefs associated with a person's religious or ethnic background is deserving of legal protection in public settings (as against the secularist republican insistence in France on treating all citizens neutrally, without taking into account particular attachments of race or creed). In its narrow form, communitarianism gives rise to appeals for special rights and privileges on the basis of a particular group's minority status within a larger society (what in the United States is sometimes called "identity politics"); see the discussion of Walzer's distinction between "thick" and "thin" identities below, at page 240.—Trans.

111. David Kessler, "Neutralité de l'enseignement public et liberté d'opinion des élèves (à propos du port de signes distinctifs d'appartenance religieuses dans les établissements scolaires)," *Revue française de droit administratif* (January–February 1993), 114, 117.

112. David Kessler, "La Laïcité en France," *CFDT aujourd'hui* (September 1996), 79–81.

113. Claude Durand-Prinborgne, "Le Port des signes extérieurs de convictions religieuses à l'école: Une Jurisprudence affirmée . . . une jurisprudence contestée," *Revue française de droit administratif* (January–February 1997).

114. Quoted in *Libération* (25 June 1997).

115. Quoted in *Le Monde* (30 November 1994).

116. Quoted in the same issue. See also *Libération* (6 November 1996) and two recent works of scholarship on this topic: Guy Coq, *Laïcité et République: Le Lien nécessaire* (Paris: Félin, 1995) and Élisabeth Altschull, *Le Voile contre l'école* (Paris: Seuil, 1995).

117. *Le Monde* (10 November 1989).

118. See Lacorne, Rupnik, and Toinet, eds., *L'Amérique dans les têtes*.

119. Altschull, *Le Voile contre l'école*, 247, 252.

120. Alain Finkielkraut, "La Laïcité à l'épreuve du siècle," *Pouvoirs*, no. 75 (1995), 57.

121. Lacorne, *La Crise de l'identité américaine*, 37. Anti-American prejudices are given free rein in parodies of degenerate American multiculturalism, as Marie-Christine Granjon has pointed out in a courageous and welcome article, "Le Regard en biais: Attitudes françaises et multiculturalisme américain (1990–1993)," *Vingtième Siècle*, no. 43 (1993).

122. Gérard Noiriel, *Le Creuset français: Histoire de l'immigration, XIXᵉ–XXᵉ siècle* (Paris: Seuil, 1988).

123. See Pierre Birnbaum, "Du multiculturalisme au nationalisme: La Nation," *La Pensée politique* (1995); also two articles by Joël Roman, "Un Multiculturalisme à la française," *Esprit* (June 1995), and "Pour un multiculturalisme tempéré," *Hommes et migrations* (April 1996).

124. See Alain Touraine, *Critique de la modernité* (Paris: Fayard, 1992), and in the same vein, Michel Wieviorka, ed., *Une Société fragmentée? Le Multiculturalisme en débat* (Paris: La Découverte, 1996).

125. Haut Conseil à l'Intégration, *Conditions juridiques et culturelles de l'intégration* (Paris: La Documentation Française, March 1992), 38.

126. Ibid., 43. See also Haut Conseil à l'Intégration, *Affaiblissement du lien social, enfermement dans les particularismes et intégration dans le cité* (Paris: La Documentation Française, March 1997), and, on French-style integration, Dominique Schnapper, *La France de l'intégration: Sociologie de la nation en 1990* (Paris: Gallimard, 1991).

127. Michael Walzer, *Thick and Thin: Moral Argument at Home and Abroad* (Notre Dame, Ind.: University of Notre Dame Press, 1994).

128. Maxime Rodinson, quoted in *Le Monde* (1 December 1989).

129. *Journal officiel* (20 June 1990).

130. *Le Figaro* (28 June 1990).

131. See Pierre de Meuse, "Qu'est-ce que l'identité?" *Identité: Revue d'études nationalistes* (June–August 1991).

132. Jean-Claude Bardet, "L'Identité française," *Identité* (June–August 1991).

133. Bruno Mégret, *La Flamme: Les Voies de la renaissance* (Paris: Laffont, 1990); see also Jean-Yves Le Gallou, "Préserver notre identité," *Identité* (June–August 1991).

134. Jean-Marie Le Pen, "Éditorial," *Identité*, nos. 1–2 (1991).

135. Jean-Marie Cardinal Lustiger, *Dieu merci, les droits de l'homme: Articles, conférences, homélies, interviews, 1984–1989* (Paris: Critérion, 1990), 114.

136. *Le Monde* (10 November 1989); see also "Contre l'assimilation," *Le Monde* (24 November 1989).

137. *Le Monde* (8 February 1980).

138. "A-t-on ou non le droit d'être français et musulman? Entretian avec Amr Helmy Ibrahim," *Esprit* (June 1995), 108–10.

139. *Le Monde* (10 April 1997).

140. Rémy Leveau and Dominique Schnapper, "Juifs et musulmans

maghrébins," in Rémy Leveau and Gilles Kepel, eds., *Les Musul-mans dans la société française* (Paris: Presses de la Fondation Na-tionale des Sciences Politiques, 1988), 128–39.

141. See my article "La Citoyenneté en péril: Les Juifs entre résistance et intégration," in Pierre Birnbaum, ed., *La France de l'affaire Dreyfus* (Paris: Gallimard, 1994).

142. See Jacques Barou, "Le Fait ethnique dans la France de demain," in George Tapinos, ed., *La France dans deux générations: Popula-tions et société dans le premier tiers du XXIᵉ siècle* (Paris: Fayard, 1992); also John McKesson, "Concepts and Realities in a Multi-ethnic France," *French Politics and Society* (Winter 1994), David Blatt, "Towards a Multi-Cultural Political Model in France? The Limits of Immigrant Collective Action, 1968–1994," *Nationalism and Ethnic Politics* (Summer 1995), and Martin Schain, "Minori-ties' and Immigrants' Incorporation in France: The State and the Dynamics of Multiculturalism," unpublished paper delivered in Florence, Italy, in April 1996.

143. *Le Monde* (13 October 1994).

144. Michèle Tribalat, *De l'immigration à l'assimilation: Enquête sur les populations d'origine étrangère en France* (Paris: La Découverte, 1996), 248, 262.

145. Ibid., chaps. 2, 3, 12, and 13. In the same vein, considering mem-bers of the younger generation born and educated in France, Joce-lyne Cesari argues that "the Islamic example occupies a place in the personal, indeed intimate, sphere, without any real effect on public behavior"; see "Demande d'islam en banlieue: Un Défi à la citoyenneté?" *Cahiers d'études sur la Méditerranée orientale et le monde turco-iranien* (January–June 1995), 175–76, and, by the same author, *Être musulman en France: Associations, militants et mosquées* (Paris: Hachette, 1997). As Jean-Pierre Worms points out, "[I]t is less a matter that 'they' are more difficult to integrate than that 'we' are less suited to the task"; see "Modèle républicain et protection des minorités nationales," *Hommes et migrations* (April 1996), 27. See also Nicolas de Lavergne, "Jeunes, français, musulmans: Identité islamique et citoyenneté républicaine" (D.E.A., Université de Paris–I, 1996).

146. *Le Monde* (7 October 1995). For a simple presentation of the facts of the case, see Franck Chignier-Riboulon, "Exclusion sociale ou exclusion nationale? L'Affaire Kelkal en banlieue est de Lyon," *Hérodote* (January–April 1996). The police denied that the Kelkal incident had any connection with the urban violence that broke out toward the end of 1995; see *Le Monde* (30 December 1995).

147. See Hervé Viellard-Baron, *Les Banlieues françaises, ou, Le Ghetto impossible* (La Tour d'Aigues: Éditions de l'Aube, 1994), 78ff. But Jean-Marie Delarue, in his official report to the ministers of urban affairs and regional development, wrote: "In the present state of affairs, no 'community' of foreigners (understood as including both [foreign] nationals and believers) threatens the established order: if democracy can show these associations that it grants them the same rights as others, citizenship will be strengthened"; see *Banlieues en difficulté: La Rélégation* (Paris: Syros/Alternatives, 1991), 179.

148. See Philippe Aziz, *Le Paradoxe de Roubaix* (Paris: Plon, 1996), 115–17.

149. See the remarkable special issue of *Les Temps modernes* (July–August 1991); also Catherine Neveu, *Communauté, nationalité et citoyenneté. De l'autre côté du miroir: Les Bangladeshis de Londres* (Paris: Karthala, 1993), chap. 3.

150. See Vincent Geisser, "Les Élus issus de l'immigration maghrébine: L'Illusion de médiation politique," *Horizons maghrébins*, no. 20 (1993), and, by the same author, "Les Élites politiques issues de l'immigration maghrébine: L'Impossible médiation," *Migrations Société* (July–October 1992).

151. See *Libération* (6 June 1995) and *Le Monde* (9 June 1995).

152. See Rémy Leveau and Fatiha Dazi, "L'Intégration par la politique: Le Vote des beurs," *Études* (September 1988).

153. See *Le Monde* (23 May 1997).

154. See Dominique Schnapper, "La Citoyenneté à l'épreuve: Les Musulmans pendant la guerre du Golfe," *Revue française de science politique* (April 1993), and in the same issue, Chantal Benayoun, "Identité et citoyenneté: Juifs, arabes et pieds-noirs face aux événements du Golfe." In this connection, two other analyses, each emphasizing the vigor of Muslim protests, are more nuanced: see Vincent Geisser, *Ethnicité républicaine: Les Élites d'origine maghrébine dans le système politique français* (Paris: Presses de Sciences Po, 1997), chap. 9, and Isabelle Rocca, "Participation politique et choix d'éthnicité: Les Élus municipaux d'origine maghrébine" (D.E.A., Université de Paris–I, 1997).

155. Algeria does not permit these persons to abandon what it regards as their primary nationality. In its view, even children born in France of Algerian immigrants after 1963, regardless of their own wishes in the matter, retain their status as Algerian citizens and can be required to perform military service. See Jacqueline Costa-Lascoux, "Quelle nationalité?" *Les Temps modernes* (March–May 1984), as well as the rest of this issue.

156. See, for example, Catherine Wihtol de Wendel, "Les Immigrés, enjeu politique," *Les Temps modernes* (March–May 1984). In this and several other articles, Wihtol de Wendel attempts to justify the application in France of the new criteria of citizenship.
157. See Rogers Brubaker, *Citizenship and Nationhood in France and Germany* (Cambridge, Mass.: Harvard University Press, 1992).
158. See Rogers Brubaker, ed., *Immigration and the Politics of Citizenship in Europe and North America* (Lanham, Md.: University Press of America, 1989). On the contrast between political communities such as France and cultural (or "ethnic") communities such as Germany, see Louis Dumont, *L'Idéologue allemande: France-Allemagne et retour* (Paris: Gallimard, 1991).
159. Danièle Lochak, "Genèse idéologique d'une réforme," *Hommes et migrations* (July 1994); see also, by the same author, "Usages et mésusages d'une notion polémique: La Référence à l'identité nationale dans le débat sur la réforme du code de la nationalité, 1985–1993," in Jacques Chevallier, ed., *L'Identité politique* (Paris: Presses Universitaires de France, 1994).
160. See *Le Monde* (29 October 1987).
161. See *Le Monde* (6 February 1996). This confirms the opinion of Marceau Long, president of the commission on nationality, who predicted in 1988 that "one will be able to become a French citizen more easily, but also more consciously"; see *Le Monde* (9 January 1989).
162. See Pierre Noreau, "L'Action collective des jeunes issus de l'immigration en France (1980–1988)" (thesis, Institut d'Études Politiques de Paris, 1991).
163. See the interview with Jean-Pierre Chevènement, the interior minister, in *Le Monde* (26 June 1997).
164. See *Le Monde* (16 September and 14 November 1997).
165. This upsurge was marked by a torrent of nationalist sentiment that the Church characterized as "fundamentally anti-Christian," pointing out that these latter-day imitators of Maurras confused French identity and Christian identity, as Maurras himself had done, thereby rendering differences in culture absolute; see *La Documentation catholique* (March 1992). Note, too, the Church's condemnation of the immigration policy pursued by the interior minister at the time, Charles Pasqua (to which Pasqua responded by declaring, "We are not in Saudi Arabia. There is no confusion in France between the churches and the state"); see *Le Monde* (26 May 1993), as well as the statement signed by four RPR deputies known for their Catholic commitment, "Les Évêques ont

tort," and published shortly afterward in *Le Monde* (16 June 1993).

166. See Diana Pinto, "Immigration: L'Ambiguïté de la référence américaine," *Pouvoirs*, no. 47 (1990).

167. See Anne-Marie Thiesse, *Ils apprenaient la France: L'Exaltation des régions dans le discours patriotique* (Paris: Éditions de la Maison des Sciences de l'Homme, 1997).

168. *Le Monde* (27 May 1996).

169. See my book *The Jews of the Republic*; also *Destins juifs: De la Révolution française à Carpentras* (Paris: Calmann-Lévy, 1995), available in English as *Jewish Destinies: Citizenship, State, and Community in Modern France*, trans. Arthur Goldhammer (New York: Hill and Wang, 2000).

170. *Le Monde* (1 October 1997).

171. From the IPSOS–*Tribune juive* poll published in the 18 March 1995 issue of *Tribune juive*.

172. See Sylvie Strudel, *Votes juifs: Itinérarires migratoires religieux et politiques* (Paris: Presses de la Fondation Nationale des Sciences Politiques, 1996).

173. See the special issue of *Hommes et migrations* (February–March 1990).

174. *Le Monde* (23 February 1990).

175. As Colette Kessler put it, writing in *La Croix* (13 April 1989): "France has become the very example of a false secularism, good in its principles, bad in applying them. Secularism, often antireligious, is experienced by Jews today as a hindrance to the expression of their identity. A secular system ought to be promoted that approves and encourages, as is the case in Anglo-Saxon countries, a denominational pluralism."

176. Yann Aguila, "Le Temps de l'école et le temps de Dieu," *Revue française de droit administratif* (May–June 1995). A systematic review of recent jurisprudence concerning the whole range of religious particularisms in France may be found in the 1995 report of the Commission Nationale Consultative des Droits de l'Homme, *La Lutte contre le racisme et la xénophobie* (Paris: La Documentation Française, 1996), 252–60.

177. See the 23 February 1994 and 17 April 1995 issues of *Le Monde*.

178. *Le Monde* (3 April 1995); see also the same paper's 17 April 1995 editorial.

179. *Le Figaro* (20 March 1995).

180. See the 23 February 1990, 10 March 1990, 19 March 1994, and 16 June 1994 issues of *Le Monde*.

181. *Libération* (26 April 1994); see also *L'Express* (17 March 1994) and *Libération* (12 April 1994). This incident gave rise to highly intelligent debate in Jewish circles: see, for example, "La Communauté juive est-elle menacée de l'intérieur?" *Les Nouveaux Cahiers*, no. 112 (Spring 1993).

182. On the top-down communitarization of this community, which remains largely "imaginary," see my *Jewish Destinies*, chap. 12.

183. Notably Pierre Joxe, Gaston Deferre, Georgina Dufoix, Georges Fillioud, Catherine Lalumière, Louis Mexandeau, and Catherine Trautmann.

184. See *Le Monde* (11 June 1997).

185. See Jean Bauberot, *Le Protestantisme doit-il mourir?: La Différence protestante dans une France pluriculturelle* (Paris: Seuil, 1988), chap. 10, and by the same author, "L'Importance de la laïcité dans les transformations internes du protestantisme français," *Revue de l'Institut catholique de Paris* (January–March 1992).

186. See Philippe Joutard, "The Museum of the Desert: The Protestant Minority," in Nora, ed., *Realms of Memory*, 1:353–77.

187. Yves Bizeul, *L'Identité protestante: Étude de la minorité protestante en France* (Paris: Méridiens Klincksieck, 1991), 229. For a more optimistic point of view on the future of a Protestant message whose prospects "seem more than threatened, [indeed] desperate," see Jeanne-Hélène Kaltenbach, *Être protestant en France aujourd'hui* (Paris: Hachette, 1997), 217.

188. See *Le Monde* (19 October 1995) and *Réforme* (21 October 1995).

189. See Claude Dargent, "La Foi, la morale et le conflit: Culture et comportements politiques et sociaux des protestants français," 2 vols. (Ph.D. diss., Université de Paris–I, 1994), 1:252ff.

190. See *Libération* (11 June 1996).

191. See *Le Monde* (30 May 1997).

192. See André Encrevé, *Les Protestants en France de 1800 à nos jours: Histoire d'une réintégration* (Paris: Stock, 1985), 268ff.

193. See Martine Hovanessian, *Le Lien communautaire: Trois générations d'Arméniens* (Paris: Armand Colin, 1992).

194. See, for example, Isabelle Taboada-Leonetti, "Territorialisation et structuration communautaire: Les Asiatiques dans le XIIIᵉ arrondissement de Paris," *Espace et société* (December 1984); Michelle Guillon and Isabelle Taboada-Leonetti, *Le Triangle de Choisy: Un Quartier chinois à Paris* (Paris: L'Harmattan, 1986); Michelle Guillon, Paul White, and Hilary Winchester, "Paris 13: Evolution of a Minority Community," *Ethnic and Racial Studies*

(January 1987); and Jacqueline Costa-Lascoux and Live Yu-Sion, *Paris XIII*, *lumières d'Asie* (Paris: Autrement, 1995).

195. See Panivong Norindr, "La Plus Grande France: French Cultural Identity and Nation Building Under Mitterrand," in Steven Ungar and Tom Conley, eds., *Identity Papers: Contested Nationhood in Twentieth-Century France* (Minneapolis: University of Minnesota Press, 1996).

196. See Christine Bard, *Les Filles de Marianne: Histoire des féminismes, 1914–1940* (Paris: Fayard, 1995). On the related diversification of community memories and common causes, see Martine Barthélemy, "Les Associations dans la société française: État des lieux," in a special issue of *Les Cahiers du CEVIPOF* (June 1996); also François Héran, "La Sociabilité, une pratique culturelle," *Économie et statistique* (December 1988), and Jacques Chevallier, "L'Association entre public et privé," *Revue de droit public*, no. 4 (1981).

197. See the special feature in the 28 June 1997 issue of *Libération*.

198. See Danièle Lochak, "Les Minorités et le droit public français: Du refus des différences à la gestion des différences," in Alain Fenet and Gérard Soulier, eds., *Les Minorités et leurs droits depuis 1789* (Paris: L'Harmattan, 1989).

199. De Certeau et al., *Une Politique de la langue*, 13, 297, 302.

200. Far away, too, seems Abbé Sieyès's injunction that "France must not be a collection of small nations that govern themselves as democracies. . . . It is a single *whole*. . . . France is, and must be, *a single whole*" ("Dire sur la question du veto royal," in *Écrits politiques*, 234, 237); also the revolutionary oath of the confederate forces of Brittany and Anjou: "We solemnly declare that, being neither Breton nor Angevin, but French and citizens, we renounce all our local privileges, abjuring them as unconstitutional. We declare ourselves proud and happy to be free!" (quoted in Ozouf, *L'École de la France*, 37).

201. See Daniel Nordman and Marie-Vic Ozouf-Marignier, *Atlas de la Révolution française: Le Territoire* (Paris: Éditions de l'École des Hautes Études en Sciences Sociales, 1989), 4, as well as Marie-Vic Ozouf-Marignier, *La Formation des départements: La Représentation du territoire français à la fin du XVIIIe siècle* (Paris: Éditions de l'École des Hautes Études en Sciences Sociales, 1992). See also Daniel Nordman and Jacques Revel, "La Formation de l'espace français," and Marcel Roncayolo, "L'Aménagement du territoire: XVIIIe–XXe siècle," both in Burguière and Revel, eds., *Histoire de*

la France; Roncayolo writes, "France offers a rather exceptional example: the partial confiscation by the state of responsibility for managing and equipping its territory."

202. Furet and Halévi, eds., *Orateurs de la Révolution française*, 1583.
203. See the 6 May 1995 and 1 October 1997 issues of *Le Monde*. The Pasqua law established for the first time the legality of "countries" (*pays*), new administrative units designating specific areas within a department—the first step toward recognizing the regionalism that had been combated by the French Revolution and the republican state.
204. Henri Giordan, *Démocratie culturelle et droit à la différence: Rapport présenté à Jack Lang, Ministre de la Culture* (Paris: Documentation Française, 1982).
205. See *Libération* (22 September 1987).
206. *Compte rendu analytique officiel de l'Assemblée nationale* (16 December 1988).
207. See *Le Monde* (6 September 1997).
208. See Erhard Friedberg and Philippe Urfalino, "La Mise en oeuvre de la culture régionale," a paper delivered at the meeting of the French Political Science Association, "The State in the Face of Regional and Community Cultures," in Aix-en-Provence, 1986.
209. See Jean-Louis Briquet, *La Tradition en mouvement: Clientélisme et politique en Corse* (Paris: Belin, 1997).
210. Maurice Agulhon, "Le Centre et la périphérie," in Nora, ed., *Les Lieux de mémoire*, 3:845.
211. Paul Thibaud, "Et si l'État venait à manquer," in Crozier and Trosa, eds., *La Décentralisation: Réforme de l'État*, 46–48.
212. Quoted in Charles Santoni, "Le Peuple corse," *Confluences en Méditerrané* (Winter 1994).
213. Marianne Lefèvre, "Il n'y a plus d'État en Corse!" *L'Histoire* (May 1996).
214. See "La République et ses territoires," *Le Monde* (12 April 1996).
215. See "Le Paradoxe des cultures régionales," *Le Monde* (21 January 1993).
216. *Le Monde* (24 June 1996).
217. *Le Monde* (1 September 1996).
218. *Le Monde* (11 September 1996).
219. *Le Monde* (17 September 1996).
220. *Le Monde* (18 September 1996).
221. *Le Monde* (18 October 1996).
222. *Libération* (15 April 1996).

223. *Libération* (22 July 1996).

224. *Libération* (2 May 1996).

225. *Libération* (30 September 1996).

226. "Les Mots pour le pire," *Télérama* (9 October 1996).

227. *Identité*, no. 12 (1991), 17.

228. See Gérard de Puymège, *Chauvin, le soldat-laboureur*, 276ff.; also Jean-Paul Honoré, "La Hiérarchie des sentiments: Description et mise en scène du Français et de l'immigré dans le discours du Front national," *Mots* (March 1986), and Michel Hastings, "La Rhétorique hygiéniste de Jean-Marie Le Pen," *Revue politique et parlementaire* (February 1988).

229. See, for example, *Le Figaro-Magazine* (26 October 1985).

230. On the alliance between fundamentalist Catholics and Le Pen's movement, see the Fall 1991 issue of *Golias*, particularly the interview with Émile Poulat. On the links between Saint-Nicolas-du-Chardonnet and the National Front, see Anglade and Costerg, *Monographie de Saint-Nicholas-du-Chardonnet*, 64ff. Anti-Christian hatred was allowed equally free rein in certain quarters of the FN. The "Crucified Blues," about "the guy with the big nose," gives some idea of the tone of this abuse:

> *Son père était un charpentier*
> *Qui voulait pas se mettre en piste*
> *Alors sa mère s'est fait draguer*
> *Par un centurion pas raciste*
> *Et dans l'étable*
> *Elle a pondu*
> *Un mec minable*
> *Un vrai faux-cul*
> *Le crucifié. . . .*
> *Marie-Madeleine allonge-toi là*
> *J'ai l'Saint-Esprit qui m'démange. . . .*
> *Le drap plein d'sueur fut revendu*
> *Le saint suaire est apparu.*

> *[His father was a carpenter*
> *Who didn't want a piece of the action*
> *So his mother got herself a soldier*
> *Who wasn't from a racist faction*
> *And in the stable*
> *She squeezed out*

A pathetic shit
A real bastard
The one they crucified. . . .
Mary Magdalene, lay down right there
The Holy Spirit's itching me you know where. . . .
The sweaty sheet was sold
The Holy Shroud appeared.]

Quoted by René Monzat in *Libération* (12 October 1995). See also *Le Monde* (1 April 1997), *Libération* (15 April 1996, 3 July 1996, and 30 March 1997), and *Présent* (10 December 1996 and 31 December 1996). Pierre Vial, writing in the 27 November 1996 issue of *Présent*, remarked: "It seems unthinkable to me that one could speak of a 'Catholic' current or a 'pagan current' within the FN. . . . Christianity managed to take root in Europe by integrating traditions and ancestral beliefs it found when it got there. . . . The problem is that the ecclesiastical hierarchy (Lustiger, for instance) no longer embodies true Catholicism."

231. See, for example, *Fideliter* (July–August 1992), as well as other issues of this journal.
232. *Le Monde* (3 March 1997).
233. See *La Vie* (12 March 1992 and 4 July 1996); also Nonna Mayer, "Le Front National consolide son enracinement," *Le Monde* (29 May 1997), and *La Croix* (13 May 1997).
234. *Le Figaro-Magazine* (5 April 1985).
235. "L'Église sur le front," *Vigilance républicaine* (January 1997).
236. Pascal Perrineau, "La Dynamique du vote Le Pen: Le Poids du gaucho-lepénisme," in Perrineau and Ysmal, eds., *Le Vote de crise*.
237. See *Le Monde* (24 October 1996).
238. See Cécile Péchu, "Le Front national à Aulnay-sous-Bois: Du vote protestaire au parti de miltants," *Les Cahiers du CEVIPOF*, no. 8 (1993).
239. See Olivier Schwartz, *Le Monde privé des ouvriers: Hommes et femmes du Nord* (Paris: Presses Universitaires de France, 1990); also Guy Groux and Catherine Lévy, *La Possession ouvrière: Du taudis à la propriété, XIXe–XXe siècle* (Paris: Éditions de l'Atelier/Éditions Ouvrières, 1993).
240. Nonna Mayer, "Du vote lepéniste au vote frontiste," *Revue française de science politique* (June–August 1997), 440.
241. See Laurent Adam, "La Réalité d'une Alsace extrémiste," *Saisons d'Alsace* (Fall 1995); also *La Croix* (27 March 1997) and *Le Monde* (31 March 1997).

242. See Jean-Luc Richard, "L'"extrême-ouest' loin de l'extrême droite: Le Vote Front national dans le Finistère," *Revue française de science politique* (October 1996).

243. See, for example, Bruno Gollnisch, "Aux sources de la modernité japonaise: La Tradition," *Identité*, no. 13 (Summer 1991). Gollnisch writes that it is necessary "to study the Indo-European heritage [rather than] the ethnography of the Araras and the Bororos. To make the moral law of our fathers who built the Palais-Royal prevail over the moral law of M. [Daniel] Buren [the artist whose remodeling of the main courtyard of the Palais-Royal in 1986–87 generated controversy]. Only if we know how to recover this heritage will we be able, with Solzhenitsyn, to overcome the terrible evil from which Western civilizations suffer and which he identifies as being 'the hypertrophy of juridical individualism. . . .' One perceives today, by comparison with the societies of the Near and Far East, that this society carries within itself the formidable seeds of its own disintegration—the very thing that we are dedicated to preventing" (30).

244. Yvan Blot, "Patrie et liberté: Le Modèle suisse," in Le Club de l'Horloge, *L'Identité de la France* (Paris: Albin Michel, 1985).

245. Yvan Blot, "La Démocratie locale en Suisse: Un Modèle pour la France," in Le Club de l'Horloge, *La Démocratie locale: Un Pari pour la France* (Paris: Albin Michel, 1990). Alain Benoist likewise frequently cites the Swiss example as a democracy rooted in a powerful community feeling that ought to inspire others: see, for example, his article in *Éléments* (Winter 1985). Pierre Gentile stresses the manner in which direct democracy has been utilized by the radical Right in Switzerland; see "Les Trajectoires de la droite radicale: 1984–1993," *Études et recherches* (Department of Political Science, University of Geneva), no. 33 (1996), 47. Pascal Sciarini and Alexandra Treschel, for their part, show how the mechanisms of direct democracy facilitate control of the "elites" by the "people," from the bottom up: see "Démocratie directe en Suisse: L'Élite politique victime des droits populaires?" *Revue suisse de science politique*, no. 2 (1996).

246. See, for example, Henri de Lesquen, "L'Expérience de la Suisse et celle de la Californie sont concluantes: Nous devons nous en inspirer," *Lettre d'information du Club de l'horloge*, no. 30 (1992), 5. See also *Identité*, no. 12 (1991).

247. Quoted by Pierre-André Taguieff, "Un Programme révolutionnaire," in Mayer and Perrineau, eds., *Le Front national à découvert*, 225.

248. Bruno Mégret, "Immigration: Mise au point du FN," quoted in Laurence Tardy and Muriel Piccamiglio, "L'Identité national dans le FN: L'Utilisation politique du thème," *Celsius*, no. 47 (1992). The expression "foreign enclaves" is common: one already finds it used, for example, in the National Front's 1985 program, *Pour la France.*
249. Le Club de l'Horloge, *L'Identité de la France*, 55. See also Emmanuel Renaud, "Analyse compréhensive de l'émergence du Front National comme force politique depuis 1980" (Ph.D. diss., Université de Paris–IV, Sorbonne, 1994), 167ff.
250. See the April 1996 *Le Monde*–RTL poll, "L'Image du Front National auprès des Français."

Conclusion: Twilight of the Utopias

1. See Numa Broc, *Regards sur la géographie française de la Renaissance à nos jours*, 2 vols. (Perpignan: Presses Universitaires de Perpignan, 1994), vol. 1.
2. Eugen Weber, "L'Hexagone," in Nora, ed., *Les Lieux de mémoire*, 3:97–116; also P. Pellegrino, G. Albert, C. Castella, and A. Lévy, "Représentations du territoire et identité," *Espaces Temps*, nos. 51–52 (1993).
3. Heinrich Heine, *De la France*, edited by Gerhard Hohn and Bodo Morawe (Paris: Gallimard, 1994), 39, 133.

Index

Index

Index

Delvolvé, Jean, 159–60, 322n13
Descartes, René, 94
Désir, Harlem, 340n84
Desmoulins, Camille, 44–45
Donegani, Jean-Marie, 221
Dostoyevsky, Fyodor, 9–10
Douste-Blazy, Philippe, 327n63
Dreyfus, Camille, 226
Dreyfus Affair, 17, 19, 23, 108, 136, 137, 161, 224; assimilationist interpretation of, 245; Catholics and, 73, 109–10, 125–28, 141, 142, 316n91; and Joan of Arc as nationalist symbol, 116; Maurras and, 94, 128, 129, 147, 148
Drumont, Édouard, 92, 95, 114, 147, 148, 164, 240, 272
Duffau, Jean-Marie, 330n92
Dufoix, Georgina, 350n183
Dumont, René, 340n84
Dupanloup, Félix-Antoine-Philibert, Bishop of Orleáns, 218
Duprat, Annie, 301n78
Durafour, Michel, 274
Durkheim, Émile, 137

École de l'Immaculée Conception, 134
École des Hautes Études Commerciales, 183
École des Mines, 202
École Libre des Sciences Politiques, 101, 134, 154, 303n11
École Nationale d'Administration (ENA), 5, 162, 164, 166–69, 172–74, 176, 179, 180, 182–91, 195–99, 201–5, 327n64, 329n86, 330n92, 331n103
École Normale Supérieure, 134, 155, 156, 162, 190, 196, 322n13
École Polytechnique, 134, 148, 191, 202
École Sainte-Geneviève, 134
education: assimilation and, 243–46; in Catholic schools, 215, 219, 235; private secular, 235; and regional identities, 268–71; secularism-multiculturalism debate in, 224–38, 243, 252, 258–62; during Third Republic, 120–24, 135,

137–39, 149, 153; Tocqueville on, 37; during Vichy regime, 145–46, 155–57
Education, Inspectorate of, 193
Education, Ministry of, 156
Eichtal, Eugène d', 101
Eiffel Tower, 109, 110
Elf-Aquitaine (firm), 330nn92, 96
Emmanuel (fundamentalist Catholic group), 215, 221
énarques, see bureaucracy
Encyclopédie, 8, 9
Enlightenment, 4, 6, 7, 10–11, 48, 55, 75, 81, 129, 209, 279; individualism of, 113; and Popular Front, 141; Scottish, 77; Third Republic policies based on, 122, 127, 139; universalism of, 5, 8, 9, 74
Errera, Roger, 342n100
Estates General, 39, 59
European Community, Commission of, 198
European Court of Justice, 159
European Union, 232, 280
exceptionalism, French, 10–11, 17–20, 191, 255; Americanization versus, 188; centralizing tradition of, 184; hatred as component of, 33, 34, 38, 43; Maistre's view of, 79–81, 83; multiculturalism as threat to, 229, 230, 236, 239; radical dualism of, 62; and Third Republic, 106–7; unifying, 65; and Vichy regime, 162

Fabius, Laurent, 174, 177, 194, 198
Faguet, Émile, 77; Le Libéralisme, 106
Fallous law, 235, 342n102
fascism, 44, 72–73, 141, 205, 272, 320nn135, 136
Fauroux, Roger, 190, 327n62, 329n76
Fédération de l'Éducation Nationale (FEN), 226, 275
Fédération National Catholique, 140
Fédération Nationale des Fonctionnaires et Employés d'Administrations Publiques, 136
Fédération Nationale des Musulmans de France, 250

Index

Index

Index

Jews (*cont.*)
Maistre on, 83; and Mitterrand's funeral, 210; National Front hatred of, 272–74; nationalism and, 75; Nazi persecution of, 13; and new secularism, 234, 255–57; and Popular Front, 142; prejudice against, *see* anti-Semitism; Dreyfus Affair; in public schools, 121, 253, 261; Vichy regime and, 97, 147, 148, 153–61, 186, 257, 320*n136*, 329*n83*, 342*n100*
Joan of Arc, 19, 115–16, 273
John Paul II, Pope, 309*n93*, 342*n97*
Joliot-Curie, Frédéric, 155
Jolivet, Benoît, 330*n96*
Jones, H. S., 136
Jospin, Lionel, 177, 196, 197, 199, 225, 228, 232–33, 243, 264, 342*n97*
Journées Mondiales de la Jeunesse, 342*n97*
Joxe, Pierre, 177, 194, 200, 225, 269, 350*n183*
Judaism, *see* Jews
Judt, Tony, 106
July, Serge, 290*n48*
Juppé, Alain, 175, 177, 183, 196, 198–99, 208, 210–11, 236, 327*nn62, 65*, 333*n130*

Kacet, Salem, 243, 250
Kahn, Jean, 261
Kant, Immanuel, 94
Kaufmann, Joëlle, 340–41*n84*
Kelkal, Khaled, 246–48, 346*n146*
Kelly, George Armstrong, 310*n8*
Kessler, Colette, 349*n175*
Kessler, David, 199, 233–36, 342*n100*
Kitzler, Catherine, 341*n85*
Kléber, General Jean-Baptiste, 285*n1*
Koen, Yonathan, 260
Kouchner, Bernard, 175
Krumeich, Gerd, 116

Laboulaye, Édouard de, 101
Labour Party, British, 249
La Bruyère, Jean de, 14
Lacordaire, Henri, 101
Lacorne, Denis, 238, 341*n91*

Lacoste, Robert, 233, 342*n96*
Lacouture, Jean, 341*n84*
La Fontaine, Jean de, 14
Lagrange, Maurice, 159–60
Lagrée, Michel, 315*n70*
Laguérie, Abbé Pierre, 216
Lalonde, Brice, 175
Lalumière, Catherine, 350*n183*
Lamassoure, Alain, 327*n63*
Langlois, Claude, 89
language, French, 270; regional variations in, education and, 268–69, 271; standardization of, 47–49, 122, 124, 267
Larkin, Maurice, 134
La Rocque, François de, 140, 141, 320*nn135, 136*
Laroque, Martine, 342*n100*
Laroque, Pierre, 342*n100*
Lasch, Christopher, 21
La Tour du Pin-Chambly, René, Marquis de, 109, 140
Lavagne, André, 146, 322*n13*
Laval, Pierre, 146, 153, 156
Lazard Frères, 192
Lazare, Bernard, 126
Lebrun, François, 286*n6*
Leconte de Lisle, Charles, 109
Lefebvre, Monsignor Marcel, 214, 217–18, 241, 273
Le Goff, Jacques, 229, 341*n88*
Leguay, Jean, 153
Lejeune, Max, 233, 342*n96*
Lelandais, Marc, 299*n28*
Leninism, 3
Lenoir, René, 184
Léotard, François, 327*n63*
Leo XIII, Pope, 93
Le Pen, Jean-Marie, 4, 23, 142, 204–5, 227, 230, 237–38, 240–42, 252, 271–76, 278, 308*n93*
Le Play, Frédéric, 95, 113
Le Pors, Anicet, 184
Leroy, Maxime, 136, 137
Leveau, Rémy, 244–45
Lévêque, Jean-Maxime, 202
Lévy-Lang, André, 333*n132*
liberalism, 8, 16, 20–23, 143; American, 21, 25, 27, 100; Catholics and, 26, 101, 112–13, 221; of Constant,

Index

101–2, 123–24; economic, 194–95; Maurras as enemy of, 130; nationalism versus, 103–5; and Third Republic, 106, 124–25, 127–28

Liénart, Cardinal, 145

Lienemann, Marie-Noëlle, 199

Ligue d'Action Universitaire Républicaine et Socialiste, 154

Ligue de la Patrie Française, 128

Ligue des Droits de l'Homme et du Citoyen, 136, 253

Ligue Française de l'Enseignement, 222–23

Lion, Robert, 331n96

Lipset, Seymour, 27

Littré, Émile, 131

Long, Marceau, 348n161

Louis IX, 12

Louis XIV, 13–15, 65, 82, 157

Louis XV, 306n59

Louis XVI, 39, 58, 59, 86, 112

Louis XVIII, 81

Lourdes, miracles of, 114

Lovecy, Jill, 291n48

Lubavitch, 261, 266

Lustiger, Jean-Marie Cardinal, 211, 213, 218–19, 225, 242, 256, 354n230

Luther, Martin, 94

Lycée Henri IV, 156

Lycée Louis-le-Grand, 154

Lycée Masséna, 260

Lycée Saint-Louis, 156

Mably, Abbé, 300n44

Machelon, Jean-Pierre, 132, 317–18n110

Madelin, Alain, 198

Madelin, Henri, 336n26

Madiran, Jean, 308n93

Maginot line, 341n87

Maistre, Joseph de, 14, 20, 23, 71–99, 163, 165, 257, 304n21, 305n38, 306nn56, 60, 308n93; Berlin on, 8–10, 72–76, 141, 304n15; Catholicism of, 73–74, 79–83, 114, 214–16, 218, 272; on executioner's role, 84–86; Le Pen and, 204, 205; Maurras influenced by,

91–95, 98, 128–30, 307n77; nationalism of, 74–75; perverse-effects thesis and, 77–78; Renan and, 103; Tocqueville and, 102; Tolstoy and, 75–76, 303n11; Vichy regime influenced by, 95–99, 308n92

Works: *Considérations sur la France*, 98; *Du pape*, 94; *St. Petersburg Dialogues*, 85–86, 96

Malraux, André, 20

Mandrou, Robert, 14

Manichaeanism, 63

Marchiani, Jean-Charles, 182

Marians, 134

Marion, Paul, 96

Maritain, Jacques, 94–95; *L'Antimoderne*, 94

Marmont, Maréchal de, 296n67

Marquet, Claudette, 225

Marseillaise, La, 145–46

Martel, Charles, 273

Martin, Monsignor, 145

Martinet, Gilles, 193

Marx, Karl, 51, 91

Marxism, 6, 75, 230

Masons, see Freemasonry

Matignon agreements, 142

Mauroy, Pierre, 174, 268

Maurras, Charles, 20, 22, 23, 73, 113, 133, 140–41, 165, 196, 319n131, 320n135, 348n165; anti-Protestantism of, 82, 278; England demonized by, 240; fundamentalist Catholics influenced by, 215, 217; Maistre's influence on, 91–95, 98, 128–30, 307n77; during Vichy regime, 95, 147–50, 161

Works: *Enquête sur la monarchie*, 94; *La Seule France*, 95

Mayeur, Jean-Marie, 310n9

May 1968 events, 16, 18, 177, 188

Médecin, Jacques, 182

Médecins sans Frontières, 175

Mégret, Bruno, 205, 241, 271–72

Méhaignerie, Pierre, 327n63

Mendès France, Pierre, 164–66

Mercier, Auguste, 161

Mesguen, Monsignor, 145

Messier, Jean-Marie, 192

365

Index